The Ambivalent Partisan

Series in Political Psychology

Series Editor
John T. Jost

Image Bite Politics: News and the Visual Framing of Elections
Maria E. Grabe and Erik P. Bucy

Social and Psychological Bases of Ideology and System Justification
John T. Jost, Aaron C. Kay, and Hulda Thorisdottir

The Political Psychology of Democratic Citizenship
Eugene Borgida, Christopher Federico, and John Sullivan

On Behalf of Others: The Psychology of Care in a Global World
Sarah Scuzzarello, Catarina Kinnvall, and Kristen Renwick Monroe

The Obamas and a (Post) Racial America?
Gregory S. Parks and Matthew W. Hughey

Ideology, Psychology, and Law
Jon Hanson

The Impacts of Lasting Occupation: Lessons from Israeli Society
Daniel Bar-Tal and Izhak Schnell

Representing Red and Blue: How the Culture Wars Change the Way Citizens Speak and Politicians Listen
David C. Barker and Christopher Jan Carman

On Voter Competence
Paul Goren

The Ambivalent Partisan: How Critical Loyalty Promotes Democracy
Howard G. Lavine, Christopher D. Johnston, and Marco R. Steenbergen

The Ambivalent Partisan

How Critical Loyalty Promotes Democracy

Howard G. Lavine, Christopher D. Johnston,
and Marco R. Steenbergen

Oxford University Press is a department of the University of Oxford. It furthers the University's objective of excellence in research, scholarship, and education by publishing worldwide.

Oxford New York
Auckland Cape Town Dar es Salaam Hong Kong Karachi
Kuala Lumpur Madrid Melbourne Mexico City Nairobi
New Delhi Shanghai Taipei Toronto

With offices in
Argentina Austria Brazil Chile Czech Republic France Greece
Guatemala Hungary Italy Japan Poland Portugal Singapore
South Korea Switzerland Thailand Turkey Ukraine Vietnam

Published in the United States of America by
Oxford University Press
198 Madison Avenue, New York, NY 10016

Library of Congress Cataloging-in-Publication Data

Lavine, Howard.
The ambivalent partisan: How Critical Loyalty Promotes Democracy / Howard G. Lavine, Christopher D. Johnston, and Marco R. Steenbergen.
p. cm.—(Series in political psychology)
Includes bibliographical references and index.
ISBN 978–0–19–977275–9 (hardback: alk. paper) 1. Party affiliation—United States. 2. Democracy—Psychological aspects. 3. Political participation—United States—Psychological aspects. 4. Voting—United States—Psychological aspects. I. Johnston, Christopher D. II. Steenbergen, Marco R. III. Title.
JK2271.L38 2012
324.0973—dc23
2012017353

9 8 7 6 5 4 3 2
Printed in the United States of America
on acid-free paper

HL: For JaneAnne, Seamus, and Finnian

CJ: For my mom, Eileen

MS: In memory of Herman

A rational approach to the world is nuanced and grey, capable of accommodating contradictions, all of which leads to hesitancy and a lack of certainty.... An easy shortcut is to combine ignorance with straight-out endorsement of ignorance—no signs of rational inquiry, but, more important, no signs of self-doubt or contradiction.

—*Robert Trivers (2011, p. 15), The Folly of Fools*

Our righteous minds were designed by evolution to unite us into teams, to divide us against other teams, and to blind us to the truth.

—*Jonathan Haidt (2008), TED Conversation*

Contents

Preface

On December 8, 2003, George W. Bush signed into law the most significant piece of social welfare legislation since the Great Society. The Medicare Modernization Act, which provides an entitlement for prescription drugs to seniors, is estimated by the Department of Health and Human Services to come at an annual cost of approximately $1,500.00 per beneficiary, or $750 billion over the next decade. By any reckoning, the law is more liberal than the status quo ante.[1] It builds on Medicare itself, provides extra subsidies to the poor, and has reduced the percentage of Americans who forgo medications due to cost. According to polls taken at the time, however, the public largely ignored the ideological dimension of the policy. Averaging over several CNN/Gallup polls conducted in 2003, 2004, and 2006, about 70 percent of Republicans supported the policy, whereas only about 40 percent of Democrats did.

That the president advocated for the law is not a surprise; its passage represented a fulfillment of his stance as a "compassionate conservative," and it helped to ensure the allegiance of older voters in his re-election bid, less than a year away. However, the inverse partisan divide in the electorate is puzzling. Why was the pattern of support for Bush's prescription drug bill opposite to similar attempts to expand health care under presidents Clinton and Obama? If party identification captures, at least crudely, systematic differences in the public's policy goals, in what way can we make sense of this mass preference "reversal?"

The answer, of course, is that partisan cue-taking trumped closer scrutiny of the substantive policy details. As political scientists have long recognized, people lead busy lives, and their interests, by and large, lie outside of politics. Moreover, political debates are often complex, leading many and perhaps most citizens to succumb to uncertainty and confusion. Therefore, when motivated

1. Although the bill was not all that Democrats in Congress would have liked, they did not expect to be able to pass an alternative—that is, more liberal—bill.

to form a judgment on some matter of public interest, most people would like to do so without expending too much cognitive effort. Moreover, as theories of cognitive consistency have taught us, we prefer to avoid having our beliefs upset and faced with contradiction. In the context of partisan politics, this often boils down to the desire to form beliefs and preferences that affirm the validity of our partisan loyalties. We therefore look for cues in the political environment that allow us to glean more detailed information (without having to acquire it piecemeal), and to form beliefs that allow us to side with the partisan in-group. As nearly all Republicans in the House voted for the prescription drug bill and nearly all Democrats voted against it, why take the time to consider the policy details when the cue of partisanship provides a ready-made judgmental shortcut, one that allows citizens to make it easy *and* stay loyal to the team? The belief that citizens routinely avail themselves of such cost-saving devices for precisely these reasons—including, most of all, the heuristic of *partisanship*—has long been conventional wisdom in political psychology.

Beyond making it easy and sticking with the in-group, we argue that citizens would also like to have a certain measure of *confidence* in the "correctness" of their judgments. The public is not oblivious to the fact that politicians and partisan-oriented news jocks slant the political world to their advantage, and in doing so disseminate information of doubtful veracity. At times, then, getting it right means having to try harder—acquiring and deliberating about more diagnostic (but costly) information—and that often requires a willingness to shake off our partisan lenses. *This book is about the conditions under which citizens are willing to make such an effort and why.* More specifically, this book is focused on the relationship between partisan attachment, the nature of citizens' multiple and conflicting political judgment goals, and the normative quality of their perceptions, preferences, and choices. Given the preeminent role that partisanship plays in how citizens negotiate the world of politics, we ask whether heuristically toeing the party line tends to facilitate "high-quality" judgments. For example, do partisan cues facilitate accurate perceptions of the political world? Do they lead voters to make electoral choices in line with their "fully informed preferences?" That is, are partisan cues an effective *substitute* for more diagnostic campaign information, or in the case of policy debates, do partisan cues lead citizens to adopt preferences in line with their material interests, social values, and relevant facts? And finally, do citizens understand when party cues are irrelevant (e.g., in judging the performance of the economy), or when they conflict with substantive information, and should therefore be discounted or set aside altogether?

The results of our analysis, experimental and observational, are not encouraging. We find that partisanship facilitates severe biases in the perception of political reality; it leads citizens to ignore their material interests and social values in forming, updating, and organizing their policy preferences; and it leads them to privilege partisan attachment over substantive preferences in the voting booth, especially when the two factors conflict (and they often do). An electorate composed of such individuals is incapable of sending meaningful policy signals to elites or holding them accountable for their performance in office.

Perhaps, then, we are faced with a Hobson's choice: in the absence of a partisan attachment (i.e., a stake in the game), attention to politics is lacking, and judgments are perforce suboptimal. But partisanship seems to ensure that people will view the political world through a crooked lens, leading to a different but equally negative outcome. The choice is that people either tune out politics altogether, or they interpret information in a biased manner due to their virtually unbounded proclivity to yield to the pronouncements of co-partisan elites. Although we find this to be true—independents are not good citizens in nearly any respect and partisans are flagrantly biased, even on matters of objective fact—it is not the whole story. Our most important conclusion is that a nontrivial portion of the electorate manages to escape the vicissitudes of apathy or wanton bias, and it is these citizens—who we refer to as *ambivalent partisans*—that reliably approximate a more desirable standard of democratic citizenship.

Ambivalent partisanship occurs when long-standing *identifications* are contradicted by short-term *evaluations* of the parties' capacities to govern and deliver benefits to the public. This disequilibrium arises when the parties behave out of step with normal expectations: it occurs when the in-party is plagued by scandal, when it fields poor candidates, presides over economic downturn, or mismanages an international conflict or a domestic emergency. It can also occur when the other party is perceived to be doing a competent job in managing the affairs of government. Like traditional partisans (who we refer to as *univalent* partisans), ambivalent partisans have a stake in the game; their attachments are no less strong than those of univalent partisans, and they are no more (or less) knowledgeable about or engaged in politics. Rather, the principal difference between the two types of partisans is that the ambivalent variety derives less judgment confidence on the basis of partisan loyalty. That is, while univalent partisans manage to simultaneously conserve cognitive energy, validate their partisan loyalties, and reach their desired confidence thresholds on the basis of partisan cue-taking, ambivalent partisans cannot manage the last of these judgment goals. The *normative* upshot is that by engendering doubt and uncertainty, the internal conflict between deep-seated identities and contemporaneous party evaluations provides fertile ground for learning and open-mindedness and, as we shall demonstrate, a willingness to assume the cognitive burden of deliberative political thought.

Our findings upend an important piece of conventional wisdom regarding the primary basis of "heterogeneity" in mass politics, namely that variation in how people make up their minds turns on political sophistication, or more generically, "cognitive ability." As we read the literature, the traditional view is that a small number of "able" citizens are more likely than the ill-informed masses to form their political judgments using complex decision rules that focus on the most diagnostic information. Our empirical work suggests two problems with this view. First, sophistication (qua objective knowledge of politics) turns out to be a double-edged sword. While it facilitates political understanding, it also makes it easier for citizens to defend their political attitudes through motivated bias. Sophistication can thus increase the ability—and perhaps even the desire—to reach predetermined conclusions at the expense of forming accurate judgments that square with the "evidence." Second, ability-centered approaches generally ignore citizens' *motivation* to acquire and use political information. If well-informed individuals can manage to attain sufficient confidence through reliance on cost-saving cues alone (e.g., party identification), they should rationally choose to ignore other relevant information, even if that information is highly diagnostic to the decision, and even if they are capable of acquiring it. As it turns out, these two factors (greater bias and unreliable incentives to utilize effortful judgment strategies), as we document in numerous empirical analyses presented throughout the book, lead us to conclude that political sophistication exerts only a minor influence on the nature and quality of mass political judgment.

Thus, contrary to conventional wisdom, poor citizen performance is not inextricably linked to a lack of formal education or political knowledge. In fact, our results quite clearly indicate that cognitive capability is not the primary problem. Instead, what is at issue is *motivation*. As Downs (1957) argued, once a person comes to a confident decision, there is little practical reason to devote further effort to the task. The main impediment to good political judgment, as we see it, is that a majority of citizens are able to come to confident political decisions on the basis of partisan cues alone, even when those cues have no logical value, or when they contradict the individual's values, interests, or well-established facts. To understand why this should be the case, we rely on a psychological insight at the heart of the theory of motivated reasoning: that cognition is driven by goals. Specifically, by toeing the party line, citizens can subjectively maximize three primary desiderata: making it easy, getting it right, and maintaining cognitive consistency. This is a feat not otherwise readily accomplished. At a deeper level, if (as seems to be the case) people pay no real cost for engaging in delusional thinking, they are free to gravitate to those beliefs that provide attractive *psychological* benefits, most prominently those linked to siding with the partisan in-group. The thrust of our analysis is that breaking out of this disciplined mindset requires critical involvement, and this requires *critical partisan loyalty*.

Acknowledgments

In writing this book, we were extremely fortunate to have supportive colleagues at our home universities: Stony Brook, Minnesota, Zurich, Duke, and Bern. Early versions of several chapters were presented at the regular political psychology wine and cheese gatherings at Stony Brook University. Stanley Feldman, Leonie Huddy, Matthew Lebo, Lindsey Levitan, Milton Lodge, Helmut Norpoth, Jeff Segal, Chuck Taber, and graduate students too numerous to mention—though let us name two, David Perkins and Julie Wronski—provided suggestions that fundamentally shaped our thinking. We are privileged to have participated in the intellectual fabric of this hotbed of political psychology during the research and writing of this book.

We have also accumulated debts of gratitude for the advice of several other colleagues—on both sides of the disciplinary divide—who read and commented on portions of the book and who provided constructive critiques at conferences, workshops, and seminars. These include Gene Borgida, Chris Federico, Paul Goren, Jamie Druckman, Jennifer Jerit, John Jost, Arie Kruglanski, Bob Huckfeldt, Joanne Miller, Kathryn Pearson, Dave Redlawsk, Wendy Rahn, Tom Rudolph, Paul Sniderman, Mark Snyder, John Sullivan, and Jenny Wolak. Scott Basinger, who co-wrote (with Lavine) the original article on which this book is based, shared with us valuable insights on how political institutions shape the incentives and cognition of voters. We would also like to thank Jon Krosnick and Skip Lupia for helping us craft items to measure partisan ambivalence and for including them in multiple waves of the 2008 ANES panel study.

We owe deep thanks to three individuals who provided continuous guidance, feedback, and encouragement on the project: Milton Lodge, Jamie Druckman, and Paul Goren. Milt, who at critical points in each of our respective careers served as a mentor, engaged us in many generative debates about the psychological foundations of politics. Milt's wide-ranging insights and suggestions, along with his consistent willingness to put aside his own work and concentrate on ours, vastly improved all aspects of the book. Jamie gave generously of his time in aiding in the development of this project. In particular, our presentation of the material in Chapter 4—on the formation, updating, and organization of policy preferences—benefited immensely from Jamie's comments. Last, but not least, we are greatly indebted to Paul Goren, who read the book from cover to cover, and who provided detailed suggestions on each chapter. Paul's incisive comments saved us, time and again—we hope—from embarrassment, and we thank him for providing wise counsel throughout.

We would also like to thank our editors at Oxford University Press. John Jost, the Political Psychology series editor, enthusiastically courted the project and prodded us to write a book that would speak to both social psychologists and political scientists. This, frankly, was not an easy task, as the field of political psychology (as we see it) remains deeply fractured along disciplinary lines. Works of renown in political science are routinely ignored by psychologists, and the same is true—if perhaps to a lesser extent—of highly visible work in psychology. With John, we believe that the success of political psychology depends critically on interdisciplinary cross-talk, and we have endeavored to write across traditional boundary lines. We are also grateful to Abby Gross and Lori Handelman, who graciously helped to make the editorial process clear, efficient, and enjoyable.

Finally, on a more personal note, we would like to acknowledge our families, who have given us tremendous support and encouragement. Lavine would like to thank JaneAnne Murray, who read large portions of the manuscript and (thankfully) did not take us at our word that we knew what we were talking about. Lavine would also like to thank Seamus and Finnian Lavine, each of whom was born around the time this project was conceived and who make life sweet. Johnston would like to thank his mom, Eileen, who made this life possible; she is a model of strength and perseverance. Johnston would also like to thank Erin and Cory Johnston, and Amy Lee, for their love and support, and for their willingness to listen to his (unsolicited) rants. Finally, Steenbergen would like to thank Elaine Sieff, who gave her support despite being seriously ill for part of the project and who is responsible for several of the graphs in the book. Steenbergen dedicates the book to his late brother Herman, who, although not an academic, showed great interest in and enthusiasm for the project and who, more generally, encouraged Steenbergen in the pursuit of his academic interests.

The Ambivalent Partisan

CHAPTER 1

Partisan Ambivalence and the Contingent Nature of Political Judgment

> I was a military man, and John McCain has always stood up for the military. But Barack Obama is a good man. I voted for Bush twice and was let down in the second term. My godfather is African American, so I'd like to see a change in the guard, too, to see that the doors are open for everyone. But my wife is a doctor, and an attempt to nationalize health care could affect her pay.
>
> *—voter in Sparks Co., Nevada, interviewed by The New York Times, September 23, 2008*

Deliberation and conflict are the essence of political life in a democratic polity. Debates about taxes, war, abortion, and much else divide citizens with contrasting visions of the good society. As the Nevada voter quoted above illustrates, however, conflict is also something that occurs within the minds of individual citizens, as they wrestle with strongly held but incompatible beliefs and feelings. Despite the fact that political elites have become ideologically polarized, average citizens are often torn about matters of politics, seeing both good and bad in policies, candidates, the political party labels, and even government itself. For example, many Americans support the conflicting values of individual effort and social equality on the question of welfare spending, the right to privacy and the sacredness of human life in deciding whether abortion should be legal, and tolerance and tradition on matters of gay rights. It isn't hard to understand why people experience internalized conflict, or *ambivalence,* in the political domain. Political disputes often activate widely shared but inherently clashing values; people hold political attitudes that do not line up with ideological or party stereotypes; they discuss politics with friends and coworkers who hold different worldviews; and the flow of information during election campaigns and policy debates is naturally two sided, casting each side in both a favorable and an unfavorable light.

People may experience ambivalence toward a variety of political objects. In presidential campaigns, it is the candidates themselves who are the most salient; they receive the lion's share of attention from the news media, and contemporary campaigns produce a staggering amount of political advertising.[1] Voters form impressions of candidate character, they react to the candidates' stands on key issues and to their performance in interviews, speeches, and debates, and they develop feelings about them as a natural part of the appraisal process. Given the media's tendency to frame stories in ways that highlight controversy and the fact that most candidates are complex individuals possessing distinct strengths and weaknesses, voters often react to them with at least a modicum of ambivalence. In 1980, for example, Jimmy Carter was seen as being an honest fellow with compassion for the poor, but many voters questioned whether he was up to the job of managing a faltering economy and an acute set of foreign policy problems. By the end of Bill Clinton's presidency, his integrity in private matters was in tatters, but he was widely seen as being a competent steward of the economy. And as for Ronald Reagan, many voters who disagreed with his policies nevertheless experienced positive emotion toward him and admired his leadership qualities.

As central as individual actors are, it is the political *parties* that are the enduring foundation of American political conflict. Political leaders enter and exit the public stage, but the parties and their symbols, platforms, and group associations provide a long-term anchor to the political system. For all the talk of their decline (e.g., Norpoth & Rusk, 1982; Wattenberg, 1998), recent evidence suggests that, if anything, the influence of partisanship has grown stronger over the past two decades (Bartels, 2000; Hetherington, 2001). In fact, partisan identification is the single strongest indicator of electoral preference. It is the principal long-term force that governs how we view candidates and election campaigns; it is a prime determinant (and organizer) of other political attitudes; and it dominates our perceptions of political leaders and events during off-election periods. Brader (2006, p. 109) echoes a strong consensus among political scientists in writing that "when voters attend to politics at all, they rely overwhelmingly on partisan habits and well-worn criteria to choose a candidate, disregarding much of what campaigns have to say."

Partisanship also serves as a powerful device in simplifying the task of political judgment: By relying on knowledge, expectations, and beliefs about

1. For the first time in American history, the candidates for president in 2008 spent more than $1 billion. To see where the money came from, see the Web site of the Center for Responsive Politics, http://www.opensecrets.org/pres08/index.php. Accessed on July 12, 2010.

the two major political parties, partisan cues can allow citizens to make reasonable choices without having more detailed information. As Rahn (1993, p. 474) explains, "partisan stereotypes are rich cognitive categories, containing not only policy information but group alliances, trait judgments, specific examples of group members, and performance assessments." In one of the most influential statements on how ordinary citizens make political judgments, Zaller (1992, p. 45) argued for the preeminence of partisan cue-taking:

> The[re is] no allowance for citizens to think, reason, or deliberate about politics: If citizens are well informed, they react mechanically to political ideas on the basis of external cues about their partisan implications, and if they are too poorly informed to be aware of these cues, they tend to uncritically accept whatever ideas they encounter.

More recent work similarly echoes the reflexive nature of partisan influence:

> If the cue giver and recipient share a party label, the latter will trust the former and accept the message without reflecting much on message content. But if the cue giver and recipient lie across the partisan divide, the recipient will mistrust the source and reject the message, again without much reflection. (Goren, Federico, & Kittilson, 2009, p. 806)

According to this dominant view, so long as citizens are capable of detecting the partisan coloration of political messages, judgments should rationally reflect their interests and values.

PARTISAN AMBIVALENCE

Despite a wealth of research demonstrating the importance of partisanship as an informational shortcut, we will show that many citizens experience internalized conflict toward the party labels. While this may take different forms, the most politically potent manifestation stems from a disjuncture between an individual's long-term *identification* with a political party and his or her short-term *evaluations* of the parties' capacities to govern and deliver benefits to the public. This disequilibrium arises when the parties behave out of step with normal expectations: It occurs when the in-party (i.e., one's own party) is plagued by scandal, when it embraces issue positions that are inconsistent with core ideological principles, or when it fields poor candidates, presides over economic downturn, or mismanages an international conflict or a domestic emergency. For example, as Figure 1.1 illustrates, the public's increasing opposition to the Iraq War and the Bush administration's inept response to

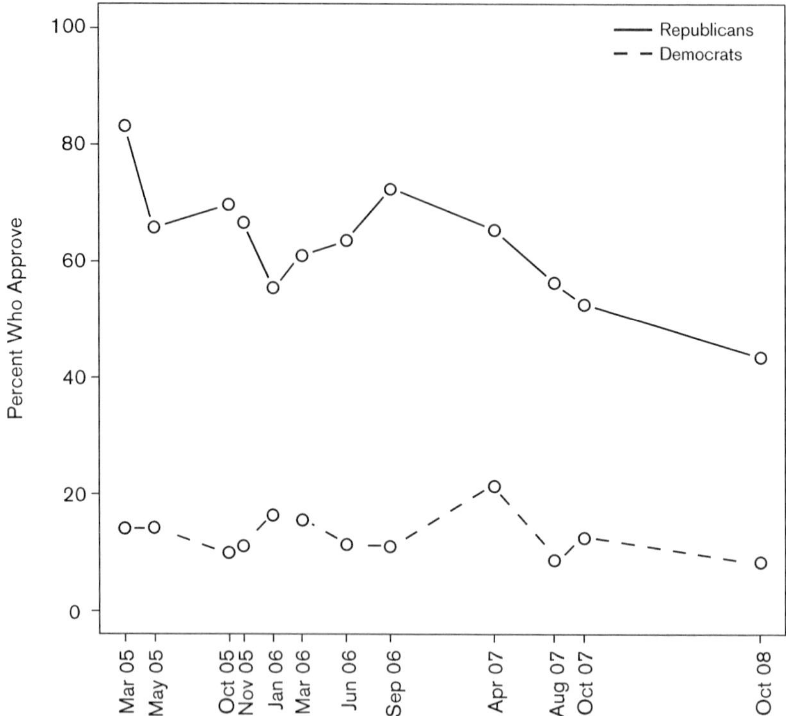

Figure 1.1 Approval of the Republican Party in Congress Among Democrats and Republicans, 2005–2008.

Notes: Pew: 3/05, 5/05, 11/05, 1/06, 3/06, 6/06, 9/06; Gallup: 10/05, 8/07; ABC: 4/07, 10/07; CNN: 10/08. *Pew*: Do you approve or disapprove of the job the Republican leaders in Congress are doing? *Gallup*: Do you approve or disapprove of the way the Republicans in Congress are handling their job? *ABC*: Do you approve or disapprove of the way Republicans in Congress are doing their job? *CNN*: Do you approve or disapprove of the way the Republican leaders in Congress are handling their job?

Hurricane Katrina preceded a wider disenchantment among Republicans with their own party. A disjuncture between partisan identity and party evaluations can also occur when the other party is perceived to be doing a commendable job in managing government affairs. This was the case among Democrats who helped to reelect Ronald Reagan in 1984 and among Republicans during the economic boom of the late 1990s (see Lebo & Cassino, 2007).

Whether it is a negative evaluation of one's own party, a positive evaluation of the other party, or both, the outcome is that identity and evaluation do not point in the same direction. We refer to this splintering as *partisan ambivalence*;

the people who experience it are *ambivalent partisans*. Figure 1.2 provides an initial glimpse of the prevalence of this disjuncture in the American electorate. The two panels rely on different measurement strategies to tally the percentage of citizens possessing at least one identity-conflicting thought or feeling (either a negative reaction toward their own party or a positive reaction toward the other party). Panel A is based on pooled data from the biennial American National Election Study (ANES) series between 1980 and 2004 (the period covered by much of our ensuing empirical work). It aggregates responses to open-ended questions that ask respondents what they like and dislike about each of the two parties. Panel B relies on measures that we wrote ourselves for multiple waves of the 2008 ANES panel study.[2] Here, respondents are separately asked whether they have any positive and negative thoughts or feelings about each party (with follow-up questions about their intensity). The different item formats yield a highly similar result: Somewhere between a third and half of the electorate experiences some discrepancy between identity and evaluations. We will present a more detailed portrait of the prevalence, antecedents, and challenges of measuring partisan ambivalence in Chapter 3; suffice it to say here that the discrepancy is not a marginal phenomenon but one that occurs widely in the electorate.

THE PURPOSE OF THIS BOOK

The central purpose of this book is to demonstrate that partisan ambivalence is a fundamental—but largely unappreciated—aspect of mass belief systems and a principal determinant of the way people make up their minds in matters of politics. We will marshal a broad array of experimental and survey evidence to demonstrate that this form of ambivalence is (a) prevalent in the American electorate; (b) irreducible to other voter attributes such as the strength of party identification, political sophistication, or anxiety; and (c) a primary determinant of variation in two key dimensions of political reasoning: its *depth* and *objectivity*. Specifically, ceteris paribus, ambivalent partisans engage in more careful deliberation than their univalent (i.e., nonambivalent) counterparts; they are more responsive to the political environment; and they rely on more valuable—but cognitively costly—criteria in forming their judgments. They also hold more *accurate* perceptions of the political world, as they are less prone to view it through a partisan lens. In sum, we will demonstrate that—whether judging candidates, issues, or political events—partisan ambivalence is a powerful determinant of how citizens "decide how to decide." Most important, and

2. We are grateful to Jon Krosnick and Skip Lupia for helping us craft these items.

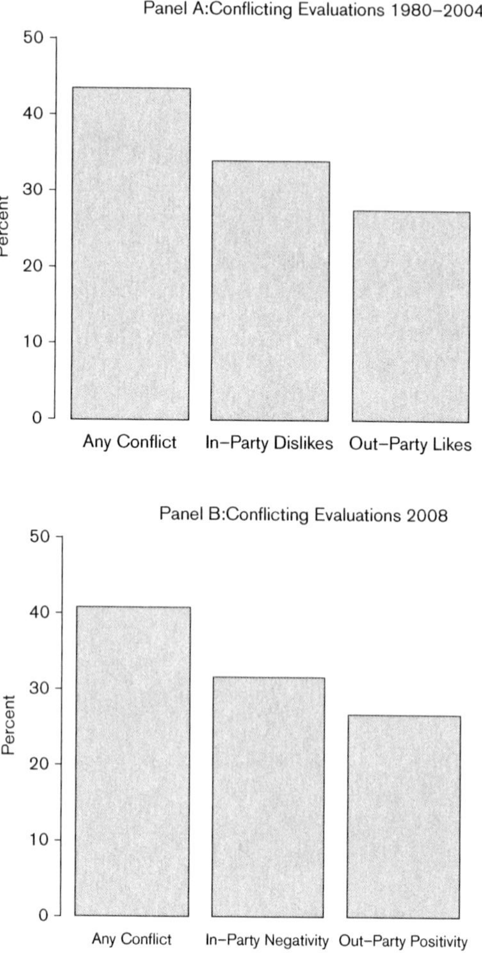

Figure 1.2 Prevalence of "Conflicting" Partisan Evaluations (*Source*: ANES). (A) "Any Conflict" refers to the percentage of respondents reporting at least one identity-conflicting consideration, either a negative reaction toward the in-party or a positive reaction toward the out-party. (B) "Any Conflict" refers to the percentage of respondents reporting at least some identity-conflicting thoughts or feelings, either in-party negativity or out-party positivity.

contrary to popular conceptualizations of mass political judgment (e.g., Zaller 1992), we will show that ambivalent partisans do not simply react mechanically to the political ideas they encounter; rather, they approximate the type of critical, systematic, and open-minded thought praised by democratic theorists (e.g., Dewey, 1933/1997; Habermas, 1998; Mill, 1859/1998). Finally, as we will elaborate on later, a consideration of the consequences of partisan ambivalence leads to a very different normative conception of the "good citizen" than conventionally suggested by research focusing on political sophistication (Converse, 1964; Delli Carpini & Keeter, 1996).

AMBIVALENCE AND THE DEBATE OVER THE NATURE OF PARTISANSHIP

The concept of partisan ambivalence draws on the insights of two schools of thought about the nature of partisanship: one focusing on social identity and the ubiquity of partisan bias, and the other on a dispassionate process of policy agreement and ongoing performance evaluation (for reviews, see Green, Palmquist, & Schickler, 2002; Johnston, 2006; Weisberg & Greene, 2003). The authors of *The American Voter* (Campbell, Converse, Miller, & Stokes, 1960) proposed that party identification is founded on a deeply rooted affective bond, developed through socialization in childhood and resulting in a sense of belongingness in which the group is incorporated into the self-concept. The identification process also reflects a cognitive representation of the parties in terms of linkages to salient social groups, and a matching of one's self-conception to an image of the groups associated with each party (Campbell, Gurin, & Miller, 1954; Key, 1955; Miller & Wlezien, 1993). For example, positive feelings toward evangelical Christians or the upwardly mobile should facilitate identification with the Republican Party, whereas positive feelings toward the working class or racial minorities should promote identification with the Democrats. In reflecting on whether they are Democrats or Republicans, Green et al. (2002, p. 8) contend that people ask themselves the following questions: "What kinds of social groups come to mind as I think about Democrats, Republicans, and Independents? Which assemblage of groups (if any) best describes me?"

In addition to viewing partisanship as an affective bond rooted in feelings toward party-linked groups, the traditional conceptualization holds that partisanship serves as a filter of political information, that it "raises a perceptual screen through which the individual tends to see what is favorable to his partisan orientation" (Campbell et al., 1960, p. 133; see also Berelson, Lazarsfeld, & McPhee, 1954). In other words, partisanship is hypothesized to produce systematic biases in what political information citizens attend to and how that information is interpreted and evaluated. Research on perceptions of the economy illustrates just how powerful this filter can be. In one analysis, Bartels (2002) examined perceptions of trends in unemployment and inflation over the 8 years of Reagan's presidency. While both indicators improved sharply during this period, Democrats were more likely than not to report that each had actually worsened. In an example of more recent vintage, as late as 2006, nearly half of Republicans—but nearly no Democrats—believed that Saddam Hussein possessed weapons of mass destruction prior to the start of the Iraq War (Gelman, Park, Shor, & Cortina, 2008). Even reactions to the most significant political scandal in modern American history were shaped by partisanship: after Watergate broke in June of 1972, Republicans reported being less interested in reading about it, knew less about it, and judged it to be less serious than did Democrats (Sweeney & Gruber, 1984).

Although the mechanisms underlying partisan bias were not clearly spelled out in *The American Voter*, several contemporary scholars have interpreted them within the framework of *social identity theory* (Huddy, 2001, 2003; Tajfel, 1978; Tajfel & Turner, 1979; Weisberg & Greene, 2003). According to the theory, people derive a portion of their self-concept through identification with social groups, including ethnic, religious, and national groups, as well as political groups, that is, Democrats and Republicans. At the heart of the theory is the idea that group identification typically occurs within an intergroup context and is motivated by a desire for "positive distinctiveness," that is, a desire to view the "in-group" as distinct from and more positive than other relevant groups ("out-groups"). Self-categorization as an in-group member thus leads to exaggerated comparisons between in-group and out-group that are designed to favor the former, particularly when the intergroup context is highly salient. In their day-to-day lives, Americans tend to be disengaged from politics, and identification with a political party is only a minor aspect of their self-conceptions. However, election campaigns, especially at the presidential level, as well as heated policy debates increase the relevance of *partisan* identities, leading citizens to think about politics from an "us" versus "them" perspective.

By viewing the group as part of who we are, we share in its successes and failures. For those who have ever felt the disappointment of losing an election, or alternatively, celebrating a close victory, this surely rings true. It is this intimate connection between the group and the self that explains why we readily distort, counterargue, or simply ignore uncongenial political news. There are two conditions, however, in which an individual may come to hold identity-conflicting partisan evaluations. The first is when party behavior and performance impinge on an area of personal importance to a voter. For example, as Iyengar and Kinder (1986) have shown in their research on agenda setting, the unemployed are more sensitive to news stories about unemployment, African Americans to stories about civil rights, and the elderly to stories about Social Security (see also Boninger, Berent, & Krosnick, 1995; Hillygus & Shields, 2008; Thomsen, Borgida, & Lavine, 1995). The influence of party performance on partisan evaluation should thus depend on one's circumstances and priorities. For example, it was *fiscal* conservatives who were dismayed when the Republicans passed a nearly trillion dollar prescription drug bill in 2003, but *religious* conservatives who looked askance at the sex scandals that plagued the Republicans during George W. Bush's second term.

Second, identity-conflicting partisan evaluations arise when a party is plagued by a long stretch of difficulties. Consider, for example, the predicament of the Democrats in 1968. Among conservative Southerners, the party was criticized for its support for civil rights. Among liberals, it had come under attack from opponents of the Vietnam War.[3] As a result, Democrats began to view their own party less favorably. Or take the Republicans during the latter part of the last decade. Appearing all but unbeatable after the terrorist attacks in 2001, mounting performance failures during Bush's second term eventually took a toll on the positivity of the party label among Republicans. As Figure 1.1 shows, the party had a favorability rating of over 80 percent among Republican voters after the presidential election in 2004. Soon thereafter, however, the American death toll in Iraq rose sharply; the administration fumbled the response to Hurricane Katrina; three leading Republicans in Congress were indicted or convicted on public corruption charges (including the majority leader in the House), and six more were involved in high-profile sex scandals.[4] If all of that were not enough bad news for the party, the economy went into a free fall just before the first debate of the 2008 presidential election. These events coincided with a seismic wave of negativity *toward the party itself* among Republicans. By Election Day 2008, the percentage of Republicans who approved of their own party had been cut in half. In sum, despite the motivation to maintain harmony between identity and evaluations, political reality can sometimes make this difficult to do.

At times, then, citizens are capable of evaluating party performance objectively. This insight led to a second, "revisionist" perspective on the nature of

3. Moreover, Lyndon Johnson, a president who had won by a landslide 4 years earlier, was compelled not to seek reelection. The primaries in 1968 had been tumultuous even before the assassination of Robert Kennedy, and they culminated in one of the most chaotic nominating conventions ever.

4. Randy Cunningham (Rep. California) and Robert Ney (Rep. Ohio) were convicted and sent to prison on corruption charges, and Tom DeLay (Rep. Texas) was indicted in 2005 on a felony conspiracy charge. The sex scandals involved Mark Foley (Rep. Florida), Larry Craig (Sen. Idaho), David Vitter (Sen. Louisiana), John Ensign (Sen. Nevada), Vito Fossella (Rep. New York), and John Sanford (Gov. South Carolina).

partisanship, one more congenial to the notion of citizens as rational actors. Scholars working within this tradition view partisanship as an ongoing running tally of evaluation based on the accumulation of information about each party's capacity to govern and the individual's level of policy agreement with the two parties (Downs, 1957; Fiorina, 1981). From this perspective, partisanship is not an enduring aspect of citizens' political self-conceptions but an ephemeral "expression of beliefs about which party will best pursue one's interests" and govern most effectively (Green et al., 2002, p. 8). Its origins, moreover, lie not in the remoteness of childhood or in feelings toward party-linked groups, but in the contemporary actions of the parties themselves—whether they preside over peace and prosperity, or corruption, economic recession, or the failure to deliver on desired policy change. For revisionists, then, partisanship is little more than a summary judgment of past experience and is always subject to adjustment. In sum, whereas the traditional approach is about *identity*, the revisionist approach is about *evaluation*.

Much of the contemporary literature centers on which of these conceptualizations better captures what partisanship really is, or which of the two components—identity or evaluation—is *causally* prior and thus of greater political importance. Yet to a large extent, these two visions have always represented a false dichotomy. For one thing, their relationship is bidirectional: Party identification both responds to and shapes substantive political opinion (Abramowitz, 2010; Carsey & Layman, 2006; Johnston, 2006). Moreover, psychological research indicates that social identification—the process of linking the self to social groups—involves both an *affective* dimension, which refers to feelings of belonging, commitment, and attachment to the group, as well as an *evaluative* dimension, which refers to holding positive or negative attitudes toward the group (e.g., Cameron, 2004; De Weerd & Klandermans, 1999; Duckit et al., 2005; Ellemers et al., 1999). The first aspect dovetails with the traditional notion of partisanship laid out in *The American Voter* and with contemporary formulations rooted in social identity (Green et al., 2002; Greene, 2002, 2005; Weisberg & Greene, 2003). The second aspect corresponds to the revisionist focus on dynamic evaluations of contemporary party performance (Downs, 1957; Fiorina, 1981; Erikson, MacKuen, & Stimson, 2002).

We believe that partisanship functions both as a stable *psychological* construct involving affective group attachment and as a temporal *political* summary judgment of group performance. In line with the general theory of cognitive consistency (Festinger, 1957; Greenwald et al., 2002; Heider, 1958), we expect that citizens have a strong preference for harmonizing these components. However, when the information flow about one's own party becomes persistently negative, efforts to maintain equilibrium inevitably break down. Under normal circumstances, partisans may be quick to blame the out-party and credit the in-party, but they are not entirely immune to how economic swings, scandal, and the quality of domestic and foreign policy management reflect on party competence and leadership. Expressed in psychological terms, the process of motivated reasoning is not *unbounded*. As the late Ziva Kunda (1990, pp. 482–483) observed in a widely read article on social judgment motives:

> People do not seem to be at liberty to conclude whatever they want to conclude merely because they want to. Rather, I propose that people motivated to arrive at a particular conclusion attempt to be rational and to construct a justification of their desired conclusion that would persuade a dispassionate observer. They draw the desired conclusion only if they can muster up the evidence necessary to support it... In other words, they maintain an "illusion of objectivity."

Gradually, once reality constraints become overpowering and the illusion of objectivity no longer tenable, a disequilibrium emerges—and partisans become ambivalent. The speed at which this occurs will vary from person to person and across political contexts. But given sufficiently long stretches of negative news about one's own party, or positive news about the other party, even the most resistant of individuals will experience a disjuncture. *Partisanship becomes ambivalent partisanship.*

Despite a general tendency to bring evaluations into line with identity, we believe that ignoring processes of objective assessment obscures a distinction between two fundamentally different forms of democratic citizenship, with important consequences for the quality of political judgment. Green and his collegues (2002) argue that people adjust their beliefs about party competence in light of new evidence but quickly return to their "baseline" or equilibrium level of partisanship in subsequent periods. Such a model leaves room for both objective assessment and long-term stability, a dynamic we label *critical loyalty*. In our empirical work, we document what happens in the period between critical evaluations of party performance and the return to long-term equilibrium. Ultimately, we hope to have put together a convincing case that we need to rethink the origins and dynamics of good citizenship in American politics.

MOTIVATION, HEURISTICS, AND THE NORMATIVE VALUE OF PARTISANSHIP

There are numerous ways to study differences in how citizens decide how to decide, and several ways in which "good" or "rational" decision making might be defined (e.g., Bartels, 1996; Delli Carpini & Keeter, 1996; Kuklinski

& Quirk, 2001; Lau & Redlawsk, 1997, 2006). The standard scholarly understanding is that variation in how people make up their minds turns on one's store of information about politics.[5] Whether referred to as "level of conceptualization," "sophistication," "awareness," or "knowledge," or measured simply as years of education, the traditional view is that a small number of "able" citizens are more likely than the ill-informed masses to form their political judgments using complex decision rules that focus on the most diagnostic information. For example, in building on Dewey's (1927/1954, 1933/1997) intuition about the importance of formal schooling in shaping the individual's aptitude for democratic citizenship, Sniderman and colleagues (1991, p. 9) argue that "the ability to manipulate information efficiently and to gather it effectively" depends on cognitive ability. They document a variety of circumstances in which well-informed individuals form their opinions on the basis of commitments to ideological abstractions, whereas the less sophisticated, who by all accounts are "innocent of ideology," rely on more issue-specific considerations.

For reasons that we discuss more fully in Chapter 2, we believe that understanding why citizens choose the judgment strategies they do requires greater attention to motivation. The key question thus becomes: When people turn their attention to public affairs, what are they trying to accomplish? What are their goals? The core of our perspective holds that people operate according to three motivational principles when forming political judgments: (1) least effort, (2) sufficiency, and (3) belief perseverance. The well-known *least effort* principle holds that citizens minimize the cognitive resources spent on making judgments (Allport, 1954; Kahneman, 2011; Simon, 1955). Given the far more immediate and personal concerns that people face in their day-to-day lives (e.g., raising children, working, engaging in social relationships), politics rarely rises to the level of a compelling spectacle. As Mondak (1994, p. 118) put it, "despite the best efforts of officials in Washington to involve themselves in glamorous scandals, Hollywood still produces far more interesting material." Hence, in those instances when people cast an eye on public affairs, they should try to get by spending as little time and effort as possible.

However, the *sufficiency* principle holds that people would like to be confident in their judgments. They want to feel that they are making the right choice, especially if the decision is important to them. Together, the two principles

5. For evidence, see Delli Carpini and Keeter (1996); Kam (2005); Krosnick (1990); Lau and Redlawsk (2006); Luskin (1987); Neuman (1986); Sniderman, Brody, and Tetlock (1991); and Zaller (1992).

imply a trade-off between conflicting goals: *Accuracy* requires that people's judgments reflect reality and their substantive values and interests; *efficiency* requires that they conserve cognitive resources. Last, citizens would like to form judgments that affirm (rather than challenge) the validity of their political predispositions, thus satisfying the *belief perseverance* principle. Ideally, then, when forming a political judgment, we would like to simultaneously make it easy, get it right, and avoid disturbing our prior beliefs or the positivity of our partisan identities. What do these conflicting goals imply about the nature of the political judgment process? Rationally, they imply that if low-effort strategies allow citizens to obtain sufficient confidence in the "correctness" of their judgments, they will be unwilling to assume the cognitive burden of obtaining more diagnostic information.

Despite the plethora of potentially useful informational shortcuts, one stands out in terms of its breadth, inferential power, and cognitive efficiency: party identification. Accumulated research over the past half century indicates that partisanship is the most "stable and influential political predisposition in the belief systems of ordinary Americans" (Goren et al., 2009, p. 805). As we noted at the outset of the chapter, partisan identity shapes a wide range of political judgments, including presidential approval, candidate appraisal, vote choice, policy attitudes, and even core values.[6] While each presidential election and national issue debate highlights a unique set of concerns, political conflict in the United States is fundamentally structured by *partisan* competition, such that Democratic values, policies, and candidates are pit against those offered by the Republicans. Sniderman (2000) argues that the preeminence of partisanship as a judgment cue arises because the party system constrains the "menu of choices" available for consideration by the public and attaches well-known, easily identifiable "brand names" to these options. As Jackman and Sniderman (2002, p. 214) explain:

> Citizens do not make the political world anew because, save for the most extraordinary of circumstances, they are not required to. The political world is presented to most citizens largely "prefabricated": in mature democracies like the United States, political institutions and actors are well defined, with parties and party leaders figuring prominently. Party identification figures so prominently ... because political parties are the way that elites have organized competition among themselves for public power.

6. For the evidence, see Bartels (2000); Conover and Feldman (1989); Goren (2005); Goren et al. (2009); Jacoby (1988); Lodge and Hamill (1986); Miller and Shanks (1986); and Rahn (1993).

From this *institutional* perspective, the power of partisanship as a heuristic lies in its goodness-of-fit to the "choice space" of most political debates. This view echoes a basic tenet of behavioral decision theory, that "the structure of a decision environment can determine the likelihood that various strategies will yield a good solution to the problem" (Payne et al., 1993, p. 71).

Partisanship is equally powerful at the level of individual psychology. Its usage not only entails minimal informational cost but potentially provides a solution to complex trade-offs between the desire for cognitive efficiency and two additional goals: the need for sufficient confidence in the accuracy of one's judgments, and the desire to reach judgments that affirm the validity of one's standing political commitments. The desire for confident knowledge reflects a well-established preference for cognitive clarity and an aversion to ambiguity, uncertainty, and doubt, and the desire to affirm one's priors reflects the negative existential value of having one's beliefs upset and faced with contradiction. By viewing politics through a partisan lens, citizens can assume that they are making judgments consistent with their values and interests (especially as the parties have become better "sorted" along the liberal-conservative dimension; see Abramowitz, 2010), thus satisfying the need for sufficient confidence. And, by ignoring (or distorting or counterarguing) other readily available information, some of which may contradict their partisan commitments, citizens can both conserve cognitive resources and maintain cognitive consistency.

It is not our intention to imply that partisanship completely engulfs the perceptual field, or that political judgments follow deterministically from prior partisan commitments. That would be a caricature of the evidence. However, for those who identify with one of the major political parties—which, if one includes those who "lean" toward one party or the other, constitutes roughly 90 percent of the electorate—partisan loyalty serves as an *anchor* from which adjustments, typically insufficient ones, are made in judging policies, candidates, and other elements of politics (e.g., the economy). Moreover, so long as party images are relatively static over time, citizens should see little reason to carefully monitor the political environment, thus inhibiting political learning and belief updating. Under normal circumstances, then, and for reasons both structural and motivational (as outlined earlier), standing partisan commitments should exert a broad and powerful influence on political judgment and choice.

Does Toeing the Party Line Lead to "Good" Judgments?

Despite the occasional expression of doubt among political scientists regarding the *normative* utility of heuristics (e.g., Bartels, 1996; Kuklinski & Hurley, 1994; Kuklinski & Quirk, 2000; Lau & Redlawsk, 2001), the conventional wisdom is that they "elevate the ordinary citizen from a hopeless incompetent to a reasonably capable participant in democratic politics" (Kuklinski & Quirk, 2000, p. 295). By providing a plausible account of how a chronically inattentive electorate can manage to make political judgments in line with its values and interests, partisanship and other cognitive shortcuts have undeniable appeal. Much to our surprise, however, there appears to be a dearth of direct empirical evidence on whether citizens typically use partisan cues *appropriately*; that is, whether they improve the *quality* of political decisions. For example, do partisan cues facilitate accurate perceptions of the political world? Do they lead voters to make electoral choices in line with their "fully informed preferences?" That is, are partisan cues an effective *substitute* for more diagnostic information, or in the case of public opinion, do partisan cues lead citizens to adopt policy positions in line with their general political outlooks? And finally, do citizens understand when party cues are irrelevant, or when they conflict with substantive information, and should therefore be discounted or set aside altogether? In writing that "we *hope* that the shortcuts citizens take will get them to the same place that they would have arrived at if they had taken the 'long way around,'" Kam (2005, p. 177) acknowledges the thin evidential base on which the normative utility of heuristics rests.

We believe there is ample reason to be skeptical. First, for all its advantages in terms of efficiency, reliance on partisan identity carries a major liability: It disposes citizens to a distorted view of the political world. Partisans expect their party to perform better, to produce high-quality candidates, and to take appropriate issue stands. To preserve those beliefs and to protect their partisan identities, people often engage in motivated reasoning.[7] They selectively expose themselves to information that validates their identities, and when confronted with uncongenial information, they often ignore, discount, or counterargue it. In Chapter 5, we will demonstrate that among *univalent* partisans—the majority of the electorate for whom partisan identity and evaluation are in perfect sync—political perceptions are subject to substantial amounts of bias on a wide range of *factual* matters, including the voting records of legislators, the policy stands of candidates, various aspects of economic performance (e.g., growth, inflation, unemployment), and crime rates.

7. For the evidence, see Achen and Bartels (2006); Bartels (2002, 2008); Cohen (2003); Fischle (2000); Goren (2002); Iyengar and Hahn (2009); Iyengar et al. (2009); Knobloch-Westerwick and Meng (2009); Lodge and Taber (2000); McGraw et al. (1996); and Sweeney and Gruber (1984).

A second reason to be skeptical of partisan cues is that when they are available, people often ignore more valuable information (Cohen, 2003; Druckman, 2001; Kam, 2005; Ottati & Wyer, 1990; Rahn, 1993). The presence of a powerful shortcut can thus undermine the motivation to engage in deliberative reasoning. Third, in laboratory experiments of mock elections in which participants choose what information to look at from a scrolling "information board," accessing the candidates' party affiliations does little to facilitate the learning of their policy stands; nor does it reliably increase the likelihood of "voting correctly" (Lau & Redlawsk, 2001). These failures are especially likely to occur when a candidate is not representative of the party stereotype (e.g., a pro-choice Republican) or when the voter is unfamiliar with partisan differences on relevant policy issues.

Partisan cue-taking is not a panacea for citizen competence for yet another reason: The American public is often more *pragmatic* than it is *ideological* when it comes to public policy. Despite the fact that most citizens have stable and coherent political principles (Goren, 2012), in practice they are flexible when it comes to applying them in particular contexts. In a recent analysis of citizens' attitudes toward inequality, Page and Jacobs (2009) argued that the public functions as "conservative egalitarians." By this, they mean that while citizens are generally skeptical of government intervention in the economy, they are willing to support such involvement in special circumstances (e.g., during a financial collapse), even when it means a rise in their own taxes. During the budget debates of 2011, for example, many Republican voters reflexively toed the party line in calling for massive cuts in spending to reduce the deficit. Other Republicans, however, sampled a broader range of elite opinion—much of it calling for immediate spending increases to stimulate economic growth—and they formed more centrist (and pragmatic) preferences.

Our conclusion is that while partisan cue-taking is a pervasive political judgment strategy, the heuristics literature has oversold its utility in producing a competent electorate (see also Bartels, 1996; Kuklinski & Hurley, 1994; Kuklinski & Quirk, 2000, 2001). While we agree that reliance on party *can* increase the quality of citizen judgment, it is unclear when and how often this will be the case among ordinary citizens. Given the considerations raised earlier, we believe that failed delegation will be the result a good deal of the time. In effect, this means that information matters, and that rational choice cannot be purchased on the cheap. Unfortunately for our desire to make it easy when forming political judgments, getting it right often requires a willingness to engage in critical and open-minded thought.

PARTISAN AMBIVALENCE AND ADAPTIVE JUDGMENT

The fundamental question, then, is *when*—under what conditions—will citizens be motivated to think more deeply and more evenhandedly about their political options? When will judgments be quick, reflexive, and shallow, reflecting little more than partisan bias, and when will they reflect more extensive thought and consideration? Second, what factors contribute to *accuracy* in political perception? Under what conditions will citizens be willing to accept information that challenges their partisan identities?[8] And third, given the mechanism(s) responsible for producing it, what are the theoretical and normative implications of this distinction in judgment strategy?

In line with the considerations raised earlier, we find that under "normal" circumstances—that is, when citizens view their own party favorably and the other party unfavorably—political judgment is marked by three interlocking characteristics: shallowness, bias, and early decision foreclosure. Political scientists have hotly debated the question of whether partisanship leads to, as Green et al. (2002, p. 110) put it, "a defensive psychological reaction whereby partisans resist political information that paints their group in a negative light," causing citizens to "avoid or ignore information that fails to correspond to their preconceptions." As we implied earlier, partisan bias is not ubiquitous; however, we find strong, unequivocal, and consistent evidence for it among *univalent* partisans, extending even to judgments on matters of objective fact. For example, in a series of experiments presented in Chapter 4, we find that univalent partisans will persist in choosing policies said to be endorsed by members of their own party, even when accompanying substantive information clearly indicates that an alternative policy option is closer to their own values. In general, the behavior of univalent partisans is well described by ancient Talmudic Law (where it is written): *We do not see things as they are; we see things as we are* (Moskowitz, Skurnik, & Galinsky, 1999, p. 12).

Beyond their proclivity for bias, the judgments of univalent partisans tend to be remarkably superficial. As we will show, they pay little heed to information about unemployment and growth when forming judgments about the

8. Although "systematic" processing might seem to have the connotation of being ubiquitously open-minded and unbiased, this is not the case. Both heuristic and systematic processing can be either objective or biased, depending on the individual's goals (e.g., accuracy vs. the desire to reach specific conclusions) and on the accessibility and reliability of heuristics that influence the interpretation and evaluation of information (Chaiken, Lieberman, & Eagly, 1989).

economy; they ignore the substance of policy proposals when partisan cues are present; they disregard the ideological leanings of legislators when making inferences about their roll-call behavior; they fail to vote on the basis of policy agreement in congressional and presidential elections, and their beliefs about crime reflect inattention to widely reported news on the subject. Overall, univalent partisans show remarkably little learning or attitudinal updating during political campaigns or salient policy debates. In sum, when contemporary party evaluations coincide with long-term identities, political judgments are by and large a reflection of partisan loyalty, with little contribution from other sources.

Finally, univalent partisans tend to foreclose quickly on their judgment options. In experimental contexts, our findings reveal that they require comparatively little information to reach their confidence thresholds, and in real electoral contexts, univalent partisans report forming their voting intentions early in the campaign. This explains why the public is often unresponsive to campaigns and to exogenous shocks to the political environment. Moreover, as we will demonstrate throughout the book, this style of decision making among univalent partisans is highly robust: It is just as likely to occur among political sophisticates and those with strong partisan attachments as among the uninformed and the weakly attached.

Partisan cues are not always perceived as useful decision guides, however. As we will discuss in Chapter 2, the subjective utility of any informational shortcut depends on the extent to which it is viewed as a *reliable* yardstick in leading to good decisions (Chaiken, 1987; Eagly & Chaiken, 1993; Lupia & McCubbins, 1998; Petty, 1994; Pierro et al., 2004). If a cue fails to heighten decision confidence, it will be disregarded as a reason to favor one course of action over another. We will demonstrate in Chapter 4 that when contemporary political evaluations are out of step with long-term (identity-based) expectations, partisan cues lose their heuristic value. We hypothesize that this prompts four fundamental changes in how citizens form their political judgments in a wide variety of settings.

First, and most directly, it should lead them to turn away from partisanship, as it is no longer seen as facilitating "accurate" decisions. Second, to pick up the slack in confidence, we expect citizens to engage in more careful thought about their political options. For example, they should be more likely to seek out information about candidates' policy stands and past voting records in deciding whether to support them. Third, we expect that when citizens distrust partisan cues, their judgments are less demonstrably plagued by partisan bias. Fourth, we expect individuals to take longer to make their decisions, allowing for greater responsiveness to campaigns. In sum, by motivating deeper and more evenhanded thought, we expect that a disjuncture between citizens' primary, long-term political identities and their contemporary evaluations of party performance will be a primary mediator of rational choice.

The upshot of our analysis is that people are adaptive political decision makers who make strategic use of their cognitive resources. Consistent with a great deal of evidence in the psychological literature and with the rational choice framework of Downs (1957; see also Lupia & McCubbins, 1998), we argue that individuals will minimize their decision effort by relying on simple rules of thumb when they can but will switch to more effortful thinking when decision confidence falls too low. Our empirical analysis in Chapters 4–7 leads to some new conclusions about the bases of citizen competence. Our most important finding is that political responsiveness follows most powerfully from ambivalent partisanship. Across a diverse range of political judgment contexts, we find that ambivalent partisans exhibit two core motivations required of effective democratic citizenship: a willingness to devote substantial cognitive resources to making political judgments, and a stronger desire to form judgments that are objectively accurate—that is, that respect the available "evidence"—than those that gratify partisan expectations.

NORMATIVE AND THEORETICAL IMPLICATIONS

Political sophistication has been widely embraced as the key moderator of judgment strategies. Well-informed citizens are more likely to attend to and receive political messages, and they process information more efficiently than political novices (Fiske, Kinder, & Larter, 1983; Lau & Redlawsk, 2001, 2006; Zaller, 1992). Moreover, they appear to rely on more diagnostic criteria in making their judgments (Delli Carpini & Keeter, 1996; Sniderman et al., 1991). Despite these well-researched findings, we believe there are two important but largely unexamined shortcomings of an ability-centered approach for predicting when citizens will think both *deeply* and *objectively* about their political options. First, sophistication turns out to be a double-edged sword. While it facilitates political understanding, it also makes it easier for citizens to defend their political attitudes through motivated bias. Sophistication can thus increase the ability – and perhaps even the desire – to reach predetermined conclusions at the expense of forming "accurate" judgments that square with the "evidence" (Bartels, 2008; Duch, Plamer, & Anderson,

2000; Gaines, Kuklinski, & Quirk, 2007; Jacobson, 2010; Kuklinski et al., 2008; Taber & Lodge, 2006; Wells et al., 2009).[9]

A second limitation of the traditional ability-centered approach is that it ignores citizens' *motivation* to acquire and use political information. Kuklinski and his colleagues (2001, p. 413) observe that political scientists have "almost entirely overlooked issues of effort and responsibility, as opposed to information and skill, in political judgment." If, as we argue in the following chapter, political judgment strategies are selected to solve the problem of complex goal conflict, well-informed citizens (like anyone else) may often be able to reach confident judgments without the need to resort to effortful thinking. In particular, if sophisticated citizens can manage to attain sufficient confidence through reliance on cost-saving cues alone (e.g., party identification), they should rationally ignore other relevant information, even if that information is highly diagnostic to the decision, and even if they are capable of acquiring

9. In a powerful demonstration of the relationship between sophistication and bias, Taber and Lodge (2006) presented participants in a lab experiment with access to a variety of pro and con arguments on a policy issue. When given the chance to choose what information to look at, nonsophisticates chose evenhandedly: They tended to read an equal number of pro and con arguments. By contrast, sophisticated participants were apt to ignore information from the opposing side and to selectively seek out information from sympathetic, nonthreatening sources. On average, sophisticates chose to read three arguments favoring their own side of the issue for every opposing argument read. As a result, their attitudes polarized. That is, after acquiring—by choice—proportionally more ammunition for their prior opinions, sophisticates became more entrenched in their original views, even as they were given the opportunity to examine contrary evidence (see also Kunda, 1987; Lord, Ross, & Lepper, 1979). Political interest also appears to magnify partisan bias. For example, Iyengar and Hahn (2009) randomly attributed political news stories on a variety of topics to one of four media sources: Fox News, NPR, CNN, or the BBC. Participants in the study were provided with a brief headline of each story along with the news organization's logo and were then asked to indicate which of the four reports on each issue they would most like to read. The authors found that Republicans preferred to read about a story when it was attributed to Fox News, whereas Democrats preferred to read the same story when it was attributed to NPR, CNN, or the BBC (i.e., any outlet but Fox). They also included a control condition in which a story was not attributed to any news source and found that partisans of both stripes expressed greater interest in reading a story when it was attributed to a desired source than when it contained no attribution. Importantly, they found that this selectivity bias was substantially enhanced—and to an equal extent among Republicans and Democrats—for those high in political interest (see also Jacobson, 2010).

it (Downs, 1957; Lupia & McCubbins, 1998). In fact, once citizens reach their confidence thresholds, they should no longer be motivated—other than by, as Downs (1957) put it, "entertainment value"—to obtain additional political information. In line with this reasoning, we find that political sophistication often fails to prompt more extensive thinking.

The conventional wisdom thus suggests an intractable tension: We would like citizens to be informed and engaged; however, we would also like them to set aside partisan passion, think for themselves, and privilege the common good over narrow partisan interest (Mill, 1869/1989; Muirhead, 2006; Schudson, 1998; Schumpeter, 1942). Conventional wisdom holds that these two goals are incompatible. If we remove their stake in the game, citizen involvement in public affairs goes down. We are thus seemingly left with two unappealing outcomes: People either tune out politics for lack of interest or respond to the political world in a biased manner. As Levendusky (2009, p. 139) bemoans in *The Partisan Sort*, "the price for more engagement [and] enthusiasm...is a heightened partisan spirit in the electorate."

Our empirical analysis in Chapters 4–7 indicates that this is an accurate description of the behavior of univalent partisans. However, we also find that a nontrivial portion of the electorate manages to escape the vicissitudes of apathy and wanton bias, and it is these citizens—these *ambivalent partisans*—who reliably approximate the "good citizen." The doubt engendered by internal conflict between deep-seated identities and contemporaneous evaluations provides fertile ground for learning and open-mindedness and, as we shall demonstrate, a willingness to assume the cognitive burden of deliberative political thought. Whereas univalent partisans—even sophisticated ones—often reflexively toe the party line in forming their judgments, ambivalent partisans pause, acquire information, and reflect. It is only in this way that citizens can take accurate stock of where the parties stand and how well they perform, and it is only when these realities are accurately perceived that there can be some hope of ensuring accountability in a democratic polity.

Scholars of voting behavior conceptualize elections as having two distinct forces: the long-term influence of partisanship, and various short-term "dynamic" factors, such as the performance of the economy, the quality of the respective candidates (and their campaigns), and "exogenous shocks" to the political system (Converse, 1966). Ambivalent partisanship uniquely affects political choice in two ways: (1) by shifting the balance of power between these two forces so that partisanship matters less and short-term factors matter more; (2) by increasing the accuracy with which the latter are perceived. For example, the quality of economic voting depends on whether the president's partisan supporters recognize and respond to economic deterioration, and whether his opponents acknowledge economic improvement. Most economists credit the Obama administration's 2009 stimulus plan with preventing a steeper economic decline. A majority of Republicans, however, believe that the stimulus either failed to improve conditions or actually made them worse. If the electorate fails to perceive national conditions as they really are, it cannot appropriately reward and punish the incumbent party as accountability demands. Similarly, if voters systematically misperceive the issue positions of candidates or the voting records of legislators, the normative value of issue voting—and therefore popular control over the direction of public policy—loses its meaning.

Finally, if ambivalent partisans are more responsive to the ebb and flow of political campaigns—and if they do not foreclose early on their options (as univalent partisans do)—their votes should exert a disproportionate influence on election outcomes. Conventional wisdom holds that late-deciding citizens are generally uninformed and disengaged. This has spawned the widespread (and disconcerting) belief that elections are "swung" by voters who are the least equipped to carry out the obligations of democratic citizenship. Although there is some truth to this pessimistic claim, it is only a side story. The proportion of disengaged "undecideds" is small compared to that of ambivalent partisans, and the influence of the former is further diminished by the fact that they often abstain from voting. We will show that ambivalent partisans comprise a disproportionate number of persuadable voters in the final weeks leading up to a presidential election.

OLD WINE IN NEW BOTTLES?

To identify the unique political consequences of ambivalence, it is essential that we stringently control for a host of factors that might otherwise magnify or distort its influence. For example, if ambivalent partisans are less strongly attached to their party than other citizens (this happens to be true, but barely so), perhaps the findings that we attribute to ambivalence are simply manifestations of differences in partisan strength. We take several pains throughout our empirical analysis to demonstrate that we are not falling prey to serving old wine in new bottles. First, and most obviously, we control for potentially biasing factors in our statistical models. These include partisan strength, political sophistication, and interest in politics, as well as a host of ideological and demographic factors.

As we will discuss in greater detail in the following chapter, Marcus and colleagues' theory of affective intelligence (Marcus, Neuman, & MacKuen, 2000; see also Brader, 2006) provides an alternative explanation of our findings. Specifically, they hold that voters will switch from heuristic to deliberative thinking when they experience anxiety toward their own party's candidate. We do not dispute that anxiety is one potential trigger of ambivalence; however, effortful thinking may also result from any of a variety of other identity-conflicting evaluations, including feelings of anger or shame toward one's own party, positive feelings of enthusiasm toward the other party, or cognitively flavored reactions toward either party. We will demonstrate in Chapter 6 that feelings of enthusiasm produce the same impact on choice strategy that Marcus et al. (2000) reserve exclusively for anxiety. We will conclude that it is not the quality of the discrete emotion that matters (as affective intelligence theory holds), but whether the emotional response dovetails or conflicts with one's partisan identity.

A second way in which we identify the causal impact of partisan ambivalence is to manipulate it experimentally. In two of our studies in Chapter 4, we demonstrate that experimental variation in ambivalence produces effects comparable to those in observational studies. Third, we demonstrate that the empirical dynamics instigated by ambivalence are *qualitatively* different from those generated by standard measures of political engagement. For example, interest in politics tends to produce *offsetting* effects on the accuracy of economic perceptions: It simultaneously strengthens the impact of both partisan bias (decreasing accuracy) and real economic signals (increasing accuracy). Partisan ambivalence, by contrast, has *cumulative* effects on accuracy: It simultaneously inhibits partisan bias and strengthens reliance on real economic news.

OVERVIEW OF CHAPTERS

In Chapter 2, we lay out a general theoretical framework of the cognitive, motivational, and political dynamics through which partisan ambivalence regulates how judgments are made. The theory is stated at a high enough level of abstraction to capture judgments about candidates and issues, as well as other elements of the political landscape. Consistent with contemporary assessments of the nature of social thinking, we find that citizens are less aptly characterized as "cognitive misers" than as *motivated tacticians* who are strategically flexible—through prone to self-gratifying distortion—in the way they allocate cognitive resources and construct their political judgments (Fiske & Taylor, 2008).

In Chapter 3, we take up several basic questions about the nature of ambivalent partisanship. First, we note how our conceptualization of it differs from the traditional definition as "a mix of positive and negative reactions"

(Basinger & Lavine, 2005; Zaller & Feldman, 1992). Next, we investigate the latent structure of party evaluations. We find that attitudes toward the parties are two-dimensional, with one dimension representing *identity-conflicting* feelings and the other capturing *identity-consistent* feelings. Having established its dimensional structure, we then explore the substantive *content* of citizens' party likes and dislikes. Here, we find that the public considers a fairly constrained set of factors in expressing its pleasure and displeasure with party elites. Last, we consider the circumstances in which partisan ambivalence arises.

In Chapter 4 we address whether ambivalence conditions the normative quality of citizens' policy preferences. In the first part of the chapter, we present the results of four experiments documenting the hypothesized mechanisms by which ambivalence alters how judgments are made. We then turn to panel data, where we test the hypothesis that ambivalent partisans judge the merit of public policies through the lens of values and material interests, whereas univalent partisans ignore these factors in favor of simple partisan cue-taking. Our focus in Chapter 5 is on political perception. Here we examine how partisan ambivalence stacks up against a variety of traditional explanatory variables in conditioning the magnitude of partisan bias, responsiveness to information in the environment, and overall perceptual accuracy. We examine perceptions of several key short-term election factors, including those related to economic performance, the policy stands of presidential candidates, the roll-call votes of US Senators, and crime rates.

In Chapter 6, we test a number of hypotheses about how ambivalence shapes voting behavior. Our general prediction is that ambivalence, all else equal, decreases voters' reliance on party and increases their reliance on issues and performance. We also demonstrate that while ambivalent partisans face a more difficult decision task, this does not deter them from going to the polls. We conclude the chapter with several critical tests between partisan ambivalence theory and affective intelligence theory.

In our final empirical effort, we examine in Chapter 7 a question that has recently received attention in the debate about the nature of partisanship, namely, whether partisan identity constrains individuals' policy opinions and core values or whether partisan loyalties shift as the result of discrepancies with these aspects of political belief (Carsey & Layman, 2006; Dancey & Goren, 2010; Highton & Kam, 2011; Levendusky, 2009). The traditional view stemming from *The American Voter* holds that partisan loyalty is a deep-seated and enduring psychological attachment, and that it serves as a perceptual screen through which other elements of politics are evaluated. By contrast, the revisionist perspective holds that partisan identity is less a psychological attachment than an informational shortcut that summarizes an individual's broader political evaluations formed over time. Thus, rather than acting to shape other attitudes, partisanship is regarded as *responding* to changes in them. Using panel data, we examine whether the causal pathways between these two factors are heterogeneous, and whether they depend on ambivalence. Presumably, party-based issue conversion is mediated (at least partly) by the mechanism of the perceptual filter: By biasing perceptions of other objects, attitudes toward them are brought into line with one's partisan identity. If, however, ambivalent partisans derive less confidence from party cues—and if their policy preferences are rooted more firmly in core values and interests (in Chapter 4 we show this to be true)—we expect that ambivalent partisans with "unsorted" policy preferences will be especially likely to manifest partisan change.

Finally, in Chapter 8, we take a critical perspective on what we have learned, raise a number of potential objections to our theory and empirical work, and discuss how partisan ambivalence heightens the quality of democratic citizenship. We hope to have convinced readers that the disjuncture between one's stable identification as a Democrat or a Republican and one's evaluations of contemporary party performance provides new insights into the ways that ordinary citizens make up their political minds in a wide variety of judgment settings. We also hope to persuade readers that the burden of citizenship cannot be met simply by encouraging political interest and attachment, but that it must include a willingness to temper one's partisan loyalty by casting a sober eye on the political world.

CHAPTER 2

Getting It Right, Making It Easy, and Validating Our Partisan Commitments

A Motivational Theory of Political Judgment

Among the most important insights in the psychology of decision making is that preference judgments are reached through a diverse and flexible set of strategies. The strategy adopted in a given setting depends on the task environment and on the individual's processing capabilities and goals (Chaiken & Trope, 1999; Druckman & Lupia, 2000; Lau, 2003; Payne et al., 1993). To better understand the consequences of partisan ambivalence, we outline a more general theoretical framework of the political judgment process, one that considers how decision strategies are contingent on the accessibility and reliability of partisan cues, on aspects of the political environment (e.g., party performance, exogenous events), and on the nature of citizens' multiple motivations as they acquire information about candidates, issues, and events.

Psychologists have long argued that cognition is driven by goals (Bruner, 1957; Fiske, 2003; Kruglanski & Webster, 1996). Broadly speaking, human reasoning can be characterized as a tension among strivings for three distinct and generally conflicting motivations: efficiency, accuracy, and belief perseverance. Among the most well-established axioms of human thought is the *least effort principle*, which states that people are economy-minded souls who wish to avoid expending cognitive energy in making decisions (for a review, see Kahneman, 2011). The least effort principle has given rise to the popular cognitive miser metaphor of the human mind, and it explains why people rely on such simplifying strategies as stereotypes, heuristics, assimilation, implicit theories, and automatic processing.

In laboratory experiments on attitude change, for example, social psychologists have shown that message recipients often lack the willingness to carefully scrutinize the central merits of a persuasive communication (Petty & Wegener, 1999). Instead, they attempt to infer its validity on the basis of low-effort cues, including aspects of the message source (e.g., experts' statements can be trusted), superficial features of the message (e.g., argument length equals argument strength), consensus information (e.g., consensus implies correctness), attributional reasoning (e.g., does the communicator have an ulterior motive for the position taken?), or simple affective mechanisms (e.g., classical conditioning) in which a persuasive message is accompanied by evocative images and music. In a real-world example that simple decision cues can be highly effective when more diagnostic information is either unavailable or difficult to acquire, Lupia (1994) conducted an exit poll of California voters who were confronted with a complicated set of insurance reform ballot initiatives. Reasoning that voters desired lower rates and broader coverage, Lupia found that uninformed voters could make choices in line with their interests if they were aware of one simple fact: which position the insurance industry favored on each initiative.[1]

While the goal of *efficiency* requires that people make judgments without expending too much effort, the goal of *accuracy* prescribes a thorough and balanced evaluation of information. This concern with decision quality gives rise to a second axiom that we call the *sufficiency principle,* which states that people desire a certain measure of confidence in the "correctness" of their judgments (Baumeister & Newman 1994; Chaiken et al., 1989; Payne et al., 1993; Petty & Cacioppo, 1986). Together, the sufficiency and least effort principles imply a trade-off between conflicting goals: *Accuracy* requires that people make "correct" judgments that reflect reality and their substantive values; *efficiency* requires that people make judgments without undue taxing of the cognitive system. We argue that people decide how to decide by identifying strategies that promise to yield the most accurate decisions without requiring an unreasonable amount of cognitive effort (see also Lau & Redlawsk, 2006). This trade-off is highlighted by the concept of *bounded rationality* (Simon, 1957), whereby all reasoning and decision making are constrained by time, knowledge, information costs, and computational power (see Gigerenzer et al., 2001; Kahneman, 2011). Thus, we should expect all political judgments to reflect a compromise—what Simon (1957) called "satisficing"—between the desire

1. Brady and Sniderman (1985) considered the more general question of how ordinary citizens can manage to figure out where they stand politically given their sporadic attention to politics. They argued that people simplify the political world by considering their feelings toward "politically strategic groups" such as Blacks, big business, the poor, evangelical Christians, and homosexuals. By knowing which social groups they like and which they dislike, and which parties and policies are likely to provide benefits or deprivations to specific groups, citizens can mimic ideologically informed behavior (see also Campbell et al., 1960; Nelson & Kinder, 1996).

to get it right and the necessity of relying on fallible (but efficient) judgment strategies.

As we suggested in the preceding chapter, however, people do not always judge the political world with an open mind and a willingness to follow the evidence wherever it leads. If the desire for accuracy leads to reasoning from "the bottom up" in an attempt to draw conclusions that respect the facts, the *belief perseverance principle* holds that reasoning can also occur from "the top down" in an attempt to draw prefabricated conclusions designed to uphold standing political commitments. From a normative perspective, the interpretation and evaluation of new information should be kept independent of one's "priors." It appears, however, that people often do otherwise, especially when information threatens cherished values and identities. Under these circumstances, we tend to selectively seek out information that validates our attitudes while actively avoiding information that challenges them, and we critically scrutinize and counterargue incongruent information while accepting congenial information at face value (Ditto & Lopez, 1992; Kruglanski & Webster, 1996; Lord, Ross, & Lepper, 1979; Taber & Lodge, 2006). Although maintaining discredited beliefs can be costly to both the individual and society at large, protective information processing strategies are a form of implicit affect regulation serving to maintain psychological equanimity (Festinger, 1957; Sherman & Cohen, 2002). As Markus and Zajonc (1985, p. 140) note in their review of the "New Look" in perception (Bruner & Goodman, 1947), "perception and cognition are obedient to goals, needs, and fears and at times are more subservient to these inner states than to the constraints of reality."

Psychologists argue that belief perseverance stems in part from a "fundamental motivation to protect the perceived worth and integrity of the self" (Sherman & Cohen 2002, p. 120). In experiments employing *self-affirmation theory* (Steele, 1988), Cohen and his colleagues demonstrated that biases in political judgment can be substantially reduced when people receive an affirmation of a valued self-attribute. In one experiment, Cohen et al. (2000) presented devout supporters and opponents of capital punishment with scientific evidence that contradicted their beliefs about the policy's effectiveness in deterring crime. As in prior research (e.g., Lord et al., 1979), participants exhibited the typical "disconfirmation" bias: They found flaws in the study's methodology, they doubted the integrity of the authors of the report, and most important, they maintained their initial attitudes toward the policy. The key question that Cohen et al. (2000, p. 121) address is this: Would people be less defensive "if their self-integrity were secured by an affirmation of some alternative source of self-worth? If the motivation to maintain self-integrity is thus satisfied, [would] people be more willing to give up a cherished belief when reason or experience dictates that they should?"

To test this hypothesis, participants in a self-affirmation condition either wrote about a personally important value or were given positive feedback on a valued skill. The results indicated that momentarily bolstering feelings of self-esteem through self-affirmation liberated individuals from responding in a defensive way to the attitude-incongruent report on capital punishment. Compared to participants in the control (no affirmation) condition, they were less critical of the evidence, less likely to suspect bias on the part of the study's authors, and more likely to change their attitudes in the recommended direction. This line of research suggests that biases in political perception and judgment can be seen as manifestations of ego-protective defensiveness.

RESOLVING GOAL CONFLICT

This brief foray into psychological dynamics suggests that the motivational underpinnings of political choice are quite complex. Whether in judging the performance of the economy, the efficacy of alternative policy options, or the leadership qualities of a presidential candidate, we expect that citizens would like their judgments to reflect a fair and balanced weighing of the evidence, while at the same time making frugal use of cognitive resources and leaving partisan expectations intact. This is a rather tall order and one that cannot always be achieved. A thorough and evenhanded review of relevant information can require substantial cognitive energy and compel the acknowledgment of inconvenient political realities. If maximizing all three goals is often not an available option, deciding how to decide requires a mechanism for determining goal priorities. How might citizens go about doing this? We believe that those who are prepared to assume the cost of attending to a campaign would like to cast a "correct" vote, that is, a vote for the candidate perceived as providing the most attractive political outcomes. We expect the same is true when taking the time to follow an important policy debate. Citizens would like their efforts to lead to "accurate" opinions, ones that square with the facts in addition to their values and interests. We therefore argue that citizens' foremost motivational concern is to attain a sufficient degree of confidence in the accuracy of their decisions.

The desire for confident knowledge reflects a well-established psychological preference for cognitive clarity and an aversion to ambiguity, uncertainty, and doubt (Frenkel-Brunswik, 1949; Kruglanski & Webster, 1996). The process of political judgment is thus one of belief crystallization in which a person moves from an unsettled state of hesitant conjecture to an equilibrium state of subjectively firm "fact." The pragmatist philosopher Charles Peirce (1877, p. 66) argued that the primary object of thought itself is the elimination and active avoidance of doubt:

> Doubt is an uneasy and dissatisfied state from which we struggle to free ourselves and pass into a state of belief, while [the feeling of believing] is a calm and satisfactory state which we do not wish to avoid... The irritation of doubt causes a struggle to attain a state of belief. I shall term this struggle inquiry... With the doubt, therefore, the struggle begins, and with the cessation of doubt it ends.

According to Peirce, our willingness to exert cognitive energy in forming beliefs is motivated not by the attainment of "truth," but rather by the desire to achieve constancy and consistency of meaning. This provides a powerful epistemic explanation for why people cling tenaciously to their political beliefs, often despite the presence of dispositive evidence contradicting their validity (see Kruglanski & Webster, 1996).

To understand how citizens resolve the multiple tensions between the desire for confident knowledge and the needs to conserve cognitive resources and maintain cognitive consistency, we adopt the concept of a *sufficiency threshold*, defined as the degree of confidence a person aspires to attain in a given decision setting (Chaiken et al., 1989; Downs, 1957; Payne et al., 1993). Actual levels of confidence that fall below the threshold will be viewed as insufficient, producing a *confidence gap*. This gap represents the difference between one's subjectively experienced level of confidence in a decision and one's desired level of confidence in that decision. When such a gap exists, people experience uncertainty about the right course of action, motivating them to seek out additional information until actual confidence matches or exceeds the threshold. In dual-process terms, if heuristic processing fails to furnish sufficient confidence, systematic processing will occur. The sufficiency principle embodies the idea that people must strike a balance between minimizing their processing efforts and maximizing their decision confidence (Chaiken et al., 1989).

ACCESSIBILITY AND THE PERCEIVED RELIABILITY OF HEURISTICS

According to this perspective, reliance on effortful political judgment strategies should occur when factors are present that either heighten one's sufficiency threshold or undermine one's actual confidence.[2] Despite the power of partisan cues in raising judgment confidence, psychological research suggests that like other heuristics, their use is subject to two important constraints. First, to influence judgment, a cue must be *accessible* in memory. Accessibility refers to the ease with which a stored item of knowledge can be retrieved from long-term memory and utilized in information processing. Highly accessible concepts come to mind *automatically* in relevant situations (i.e., without effort, intention, or control), whereas those low in accessibility require conscious effort to retrieve (Fazio et al., 1986).

Persuasion research indicates that an attitude (or an identity) will bias perceptions of other information only if it comes to mind automatically in relevant situations (Fazio, 1990). In one study, Huckfeldt and his colleagues (1999) demonstrated that individuals with highly accessible ideological orientations—measured by the speed with which they were reported—were more likely to resist attempts to change their policy preferences than were those with less accessible orientations. In another study, Houston and Fazio (1989) found that judgments about whether capital punishment is an effective homicide deterrent were biased by prior attitudes toward the policy, but only among those for whom attitude accessibility was high.

In addition to accessibility, the value of a heuristic cue depends on whether it is viewed as a *reliable* (or applicable) guide in producing a good decision

2. At the individual level, sufficiency thresholds should be higher among voters who are engaged in politics, and among those for whom the decision is seen as impinging on important interests, values, or social identifications (see Boninger et al., 1995; Thomsen, Borgida, & Lavine, 1995). Confidence thresholds should also be influenced by personality traits such as the *need for cognition* and *personal fear of invalidity*. Individuals high in the need for cognition have been shown to engage in greater elaboration of persuasive messages and to show a general preference for cognitively demanding tasks. Those high in personal fear of invalidity are more likely to see different alternatives when making a decision and to vacillate between options (Cacioppo et al., 1996; Haugtvedt & Petty, 1992; Thompson & Zanna, 1995). On the contextual side, sufficiency thresholds should be heightened at the national level by high-stakes elections, such as when the nation is at war or during an economic recession, and in battleground states, where voters may believe their decisions exert a greater impact on the election outcome and thus feel a greater sense of accountability (Duffy & Tavits, 2008; Palfrey & Rosenthal, 1983).

(Chaiken, 1987; Eagly & Chaiken, 1993; Lupia & McCubbins 1998). If a cue is perceived as failing to increase confidence, "it will be disregarded as an argument in favor of or against a particular course of action" (Fabrigar et al., 2005, p. 107; see also Althaus & Kim, 2006; Chong & Druckman, 2007). Persuasion theorist Shelly Chaiken (1989, p. 218) discusses the role of reliability in the context of the liking-agreement heuristic:

> A person whose past experience with likable and unlikable persons has yielded many confirmations and few disconfirmations of the liking-agreement rule [that we tend to like people we agree with more than those we disagree with] should perceive a stronger association between the concepts of liking and interpersonal agreement than a person whose experience has yielded proportionately more disconfirmations. Because the former person should attribute greater reliability to the liking-agreement heuristic, he or she may be more likely to use it in relevant persuasion settings, and hence more likely to express agreement with likable (vs. unlikable) communicators.

In several persuasion experiments, Chaiken and her colleagues demonstrated that the use of heuristic cues depends on their perceived reliability. In one experiment, Chaiken (1987) manipulated participants' perceptions of the reliability of the cue "message length corresponds to message strength"—a variation on the rule of thumb that "more is better." To do this, she conducted two ostensibly unrelated studies. In the first, participants were asked to judge the quality of several persuasive messages that differed in length. In the high-reliability condition, the longer messages were designed to contain many strong arguments and few weak arguments, whereas in the low-reliability condition the correlation between message length and message quality was zero. After completing this phase of the experiment, participants were "debriefed" and asked to participate in a second study in which a speaker argued in favor of mandatory comprehensive exams for college seniors. In one condition of the study, the speaker claimed to have nine reasons to support his position while in the other version the speaker claimed to have three reasons (in both conditions, the actual message contained six distinct arguments). In the analysis of the post-message opinion data, Chaiken found that participants agreed more with the message that purported to contain nine (vs. three) message arguments. The punch line, however, is that this occurred only among participants for whom the reliability of the "more is better" cue had been experimentally strengthened in the first study. This study illustrates that people can be attentive to the *quality* of a heuristic cue.

A MODEL OF PARTISAN AMBIVALENCE AND POLITICAL JUDGMENT

How do the concepts of cue accessibility and reliability, sufficiency thresholds, and the trade-offs among efficiency, accuracy, and cognitive consistency help us understand how partisan ambivalence regulates the political judgment process? In particular, how do these ideas explain why ambivalent partisans think more deeply about their political options and why their judgments tend to be untainted by partisan bias? An overview of a model of political judgment based on an integration of these ideas is depicted in Figure 2.1. Consistent with contemporary research (Forgas, 1995; Gawronski & Bodenhausan, 2006; Kahneman, 2011; Zaller, 1992), the top left portion of the schematic indicates that a relevant prior attitude or belief will guide the initial stage of the judgment process if it is automatically activated.

Once activated, this information, like all judgment considerations, is weighted by its "reliability," which is intended to reflect the extent to which it (1) moves a decision maker toward a given judgment option and (2) reduces the gap between current and desired levels of confidence. Thus, like dual-process models in psychology, our framework incorporates both automatic and controlled components of information processing. As the schematic illustrates, larger reliability weights provide for greater confidence and increase

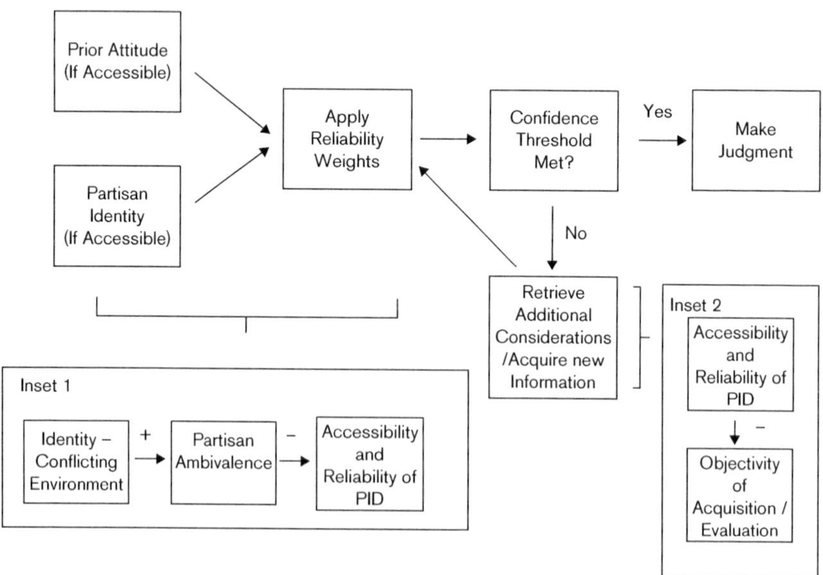

Figure 2.1 A Model of Political Judgment. PID, party identification.

the likelihood that the individual's sufficiency threshold will be met. If this initial information is seen as strong enough to eliminate the confidence gap entirely, a judgment will be made and cognitive resources will be channeled elsewhere. A process of this sort was originally conceived by Downs (1957, p. 85), who argued that:

> voters who are certain about how they want to vote [do] not know every fact relevant to their voting decision, nor [are] they absolutely sure it is the best one they can make. It means they know enough to have reached a definite decision, and they regard as negligible the probability that any further information would cause them to change it. Hence, they do not deliberately seek further information.[3]

This portion of the model is intended to capture the "top of the head" judgment process described by Zaller (1992; see also Taylor & Fiske, 1978).

Simultaneous to the activation of domain-specific information, an individual's partisan identity may also be automatically activated, even in circumstances in which partisan brand names are not explicitly attached to the competing options. As with any consideration, we expect the weighting of partisanship to be a function of its subjective likelihood in raising judgment confidence. According to the model, partisanship should lay the foundation for political judgment when partisan identity is both highly accessible and deemed to be a reliable decision guide. Under these circumstances, judgments should not only reflect little deliberation; they should also be biased by partisan expectancies. Figure 2.2 illustrates "strong" and "weak" versions of a *partisan cue-taking* heuristic strategy. In the strong form (Panel A), partisanship itself provides the bulk of judgment confidence, with little contribution from other "top of the head" considerations. In the weak form (Panel B), the latter contribute more to narrowing the confidence gap, with partisanship playing only a secondary role. In either case, the judgment process is driven solely by automatically activated information, reflecting little deliberative reasoning (beyond the assigning of reliability weights) or acquisition of new information.

The concept of the sufficiency threshold provides a commonsensical mechanism for predicting when—and more important, understanding *why*—decision makers will transition from heuristic to deliberative thinking. In our

3. This assumes that reaching one's confidence threshold is the only reason to acquire political information. Clearly there are other reasons, which we subsume under Downs's notion of "entertainment value," or the idea that people pay attention to politics because they find it enjoyable.

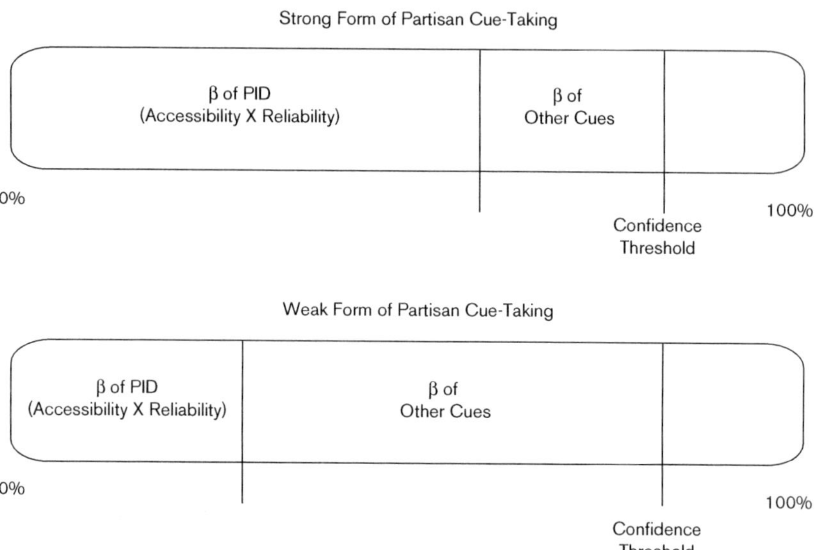

Figure 2.2 Two Forms of Heuristic Thinking. PID, party identification.

framework, this occurs primarily when partisan cues (and other automatically activated information) fail to furnish enough confidence to create an equilibrium state of settled preference in a given judgment option. For example, just as circumstances might lead people to place little trust in the "more is better" heuristic (as in Chaiken's experiment), they can also undermine one's belief in the utility of partisanship as a valid judgment cue. When one's own party presides over a poor economy, performs ineptly during a crisis, becomes mired in scandal, or fails to deliver on desired policy change—or equally, when one's partisan opponents govern well—contemporary partisan evaluations may become out of step with long-term expectations, generating partisan ambivalence. The crux of our argument is that this state of critical loyalty signals that something is amiss, and that the habit of partisanship will need to be supplemented with—or even supplanted by—alternative means for raising judgment confidence.

In the case where ambivalence blocks the activation of partisan identity entirely, the latter will make no contribution to reducing the gap between actual and desired confidence (i.e., its weight will be zero). The same will be true when partisan identity is automatically activated but assigned a low reliability weight (reflecting doubt about its utility). Whether partisan identity is inaccessible or judged to be an inapplicable yardstick, we hypothesize that citizens will be motivated to turn to other sources of information to reach their sufficiency thresholds. Specifically, they should be willing to search their memories for relevant considerations and to acquire new information from the political environment. Moreover, contingent on cognitive ability or a political environment that subsidizes information costs (e.g., a high-stakes election), citizens should be especially motivated to seek out the most diagnostic information available, as this is the most effective means of raising judgment confidence. Thus, rather than simply switching from partisanship to other low-effort cues (e.g., incumbency, group membership), we expect that able or subsidized ambivalent partisans will engage in a deeper, more thorough information search. In voting contexts, for example, they should be more likely to seek out information about the candidates' policy stands, experience, and voting records, or more carefully scrutinize the quality of a president's performance during a crisis.

However, the transition from heuristic to deliberative thinking does not require that citizens engage in a *representative* search of memory, or that they will interpret or evaluate new information in an *evenhanded* manner. As we noted earlier, citizens can be motivated more by directional goals than by getting it right. There is a consensus in the psychological literature (e.g., Dunning, 1999; Kruglanski, 2003; Kunda, 1990) that neither goal drives information processing in the complete absence of the other; rather, people attempt to "strike a workable balance" between getting it right and leaving their prior beliefs intact (Fiske, 1992, p. 880). The question, then, is what determines the priority of each goal? Under what conditions will directional goals dominate accuracy goals and vice versa? That is, when will political judgments be biased by partisan expectations, and thus reflect *motivated reasoning*, and when will they be evenhanded, thus approximating *rational choice*?

We hypothesize that the degree to which effortful thinking is biased or objective will depend largely on the extent to which party identification reduces the gap between actual and desired judgment confidence. As illustrated in Inset 2 of Figure 2.1, when partisanship is highly accessible and provides for ample (though not sufficient) confidence, we expect that it will direct how subsequent information is gathered, evaluated, and combined with existing knowledge. By directing attention *selectively*, partisan stereotypes should lead to a belief-confirming strategy whereby incongruent information is ignored or counterargued to fit with existing partisan beliefs. This process is wholly consistent with Campbell et al.'s (1960) notion of a "perceptual screen" and with Taber and Lodge's (2006, p. 756) argument that people are "unable to control their preconceptions." By contrast, when partisanship provides for comparatively little judgment confidence, subsequent information processing should be more objective. Biased and objective forms of deliberative reasoning

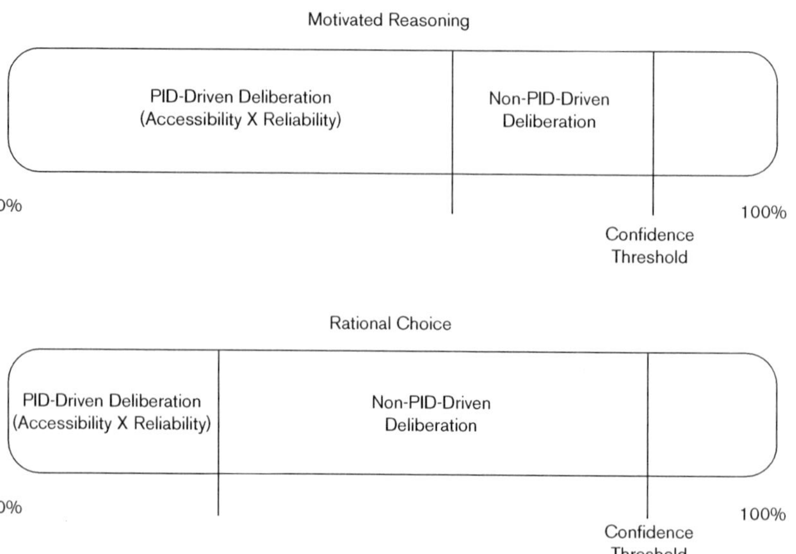

Figure 2.3 Two Forms of Deliberative Thinking. PID, party identification.

are depicted in Figure 2.3. In Panel A, the confidence gap is reduced primarily by an information search guided by partisanship, leading to judgments that are congruent with existing beliefs. In Panel B, a greater proportion of judgment confidence is derived from an information search that is not constrained by directional (i.e., partisan) goals, thus producing more evenhanded judgments.

To summarize, once ambivalence is aroused, partisan identity should come less readily to mind in making political judgments, and it should be viewed as a less reliable proxy for one's values and interests. In the empirical chapters to follow, we compare how partisan ambivalence stacks up against traditional explanatory factors (e.g., political sophistication) in fostering deliberative and unbiased judgments about policies, candidates, and other aspects of the political landscape. Using both experimental and survey methods and relying on a wealth of primary and secondary data sources, we test two general hypotheses: First, we expect ambivalent partisans to engage in more extensive thinking than their univalent counterparts, and to rely on more valuable—but cognitively costly—criteria in forming their political judgments. We test this hypothesis in the domain of policy preferences in Chapter 4 and in the domain of voting behavior in Chapter 6. Second, we expect ambivalent partisans to hold political perceptions that are less contaminated by partisan bias and more responsive to objective conditions. We test this hypothesis in Chapter

5. In each domain, we examine whether ambivalent partisans, ceteris paribus, approximate the kind of reasoning praised by normative theorists.

EVIDENCE FOR THE MODEL

Experimental work in cognitive, social and political psychology provides support for several aspects of our model, including that ambivalence (a) reduces both attitude accessibility and judgment confidence; (b) motivates individuals to devote additional cognitive resources to judgment tasks, and; (c) increases judgmental accuracy. In one study, Bassili (1995) examined how priming party identification within a naturalistic context—the calling of a federal election in Canada in 1993—altered the accessibility of partisan feelings among "conflicted" and "unconflicted" partisans. Reasoning that an impending election would heighten the situational salience of partisan identity, Bassili hypothesized that unconflicted partisans would express their partisan feelings faster *after* than *before* the call of the election, but that conflicted partisans would find it more difficult (and thus take longer) to express their partisan feelings once the election had been called. Bassili's data nicely supported this interactive priming hypothesis. In related priming research, Lodge and Taber (2005) found that ambivalence toward the party labels ("Democrats" and "Republicans") eliminated their effectiveness in priming responses to affectively congruent target words.[4]

In addition to creating sluggishness in the retrieval of attitudes, there is evidence that ambivalence decreases people's confidence in them. For example, the 1996 American National Election Study asked respondents to place the presidential candidates (Clinton and Dole) on issue scales and then to rate their level of certainty in the correctness of each placement. Controlling for a variety of standard explanatory variables related to cognitive ability and political engagement, Meffert, Guge, and Lodge (2004) found that ambivalence toward the candidates was associated with less

4. In the affective priming procedure used by Lodge and Taber (2005), "automatic activation" of a prime is thought to occur if evaluative responses to a target word (typically a noun with consensually positive or negative connotations, e.g., "rainbow," "cancer") are made more quickly when it follows an affectively congruent prime (Fazio et al., 1986). For example, automatic positive attitudes toward the concept "Democrats" would be manifested in faster evaluative responses to positive than negative target words, whereas automatic negative attitudes toward the party label would be indicated by faster responses to negative than positive target words.

confidence but greater accuracy in candidate perceptions.[5] While this pattern may seem counterintuitive, it conforms precisely to the expectations of our theoretical model.

Laboratory experiments indicate that ambivalence can undercut initial judgment confidence and thus instigate more extensive thought. In one study, Jonas et al. (1997) manipulated ambivalence toward a consumer product by associating it with either evaluatively consistent or inconsistent features (creating univalent and ambivalent conditions, respectively). Just after hearing the product description, participants' levels of actual and desired confidence were assessed by asking "how certain *would you be*..." and "how certain *would you like to be*... if you were to indicate your attitude [toward the product] right now?" The authors found a substantially larger confidence gap—calculated as desired minus actual confidence—among those assigned to the ambivalent than the univalent condition. To assess the degree of deliberative thinking, respondents listed their thoughts while reading about the product.[6] The authors found that those assigned to the ambivalent condition listed a larger proportion of *message-relevant* thoughts, and that ambivalence-based differences in initial judgment confidence mediated this effect. That is, ambivalence initially diminished participants' confidence about whether to purchase the product, and this in turn prompted more extensive thought about the decision.

In a similar experiment focusing on intergroup attitudes, Maio and Olson (1996) presented Canadian participants with either strong or weak arguments in favor of increased immigration from Hong Kong. If participants carefully scrutinized the arguments, they should have formed more supportive attitudes toward immigration when assigned to the strong (vs. the weak) arguments condition. This is exactly what occurred, but only among those with ambivalent attitudes toward the immigrant group. By contrast, the post-message attitudes of univalent respondents were unrelated to the strength of the arguments they received; rather, their attitudes were determined largely by prior feelings toward the group, indicating heuristic processing.

---

5. From the perspective of the least effort and sufficiency principles, the accuracy finding can be explained by either greater attention to and elaboration of campaign information about the candidates' preferences, less bias induced by the respondent's own candidate and policy attitudes, or both (see Conover & Feldman, 1989).

6. Thought listing is a standard technique for assessing "systematic" message-related thought (see Petty & Cacioppo, 1979).

Support for the ambivalence model also comes from recent work on the neural substrates of automatic and deliberative information processing. In particular, several studies have shown that the anterior cingulate cortex (ACC)—a structure in the brain that detects the violation of expectations and triggers deliberative thinking—is activated by cognitive conflict (e.g., ambivalence; Amodio et al., 2007; Botvinick, Cohen, & Carter, 2004; Cunningham et al., 2003; Kerns et al., 2004; Lieberman, 2007). As Lieberman et al. (2003, p. 685) note, "when nonconscious habit cognition cannot accommodate the conflicting considerations activated in response to a survey item, the brain has a mechanism [i.e., the ACC] for sounding an alarm that will engage conscious cognition. Consequently, the number of conflicting considerations accessible... will play a major part in determining which mental mechanism(s) contribute to the reported attitude." In a Stroop experiment, Kerns et al. (2004) found significantly greater ACC activity on conflict trials (e.g., when the word "blue" is printed in the color green) than on congruent trials (when word and color match). They also found that ACC activity was associated with greater activity in regions of the prefrontal cortex (PFC; a brain region associated with effortful cognition). In a related functional magnetic resonance imaging (fMRI) study, Cunningham et al. (2003) found that processing ambivalent stimuli activated both the ACC and the ventrolateral PFC. Taken together, this work indicates that ambivalence activates brain regions known to be associated with conflict monitoring (the ACC) and effortful cognition (the PFC).

In sum, prior work indicates that ambivalence moderates the occurrence of both automatic and deliberative attitudinal processes. It renders attitudes and identities less accessible and less likely to be automatically activated, thus requiring conscious effort to retrieve (and use) them in relevant judgment situations. Moreover, it undermines judgmental confidence, thus providing the motivation for more extensive thought. Most important, ambivalence leads people to scrutinize more carefully the merits of the communications they receive.

DISTINGUISHING PARTISAN AMBIVALENCE FROM PAST RESEARCH ON HETEROGENEITY

We are not the first to suggest that people make up their minds about politics in different ways. Political scientists have often acknowledged that in constructing their judgments, citizens take account of different considerations and attach different weights to them (e.g., Lau & Redlawsk, 2006; Sniderman et al., 1991). There are two existing frameworks that provide competing explanations for our findings. The first is Marcus and colleagues' (2000) theory of *affective intelligence,* which builds on work in the neurosciences linking positive and negative emotion to independent biobehavioral systems in the brain. In particular, the withdrawal system, which mediates the experience of negative affect, provides an alternative explanation to the dynamics we ascribe to partisan ambivalence. Labeled by Marcus et al. (2000) as the surveillance system, its focus is to maximize attention on the physical and social environment for the presence of threat and danger. Activation of the surveillance system results in the emotion of anxiety, which interrupts ongoing habitual action, redirects attention to novel stimuli, and promotes increased thoughtfulness and greater motivation for learning. Applied to the political realm, anxiety is expected to lead voters to reduce their reliance on existing predispositions (such as party identification) and to pay greater attention to relevant information in the environment. Marcus et al. (2000) have shown that when voters are anxious about their party's presidential candidate, they (a) pay greater attention to the political environment and acquire more information about candidates' policy stands; (b) rely less on partisanship and more on policy and assessments of candidate character in forming candidate evaluations; and (c) defect at higher rates from the party's candidate.[7]

On the surface, the partisan ambivalence and affective intelligence frameworks are highly similar. They highlight a similar mechanism—uncongenial

7. Brader (2006) provided more powerful evidence of the role of anxiety on how candidate judgments are made by manipulating it experimentally in the context of political ads. He embedded two versions of a negative ad script for a gubernatorial primary in Massachusetts—one that evoked the emotion of fear and one that was emotionally pallid—within an evening news program. To distinguish the persuasive effects of emotionality from the ad's informational content, Brader packaged the same verbal script—which contained references to crime, drugs, and children—with two different sets of audiovisual cues. In the *fear* condition, the verbal text was accompanied by grainy black-and-white images, including a crime scene, a woman being attacked by an intruder, a crack pipe and a gun, and by "high-pitched, dissonant instrumental chords pulsating beneath the narration" (2006, p. 84). The control condition featured mostly impersonal images (e.g., buildings) and no aural accompaniment. Brader found that compared to the pallid ad, the fear ad led to greater attentiveness to the ad script, greater reliance on information included in the ad on vote choice, better memory for information about the campaign in the news, increased interest in contacting the campaigns for more information, and less reliance on initial preferences. When taken together, these consequences of experimental condition indicate that anxiety stimulates attentiveness and interest and leads to voting decisions that are more informed by contemporary information and less by prior predispositions.

party evaluations and in-candidate/party anxiety, respectively—as the motivational basis for greater responsiveness. Perhaps, then, the consequences we ascribe to ambivalence simply reflect the operation of the surveillance system and the experience of anxiety. Or perhaps the influence of partisan ambivalence on political judgment is mediated by anxiety. While these are both plausible scenarios, they run into several problems: (a) partisan ambivalence does not require the occurrence of anxiety; (b) psychological research indicates that anxiety more often *impairs* (rather than enhances) performance on capacity-demanding tasks; and (c) the evidence we present in Chapter 6 (on political behavior) does not support either possibility.

Affective intelligence holds that the motivation to engage in deliberative thinking hinges specifically on the experience of anxiety. Our framework makes the broader claim that negative evaluations of one's own party—resulting in anger, sadness, or anxiety, or in more cognitively flavored evaluations—should result in insufficient judgment confidence, thus prompting more careful thinking and less bias. However, disappointment in the performance of one's co-partisan elites is only one route by which ambivalence may be aroused. It may also result from positive reactions stemming from an unexpectedly good performance by the other party. For example, in signing NAFTA and welfare reform and in acknowledging that "the era of big government is over," President Clinton improved the Democratic Party brand among moderate Republicans. The experience of partisan ambivalence thus does not depend on holding negative evaluations of the in-party. In fact, as we will demonstrate in Chapter 6, the effects of ambivalence are just as powerful when it is based on the presence of positive evaluations of the other party. As the latter does not logically entail the activation of the surveillance system or the experience of anxiety (just the opposite we would think), the results are difficult to square with affective intelligence theory.[8]

Our perspective also bears resemblance to Hillygus and Shields's (2008) work in *The Persuadable Voter*. They posit that partisan defection in presidential

8. Moreover, a good deal of psychological research indicates that anxiety, especially situationally induced or "state" anxiety, interferes with the ability to engage in a variety of working memory and decision tasks. In fact, it appears that anxiety often has precisely the opposite effects on information processing and judgment that we ascribe to ambivalence. For example, recent experimental work indicates that anxiety reduces the desire for open-ended information search (Thorisdottir & Jost, 2011) and impairs the ability to elaborate evenhandedly on persuasive information (Sengupta & Johar, 2001). From a theoretical perspective, then, ambivalence and (real) anxiety should induce quite different judgment strategies.

elections will occur when voters disagree with their party on a policy issue that is (a) primed by the campaign and (b) regarded as personally important. As in our framework, they hold that such cross-pressured voters will pay greater attention to the campaign environment. They write that:

> When partisans with reinforcing policy preferences encounter campaign information from the opposing party candidate, we expect that they will counterargue it as previous studies have predicted. But for those partisans who disagree with their party on an issue, we expect them to be more receptive to information from the opposition party on that conflicting issue. (p. 21)

Consistent with their hypothesis, Hillygus and Shields find that defection increases dramatically among cross-pressured partisans if they are exposed to campaign information on the relevant issue. In one major respect, their approach and ours are similar: We both hypothesize that holding identity-conflicting evaluations leads to greater responsiveness to campaign messages, and in particular, to greater openness to messages sponsored by one's partisan opponents.

Overall, however, our conceptual perspectives are strongly divergent. Hillygus and Shields's (2008) conception of cross-pressures is based on a specific conflict between partisan identification and an incongruent position on a personally important policy issue. By contrast, partisan ambivalence is more broadly conceived as a disjuncture between the long-term *identification* and short-term *evaluative* components of partisanship. The conflicting evaluations can reflect any of a variety of considerations, including, but not limited to, policy issues. For example, they can refer to judgments about domestic or foreign policy stewardship, performance in a crisis (e.g., Katrina, 9/11), candidate quality, scandals, or changes in the perceived linkages between the parties and specific social groups (see Miller & Wlezien, 1991; Valentino & Sears, 2005). A central assumption of our framework is that citizens vary widely in the political considerations that matter to them, and that contextual factors can alter what considerations receive the greatest attention and weight. What we believe is most important in shaping the nature and quality of political judgment is whether citizens have *some* reason—and not just a policy-based one—to doubt whether they should toe the party line.

An additional difference between *The Persuadable Voter* and our work lies in the scope of our respective empirical inquiries. Hillygus and Shields are concerned specifically with voting behavior in presidential elections, and their primary dependent variable is partisan defection. Our purpose, by contrast, is considerably broader. We are interested in building a general model of the political judgment process that applies to a range of settings, including evaluations of candidates and issues, and reactions to salient events (e.g., scandals, economic collapse, terrorism). In particular, our model is focused on the conditions under which citizens will relinquish their reliance on partisanship and think more carefully about their political options. In line with the theory of affective intelligence or *The Persuadable Voter*, this might occur if citizens experience anxiety or if they hold a policy preference that conflicts with their party's position. However, as we have outlined, it may—and as we shall show, actually does—occur for a variety of other reasons. Finally, our concern is not only with the depth of political information processing but also with the accuracy of political perception. Democrats and Republicans not only hold different political values, they often disagree about the facts, about political reality itself. Among our tasks is to identify the conditions under which partisans will privilege reality over the gratification of their partisan commitments.

CHAPTER 3

Conceptualization, Measurement, and Antecedents

Before testing our theoretical model in Chapters 4–7, we first lay out in greater detail our conceptualization of partisan ambivalence and how we propose to measure it. As our conception represents a departure from past work, we begin with a brief overview of how ambivalence has been traditionally defined and explain why the variety that occupies us is unique. We then turn to two important questions of measurement: How can citizens' positive and negative reactions toward the parties be assessed, and how should these evaluative responses be integrated with partisan identity (and with one another) to form a measure of ambivalence that comports with our theoretical conception?

To preview a part of our argument, we hold that partisan evaluations are two-dimensional, with one dimension representing *identity-conflicting* reactions and the other capturing *identity-consistent* reactions. We expect the former to heighten the experience of ambivalence and the latter to decrease it. Once we have established the empirical validity of this bivariate structure, we inquire into the substantive content of citizens' party evaluations. As it turns out, the public considers a fairly constrained set of factors in expressing its pleasure and displeasure with party elites. Last, having disposed of matters of conceptualization and measurement, we examine how someone becomes an ambivalent partisan.

CONCEPTUALIZATIONS OF AMBIVALENCE: PAST AND PRESENT

The proliferation of contemporary research on ambivalence has been fueled by recent developments in attitude theory and neuroscience on the structure of evaluative responses. Until recently, it was assumed that attitudes were unidimensional and bipolar, ranging on a single evaluative continuum from maximally negative to maximally positive. This assumption constrains positivity and negativity to be diametric opposites: the more one likes an object, the less one must dislike it. In this sense, attitudes are like the bipolar concepts of hot and cold and bright and dim (as cold is literally equivalent to the absence of heat and dimness to the absence of brightness). Noting the strong intuition behind perceiving the world in dichotomies and bipolarities, Cacioppo, Gardner, and Berntson (1997, p. 5) write that:

> Is the dichotomy between positive and negative not obvious, stable, expected, and psychologically harmonious? Is it not self-evident that the opposite of harmful is beneficial, optimism is pessimism, wise is foolish, and good is bad? Is not the bipolarity of attitudes one of the few generally accepted principles across the social sciences?

Cacioppo and his colleagues go on to argue that while behavior itself is logically bipolar (e.g., voting Democrat or Republican), the underlying hedonic processes that drive behavior may be more complex:

> Physical limitations may constrain behavioral expression and incline behavioral guides toward bipolar (good/bad; approach/withdrawal) dispositions, but these constraints do not have the same force at the level of underlying mechanism. That is, the fact that approach and withdrawal tend to be reciprocally activated behavioral manifestations does not mean that they were derived from a single bipolar evaluative channel; it only means that the outputs of all of the evaluative processors comprising the affect system are combined in order to compute preferences and organize action. (Cacioppo & Gardner, 1999, p. 201)

In line with Cacioppo and Gardner, the patterns of positive and negative activation evoked by numerous social stimuli often depart from the reciprocal pattern expected by the bipolar model (i.e., more positivity covarying with less negativity, and vice versa). This led to the argument that positive and negative evaluation have separable motivational and neurological substrates and that under certain circumstances the two may be coactivated (e.g., Holbrook, Krosnick, Visser, Gardner, & Cacioppo, 2001).[1] To take a simple example, going to the dentist may arouse both positive and negative feelings.

1. For example, neurophysiological evidence indicates that goal-directed approach and withdrawal behaviors (i.e., positivity and negativity) are generated by two independent systems of arousal residing in the limbic area of the brain. The withdraw system that mediates the experience of negative affect is referred to as the *behavioral inhibition system* (BIS; Carver & White, 1994; Gray, 1987; Marcus, 1988; Marcus, Neuman, & MacKuen, 2000; Tomarken & Keener, 1998; Watson & Tellegen, 1985). The primary function of the BIS is to focus maximum attention

Most relevant to political scientists are studies showing that positive and negative reactions to presidential candidates are largely independent. Marcus et al. (2000) examined how voters' feelings of enthusiasm and anxiety were influenced by events during the 1980 election. Early in the campaign, the Iran hostage crisis and the Soviet invasion of Afghanistan led to sympathy and support for Carter as the public rallied around the president. By June, however, the hostage rescue attempt had failed, the energy market had exploded (producing double-digit inflation), and—if this weren't enough—the president's hapless brother became embroiled in a scandal involving Libyan dictator Muammar al-Qaddafi. In July, Carter addressed the nation in what was later dubbed his "malaise speech," where he told the American people "we can see this crisis in the growing doubt about the meaning of our own lives and in the loss of a unity of purpose for our nation." These events led to a precipitous decline in enthusiasm for the president, as voters began to doubt his capacity to solve the country's problems. According to the bipolar model, this decline in enthusiasm should have been accompanied by an equally strong surge in anxiety, as the activation functions of positivity and negativity in the bipolar model are mirror images of one another.

However, this bipolarity failed to materialize. Carter may have disappointed voters, leading to a loss of enthusiasm, but they did not see the president's behavior as erratic or threatening, thus leaving anxiety levels

---

on the physical and social environment for the presence of novelty, threat, and danger. As Marcus and colleagues (2000) note, the BIS interrupts ongoing habitual action, redirects attention to novel stimuli, and promotes increased thoughtfulness and greater motivation for learning. Activation of the BIS regulates the unipolar dimension of negative affect, which ranges from calm and placid when activation is low to nervous and anxious when activation is high. The approach system that mediates the experience of positive affect is called the *behavioral activation system* (BAS). The BAS is a reward-seeking system that responds to positive incentives by directly initiating behavior. Its primary adaptive function is to direct the individual to situations and experiences that may yield pleasure and reward (Watson, Wiese, Vaidya, & Tellegen, 1999). The BAS serves a key role in providing ongoing feedback about goal attainment and reward acquisition. When current behavior is judged to be successful, the BAS is activated, resulting in feelings of enthusiasm and excitement. In contrast, when behavior is unsuccessful in reaching a goal, BAS activation is low, resulting in feelings of sadness and depression. Thus, like the BIS, the BAS is associated with unipolar emotionality, ranging from sadness, depression, and resignation when activation is low to enthusiasm, excitement, and joy when activation is high.

unchanged. Emotional responses toward Reagan also failed to fit the bipolar pattern. Partly as the result of a Democratic scare campaign, anxiety levels toward Reagan rose throughout the fall. But contrary to the bipolar model, this did not produce a concomitant decrease in enthusiasm (which remained relatively high throughout the campaign). Marcus et al. (2000) also examined the correlation between individual-level *changes* in enthusiasm and anxiety from January to October of 1980. As they note, the bipolar model predicts that as enthusiasm goes up, anxiety should go down: "when people start to 'like' a candidate they should simultaneously abandon their 'dislikes'" (p. 73). Again, this basic prediction failed to receive support: For both Carter and Reagan, changes in enthusiasm and anxiety were entirely independent of one another. Thus, for every voter who experienced more anxiety and less enthusiasm, another voter experienced more anxiety and more enthusiasm.[2]

Intergroup attitudes also adhere more to a bivariate than a bipolar structure. Katz and Hass (1988) proposed a *racial ambivalence hypothesis*, in which the attitudes of Whites are thought to contain both pro-Black and anti-Black elements. They argue that:

> Blacks, having a history of exclusion from the main society, are often perceived by the majority as both *deviant* in the sense of possessing certain disqualifying attributes of mind or body and *disadvantaged*, either by the attributes themselves or by the social and economic discrimination that

2. Abelson et al. (1982) extended this analysis to a broader range of presidential candidates and a larger number of affective terms. In two studies carried out in 1979 and 1980, they asked respondents "Now, has (candidate)—because of the kind of person he is or because of something he has done—ever made you feel: (afraid, angry, disgusted, disliking, frustrated, sad, uneasy, hopeful, happy, liking, proud, sympathetic)?" According to the bipolar model, feeling "afraid," "angry," and "disgusted" about a candidate should be strongly associated with the absence of feeling "hopeful," "proud," and "sympathetic." It should thus be possible to project both the negative and positions emotions onto a single evaluative continuum. However, analyses of the latent structure of respondents' feelings revealed two distinct and largely independent factors: one constituting positive emotion and the other constituting negative emotion. This bidimensional, unipolar latent structure indicates that respondents who experienced one positive emotion toward a candidate were likely to experience other positive emotions, but this had little to do with the number of negative emotions evoked by the candidate (and vice versa). Marcus (1988) replicated the two-dimensional model for Reagan and Mondale in 1984.

> having them entails. The dual perception of deviance and disadvantage likely generates in the observer conflicting feelings of aversion and sympathy. (p. 894)

Katz and Hass found that pro-Black and anti-Black attitudes were uncorrelated and linked to distinct antecedents: the former to egalitarianism and humanitarianism, and the latter to individualism (i.e., the Protestant work ethic). In a priming experiment, they found that participants who first completed measures of egalitarianism and humanitarianism subsequently expressed more pro-Black beliefs, while anti-Black beliefs remained the same. Conversely, participants who first completed a measure of individualism subsequently expressed more anti-Black beliefs, leaving pro-Black beliefs unchanged. This study is consistent with a now sizable literature showing that positive and negative racial attitudes are not opposite ends of a bipolar continuum, but that Whites often experience both aversion and sympathy toward Blacks (Gaertner & Dovidio, 1986). These studies illustrate a more general insight: The bivariate model of evaluation provides a better description of the nature of social and political attitudes than the traditional bipolar model (for more comprehensive reviews, see Cacioppo et al., 1997; Watson & Tellegen, 1985).

As social psychologists worked out the structure of evaluative space, Zaller (1992) proposed a general model of public opinion with ambivalence as a first principle. He argued that individuals often endorse both pro and con considerations on an issue because they are unable to distinguish between value congruent and incongruent communications. In normal (i.e., competitive) political environments, citizens are exposed to both sides of a debate, and those who are unaware of the partisan coloration of a given message tend to uncritically accept whatever ideas they encounter. Thus, they end up "mistakenly" accepting some arguments that contradict their political values. Zaller and Feldman (1992) demonstrated that issue ambivalence is widespread, with up to 50 percent of respondents in national surveys expressing some degree of cross-pressure.[3] This work persuaded many political scientists that ambivalence was a critical factor in public opinion and electoral behavior, and it prompted numerous investigations of its antecedents and political

3. See also Feldman and Zaller (1992) and Hochschild (1981); for dissenting perspectives, see Alvarez and Brehm (2002), Jacoby (2006), and Steenbergen and Brewer (2004); for estimates of the prevalence of ambivalence toward candidates, see Lavine (2001) and Meffert, Guge, and Lodge (2004).

consequences.[4] These studies indicate that attitudes marked by ambivalence are held with less certainty and are more difficult to retrieve from memory than one-sided attitudes. They are also less stable over time, more vulnerable to both message-based persuasion and context effects in surveys, and less predictive of future behavior.[5]

4. For a representative sampling, see Alvarez and Brehm (1995, 1997, 2002); Basinger and Lavine (2005); Cantril and Cantril (1999); Craig and Martinez (2005); Craig, Martinez, and Kane (2005); Feldman and Zaller (1992); Huckfeldt, Johnson, and Sprague (2004); Keele and Wolak (2008); Lavine (2001); Lavine, Thomsen, Zanna, and Borgida (1998); McGraw, Hasecke, and Conger (2003); Mulligan (2011); Nelson (1999); Rudolph (2011); and Rudolph and Popp (2008).
5. The idea of citizens being pulled in different political directions is actually quite an old one. Some of the earliest studies of voter choice recognized this phenomenon. In their seminal work, *The People's Choice* (Lazarsfeld, Berelson, & Gaudet, 1944), and their follow-up study, *Voting* (Berelson, Lazarsfeld, & McPhee, 1954), Lazarsfeld and his colleagues observed that citizens may experience "cross-pressures" (their term for ambivalence) arising from a variety of sources during an election campaign. Their sociological model emphasized the role of demographic factors, specifically economic class, level of urbanization, and religion (Protestant vs. Catholic) as the primary determinants of vote preference. Working-class voters, Catholics, and urban dwellers tended to vote Democratic, while the middle class, Protestants, and those residing in rural areas favored the Republicans. Voters with overlapping social identities (e.g., middle-class Catholics; urban Protestants) were assumed to be "attracted to each party by one set of opinions and repelled by another" (p. 190), producing "conflict within the individual" (Berelson et al., 1954, p. 200). They also explored the effects of cross-pressures stemming from interpersonal disagreement (i.e., differences in political views with friends, coworkers, and family members), and from holding ideologically inconsistent policy attitudes on salient campaign issues (e.g., Taft-Hartley, price controls). Lazarsfeld and his colleagues found that the presence of cross-pressures—stemming from demographic, interpersonal, or attitudinal sources—was related to a delay in the formation of citizens' voting intentions, temporal instability in their candidate preferences, and a greater probability of ultimately defecting to the other party (i.e., Democrats voting for Republicans and vice versa). Six years after the publication of *Voting*, the authors of *The American Voter* (Campbell et al., 1960; see also Campbell & Miller, 1957) extended the concept of ambivalence to conflict "among several psychological forces acting on behavior" (p. 79), including perceptions of the personality traits of the candidates and the groups linked to each of the parties, attitudes toward domestic and foreign policy issues, and judgments of the comparative record of

Partisan Ambivalence: Conflicted Evaluations or Identity-Evaluation Disjuncture?

The standard "mixed feelings" conceptualization makes sense when applied to objects such as candidates or issues, for in such cases ambivalence arises entirely from conflict along the *evaluative* dimension (i.e., the endorsement of pro and con considerations). However, as we discussed at length in Chapter 1, partisanship is not just any old belief element; it is the individual's primary link to the political system. Nor does it function solely as an attitude; beyond a sense of liking or disliking (or some of both), partisanship includes feelings of belonging, commitment, group attachment, and common fate. While partisan *identification* and partisan *evaluation* likely serve overlapping functions (e.g., facilitating a coherent view of politics), the two are conceptually distinct. The identification component is rooted in symbolic needs for positive group and self-evaluation, whereas the evaluative component reflects a more utilitarian concern with the parties' platforms and performance in office (see Green et al., 2002).

It seems to us that conceiving of a specifically *partisan* form of ambivalence in strictly evaluative terms is to ignore the role of partisanship as a primary social bond. To our knowledge, however, all previous studies of partisan ambivalence, including our own, have done exactly that (see Basinger & Lavine, 2005; Keele & Wolak, 2008; Mulligan, 2011; Rudolph & Popp, 2008). Specifically, they have relied on Basinger and Lavine's (2005) mixed evaluations measure:

$$\text{Ambivalence} = \frac{D + R}{2} - |D - R|$$

where D is the average of the positive reactions to the Democrats and the negative reactions to the Republicans and R is the average of the positive reactions to the Republicans and the negative reactions to the Democrats (D thus represents the pull toward the Democrats and R represents the pull

---

the two parties in managing the affairs of government. They argued that orientations toward these objects comprise a system of partisan forces marked by the presence or absence of internal conflict. They found that such conflict was quite prevalent, as less than half of the electorate favored one party over the other by a margin of two or more attitudes. Like Lazarsfeld and colleagues, Campbell et al. (1960) found that voters experiencing conflict in their attraction to the two parties were less likely to have formed voting intentions before the start of the campaign and more likely to remain undecided within 2 weeks of the election. They also found that ambivalent voters were more likely to cast split ballots (i.e., voting for one party for president and the other for Congress).

toward the Republicans). The intensity of feeling is captured on the left by the average number of reactions; the similarity of feeling is captured on the right by the absolute difference between the D and R terms. Like Thompson, Zanna, and Griffin's (1995) original measure, this formula treats ambivalence as the intensity of the conflicting evaluations corrected by their dissimilarity. Ambivalence is thus maximized when a person experiences strong liking and disliking toward both political parties simultaneously.

The problem with this measurement approach, as we have just noted, is that it ignores partisanship as an *identity*. Moreover, when identity is introduced, the Basinger and Lavine procedure yields counterintuitive scores. Why, for example, if a person has *negative* feelings toward one's own party should ambivalence rise if the person also has *positive* feelings? That is, why should someone be more ambivalent (rather than less) as partisan-*consistent* evaluations become stronger? It seems intuitive to us that when identity is explicitly taken into account, maximal ambivalence occurs not when identity-conflicting and consistent evaluations are both high (as Basinger and Lavine's original measure would have it), but when the former are high and the latter are low. It is therefore not mixed feelings that should instigate partisan ambivalence, but rather a *disjuncture* between the identification and evaluative components of partisanship.

Having thus defined ambivalence in this way, our next three questions are (a) How can these components be measured in surveys? (b) Is this bidimensional structure empirically valid? and (c) How should the conflicting and consistent forces be integrated to form a concrete operational measure? In the next section, we address these questions in turn.

TESTING THE BIDIMENSIONAL STRUCTURE OF PARTISAN EVALUATION

To examine the impact of partisan ambivalence on the political judgment process, we require data containing large, representative samples, measures of a variety of substantive political phenomena (congressional voting, economic perceptions, policy preferences), and a time span sufficient to model the influence of macro-level factors such as economic performance. The data must also contain items allowing for the independent assessment of positive and negative party evaluations. The most comprehensive vehicle for this purpose is the American National Election Study.

Beginning in 1952 and continued biennially up to the present,[6] each ANES survey has gathered data on a nationally representative sample of about 1,500

6. With two exceptions: 1954 and 2006.

in size. Almost every survey carries items in which respondents are asked what they like and dislike about the two parties. The typical introduction to these items reads as follows: "I'd like to ask you what you think are the good and bad points about the two national parties." Respondents are then invited to report their likes and dislikes for each party separately, generating four independent counts (number of in-party likes, in-party dislikes, out-party likes, and out-party dislikes). For each item, respondents are first asked, "Is there anything in particular that you [like/dislike] about the [Democratic/Republican] party?" If the respondent says "no," the survey moves to the next component. If the respondent says "yes," she is asked, "What is that?" and her verbatim response is recorded. Respondents are then asked whether there is "anything else," and this process is repeated up to four times for each component. Respondents can thus register up to five likes and five dislikes toward each party.

This unipolar format comports with the measurement requirements of the bivariate model. However, there are two drawbacks to asking respondents to actively generate (i.e., recall) their own likes and dislikes instead of simply recording *degrees* of liking and disliking on a scale. First, the distributions on all four count variables are positively skewed due to a large proportion of voters who cannot think of anything good or bad to say about either party. The distribution in Figure 3.1 displays the number of open-ended likes/dislikes summed across the four components (i.e., # of Democratic likes + # of Democratic dislikes + # of Republican likes + # of Republican dislikes) based on a pooling of ANES surveys from 1980 to 2004. As the figure indicates, fully a quarter of the sample failed to report a single evaluative reaction. The four panels of Figure 3.2 show the separate distributions of likes and dislikes for the in- and out-parties (i.e., one's own party and the opposition). The distributions of in-party likes and out-party dislikes—shown in Panels A and D—represent identity-consistent reactions; the graphs indicate that 30 to 40 percent of respondents generated no reactions at all. Unsurprisingly, the identity-conflicting distributions—shown in Panels B and C—indicate that an even larger percentage had nothing nice to say about the other party (70 percent) or nothing untoward to say about their own party (65 percent). In Figure 3.3 we combine Panels A and D from Figure 3.2 to form a distribution of identity-consistent reactions; we do the same with Panels B and C from Figure 3.2 to form a distribution of identity-conflicting reactions. These distributions, which constitute our final measures of partisan ambivalence (more on that below), include fewer entirely mum respondents. In particular, 44 percent of the pooled sample reported at least one identity-conflicting reaction, and more than half of those reported two or more.

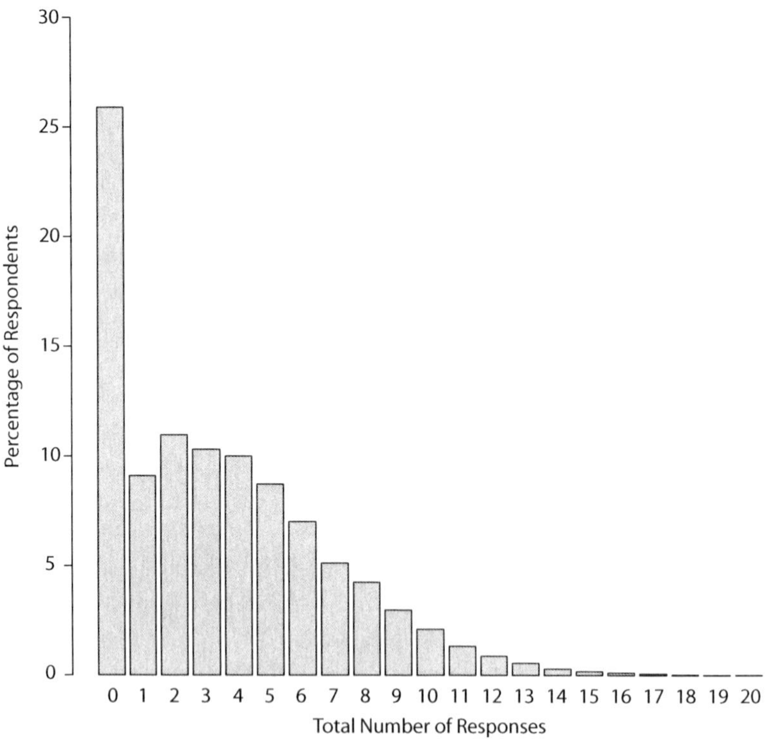

Figure 3.1 Distribution of Summed Open-Ended Party Likes and Dislikes, ANES 1980–2004.

Beyond the problem of distributional skew, requiring respondents to spontaneously generate (or retrieve) partisan evaluations creates a built-in confound between the number of responses reported and citizen characteristics related to political engagement. As those who profess an interest in politics are more knowledgeable about the subject, they are likely to report more reactions—irrespective of type—than less interested/well-informed citizens (Glass, 1985; Kessel, 1980; Smith, 1989).[7] While this may seem like an important drawback, it is far from devastating for our inquiry. In all analyses in which we rely on the open-ended likes/dislikes terms, we control for political sophistication, partisan strength, and interest in politics (which together account for 13 and 21 percent of the variance in the identity conflicting and

7. Smith (1989) has gone so far as to argue that the total number of open-ended likes and dislikes is effectively a measure of political sophistication.

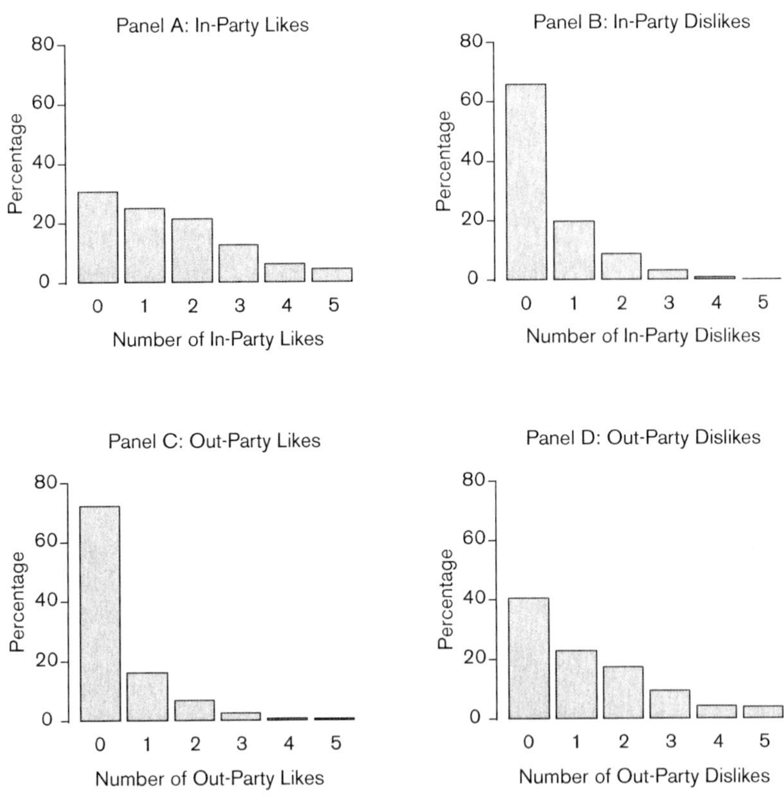

Figure 3.2 Distribution of In-Party and Out-Party Likes and Dislikes, ANES 1980–2004.

consistent components of ambivalence, respectively; the verbatim items for these standard engagement factors are presented in Appendix B).

An Alternative Measure of Partisan Ambivalence

Fortunately, we have at our disposal a second measure of partisan ambivalence, one that preserves the main benefit of the open-ended format (the ability to compute identity consistent and conflicting evaluations) but comes with better distributional properties and less of a concern about confounding. This measure—which we wrote and were able to place in the February and November waves of the 2008 ANES panel study—is introduced to respondents with the following stem:

> You might have some favorable thoughts or feelings about the [Democratic/Republican] Party. Or you might have unfavorable thoughts or feelings about the [Democratic/Republican] Party. Or you might have some of

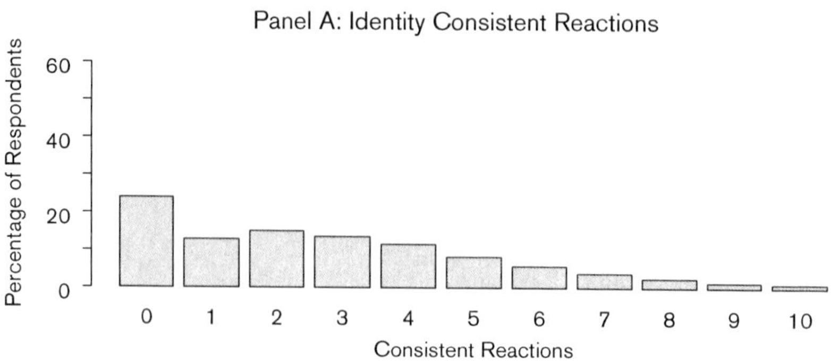

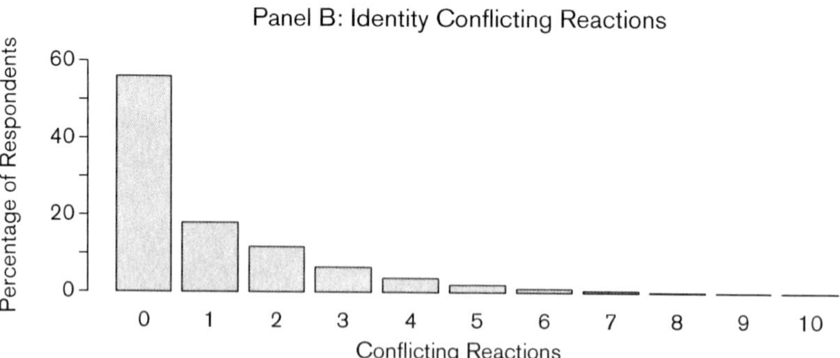

Figure 3.3 Distribution of Identity Consistent and Conflicting Reactions, ANES 1980–2004.

> each. We would like to ask you first about any favorable thoughts and feelings you might have about the [Democratic/Republican] Party. Then in a moment, we'll ask you some separate questions about any unfavorable thoughts and feelings you might have.

Respondents are then asked: "First, do you have any favorable thoughts or feelings about the [Democratic/Republican] Party, or do you not have any?" Negative responses are given a score of "0." Affirmative responses are followed by the question: "How favorable are your favorable thoughts and feelings about the [Democratic/Republican] Party?" Response options include "extremely favorable," very favorable," "moderately favorable," and "slightly favorable" (these responses are given scores of 1.0, .75, .50, and .25, respectively). This process is repeated for unfavorable responses, and then for both favorable and unfavorable responses toward the other party.

These questions were written to parallel the format used in psychological studies of ambivalence, and they were intended to capture degrees of positive and negative evaluation without demanding the higher level of cognitive investment required by the open-ended format. The distributions of positivity and negativity toward the in- and out-parties—shown in the four panels of Figure 3.4—indicate that this alternative format dramatically reduces the proportion of respondents who report having zero affect. Looking at Panels A and D—those that capture identity-consistent feelings—we see that this format decreases by half (vis-à-vis Panels A and D of Figure 3.2) the proportion of mum respondents (to 15 percent for in-party positivity and 23 percent for out-party negativity). Similarly, Panel B shows that the proportion of respondents who fail to acknowledge any negativity toward the in-party is reduced by nearly half (from 65 percent in Panel B of Figure 3.2 to 39 percent in Panel B of Figure 3.4). Finally, the proportion expressing no positivity toward the out-party is also reduced, but less drastically (from 71 percent in Panel C of Figure 3.2 to 61 percent in Panel C of Figure 3.4).

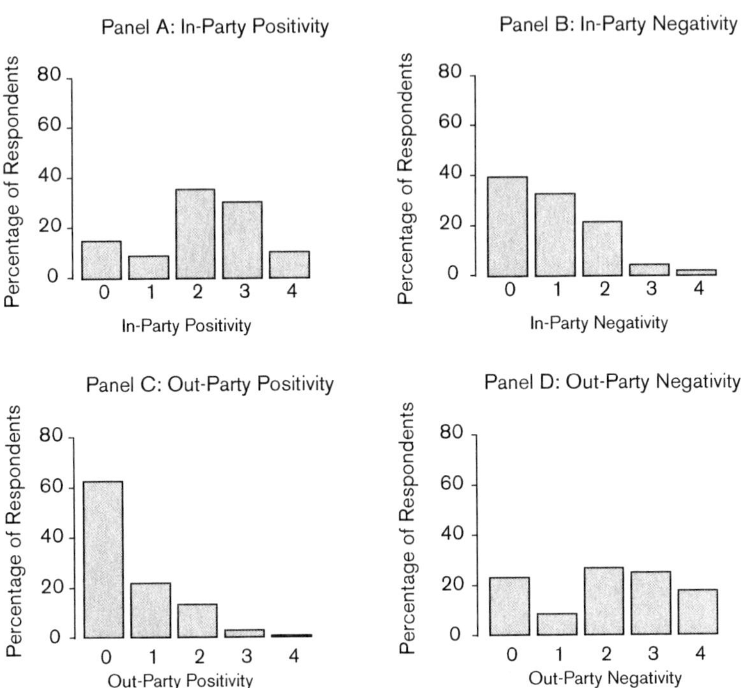

Figure 3.4 Distribution of In- and Out-Party Positivity and Negativity, 2008 ANES.

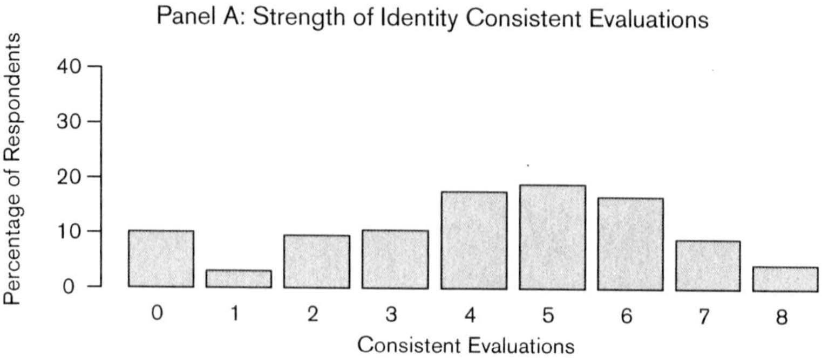

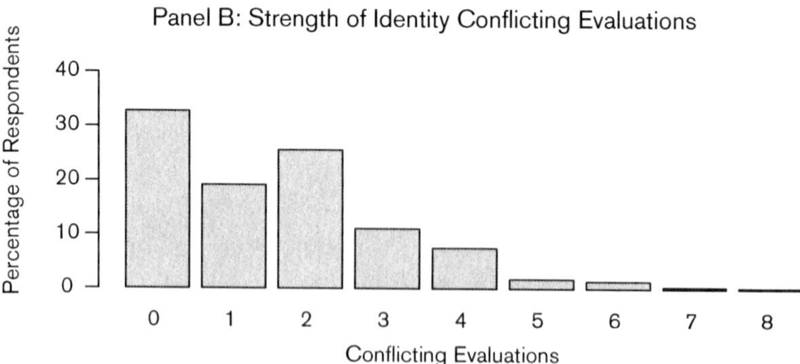

Figure 3.5 Strength of Identity Consistent and Conflicting Evaluations, 2008 ANES.

As we did with the count format, in Figure 3.5 we combine Panels A and D from Figure 3.4 to form a distribution of identity-consistent reactions; we do the same with Panels B and C to form a distribution of identity-conflicting reactions. These distributions are far less skewed than those in Figure 3.3. Most important, the proportion of respondents with zero affect drops dramatically: from 25 percent to 10 percent for identity-consistent feelings, and from 55 percent to 33 percent for identity-conflicting feelings. We utilize this alternative measure whenever possible, including in all analyses performed on the 2008 ANES panel study.[8]

8. In addition to these two measures, we created a third one for analyses conducted on the 2006 Cooperative Congressional Election Study. As the measure is quite distinct from the other two and is used only once (in Chapter 5), we will describe it in more detail at the appropriate time.

How Are Partisan Evaluations Structured?

Having distinguished between identity consistent and conflicting assessments, we now test whether it is empirically defensible to do so. In particular, we examine whether these are truly independent components, or whether they covary (negatively) to such a high degree that they form a single evaluative continuum (from perfectly consistent to perfectly conflicting evaluation). Should we expect to see a critical mass of citizens with high levels of both consistent and conflicting reactions?

If our breakdown is valid, we should observe two things: (1) the correlation between in-party likes and out-party dislikes (representing the two aspects of identity-consistent evaluation) is stronger than the correlation between either of these and either out-party likes or in-party dislikes (similarly, the correlation between in-party dislikes and out-party likes—representing the two aspects of identity-conflicting evaluation—should be stronger than the correlation between either of these and either out-party dislikes or in-party likes); (2) the correlation between identity consistent and conflicting reactions, generated as the sum of their respective components, should be small.

We turn first to the ANES cumulative file from 1980 to 2004 and examine the pattern of correlations for the separate likes and dislikes components.[9] As shown in the top section of Table 3.1, the correlation between in-party likes and out-party dislikes (the components of identity-consistent evaluation) is .49, and the correlation between in-party dislikes and out-party likes (the components of identity-conflicting evaluation) is .39. These are substantially larger than the other correlations in the table. An exploratory factor analysis provides stronger support for the bivariate structure. In a principal components analysis, the first two extracted factors account for 46 percent and 26 percent of the variance in partisan evaluations. Using principal factors analysis, we then extracted two factors and rotated these using a promax solution. The loadings of the four components on the two factors, shown in the bottom section of Table 3.1, strongly support the proposed bivariate structure. In-party likes and out-party dislikes load highly on the first factor (.59 and .61, respectively), whereas in-party dislikes and out-party likes have loadings near zero (.09 and –.03, respectively). Conversely, in-party dislikes and out-party likes load highly on the second factor (.51 and .53, respectively), while the other two components have minimal loadings (.03 and .02, respectively). The

9. In an attempt to purge the scores of variance in political engagement, we residualized them of variation in partisan strength, political interest, and sophistication.

TABLE 3.1. *CORRELATIONS AND FACTOR LOADINGS FOR AMBIVALENCE COMPONENTS, 1980–2004 ANES*

	Correlations		
	In-Party Likes	**In-Party Dislikes**	**Out-Party Likes**
In-party likes	1		
In-party dislikes	.22	1	
Out-party likes	.19	.39	1
Out-party dislikes	.49	.28	.14
	Factor Loadings		
	Loading on Factor 1	**Loading on Factor 2**	
In-party likes	.59	.03	
In-party dislikes	.09	.51	
Out-party likes	−.03	.53	
Out-party dislikes	.61	.02	

Notes: ANES Cumulative File, 1980–2004. $N = 13{,}067$. Components were first residualized by regressing each one on partisan strength, sophistication, and interest in politics. The two-factor solution was rotated using a promax rotation.

correlation between the two (unit summed) scales formed by the four components is actually moderately positive, at $r = .29$ (even after residualizing on the basis of political engagement).

We repeated this analysis using our alternative measure of partisan evaluation.[10] The correlations, shown in the top section of Table 3.2, indicate even stronger support for the bivariate structure. The correlation between in-party positivity and out-party negativity is .42, and the correlation between in-party negativity and out-party positivity is .34. The other correlations are minimal. The first two factors of a principal components analysis accounted for 37 percent and 33 percent of the variance in the items, and the rotated loadings indicate that in-party positivity and out-party negativity load highly on the first factor (.54 and .61), while in-party negativity and out-party positivity load highly on the second factor (.55 and .46; see bottom section of Table 3.2). The other loadings were all close to zero. Finally, the correlation between the two scales (identity consistent and conflicting reactions) is trivial ($r = -.04$). In sum, the two measurement formats submit to the same bivariate structure of

10. We rely on the second wave of the 2008 ANES panel study in February for this analysis, as this is the wave utilized to operationalize ambivalence throughout the book.

TABLE 3.2. *CORRELATIONS AND FACTOR LOADINGS FOR AMBIVALENCE COMPONENTS, ANES 2008 PANEL STUDY*

	Correlations		
	In-Party Likes	**In-Party Dislikes**	**Out-Party Likes**
In-party likes	1		
In-party dislikes	−.10	1.00	
Out-party likes	−.10	.34	1
Out-party dislikes	.42	−.12	.17
	Factor Loadings		
	Loading on Factor 1	**Loading on Factor 2**	
In-party likes	.54	−.10	
In-party dislikes	.10	.55	
Out-party likes	−.11	.46	
Out-party dislikes	.61	.11	

Notes: ANES 2008 Panel. $N = 1{,}303$. The two-factor solution was rotated using a promax rotation.

unipolar evaluation, distinguishing in each case between reactions that mesh and those that conflict with one's partisan identity.

Operationalizing Partisan Ambivalence

Thus far we have provided a conceptual definition of partisan ambivalence and discussed two procedures for measuring its two components. The question we take up now is whether and how these two components can be integrated into an overall empirical realization. The Basinger-Lavine procedure, based on the mixed evaluations definition of ambivalence, subtracts the absolute difference in the "pull" toward the two parties from their average intensity. Can we substitute our identity consistent and conflicting components for Basinger and Lavine's D and R terms, and thus retain the standard intensity-similarity formula? Unfortunately, given our conceptual definition, this would produce nonsensical scores. As we reviewed earlier, Basinger and Lavine's (2005) formula produces maximal ambivalence when the pull toward both parties is strong. According to our definition, however, maximum ambivalence occurs when identity-conflicting evaluations are strong and identity-consistent evaluations are weak.

Perhaps, then, a simple difference score (i.e., conflicting-consistent evaluations) would do the trick, with larger values reflecting greater ambivalence. Although this works well for highly asymmetrical values (i.e., many conflicting and no consistent feelings or vice versa), in most instances it prevents us from distinguishing between individuals with equal *relative* numbers of conflicting and consistent reactions but different *total* numbers. Moreover, the difference score is valid only under the restrictive assumption that the two components exert equally strong impacts on political judgment. While this is an empirical question, there is reason to believe that their effects may be asymmetric in magnitude.

Specifically, Priester and Petty (1996) examined the validity of several ambivalence formulas by regressing positive and negative reactions toward an object onto a measure of the subjective experience of internalized conflict (e.g., rating whether one has "one-sided" or "mixed" feelings). They dubbed as "dominant" the more prevalent type of reaction—either positive or negative—and as "conflicting" whichever type was less prevalent. They found that "conflicting" reactions exerted a far stronger influence on subjectively felt ambivalence than did "dominant" feelings.[11] As our identity-conflicting reactions are conceptually akin to Priester and Petty's "conflicting" component and our identity-consistent reactions akin to their "dominant" component, their finding implies that the former may trump the latter in conditioning how political judgments are made. To the extent that this is true, integrating them into a single difference score would lead to biased estimates (i.e., it would underestimate the impact of conflicting reactions). Thus, our approach is to include each component as a separate predictor in our statistical models, rather than attempt to combine them into a single variable.

To avoid bogging down the reporting of our empirical findings, however, we present predicted values and probabilities on our dependent variables by varying both terms simultaneously, and we refer to the effect simply as "ambivalence." If conflicting reactions have a larger influence than consistent ones, this approach will take the asymmetry into account in estimating the marginal effects. More specifically, when we use the ANES likes and dislikes count measure, we will refer to "ambivalent partisans" as those with *four*

11. Priester and Petty's (1996) also found that the influence of "dominant" reactions was conditional on the number of "conflicting" reactions. Specifically, they found that once the level of conflicting reactions approaches a threshold (which they found to be equal to one such reaction), dominant reactions exerted no influence at all on the subjective experience of ambivalence. This suggests that we might include an interaction term consisting of the product of identity-conflicting and identity-consistent evaluations. We decided against this because it would create a great deal of added complexity to our already stringently controlled models.

identity-conflicting reactions and *two* identity-consistent ones; to "mixed partisans" as those with *four* consistent and *two* conflicting reactions; and to "univalent partisans" as those with *six* consistent and *zero* conflicting reactions.[12] This strategy has the virtue of holding constant (at six) the total number of

12. While these specific values may seem arbitrary, they are based on a consideration of the joint distribution of conflicting and consistent assessments. To derive these specific operational definitions, we attempted to identify the reasonable bounds of each component, as well as take into account the fact that the two components are correlated (due to "loquacity," or citizens' tendency to talk). If the two components were uncorrelated (as they are in our 2008 operationalization), we would simply vary each from its 5th to its 95th percentile, as is common practice in political science (e.g., "ambivalent" partisans would be defined as those respondents at the 5th percentile of consistent reactions and the 95th percentile of conflicting reactions). For the likes/dislikes measure, we attempted to identify individuals with high percentile values on one component and low percentile values on the other. Using the ANES cumulative file from 1980 to 2004, for "univalent" partisans, the 90th percentile of the number of consistent reactions is six, and about 5 percent of respondents give six or more consistent reactions and zero conflicting reactions. This seems a reasonable lower bound on ambivalence. The opposite situation, however, is rarely observed. Citizens, all else equal, tend to say more identity consistent than conflicting things, and when combined with the positive correlation between the two, it is relatively unlikely to observe a person who reports a large number of identity conflicting but no consistent reactions to the parties. While needless to say, any choice made is here bound to be somewhat arbitrary, we chose to define points on the ambivalence continuum as follows: Univalent partisan equals six consistent and zero conflicting reactions, mixed partisan subtracts two consistent reactions and adds two conflicting reactions, and ambivalent partisan subtracts two more consistent reactions and adds two more conflicting reactions. This is pleasing on its face for being linear; moreover, it generates a face-valid moderate level of ambivalence at four consistent and two conflicting reactions, and an "ambivalent" endpoint that stays within the observed data. With respect to the latter, the 95th percentile of conflicting reactions is four, and about 2 percent of the sample simultaneously possesses four or more conflicting reactions along with two or fewer consistent reactions. One should thus view "univalent" and "ambivalent" as the effective bounds of the scale, and, as most of our models are linear (or approximate linearity), marginal effects using smaller changes can be readily interpolated by the reader. Perhaps most important, these operational definitions hold the total number of open-ended responses the same (at six) across the three categories.

open-ended responses.[13] When we utilize our own measure in the 2008 ANES panel study, we will refer to "ambivalent partisans" as those who score at the 95th percentile on identity-conflicting reactions and the 5th percentile on identity-consistent reactions; to "mixed partisans" as those at the 50th percentile of each component; and to "univalent partisans" as those respondents with the reverse profile of ambivalent partisans.[14]

THE CONTENT OF PARTY LIKES AND DISLIKES

Since much of our analysis in the next several chapters relies on open-ended responses to measure ambivalence, we think it is important to inquire into their substantive content. Respondents' verbatim answers were recorded by the ANES staff, and then coded into a large number of categories such as "economic policy" or "groups." By combining similar topics, we reduced the number of distinct categories to twenty, eight of which constituted a nonnegligible proportion of the total. These eight categories, which are listed and defined in Table 3.3, are "economic policy," "groups," "general performance," "party traits," "party leaders," "general ideology," "foreign policy," and "social policy." Each of the three policy categories refers to issue-related comments in a specific domain; "groups" refers to comments about social categories (e.g., gays and lesbians, evangelical Christians); "party traits" refers to positive or negative adjectives pertaining to perceived party reputation (e.g., honest, incompetent, spendthrift); and "general party performance" pertains to specific examples of past behavior (e.g., scandal, stewardship in foreign affairs). Examples of each category are provided in the rightmost column of Table 3.3.

Frequencies for each of the eight categories, tallied separately for identity conflicting and consistent reactions, are shown in Figure 3.6.[15] The graph shows that the most frequently observed category for both types of evaluations is *economic policy*. These comments were wide-ranging, including broad comments about the desire for more or less government to specific comments about unemployment benefits, taxes, and health insurance. The second most populous category depended on evaluation type. For conflicting responses, the runner-up was "party traits," which constituted 21 percent of the total

13. Our results are thus uncontaminated by "loquacity," or the general tendency to talk.
14. This operationalization, in contrast to the ANES likes and dislikes approach mentioned earlier, is consistent with the minimal association between the two components using our own measures.
15. The bars represent the proportion of all responses falling within each category.

TABLE 3.3. *CONTENT CATEGORIES OF PARTY LIKES AND DISLIKES, 1980–2004 ANES*

Category	%	Description	Example
Economic policy	24	Mention of economic policies or values	Pro expansion in unemployment benefits; pro lower taxes
Groups	23	Mention of group associations	Pro labor unions; anti Wall Street
General performance	10	Broad retrospective statements about the party's performance in government	Campaign finance scandals
Party traits	9	Mention of politically relevant party traits	Too negative, always tearing down the other side; honest government, not corrupt
General ideology	8	General statements about liberalism or conservatism of the party	Too liberal; like their conservative philosophy
Foreign policy	6	Mention of foreign policies or values	Pro abolition of peacetime draft; care more about world opinion
Party leaders	5	Reference to contemporary party figures	Reference to contemporary party figures
Social policy	2	Mention of social policies or values	Pro legalization of drugs; anti legalization of abortion

(compared to just 10 percent of identity-consistent responses). This was also a broad category, encompassing a range of assessments of party behavior. Positive comments included "well organized," "sticks together," "honest government," and "stands for a clear set of goals;" negative responses included "slings mud," "always tearing down the other side," and "doesn't follow through on policies." The second most populous category for identity-consistent responses was "groups." Responses included a wide range of social categories, including common people, farmers, Blacks, old people, Whites, gays, Christians, Jews, Muslims, Hispanics, women, and the middle class. This category constituted 26 percent of identity-consistent responses and 17 percent of identity-conflicting responses. The popularity of this category among consistent responses dovetails with the finding that partisan identity itself is strongly rooted in affect toward party-linked groups, and that consistent (vs. conflicting) reactions are more strongly tied to identity (Campbell et al., 1960; Green et al., 2002; Miller et al., 1991; Weisberg, Haynes, & Krosnick, 1995).

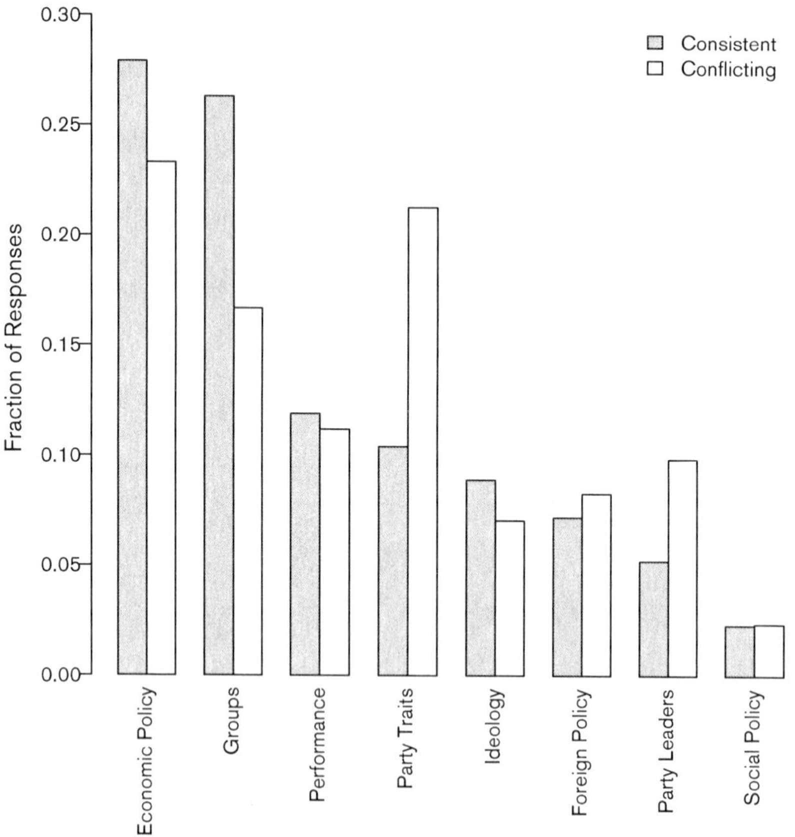

Figure 3.6 Content of Identity Consistent and Conflicting Reactions, 1980–2004 ANES.

After "economic policy," "groups," and "party traits," "general party performance" is the most populous category with about 12 percent of consistent and conflicting responses. This category refers to a range of specific performance-related outcomes, such as "inflation/cost of living better/worse," "wages/unemployment better/worse," "campaign finance scandals," and "responses to handling domestic crises or natural disaster."

The remaining four categories shown in Figure 3.6—"social policy," "foreign policy," "general ideology," and "party leaders"—represent smaller proportions. In sum, each of the eight categories comprised a nontrivial percentage of partisan evaluations. To some extent, the likes and dislikes are tied to enduring cleavages defining the party images (i.e., the "groups" category), but the vast majority—over 85 percent of the conflicting reactions—are tied to some form of party output.

THE ANTECEDENTS OF PARTISAN AMBIVALENCE

Having disposed of matters of conceptualization, measurement, and the substantive content of ambivalent partisanship, we now ask how someone becomes an ambivalent partisan.

We consider three classes of factors: party performance relevant to personal and public utility, value orientations related to contemporary issues, and the character of citizens' social networks. The bulk of our analysis will examine individual-level factors. First, however, we consider aggregate changes in ambivalence over the entire length of the ANES series. With a bit of political history as our guide, we can explain the ups and downs in perceived party fortunes.

Aggregate Changes in Partisan Ambivalence by Party, 1952–2004

The ANES has included the open-ended likes/dislikes items in almost every biennial survey it has conducted over the past 60 years. This allows us to examine a series of partisan evaluations spanning more than five decades of US political history. We present two separate series, one for identity-conflicting evaluations and one for identity-consistent evaluations. To generate the series, we subtracted the average number of responses provided by Democrats from the average number provided by Republicans. Thus, positive values indicate that Republicans outpaced Democrats; negative numbers indicate the reverse. We then transformed the yearly estimates into standard deviations from the mean of each series for purposes of comparing them.[16]

The two series are plotted in Figure 3.7. The solid line represents the standardized partisan difference in conflicting reactions, and the dashed line represents the same for consistent reactions. For the most part, the temporal patterns are in line with major historical events. Beginning in 1952, we see that Republicans provided more consistent and fewer conflicting reactions than Democrats. These differences reflect a list of self-referential grievances that Democrats expressed during this period. The Korean War—which in 1950 General MacArthur had promised would last less than 6 months—turned into a bloody stalemate by 1952 and was extremely unpopular among both Democrats and Republicans. In his "I shall go to Korea" speech made the week before the 1952 presidential election, Eisenhower implied that he would end

16. As citizens are more likely to report consistent than conflicting reactions, there is more variation in the means for the former. For purposes of comparison in terms of magnitude of differences in a given year, the standardized measure is more interpretable.

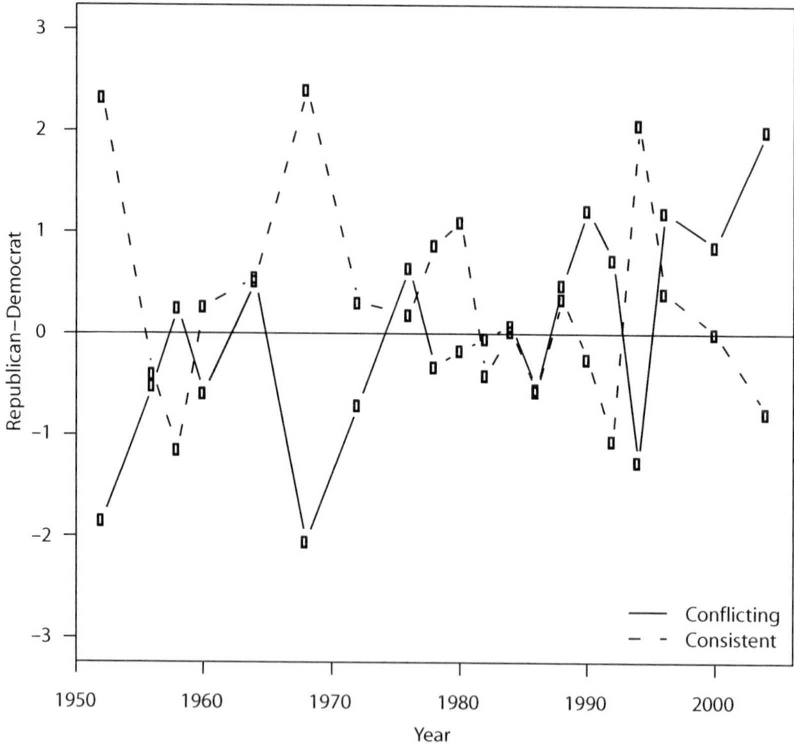

Figure 3.7 Party Differences in Aggregate Partisan Ambivalence, 1952–2004 ANES.

Notes: This figure shows the difference between Republicans and Democrats in average reported conflicting (solid) and consistent (dashed) considerations over time. These differences were standardized for presentational purposes.

the war, whereas Adlai Stevenson, his Democratic opponent, toed President Truman's line that the United States must continue the fight. A second source of in-party irritation among Democrats was the specter of communist infiltration of the US government (especially in the State Department), and the widespread furor whipped up by Senator Joseph McCarthy's red hunt. Many Democrats were sympathetic to McCarthy (the Catholic Church was a strong supporter), and being both the incumbent party and the soft-on-communism party, the Democrats experienced a wave of negativity among their own supporters. By contrast, both communism and Korea played the other way among Republicans by heightening identity-consistent reactions. Finally, Eisenhower himself, the popular World War II hero, made a substantial contribution to improving the Republican Party's image—and thus contributed to conflicting reactions among Democrats who also liked Ike.

Ambivalence among Democrats erupted again in 1968, with an equally clear story line: As the war in Vietnam dragged on, Lyndon Johnson became steadily less popular, and after being nearly defeated in the 1968 New Hampshire primary by anti-war candidate Eugene McCarthy, he withdrew from the presidential election. Division within the party about both the war and civil rights—including televised riots and violent war protests—ignited a culture war between its liberal and conservative factions that contributed strongly to in-party negativity. Perhaps nowhere was the collapse of the party more evident than at the national convention itself. Here is a segment of the events in Chicago, as described in real time by ABC's David Brinkley (as recounted by historian Rick Perlstein in his tome on the 1960s, *Nixonland*):

> The [National] guardsmen have bayonets at the end of their rifles, they're wearing gas masks; part of the central hallway of the Hilton Hotel has been made into a first aid station, sort of a receiving hospital. [Gene] McCarthy volunteers are now going out in the streets to find injured demonstrators...There's now a report that some guests in the hotel are getting mixed up in it and are throwing glasses and other things out of hotel rooms at the police. (p. 325)

Chet Huntley, Brinkley's co-commentator, says, "David, I think we can establish this without fear of contradiction: This is surely the first time policemen have ever entered the floor of a [national political] convention." In his rousing (if premature) convention speech for insurgent candidate George McGovern, Connecticut Senator Abe Ribicoff deplored Chicago Mayor Richard J. Daley's violent response to the young protestors: "And with George McGovern as president of the United States, we wouldn't have to have Gestapo tactics in the streets of Chicago!...With George McGovern, we wouldn't have to have a national guard...George McGovern is a man with peace in his soul." Perlstein (2008, p. 327) recounts ABC's television coverage:

> Quick cut to Daley, then Ribicoff, then Daley, then Ribicoff, a simpering downward turn of his mouth, then Daley, who was no longer bored. "Would like to know what the mayor is saying," Brinkley responds. Later an expert lip-reader suggests an answer: "Fuck you, you Jew son of a bitch, you lousy motherfucker, go home."

As liberals cheered Ribicoff's speech, Ohio congressman Wayne Hays spoke from the podium for the party's conservative wing about those who "substitute sideburns for sense and beards for brains" (Perlstein, 2008, p. 319). By the time Humphrey was eventually nominated, Perlstein concludes, it wasn't clear whether he was leading a party or presiding over a civil war.

Ambivalence among Republicans occurred at equally predictable times, first in 1974 (Watergate) and again in 1990–1992. The economy was in recession from July of 1990 to March of 1991, and economic downturn is always damaging to the incumbent party. Two other events plagued the Republican Party during this period. Perhaps most damaging was that a sitting Republican president committed the ultimate policy sin: raising taxes. When elected president in 1988, George H. W. Bush faced a budget deficit of $200 billion (triple what it had been when Reagan took office in 1981). Bush and the Republicans were committed to reducing the deficit, but they disagreed with the Democratic-controlled Congress about how to do it. Then as now, Republicans preferred spending cuts while Democrats favored tax increases. Raising taxes would have hurt the party's reputation (among in-partisans) under almost any circumstance, but a central part of Bush's 1988 platform—and the most memorable line from his convention speech that year—was his pledge of "read my lips: no new taxes." Bush ultimately compromised with the Democrats in the budget battle of 1990, and Republican voters reacted in a predictably (disapproving) manner.

Despite having waged a victorious war against Saddam Hussein the year before, Bush faced formidable problems again in 1992, including a challenge in the early Republican primaries by former Nixon aid and political writer and commentator Pat Buchanan. He soundly beat the president in the New Hampshire primary, ridiculing him repeatedly for backing out of his tax pledge. And quite unfortunately for Bush and the party, while the recession that plagued the Republicans at the midterms was long over, voters continued to hold negative perceptions of economic conditions. According to Hetherington (1996, p. 372), "relentless negative reporting on economic performance during the election year negatively affected voters' perceptions of the economy. These altered perceptions influenced voting behavior."

The last episode of Democratic ambivalence in the time series occurred in 1994. Like in 1968, the Democrats were divided on important issues of the day. Early in Clinton's presidency, they disagreed about gays in the military; Clinton campaigned on allowing gays to serve openly but then signed a bill championed by influential Democratic senator Sam Nunn making it illegal (it passed the Senate by a veto-proof majority in any case). They also disagreed about the North American Free Trade Agreement. Clinton, like any Democrat, depended on union support, and the unions strongly opposed NAFTA (as did a majority of Democrats in both the House and Senate). Being a "new" Democrat, Clinton was consistently for it, and so was his team of centrist economic advisors. Finally, and perhaps most important, the Democrats failed to pass heath care reform, which was Clinton's most important domestic initiatve. All of this produced a wave of negativity toward both Clinton and the party among Democrats. Their fortunes then improved rapidly after 1994, as the economy recovered and Clinton was easily re-elected. In the ensuing years, even through the Monica Lewinsky scandal and Clinton's impeachment, both the president and his party benefited from a technology-fueled economic super boom. As Figure 3.7 shows, Republicans during this period experienced heightened levels of ambivalence, generated by positive evaluations of Clinton's stewardship of the economy.

We also consider the development of partisan ambivalence over the course of the 2008 presidential election. Republicans were already at a disadvantage going into the fall campaign, but their problems were compounded when President Bush announced the possibility of imminent economic collapse. Happily for us, partisan evaluations were assessed in both the February and November waves of the 2008 ANES panel study, straddling the economic crisis in September. This natural experiment provides a particularly acute example of a shock to the system with the potential to induce strong ambivalence—in this case among Republicans (as in-partisans).[17] We estimated mean levels of consistent and conflicting evaluations for Republicans and Democrats at each time point, and we plotted these values in Figure 3.8. It is clear that the events transpiring between these points had a meaningful effect on the party evaluations of Republicans: Conflicting evaluations increased significantly from February to November (see Panel A), and consistent reactions similarly decreased over this period (see Panel B). There were no changes in either variable among Democrats.

Individual-Level Antecedents of Partisan Ambivalence

We turn now to a more rigorous examination of individual-level antecedents of ambivalence. We consider three broad classes of factors: retrospections of the performance of the incumbent party, value orientations related to contemporary policy issues, and the character of citizens' social networks. The first two categories correspond to the retrospective and prospective methods of party evaluation, respectively. The third refers to whether individuals discussed politics with those holding opposing views. We discuss our operationalization of each variable in turn.

17. Political accountability requires that *in-partisans* recognize poor incumbent performance.

Panel A: Change in the Strength of Conflicting Evaluations

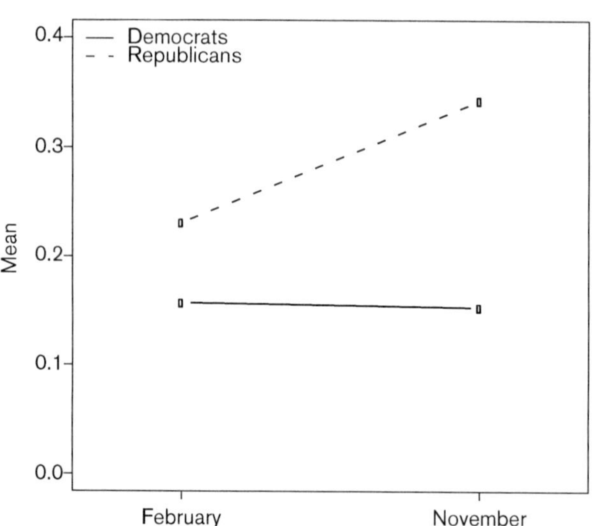

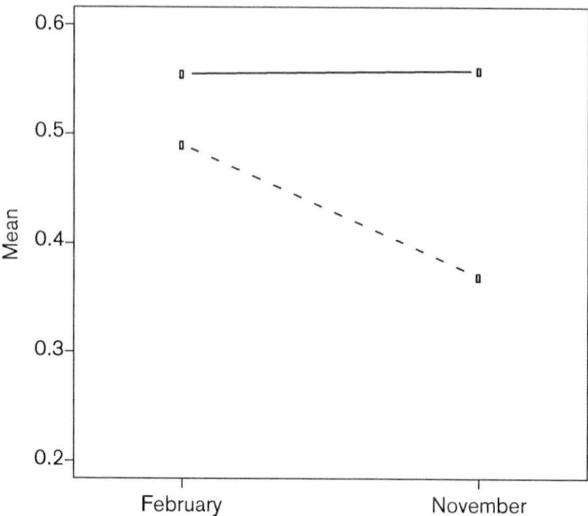

Figure 3.8 Changes in Identity Conflicting and Consistent Evaluations, 2008 ANES.

Notes: The figures depict changes in consistent and conflicting evaluations during the 2008 presidential campaign for Democrats (solid) and Republicans (dashed) separately (coded 0 to 1).

Economic Variables

We examine three variables intended to capture one's personal economic situation: an indicator of unemployment, a subjective measure of job insecurity (if employed) or the likelihood of finding a suitable job (if unemployed and searching), and an item measuring keeping up with costs over the previous year. We expect these variables to affect partisan ambivalence *conditionally*, as a function of the relationship between an individual's economic predicament and the party occupying the White House. When there is a partisan match (i.e., when the respondent and the president are of the same party), negative changes in personal circumstances should increase ambivalence, whereas positive changes should decrease it. We thus code the three variables such that negative changes are given higher values when the in-party is in power and lower values when the out-party is in power (e.g., being unemployed is coded "1" if the in-party occupies the White House and "0" if the out-party is in office).[18]

Values

As we discuss at greater length in the next chapter, core values—defined as bottom-line standards about right and wrong that inform a wide range of social and political judgments (Feldman, 1988; Goren, 2004; Rokeach, 1973)—may contribute dispositional variance in ambivalence. For example, ambivalence among Republicans may be fueled by support for egalitarian or humanitarian values, and among Democrats who support the values of limited government or moral traditionalism. We examine two broad value domains that have been included in a large number of ANES studies: egalitarianism and moral traditionalism. As with the economic variables, the effects of value orientation should be conditional: Proponents of egalitarianism should come into conflict with the Republican Party, and proponents of moral traditionalism should run into conflict with the Democrats. We thus code these two variables so that higher scores indicate more conflict with the respondent's own party.

Group Affect

According to the traditional conception, party identification reflects an affective group bond that results in a sense of social identity. It also involves a process of matching one's self-conception to an image of the social groups associated with each party (Green et al., 2002). Thus, holding negative feelings

18. This is a simplified way of testing an interaction between personal economic changes and the incumbent party.

toward groups traditionally linked to one's own party (or holding positive feelings toward groups linked to the other party) should be a powerful instigator of ambivalence (see Lavine & Steenbergen, 2005). We use the feeling thermometers asked regularly in the ANES to construct two scales representing affect toward the groups composing the two party coalitions. For the Democratic groups scale, we include feelings toward Blacks, labor unions, liberals, Hispanics, welfare recipients, environmentalists, gays and lesbians, and feminists.[19] For the Republican groups scale, we included big business, conservatives, the military, anti-abortionists, Christian fundamentalists (or evangelical Christians), and Protestants. We then generated a difference score by subtracting respondents' mean feelings toward in-party groups from those toward out-party groups. Positive values should thus increase ambivalence.

Social Networks

Respondents in the 2000 ANES were asked to list up to four individuals with whom they discuss politics, and whether each discussion partner voted for Bush or Gore. We used this information to create a single measure of face-to-face political discussion favoring the out-party.[20] Based on prior research (analyzing other forms of ambivalence), this variable should be positively associated with partisan ambivalence (Huckfeldt et al., 2004; Mutz, 2006; Visser & Mirabile, 2004).[21]

In accord with our breakdown of ambivalence into identity consistent and conflicting reactions, we estimated a pair of identical models with each component serving as the dependent variable. Our analysis is complicated by the fact that not all variables were asked in every ANES survey. Estimating

19. As not every group was included in every survey, we take the average of reported feelings for whatever groups were included in a given survey for which the respondent provided a response.
20. To do this, we created a variable coded "1" if the discussion partner voted for the out-party (vis-à-vis the respondent), "–1" if the discussion partner voted for the in-party, and "0" otherwise. We then multiplied this variable by the frequency with which the respondent discussed politics with this person. Finally, we added the four items (one for each possible discussion partner) to create a composite index with higher values indicating greater exposure to ideas favoring the opposition.
21. We also measured three other variables capturing potential heterogeneous information exposure: contact by the out-party, contact by the out-party House candidate, and the degree to which one discusses politics with other people. None of these factors influenced either component of ambivalence.

a single model would thus substantially reduce our overall sample size and generate inefficient estimates of the predictors. We employ an imperfect but workable strategy of estimating a series of models. We first estimate a baseline model that includes those variables that appear in all surveys between 1980 and 2004. Then, retaining these in all subsequent models, we add one variable at a time depending on availability. Our baseline model includes demographic information, partisanship, partisan strength, interest in politics, political sophistication, unemployment status, and our measure of group affect. The second model adds egalitarianism and moral traditionalism (they appear together in 1992, 1996, 2000, and 2004). All subsequent tests include a single additional variable. To simplify the presentation, the results are condensed into Figure 3.9 (Table A3.1 in the Appendix presents the model estimations; all tables throughout the book with an "A" prefix are relegated to the Appendix).[22]

Results

Economic Variables

We begin by examining the performance of our three economic variables: employment status (employed vs. unemployed), employment insecurity, and keeping up with costs. Each variable is coded such that higher values predict a larger number of identity-conflicting reactions and a smaller number of identity-consistent ones. As Table A3.1 indicates, two of the three variables are statistically significant and exert substantively meaningful effects on ambivalence. First, when considering an individual whose own party occupies the White House, moving from being employed to unemployed increases the expected number of conflicting reactions by 26 percent, all else equal (see Fig. 3.9).[23] The effect of unemployment on the number of consistent reactions is smaller in

22. As both components of ambivalence in the 1980–2004 ANES are count variables, we utilize negative binomial regression to estimate all parameters. This technique modifies the basic Poisson regression to allow for overdispersion (i.e., variance greater than the mean). To make the estimates readily interpretable and comparable across consistent and conflicting reactions, we report in Table A3.1 the percent change in the expected count for each ambivalence component for a 5 percent to 95 percent change in the independent variable of interest.

23. One can also consider this effect, as with the others reported later, in terms of a citizen whose party does not occupy the White House. In this case, a move from employed to unemployed status *decreases* the number of expected conflicting reactions by 26 percent.

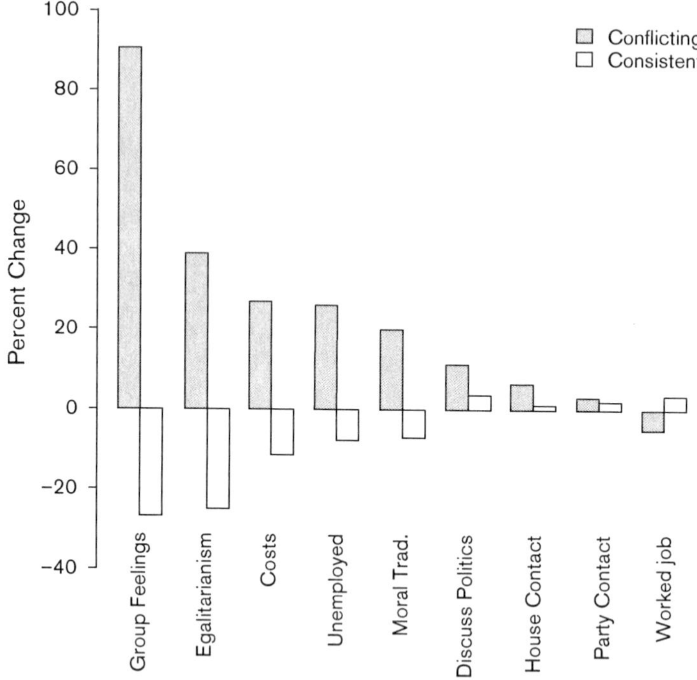

Figure 3.9 Effects of Individual-Level Antecedents on Partisan Ambivalence, 1980–2004 ANES.

Notes: The figure shows the percentage change in the number of identity-conflicting and identity-consistent considerations as various individual-level predictors are moved from their 5th to 95th percentile values.

magnitude, with an expected (negative) change of about 8 percent. The other economic factor to significantly predict ambivalence is one's ability to keep up with costs. When the in-party occupies the presidency, moving from "gone up a lot" to "fallen behind a lot" produces an expected change in the number of conflicting reactions of 27 percent, and an expected (negative) change in the number of identity-consistent reactions of 12 percent (see Fig. 3.9).

Group Affect

Our variable tapping the conflict between party identification and affect toward the group coalitions is included in all models. As Figure 3.9 shows, the results are quite strong, especially for identity-conflicting reactions. A move from the 5th to the 95th percentile on this predictor (i.e., from group feelings that range from highly consistent to highly inconsistent with party ID) entails a near doubling in the number of identity-conflicting reactions and an expected (negative) change in identity-consistent reactions of 27 percent.

Values

The results for both moral traditionalism and egalitarianism also confirm our expectations. For the former, a change from the 5th to 95th percentile of value-identity conflict produces an expected change in conflicting reactions of 20 percent, and an expected (negative) change in consistent reactions of 7 percent. As Figure 3.9 shows, the results for egalitarianism are more than twice this size.

Social Networks

Here, we examine the extent to which citizens' self-reported political discussion partners range from homogenously in-partisan to homogenously out-partisan. To the extent that information conveyed in a face-to-face context is perceived as highly credible (or simply salient), we expect it to have a strong influence on ambivalence. The results are shown in Figure 3.10. We vary the network variable from its 20th to 80th percentile, 5th to 95th percentile, and minimum to maximum values, and observe the expected change in identity

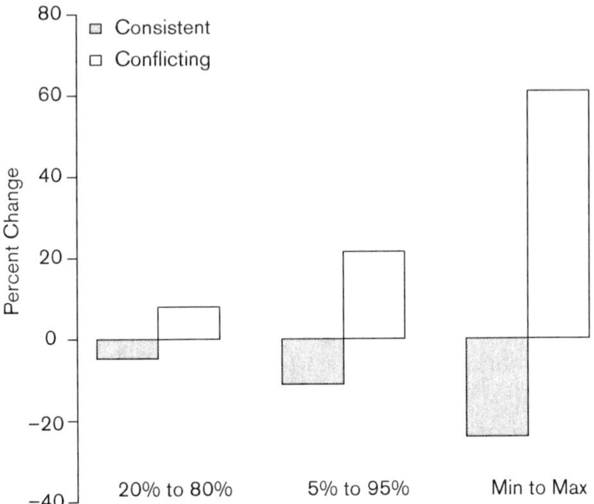

Figure 3.10 Social Networks and Partisan Ambivalence, 2000 ANES.

Notes: The figure shows the percentage change in the number of identity-conflicting and identity-consistent considerations for various changes in the partisan composition of the respondent's social network. Values of this independent variable range from a heavily in-partisan to a heavily out-partisan network.

conflicting and consistent reactions. As the figure shows, respondents who discuss politics with those holding worldviews different from their own experience substantially more identity-conflicting evaluation and less identity-consistent evaluation.

Summary of Findings

As Figures 3.9 and 3.10 readily show, the predictor variables were more successful in capturing variation in identity conflicting than consistent partisan evaluations. Although we do not have a ready explanation for this asymmetry, it is broadly consistent with a related observation made in the psychological literature. In particular, as we noted earlier, Priester and Petty (1996) found that feelings that conflicted with one's overall attitude exerted more weight in determining the subjective experience of ambivalence than did feelings that were consistent with the overall attitude. It remains to be seen (in Chapters 4–7) whether the same asymmetry holds when the two ambivalence components serve as independent variables.

In terms of the individual predictors, we found robust effects for economic insecurity: Being unemployed or viewing oneself as financially insecure each substantially increased the number of identity-conflicting reactions (if a co-partisan occupied the White House). Given that the president's party is routinely held accountable for economic outcomes, this finding is not a surprise. Moreover, it accords with the revisionist claim that voters rely on swings in the economy to judge party competence (Erikson et al., 2002). Both components of ambivalence also depended on whether values and group feelings conflicted with partisan identifications. Despite increased levels of sorting over the past few decades (Levenudsky, 2009), some Republicans continue to support egalitarian values and some Democrats continue to support traditional morality (we discuss this at greater length in Chapters 6 and 7). As Figure 3.9 shows, these discrepancies turn out to be an important dispositional basis of partisan ambivalence. Inasmuch as the parties—especially the Republicans—have emphasized core values in recent election cycles, we expect these sorts of inconsistencies to provide a stable core of ambivalent partisans in the American electorate. Finally, ambivalence depends on those with whom we regularly discuss politics. All else equal, those with heterogeneous social networks experience more ambivalence than those who discuss politics with like-minded others.

SUMMARY AND CONCLUSIONS

This concludes our discussion of the conceptualization, measurement, and antecedents of partisan ambivalence. We covered a lot of ground in this chapter. We redefined the concept of ambivalence from mixed evaluations to a disjuncture between partisan identity and party evaluations; we demonstrated the bidimensional structure of the latter in terms of identity conflicting and consistent reactions; and we examined its content and origins. These last analyses indicate that while ambivalence is partly fueled by stable factors (e.g., values and feelings toward social groups), the political environment constitutes a crucial dynamic component. The next several chapters explore the consequences of ambivalence for political preference (Chapter 4), perception (Chapter 5), political participation and vote choice (Chapter 6), and partisan change (Chapter 7). Chapter 4, to which we now turn, also examines the *causal* status of ambivalence by manipulating it experimentally.

CHAPTER 4

Partisan Ambivalence and Preference Formation

Experimental and Survey Evidence

In Chapters 1 and 2, we laid out a theoretical model centered on the argument that "good" political judgment depends on an individual's willingness to recognize and respond to inconvenient partisan realities. To briefly summarize, the model's main premises are that (1) ambivalence arises as a joint function of party performance and an individual's predicaments and priorities; (2) once aroused, ambivalence decreases the cognitive accessibility and perceived reliability of partisan cues, prompting individuals to turn to more diagnostic (but costlier) information when making political judgments; and (3) as a result, judgments are less biased, more accurate, and more firmly rooted in normatively desirable criteria (e.g., values, interests, facts). In the last chapter we confirmed the first premise, and in the next three chapters we will test the remaining components of the model using survey data on political perception and behavior.

In this chapter, we address whether partisan ambivalence conditions the normative quality of citizens' policy preferences. To do this, we examine whether univalent and ambivalent partisans systematically differ in the considerations that underlie them. Given the high degree of partisan polarization in contemporary American politics (more on that below), we expect the influence of party identification on policy preferences to be especially strong among univalent partisans. Furthermore, if such individuals derive sufficient confidence in the correctness of their policy views on the basis of partisanship alone (e.g., "If my party supports policy X, it must be the right policy"), they may be largely unconcerned with (or unaware of) whether their opinions dovetail with underlying values, material circumstances, or relevant facts. For example, univalent Republicans oppose policies aimed at the redistribution of wealth (e.g., universal health care, higher taxes on the wealthy), but they may fail to consider whether such policies harmonize with their broader view of government or their own economic position.

By contrast, ambivalent partisans are less willing to reflexively toe the party line. The evidence presented in Chapters 4–7 suggests that they place little faith in partisan cues, and that to absorb the slack in judgmental confidence they turn to more resource-demanding strategies. In this chapter, we examine whether the policy preferences of ambivalent partisans are rooted in core values and material interest, and whether they respond less on the basis of partisanship. On economic issues, we expect ambivalent partisans to consider both their broader view of government and whether they themselves would benefit from progressive taxation and expanded health care. On social issues such as abortion and gay marriage, we expect their attitudes to be rooted in orientations toward morality (i.e., traditional vs. tolerant).

We also examine whether ambivalence determines how policy attitudes are organized. As several studies have shown, the public's policy preferences are more tightly organized today than they were a generation ago (Abramowitz, 2010; Layman & Carsey, 2002; Levendusky, 2009, 2010). On the basis of Levendusky's (2009) work on the nature of partisan "sorting"—that is, that policy preferences bend toward party identification more than the reverse—we expect partisanship to be the primary basis of constraint among univalent partisans (see also Tomz & Sniderman, 2005). This should be especially true for economic issues, which are technical, pertain to means rather than ends, and are consequently more difficult for the public to grasp (Carmines & Stimson, 1980). Among ambivalent partisans, by contrast, we expect constraint to be rooted less in party attachment and more in core values.

In the next section, we present an overview of how partisan polarization at the elite level has altered the manner in which ordinary citizens construct their policy opinions. We then discuss the normative influence of values and social class, and note that despite decades of polarization, these factors are only moderately tied to party identification in the electorate. Our empirical analysis then proceeds in three sections. First, we discuss the results of several policy experiments in which both partisan ambivalence and the presence of partisan cues are manipulated. Second, we use panel data to examine how univalent and ambivalent partisans update their policy preferences over the course of a presidential election and over multiple years of partisan political conflict. Finally, we examine ambivalence-based heterogeneity in the bases of policy constraint.

BACKGROUND AND THEORY

The question of how ordinary citizens form their policy preferences has preoccupied political scientists for more than half a century. Following Converse's (1964) influential study of mass belief systems in the 1950s, a debate centered on whether citizens derived their opinions from general ideological principles such as liberalism and conservatism (for a review, see Kinder, 2006). An understanding of such abstractions is seen as a primary marker of democratic competence, as it allows ordinary citizens to respond to elite discourse. Converse found little evidence of ideological sophistication: Only a thin slice of the public made even partial use of ideological terms in reporting their likes and dislikes toward the political parties and presidential candidates; correlations between preferences on different policy issues were vanishingly small (indicating an absence of constraint); and preferences were inconsistent across time. This led many students of public opinion to conclude that there was an unbridgeable gulf between the public and its elected representatives, raising troubling questions about the former's ability to exert control over the direction of public policy. This pessimistic portrait was bolstered by a slew of research demonstrating widespread public ignorance of basic political facts (for a comprehensive review, see Delli Carpini & Keeter, 1996). Sniderman and colleagues (1991, p. 2) summed up the standard view of public opinion in this way:

> The public's knowledge of politics [is] paper thin, its views on public issues arranged higgledy-piggledy, its understanding of political abstractions like liberalism or conservatism as a rule superficial or nil. Against this backdrop, it [makes] little sense to inquire into the structure of reasoning and choice on political issues.

Converse and others interpreted the absence of ideological thought in terms of cognitive ability. According to this view, most people simply lack the wherewithal to understand the competing ideological principles underlying elite political conflict. Thus, barring an increase in formal education (and consequently in political sophistication), ideological innocence would be a permanent feature of mass politics. Other scholars, however, argued that Converse's findings were a reflection of the politically pallid nature of the Eisenhower era (when his research was conducted). For example, as Murakami (2008, p. 91) points out, the political parties in the 1950s were "ideologically heterogeneous coalitions, as much formed by historical grudges as by governing philosophies." This heterogeneity made it difficult for voters to figure out where the parties stood on salient policy debates, and to organize their own opinions accordingly.[1]

1. Although in his seminal 1964 essay Converse laid the blame for ideological innocence on citizens, he acknowledged the pivotal role of elite cues in his earlier collaboration on *The American Voter*: "There are periods in which the heat of partisan debate slackens and becomes almost perfunctory, and the positions of the parties become relatively indistinct on basic issues. In times such as these, even the person sensitive to a range of political philosophies may not feel this knowledge to be helpful in an evaluation of current politics" (Campbell et al., 1960, p. 256).

Contemporary research on elite polarization strongly supports this environmental thesis (see also Nie, Verba, & Petrocik, 1976; Sniderman, 2000). Up through the 1970s, the parties remained highly overlapping: Republicans in Congress included a healthy number of Northeastern liberals (e.g., Nelson Rockefeller), and the Democratic caucus had a large contingent of Southern conservatives (e.g., Phil Gramm[2]). In the early 1980s, however, following the election of the first modern conservative president, the bipartisan political consensus established in the wake of the New Deal finally gave way (Perlstein, 2001). Over the next two decades, the moderate Rockefeller wing of the Republican Party died out, leaving a conservative majority, and conservative southern Democrats either switched parties or were replaced by conservative Republicans, leaving the Democrats more homogeneously liberal (Black & Black, 2002; Poole & Rosenthal, 1997). This process of polarization—whereby liberal and conservative members of Congress sorted themselves into ideologically coherent parties and moved from the center to the extremes, and where the remaining moderates in each party were replaced over time by more extreme ideologues—proceeded apace through the Clinton and Bush presidencies so that today, nearly all Democrats in Congress are on the left and nearly all Republicans are on the right (Abramowitz, 2010; Levendusky, 2009; McCarty, Poole, & Rosenthal, 2006).

By providing a clear and programmatic choice between highly divergent policy packages, partisan polarization at the elite level has led to a transformation in the mass electorate. First, in moving from the center to the ideological poles, partisan elites now provide clear cues to the public about what policies are associated with the two major parties. This has increased the proportion of citizens who perceive party differences and who place the parties correctly on a variety of policy issues (i.e., Democrats to the left of Republicans; Hetherington, 2001; Layman & Carsey, 2002). Second, greater clarity at the elite level has led citizens to bring their own partisanship and policy preferences into greater alignment (Abramowitz, 2010; Layman & Carsey, 2002; Levendusky, 2009). For example, Layman and Carsey (2002) have shown that Democrats and (especially) Republicans have grown more polarized in their preferences on economic, racial, and cultural issues over the past three decades.

As elite polarization has led to a tightening in mass belief systems, parties have become more central to voters' political evaluations. Compared to the 1960s and 1970s (when parties were in sharp decline; see Bartels, 2000; Norpoth & Rusk, 1982; Wattenberg, 1998), the contemporary parties are highly salient

2. Gramm converted to the Republican Party in 1983.

to the public: Partisan identification is stronger, party-based voting is up, and split-ticket voting is down. In many respects, this transformation is a boon to democracy. Party elites are ideologically coherent; voters' belief systems have aligned accordingly, and party allegiance is the primary determinant of vote choice. As Murakami (2008, p. 106) writes:

> If responsible voting were a matter of matching one's *given* preference for government policies to the candidate or party that comes closest to agreeing, then it is hard to imagine how party polarization would be harmful. That is, if we are indifferent to the source of citizens' policy preferences, then elements in the political system that lower voters' ability to perceive partisan policy differences or that inhibit the parties from coalescing around such differences, are the chief impediments to democratic accountability. Polarization... lowers both of these barriers to simple, "matching" accountability.

But as he goes on to argue, rightly in our view, accountability requires that we do not treat the public's preferences simply as givens. Specifically, Murakami (2008, p. 105) argues that "voters may know with precision which politicians and parties favor the policies they 'prefer' without knowing which policies would achieve the *ends* they most desire." This is undoubtedly true in that voters cannot predict with any certainty the consequences of their preferences. In another respect, however, Murakami raises a more empirically tractable question about the *quality* of contemporary mass opinion: Has partisan sorting increased the extent to which citizens' policy preferences are rooted in some normatively justifiable idea(s) about public life?

Our suspicion that elite polarization has failed in this regard is fueled by the manner in which sorting has occurred. Rather than switching parties to accommodate their substantive preferences, the empirical evidence indicates that voters tend to do the opposite: They sort by altering their policy preferences to fit with their standing party attachments (Carsey & Layman, 2006; Levendusky, 2009). Thus, an unsorted liberal Republican is more likely to become a sorted conservative Republican than a sorted liberal Democrat. This appears to be true even among political sophisticates. Given the large literature on the centrality and stability of partisanship (e.g., Campbell et al., 1960; Goren, 2005; Green et al., 2002), it should come as no surprise that party loyalty trumps other elements of political belief; nevertheless, it is not a normatively pleasing outcome, as it implies that voters' substantive opinions are less a reflection of systematic thought about desired end states (or the best means of bringing about consensually desired ends) than they are reflexive accommodations to socialized partisan attachments. So rather than reasoning that "I favor a progressive tax system because I value social equality (or have a low income)," it is "I favor a progressive tax system because I am a Democrat and that's what Democrats favor."

In Chapter 7, we will examine whether ambivalent partisans are an exception to this general trend, and whether they become sorted by changing their partisan allegiances to suit their substantive preferences. The central question we raise in this chapter is whether univalent partisans rely principally on a simple partisan cue-taking approach in forming, organizing, and updating their policy opinions, and whether ambivalent partisans, ceteris paribus, rely on more substantive considerations. Having rejected the assumption that political attitudes are formed on the basis of ideological deduction, political scientists have turned to other ideas that might organize and provide "some degree of consistency and meaningfulness to public opinion" (Feldman, 1988, p. 416). Two ideas that have been widely endorsed on both normative and descriptive grounds are self-interest and core values (Kinder, 1998).

The notion that political life—and normal human behavior itself—is fundamentally grounded in the pursuit of self-interest has pervaded all areas of social science. In economics and political science the theory of rational choice holds that people are motivated to maximize "utility," which is frequently synonymous with the idea of balancing the costs and benefits of different courses of action in terms of personal advantage (Downs, 1957; Mansbridge, 1983; Schumpeter, 1994; Sen, 1978). In characterizing the essence of self-interest in politics, Kinder and Sanders (1996, p. 51) write that "working-class citizens support social welfare policies because the benefits of such policies fall to them, while the middle-class line up in opposition because they must shoulder the costs." The normative argument, especially on the political left, is that large-scale democracies with strong class differences are intrinsically adversarial (rather than possessing a unified common good), and that aggregated self-interest—implemented through the political institution of one person one vote—is the soundest formula on which to build an edifice of fairness (Mansbridge. 1990).

Human beings are more than single-minded, self-seeking egoists, however. As the economist Sen (1990, p. 37) famously said, "the *purely* economic man is indeed close to being a social moron" or, as he also put it, a "rational fool." Most social theorists agree that human selfishness is tempered by moral judgments, by "our conception of what life and what society should be" (Schumpeter, 1994, p. 251). Our preferences in politics should therefore reflect more than narrow-minded personal advantage; they should also flow from a consideration of which *societal* outcomes are to be desired and the means by which commonly desired ends can best be achieved. These social prescriptions are embodied in the concept of *values* (Feldman, 2003; Lipset,

1963; Rokeach, 1973; Schwartz, 1992). At their core, values are normative orientations; they are the standards by which we make judgments about right and wrong, and should thus serve as criteria for political judgment. Moreover, unlike the abstract terms of liberalism and conservatism, values are intuitively simple concepts to grasp, as they are thought to be absorbed into the political culture through socialization and the reinforcement of social norms (McClosky & Zaller, 1984). Ordinary citizens thus need not be politically sophisticated to understand how public policies serve to facilitate or block their attainment (Feldman, 1988; Goren, 2004, 2012). Several core values have been studied as antecedents to policy preferences, including egalitarianism, economic individualism, limited government, environmental preservation, national security, humanitarianism, and moral traditionalism.

SUMMARY OF PREDICTIONS

Throughout most of the book, we rely on observational (i.e., survey) methods to gauge the political consequences of partisan ambivalence. In the first empirical section of this chapter, however, we report on several experiments in which both ambivalence and partisan cues are manipulated. These factorial experiments test several propositions of the model, including that ambivalence (a) stratifies citizens' reliance on cues versus policy content in driving preferences; (b) leads to greater attention to the *quality* of information; (c) heightens information recall; and (d) undermines the perceived reliability of partisan cues. In the second empirical section, we use panel data from the 2008 presidential election to examine whether preference updating over the course of the campaign followed a pattern of partisan polarization—with Republicans moving to the right on policy issues and Democrats moving to the left—for univalent but not ambivalent partisans. By contrast, we examined whether updating among ambivalent partisans was tied more closely to economic position, with low-income Republicans and Democrats moving toward a preference for greater government spending, and high-income Republicans and Democrats moving in the other direction. In the final section, we test the hypothesis that univalent and ambivalent partisans organize their policy preferences in qualitatively different ways, with the former relying on partisanship and the latter relying on values.

EXPERIMENTAL TESTS OF THE MODEL

Studying how ordinary citizens make political judgments in real-world contexts has the virtue of maximizing *external* validity. This refers to whether one's research conclusions—based on samples of the population and specific research procedures—can be generalized to larger populations of people, settings, and time periods. Our empirical analysis in the following two sections and in Chapters 5 through 7 relies on large, representative samples, heterogeneous research operations (e.g., measurement strategies, statistical models), diverse substantive contexts (congressional voting, economic perceptions, policy preferences), and spans several decades of American political history. We hope to make a convincing case that the consistent pattern of findings paints a discernable portrait of when and why citizens will shift from thinking lightly about politics—with the inevitable pitfalls that we have described—to giving more serious consideration to objective political conditions and to making choices based on the best available information.

However, traditional survey methods also have distinct disadvantages. By passively observing the world of political actors, ideas, and events as they come provided in nature (especially in the chaotic world of the 24-hour news cycle), it is difficult to isolate either cause-effect relationships or the psychological processes that mediate them. The behavioral economist Dan Ariely (2009, p. xxi) nicely expresses this point:

> Life is complex, with multiple forces simultaneously exerting their influence on us, and this complexity makes it difficult to figure out exactly how each of these forces shapes our behavior. For social scientists, experiments are like microscopes or strobe lights. They help us slow human behavior to a frame-by-frame narration of events, isolate individual forces, and examine those forces carefully and in more detail.

Before we subject our model to the messy real world, we first create tidier, more manageable *experimental* contexts that provide stronger tests of causality and allow for closer inspection of the model's theoretical dynamics.[3] In four experiments in this chapter, we directly test whether the presence of partisan cues undermines citizens' attention to substantive policy information among *univalent* but not *ambivalent* partisans. In three of our experiments, we present participants with two different proposals on a single issue (either welfare or health care reform). In one randomly assigned condition, the policy arguments are presented without party labels—they are referred to simply as "Policy 1" and "Policy 2." In another condition, one of the policy proposals is attributed to "Democrats in Congress" and the other to "Republicans in Congress." The

3. For expansive discussions of the virtues and drawbacks of the experimental method in political science, see Druckman, Green, Kuklinski, and Lupia (2011).

conceit of this manipulation—which we adopted from Cohen (2003)—is that the party cues are constructed such that the liberal policy is attributed to the Republicans and the conservative policy is attributed to the Democrats. That is, the partisan cues are *counterstereotypic*. As we shall see, this design feature allows us to determine the extent to which participants rely on cues versus policy details in forming their opinions.

To triangulate further on the role of ambivalence in stimulating deliberative thought, we conducted a fourth experiment that examined whether ambivalent partisans are more sensitive than their univalent counterparts to the *cogency* of information. According to dual-process theories of persuasion in psychology (Chaiken et al., 1989; Petty & Cacioppo, 1986), the occurrence of "systematic" thinking can be documented by the extent to which attitude change follows more from exposure to strong arguments than specious ones. Someone who is paying attention to the substance of a persuasive message should be more inclined to accede to its recommendations when the arguments are forceful and convincing than when they are flimsy and weak. Thus, variables that interact positively with an argument quality manipulation—such as ambivalence—can be treated as agonists of deliberative thought. Accordingly, in our fourth experiment, we crossed a (strong vs. weak) argument quality manipulation with a partisan cue manipulation in the context of a message advocating that charter schools be allowed to compete for resources with traditional public schools in the participant's school district.

We expected that univalent partisans would accede to the message—irrespective of whether the arguments were strong or weak—when the partisan cue matched the participant's own party identification. Thus, univalent Democrats should be persuaded when the message is attributed to a Democratic source, and univalent Republicans should be persuaded when the message is attributed to a Republican source. Ambivalent partisans, by contrast, should find the cue manipulation less reliable; as a result, they should process the substantive arguments more thoroughly. Agreement should therefore depend primarily on the strength of the message. Finally, we directly assess whether the shift from cues to message arguments is mediated by perceptions of partisan cue *reliability*.

The Party-Over-Policy Versus Policy-Over-Party Experiments

As we described earlier, the purpose of our experiments is two-fold: (1) to manipulate partisan ambivalence and determine whether its causal influence on the political judgment process conforms to our model's expectations; and (2) to control the types of information to which participants are exposed, so that we can make stronger inferences about what factors influence their judgments under different conditions. We present three experiments in this section. The first is a random-digit dialing telephone survey fielded by the Stony Brook Survey Research Center, conducted in February-March of 2009 with a representative sample of residents living in Nassau and Suffolk Counties of New York ($N = 548$; $n = 321$ Democrats; $n = 289$ Republicans).[4] We will refer to this study as the Long Island study, or simply as the LI study. The second experiment was an Internet survey fielded by Knowledge Networks (KN) with a representative national sample in March of 2010 ($N = 1{,}077$; $n = 548$ Democrats; $n = 560$ Republicans). We will refer to this as the KN study. Our third experiment was an Internet survey that we fielded through the "volunteers" section of Craigslist.com in November of 2008 (just weeks after the presidential election) with a nonrepresentative sample of adults living in 23 US states and Washington D.C. ($N = 168$; $n = 124$ Democrats; $n = 41$ Republicans). The LI and KN studies focused on the issue of welfare reform; the Craigslist study focused on the issue of health care reform.

The three experiments share the same 2 x 2 between-groups factorial design: 2 (Ambivalence: low vs. high) x 2 (Information Condition: policy only vs. policy + partisan cue). The experiments were conducted in three stages. At the outset of the first stage, respondents completed questions about their political ideology, party identification, and political knowledge, and they provided demographic information (gender, race, education, income, employment status). Partisan ambivalence was then either

4. The Stony Brook University Center for Survey Research conducted the survey by telephone between February 9 and March 7, 2009. A list-assisted method of random-digit dialing (RDD) was used to obtain phone numbers in the sample. Within selected households, individuals 18 years and over were selected at random for participation. Up to six contact attempts at various times of the day and week were made at each household phone number. To assure a representative sample, all households and individuals who initially were not willing to participate in the survey were contacted again, and an attempt was made to persuade them to participate. Interviews were conducted with 810 residents of Nassau and Suffolk Counties, including 410 completed interviews with residents of Nassau County and 400 completed interviews with residents of Suffolk County. The results were weighted on gender, age, educational attainment, and race, based on the 2007 US Census American Community Survey county-level data. Weighting was done using an iterative ranking process developed to estimate joint weights for any number of demographic variables for which population percentages are known only individually, not jointly. The margin of error is plus/minus 3 percentage points.

manipulated (KN and Craigslist studies) or measured (LI study). In the KN and Craigslist studies, respondents were randomly assigned to either a high- or low-ambivalence condition, where the former elicited *dissonant* partisan evaluations and the latter elicited *consonant* partisan evaluations. Specifically, respondents assigned to the high-ambivalence condition were asked to list two things—for example, policies, performance, leaders, groups—that they disliked about their own party, and two things that they liked about the other party. Those assigned to the low-ambivalence condition were asked to list two things that they liked about their own party and two things that they disliked about the other party. Thus, in the high-ambivalence condition, respondents were asked to bring to mind four dissonant partisan evaluations, and in the low-ambivalence condition they were asked to bring to mind four consonant partisan evaluations. In the LI study, ambivalence was measured (rather than experimentally manipulated) by asking respondents to separately rate the extent to which they held positive and negative feelings toward each of the two parties (this measure was described in Chapter 3 and included in the 2008 ANES panel study).

In the second stage of the experiments, respondents were presented with two competing policy proposals (each of which was approximately 50 words in length; the verbatim text for each experiment is shown in Table 4.1). Participants randomly assigned to the Policy-Only condition read (KN and Craigslist studies) or listened to (LI study) the competing proposals with no partisan cue information. The proposals were simply referred to as "Policy 1" and "Policy 2."[5] For those assigned to the Policy + Cue condition, the proposals were linked to *mismatched* partisan labels (i.e., the liberal proposal was attributed to the Republicans and the conservative proposal was attributed to the Democrats). In the final stage of the LI and Craigslist studies, participants chose the proposal they most preferred ("Which policy do you prefer: Policy 1 or Policy 2?"). In the KN study, participants rated their attitudes toward each policy (e.g., "Now, in thinking about the policies, to what extent do you favor or oppose Policy 1? Strongly favor, somewhat favor, neither favor nor oppose, somewhat oppose, or strongly oppose").

Our expectations are straightforward. In the Policy-Only condition, where no partisan cues are attached to the competing proposals, we expect participants to choose according to their general political outlooks. In the absence of any other information, we expected both univalent and

5. The policy labels—"Policy 1" or "Policy 2"—were counterbalanced with the proposals themselves so that half of the time Policy 1 referred to the liberal policy and half of the time it referred to the conservative policy.

TABLE 4.1. *VERBATIM TEXT OF LIBERAL AND CONSERVATIVE POLICY PROPOSALS, PARTY-OVER-POLICY EXPERIMENTS*

Knowledge Networks and Long Island Studies

Now we are interested in your opinion about two policy measures. Congress has recently debated two policy measures dealing with benefits to social welfare recipients.

The first policy, POLICY 1, [proposed by Republicans,] calls for $1000 per month for a family one child, with an additional $200 dollars for each additional child. These benefits are intended to last 7 years. [Under this Republican plan,] [r]Recipients would also receive $2,000 a year in food stamps and extra subsidies for housing and child care.

The second policy, POLICY 2, [proposed by Democrats,] calls for $400 per month for a family of one child, with an additional $50 dollars for one additional child. These benefits are intended to last for 3 years. [Under this Democratic plan,] [r]Recipients would also receive $500 a year in food stamps but no extra subsidies for housing or child care.

Craigslist Study

In addition to basic political opinions, we are also interested in how people read the news. Below, you will find an excerpt from a recent article in a major national newspaper. Please read the article, and then answer the questions that follow.

The House of Representatives has recently debated the state of health care in America. Two health care reform policies were proposed. The first policy ("Policy 1")[, supported by about 90 percent of Republicans, but only 10 percent of Democrats,] seeks to increase access to health care in America—and reduce health care costs—by giving government a greater role in the provision of coverage. The plan would require large businesses to provide health care to employees or pay a tax that would go into a government fund. Individuals without employer coverage would be allowed to buy into the government employees' plan. This plan would come at a greatly reduced cost and would be partially funded using the money collected from nonproviding businesses. The second policy ("Policy 2")[, supported by about 90 percent of Democrats, but only 10 percent of Republicans,] also seeks to increase access to health care and to reduce health care costs. It seeks to do this by increasing competition between insurance providers. The plan proposes to give Americans a tax credit equal to about half the cost of covering a typical family. Families could then go out and choose a preferred provider in the market. In addition, the plan would allow individuals to purchase coverage across state lines in an attempt to increase competition between providers, thus lowering costs.

Notes: Added wording in Policy + Cue conditions in brackets. Order of policy content counterbalanced.

ambivalent respondents to absorb the policy details well enough to learn which proposal corresponds better to their overall political views. In the Policy + Cue condition, however, we expect the likelihood of choosing the ideologically consistent policy to depend on partisan ambivalence (manipulated in the Craigslist and KN studies and measured in the LI study). According to our theory, univalent partisans can expect to derive sufficient confidence in their political judgments on the basis of partisan cues alone.

The presence of such cues thus obviates the necessity of processing the policy details. However, because the cues are counterstereotypic, using them as a judgmental yardstick should move respondents' preferences in the "wrong" direction: Cue reliance should make Democrats more amenable to the (Democratic-sponsored) *conservative* policy and Republicans more amenable to the (Republican-sponsored) *liberal* policy.[6]

While univalent respondents are likely to reduce their attention to the policy details in the presence of the partisan cue, we do not expect the same to occur among ambivalent respondents. If, as our theory prescribes, a disjuncture between partisan identity and partisan evaluation renders the heuristic of partisanship less trustworthy, respondents assigned to the ambivalent condition should fail to take the cue and should rely instead on the substantive information. Thus, the preferences of ambivalent respondents should be the same across the Policy-Only and Policy + Cue conditions.

The results of the three experiments are presented in Figures 4.1 through 4.3. The y-axis in Figures 4.1 and 4.2 (Craigslist and LI studies) shows the predicted probability of choosing the "correct" policy, which for Democrats is the more generous welfare policy and the government-sponsored health care plan, and for Republicans is the the more stringent welfare policy and the tax cut-based health care plan.[7] [8] As Figure 4.1 clearly shows, our major hypothesis was borne out: The preferences of low- but not high-ambivalence respondents were influenced by the counterstereotypic cues. In the Policy-Only condition (the gray bars in Fig. 4.1), respondents assigned to either ambivalence condition were highly likely to choose the correct policy (predicted probabilities = .81 and .78). However, in the presence of the perverse cues (i.e., the Policy + Cue condition), univalent but not ambivalent partisans

6. The strong form of this hypothesis is that an outright reversal will occur. In the weak version, the probability of observing a "correct" preference is reduced.
7. While it may be more appropriate to define the "correct" policy in terms of ideology (liberal to conservative) rather than party identification, we chose to use the latter for two reasons. First, as in the ANES series, the most frequently chosen ideological category is "moderate," that is, the scale midpoint. Using ideology scores would thus require a substantial sacrifice in statistical power. Second, the correlation between ideology and party identification is quite strong ($r = .61$). And in any case, the results are substantively similar when we substitute the former for the latter.
8. The probabilities for the Craigslist and LI experiments were generated from a probit analysis; the predicted values for the KN experiment were generated from OLS regression.

eagerly took the bait. As Figure 4.1 shows, the drop in the predicted probability of a correct response (from cue absent to cue present) among those assigned to the low-ambivalence condition is a hefty .32 (i.e., .81 – .49), a statistically significant and substantively large change. Moreover, participants assigned to the low-ambivalence/Policy + Cue cell were no more likely to choose the "right" (ideologically consistent) policy than the "wrong" (ideologically inconsistent) one. By contrast, the drop in predicted probability from the cue-absent to the cue-present condition among those assigned to the high-ambivalence condition is only .09 ($p > .20$). These results support our contention that univalent (but not ambivalent) partisans will forego careful scrutiny of substantive information when partisan cues are available.

Can we replicate these conditional effects on a different issue and a more representative sample? The LI study is based on the two welfare proposals shown in Table 4.1. While it is presumably difficult for participants to judge how liberal or conservative each proposal is in an absolute sense, the policy promising $1,000 per month in benefits for 7 years and $2,000 a year in

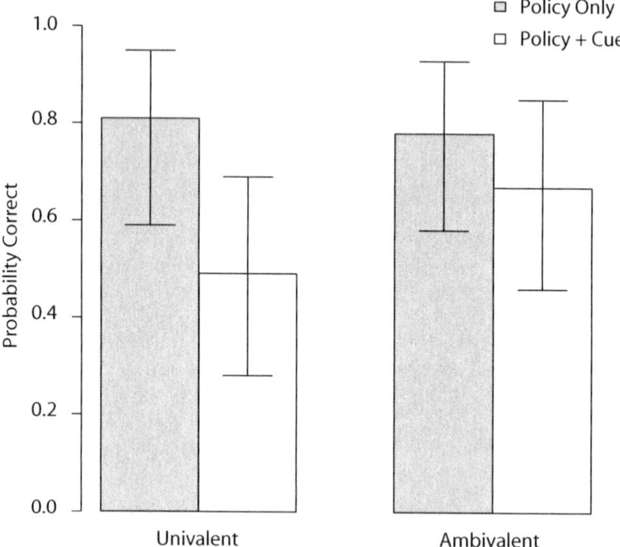

Figure 4.1 Predicted Probability of Choosing the "Correct" Policy, Craigslist Experiment.

Notes: The height of the bars corresponds to the predicted probability of choosing the correct policy as a function of the experimental manipulations. The capped lines represent the 95 percent confidence intervals. $N = 168$.

food stamps is *comparatively* more liberal than the policy promising $400 per month in benefits for 3 years and $500 a year in food stamps. The results, displayed in Figure 4.2, reveal the same pattern as before: Low- but not high-ambivalence participants altered their policy preferences in the presence of the counterstereotypic partisan cue. The one difference between the Craigslist and LI studies is that in the latter, respondents were given the option of expressing "no preference" between the two policy options. The probability of choosing this option was about .30 across conditions; therefore, the predicted probability of choosing the correct policy in Figure 4.2 is considerably lower than in Figure 4.1.

Nevertheless, the conditional *differences* in predicted probability closely replicate the Craigslist study. Among univalent partisans, the probability of choosing the correct policy in the absence of the partisan cue is .56; this drops to .14 when the cue is present. As in the Craigslist study, this change is statistically significant and substantively large. Ambivalent partisans, by contrast, were (as before) impervious to the cue. For these participants, the predicted probabilities are nearly identical across the two informational

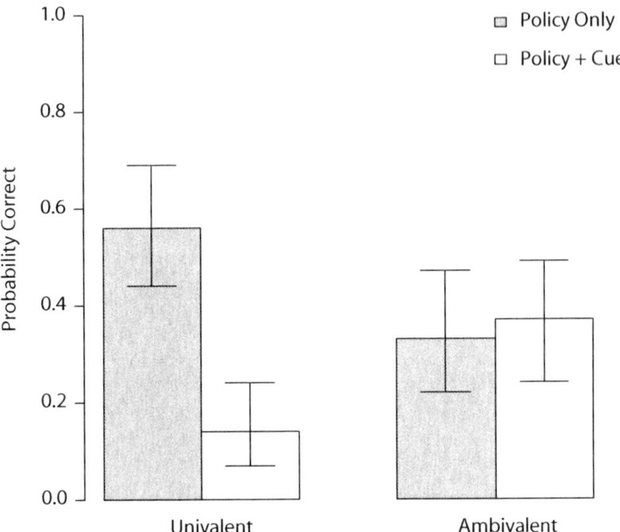

Figure 4.2 Predicted Probability of Choosing the Correct Policy, Long Island Experiment.

Notes: The height of the bars corresponds to the predicted probability of choosing the correct policy as a function of the two experimental manipulations. The capped lines represent the 95 percent confidence intervals. $N = 548$.

conditions (.33 and .37), and not statistically distinguishable from one another.[9]

Our last experiment (the Knowledge Networks study) also relied on the two welfare policies shown in Table 4.1. Participants in this study rated their favorability toward the two proposals on a five-point scale. Our dependent variable in this study is a difference score, in which support for the stringent policy was subtracted from support for the generous policy. Higher values thus indicate greater relative support for the latter.

With a continuous measure, we can examine differences in policy support across political orientation. In general, we expect that Democrats and liberals will show stronger support for the generous policy than Republicans and conservatives. Importantly, however, the size of this difference should be conditional on the two experimental manipulations (i.e., cue presence and partisan ambivalence). In the absence of partisan cues, we expect a large positive influence of political orientation on policy preference in both (low and high) ambivalence conditions. In the presence of the cues, however, we expect this relationship to decline (or reverse) for respondents assigned to the

9. Interestingly, however, there is a significant drop in the probability of a "correct" response moving from univalent partisans in the Policy-Only condition to ambivalent partisans in either condition ($p < .05$). In other words, while negating the effect of the partisan cue, ambivalence decreases the probability of a correct judgment. Why might this be the case? And why do we see a difference between this study (where ambivalence is measured) and the previous study (where it is manipulated)? The key difference is that in the LI study (in which ambivalence was measured), ambivalent respondents were less likely to possess ideological orientations consistent with their partisan attachments. The drop in "accuracy" is thus a measurement issue, and not a substantive one related to the influence of ambivalence on information processing. To further examine this possibility, we considered the effect of ambivalence on partisan-ideological consistency, defined as being both a Democrat and a self-identified liberal, or being a Republican and a self-identified conservative. While we find no relationship for Democrats, there is a strong and significant effect of ambivalence for Republicans. At low levels of ambivalence, Republicans are almost guaranteed to be consistent (i.e., to identify as conservative; predicted probability = .99). At high levels of ambivalence, by contrast, this probability drops substantially to .79. This pattern appears to be an idiosyncrasy of the Long Island sample (i.e., the finding is not replicated in our other data). When we exclude these "unsorted" Republicans, the main effect of ambivalence is eliminated. In any case, the key dynamic replicates: Univalent partisans take the perverse partisan cue, whereas ambivalent partisans do not.

low-ambivalence condition but to remain constant for those assigned to the high-ambivalence condition. We can assess these hypotheses by regressing policy support on political orientation within each of the four experimental cells. To operationalize the latter, we averaged respondents' partisan and ideological identifications, with higher values indicating a liberal orientation.

As can be seen in Figure 4.3, our expectations are supported. The y-axis in the figure represents the difference between liberals and conservatives on relative support for the generous policy. In the absence of partisan cues, this difference is positive and significant for participants assigned to both the low- and high-ambivalence conditions. When the cues are present, however, the difference is eliminated among those assigned to the low-ambivalence condition. By contrast, cue presence did not affect the difference between liberals and conservatives assigned to the high-ambivalence condition.

Summary

The results of the three experiments are the same: Cue presence reduces the attention to policy substance among univalent but not ambivalent partisans. This occurs, so we think, because the former derive more confidence from such cues. Ambivalent partisans must therefore take in more substantive detail to

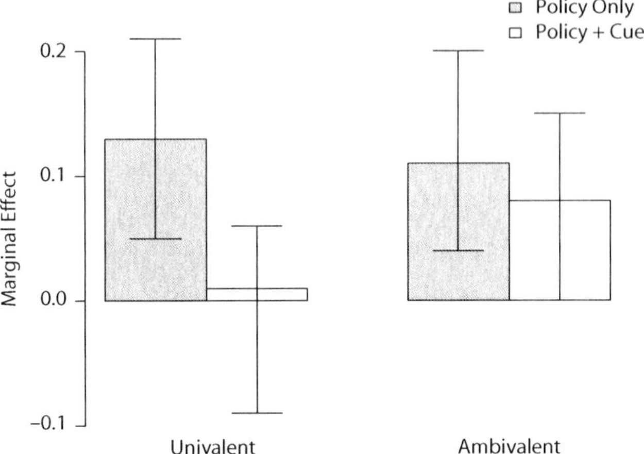

Figure 4.3 Predicted Marginal Effect of Political Orientation on Policy Preference, Knowledge Networks Experiment.

Notes: The height of the bars represent the marginal effect of left-right political orientation (or in other words the average difference in support for the generous welfare policy between strong liberals and strong conservatives) as a function of the two experimental manipulations, with capped lines indicating the 95 percent confidence intervals. $N = 1{,}077$.

reach their confidence thresholds. Fortunately, we were able to include a recall task at the end of the KN experiment, allowing us to test this "depth of processing" hypothesis directly. Specifically, after indicating their support for the two welfare proposals, participants were given a surprise recall task in which they were asked to list all the facts they could remember about them. Each fact was coded as correct or incorrect, and the number of correct responses was tallied across the two policies. The recall results were supportive: When partisan cues were present, those assigned to the low-ambivalence condition recalled fewer policy facts than did those assigned to the high-ambivalence condition (means = 3.71 vs. 4.16, respectively, $p < .05$).[10]

An important question not answered by these experiments is *why* ambivalence facilitated greater attention to the policy statements when partisan cues were present. We argued in Chapter 2 that people have a desire for confident knowledge (Kruglanski, Pierro, Mannetti, & De Grada, 2006), and that they will seek out additional information to meet their confidence thresholds when partisan cues are perceived to be unhelpful in this regard. In our next experiment, we test this proposition directly.

The Argument Quality Experiment

We have two primary goals in this experiment. First, we would like to test the claim that partisan ambivalence undermines the perceived reliability of partisan cues. Second, we would like to provide a further experimental test of the claim that univalent partisans pay less attention to the content of policy statements when partisan cues are present. In the last set of experiments, we varied the *ideological* nature of two policy statements (i.e., one policy was clearly more liberal than the other). In this experiment, we vary the *persuasiveness* of a single policy statement. Specifically, half of our participants were randomly assigned to read a statement containing strong arguments recommending that charter schools be allowed to compete with other public schools in local school districts. The other half were assigned to read a statement making the same recommendation but using arguments that are weak and unconvincing (the verbatim text of the strong and weak argument conditions is shown in Table 4.2).

We also manipulated the source of a partisan cue, such that the policy statement was attributed either to a local (Long Island, NY) Democratic or Republican political leader. We predicted that among univalent partisans, the cue would constitute sufficient information to form an opinion about

10. As we would expect, this recall difference was eliminated in the Policy-Only condition (i.e., when partisan cues were not provided).

TABLE 4.2. *VERBATIM TEXT OF STRONG AND WEAK ARGUMENT CONDITIONS, ARGUMENT QUALITY EXPERIMENT*

Strong Arguments Condition

The charter school approach uses market principles from the private sector, including accountability and consumer choice, to offer new public sector options. The key idea is that individuals who are dissatisfied with their current school's performance can simply take their business elsewhere. Over time, bad schools will either clean up their act to compete or be driven out of the market by better schools. The charter schools that already exist are getting results. Two recent scientific studies led by economist Caroline Hoxby of Harvard University found that charter school students do better on average than public school students. Their SATs are higher, and they do better in helping their students get into selective colleges than traditional public schools. It is about time that we take the education of our young people seriously and move to the charter school model.

Weak Arguments Condition

The charter school approach to education is far superior to the traditional model. We would not want to restrict ourselves to one type of car, television, or restaurant, so why should we restrict the ability of parents to send their children to the school they want? Children report having a good time at charter schools, and since they are the ones whose future is at stake, they should have some choice in the matter. Moreover, children at charter schools often make friends that can last a lifetime. It is about time that we take the education of our young people seriously and move to the charter school model.

the policy (i.e., more agreement should occur when the policy statement is attributed to a co-partisan than a partisan opponent). Univalent respondents should therefore see little reason to carefully scrutinize the merit of the statement itself. Ambivalent partisans should place less faith in the partisan cue; they should therefore be more willing to absorb the substantive arguments. If this is the case, the effect of the argument quality manipulation on policy preference should be stronger among ambivalent than univalent partisans.

Our last two hypotheses concern perceptions of cue reliability. First, we expect such cues to be perceived as more trustworthy judgment guides among univalent than ambivalent partisans. Second, we expect that ambivalence-based differences in the influence of the experimental cue manipulation will be mediated by concomitant differences in perceived cue reliability. To test these hypotheses, we recruited 136 Stony Brook undergraduates to participate in the study (105 Democrats; 31 Republicans). After completing a series of demographic questions and our survey measure of ambivalence, participants were randomly assigned to one of four experimental conditions in a 2 x 2 between-groups design: 2 (Partisan Cue: Democrat vs. Republican) x 2 (Argument Quality: strong vs. weak). After reading the (strong or weak) policy statement, participants

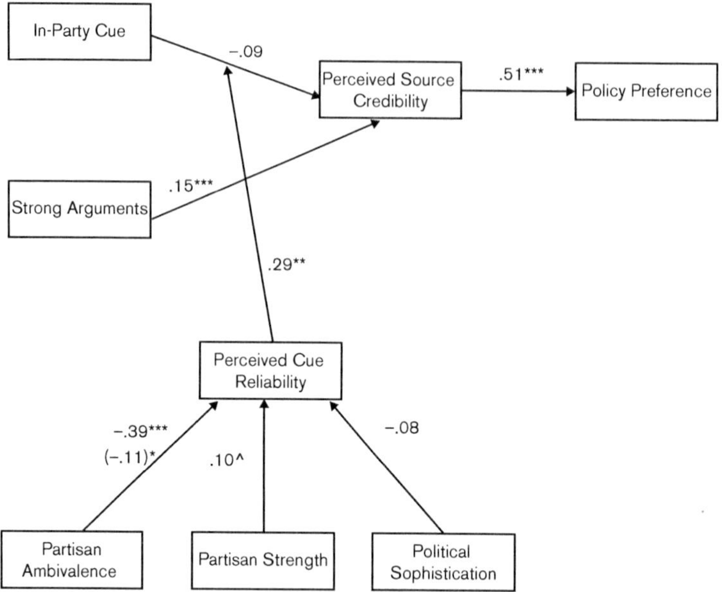

Figure 4.4 Path Model Depicting the Moderating Influences of Ambivalence and Perceived Cue Reliability on the Use of Partisan Cues, Argument Quality Experiment,

Notes: $N = 131$. (−.11) = indirect (i.e., mediated) effect of partisan ambivalence on the use of party cues. ***$p < .01$; **$p = .06$; *$p = .11$; ^$p = .14$.

completed a measure of policy support, as well as measures of cue reliability and message source credibility.[11]

As the path model in Figure 4.4 shows, our expectations were only partially met. Notably, partisan ambivalence failed to moderate the impact of argument quality on policy preferences. However, it did exert a strong (negative) influence on perceived cue reliability, which in turn conditioned the influence of the party cue manipulation on both perceived source credibility and policy preferences (perceived cue reliability was operationalized by averaging responses to the items shown in Table 4.3).[12] When the cue was viewed as unreliable, attitude change was unrelated to whether the persuasive policy statement was attributed to a fellow partisan or a partisan opponent. Among those who

11. The strong message contained 138 words, and the weak message contained 109 words.

12. As the path model shows, ambivalence influenced cue reliability more powerfully than did either partisan strength or political sophistication.

TABLE 4.3. *ITEMS ASSESSING PERCEIVED PARTISAN CUE RELIABILITY: ARGUMENT QUALITY EXPERIMENT*

(1) When it comes to forming your opinions about political issues, how reliable are the political parties as guides?
(2) For some people, simply knowing that the Democrats support one side of an issue and the Republicans support the other side is enough information to make a decision on that issue. For other people, this is not enough information to make a decision. To what degree does knowing the parties' positions on a policy help you in deciding whether to support or oppose it?
(3) Let's say that all you know about a political issue is that most Democrats support one side and that most Republicans support the other side. If you had to make a decision about the issue, how confident would you be in your decision—knowing just the parties' positions?

perceived the cue as trustworthy, however, more persuasion occurred when the source was said to be a co-partisan. In sum, ambivalence produced a substantial decline in the extent to which partisan cues were viewed as reliable judgment guides, and this in turn decreased respondents' reliance on them in deciding whether to support the policy proposal.

SURVEY-BASED TESTS OF THE MODEL I: POLICY FORMATION AND CHANGE

To test our hypotheses on observational data, we rely principally on panel studies, which allow us some measure of protection against the scourge of endogeneity. We begin with the 2008 ANES panel study to examine whether the bases of preference formation and change during an election campaign vary across levels of partisan ambivalence. We then focus specifically on economic issues and examine whether the preferences of ambivalent partisans are shaped more by objective self-interest than by partisanship, and whether univalent partisans exhibit the opposite pattern. We show here that the moderating influence of ambivalence is strikingly different from—and from a normative standpoint, more desirable than—our triad of traditional engagement variables (political sophistication, interest in politics, and partisan strength). Finally, we conceptually replicate this analysis using the 1992–1994 ANES panel study.

Preference Formation in the 2008 Presidential Campaign

The 2008 ANES panel study provides a unique opportunity to test our theory of political judgment in the realm of preference formation. The study solicited respondents' opinions on eight policy issues at two points in time, once in January and again in October. This design allows us to observe how citizens responded to the intensification of the presidential campaign and to the flood of partisan political messages. We contrast two basic processes by which citizens may have responded to this information. First, they may have chosen to receive and/or accept policy messages only from fellow partisans, leading to preference adjustments that resulted in greater alignment with co-partisan elites. Alternatively, they may have been less attuned to the *source* of a campaign message than to the *merits* of its content. If so, they should have given greater consideration to whether the information resonated with core values and material interests.

In our first analysis, we examine the bases of preference updating on the eight issues included in the survey (measured in the October wave): a constitutional amendment banning gay marriage, increasing taxes on citizens making more than $200,000 per year, government-provided prescription drugs for elderly citizens living on low income, suspension of habeas corpus for suspected terrorists, warrantless wiretapping, temporary work visas for illegal immigrants, a path to citizenship for illegal immigrants, and government-provided health insurance. We control for issue preferences in the January wave of the survey; thus, the model coefficients represent *changes* in preference over the course of the campaign. In addition to demographic controls, the model includes party identification, the engagement variables, and partisan ambivalence.[13] We form interactions between the Republican identification indicator (Democrats = 0; Republicans = 1; Independents excluded) and all four moderators (i.e., partisan strength, interest in politics, sophistication, and ambivalence). The model thus includes stringent controls.[14]

The results, shown in Table A4.1 (of the Appendix), indicate that issue preferences were highly unstable over the campaign. The effect of January partisanship on October preferences reveals that a good deal of this instability is the result of partisan cue-taking. Holding all moderators at their means, the

13. Partisanship, partisan strength, and political interest are measured in January. Ambivalence and sophistication are measured in February.

14. We estimated a multilevel model that considers all eight issues simultaneously and controls for unobserved heterogeneity in responses not accounted for by the respondent-level characteristics examined. We also include dummy indicators for issue to allow the average conservatism of the public to vary across issue domains. All variables were recoded to a zero to one scale, and coefficients represent the effect of each variable averaging over issue-specific heterogeneity.

marginal effect of precampaign partisanship on October policy preferences, averaging across issues, is .14. In other words, controlling for baseline differences in January, Republicans were 14 percentage points more conservative than Democrats by October. This is a substantively large campaign effect.

Consistent with our expectations, however, the effect of partisanship is strongly conditioned by ambivalence. Controlling for partisan strength, interest in politics, and sophistication, we find that the effect of partisanship ranges from .20 among univalent partisans to just .02—effectively zero—among ambivalent partisans. To place these conditional effects in a comparative light, we also estimated the marginal effect of partisanship at varying levels of interest in politics and sophistication (the influence of partisan strength was small in magnitude). These results—along with those for ambivalence—are plotted in Figure 4.5. As the figure shows, both interest and sophistication heightened reliance on partisanship, although their conditional impact is smaller than (and opposite in sign to) that for ambivalence.

This analysis demonstrates that the policy preferences of univalent (but not ambivalent) partisans were highly responsive to messages sponsored by the in-party during the 2008 presidential campaign. We would like now to determine whether ambivalent partisans responded to other considerations.

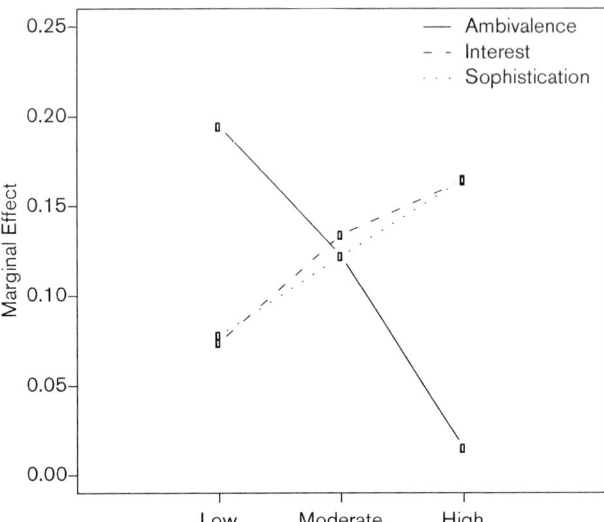

Figure 4.5 The Influence of Partisanship on Preference Formation Across Moderators, 2008 ANES Panel Study.

Notes: Lines represent predicted marginal effects of partisanship at various levels of the three moderators holding all other predictors at their central tendencies.

To do this, we consider the three issues that deal directly with economic concerns (taxes, health care, and prescription drugs) and examine whether preference updating among ambivalent partisans was driven by socioeconomic status (i.e., income).[15] According to the self-interest motive, the relationship between income and policy preference is straightforward: Less affluent citizens should be more amenable to higher taxes on wealthy citizens, as well as to greater government involvement in health care in general and prescription drugs in particular, as these policies serve redistributive and social protective functions (e.g., Meltzer & Richard, 1981). We should emphasize that mass partisanship—even after decades of sorting—only weakly captures differences in economic class. For univalent and ambivalent partisans, the correlation between partisanship and income in the 2008 panel study is .22 and .16, respectively.[16] This means that a large impact of partisanship will result perforce in many low-income citizens holding policy preferences contrary to their economic interests.

The model is identical to the last analysis, except that we add interactions of income with partisan strength, interest in politics, sophistication, and partisan ambivalence. The results are shown in Table A4.2 and indicate (again) that partisan cue-taking is responsible for much of the overtime instability in economic preferences.[17] Also, as before, we find that ambivalence substantially decreases this effect, and that political interest (but not partisan strength or sophistication) enhances it. Most important, we find that ambivalence does indeed heighten citizens' reliance on income. To better interpret the differences in how univalent and ambivalent partisans updated their opinions over the course of the 2008 campaign, we estimated the marginal effects of partisanship and income while holding all other variables at their central tendencies. The results are shown in Panel A of Figure 4.6.

15. Although prescription drugs for seniors was not a contested issue in the campaign, both taxes and health care were high-profile issues on which Obama and McCain took strongly divergent stands.

16. This weak relationship is in part a result of strategic moves by the Republican Party to break up the New Deal coalition over the past three decades (Dionne, 1991; Smith, 2007). While working-class citizens may not have completely abandoned the Democratic Party (Bartels, 2006, 2008; Gelman et al., 2008) as some have suggested (e.g., Frank, 2004), neither do they remain its staunch supporters.

17. Like the model in Table A4.1, this model is estimated within a multilevel framework to control for unobserved heterogeneity in responses, and it includes dummy terms for issue.

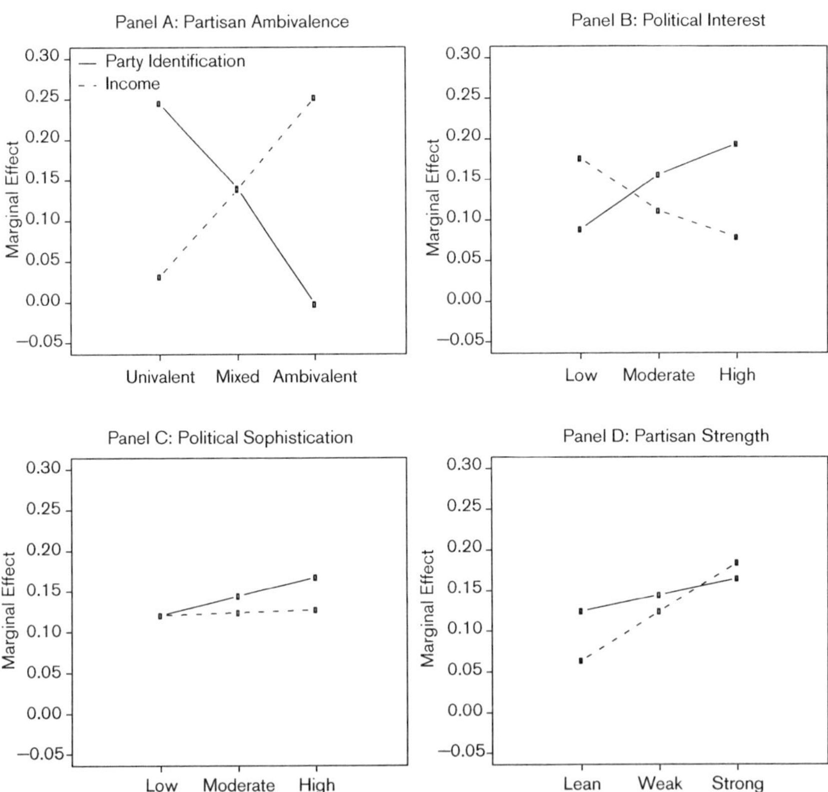

Figure 4.6 The Influence of Partisanship and Income on Economic Preferences Across Levels of Ambivalence, Sophistication, Partisan Strength, and Interest, 2008 ANES Panel Study.

Notes: Lines represent predicted marginal effects of partisanship (solid lines) and income (dashed lines) at various levels of each moderator holding all other predictors at their central tendencies.

The pattern in this figure perfectly reflects the essential dynamic of our dual-process framework. At minimal ambivalence, the marginal impact of partisanship on policy preferences is a substantial .25, one-quarter of the range of the dependent variable. Substantively, this means that on average (i.e., across the three issues and controlling for preferences in January), Republicans are predicted to be 25 percentage points more conservative in their economic policy views than Democrats by October. By contrast, at the same (minimal) level of ambivalence, the impact of income on economic preferences is essentially zero ($B = .03$). When ambivalence is moved to its moderate value, the marginal impact of the two factors is nearly equal, and when ambivalence is high, the effect of partisanship is dominated by that of income, with marginal effects of .00 and .25, respectively. Given the rarity of strong material interest effects in mass politics (for a comprehensive review, Sears & Funk, 1991), these results are striking. Moreover, as the model controls for initial preferences in January, the predicted values represent changes in preference over the course of the campaign. This means that the campaign mattered (i.e., citizens reconsidered their preferences) but in strikingly different ways for univalent and ambivalent partisans.

Finally, it is instructive to compare how our "competitor" variables—partisan strength, sophistication, and interest in politics—stack up against ambivalence in creating heterogeneity. Panels B, C, and D of Figure 4.6 display these results. As the figures show, there is no hint that any of these factors heighten reliance on self-interest (save strength). This suggests that the politically "engaged"—traditionally defined—derive sufficient confidence in their preference judgments to ignore their personal economic circumstances.

Replicating the Self-Interest Effect Using a Broader Measure of Personal Economic Well-Being

Although income level provides a reasonable basis for determining one's self-interest, we would like to replicate the ambivalence effect using a more thorough measure of personal economic well-being. Fortunately, the ANES included a battery of relevant items in the 1992 and 1994 waves of the 1992–1997 panel study. We measure personal economic insecurity in 1992 using the following battery of items, concerning whether in the past year, one (and one's family) (a) was better or worse off than a year ago; (b) put off making planned purchases (including medical and dental treatments); (c) borrowed money from relatives, friends, or a financial institution to make ends meat; (d) dipped into savings; (e) looked for a second job or worked more hours at one's present job; (f) saved money; and (g) fell behind on a rent or house payment. Together, these items provide a broad and internally consistent portrait of an individual's current economic predicament ($\alpha = .76$). We recoded each item to a 0 to 1 scale and averaged them to form a composite measure of personal economic insecurity (where 0 = insecure; 1 = secure).

We used this measure to predict attitudes toward the three economic issues carried in the 1994 ANES wave of the panel study: government services/spending, government-guaranteed jobs, and government-provided national health care (averaged and recoded to a 0 to 1 scale). Our analysis includes all the usual controls, as well as partisan ambivalence and a lagged measure of the same policy preferences (all measured in 1992).[18] Thus, our dependent

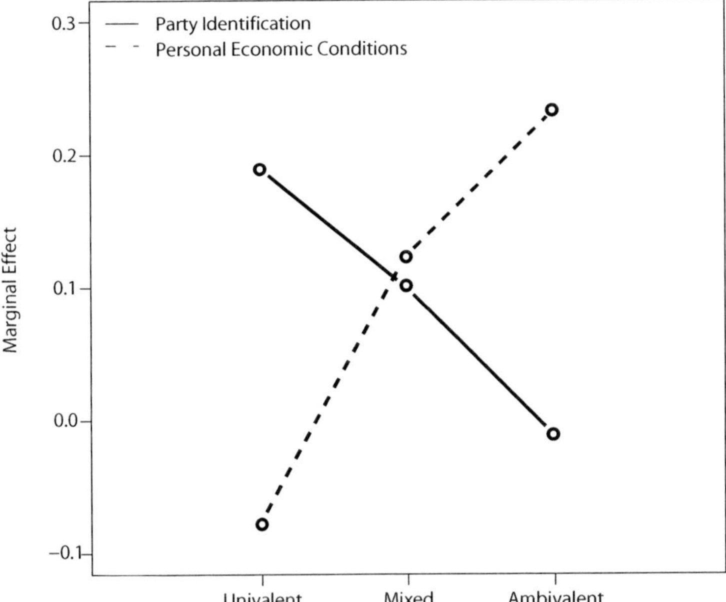

Figure 4.7 Marginal Effects of Party Identification and Economic Insecurity on Economic Preferences, 1992–1994 ANES Panel Study.

Notes: Lines represent predicted marginal effects of partisanship (solid line) and personal economic conditions (dashed line) at three levels of partisan ambivalence holding all other predictors at their central tendencies.

variable represents the change in preferences between 1992 and 1994. As Table A4.3 indicates, the effects of both party identification and personal economic insecurity are strongly conditioned by ambivalence. As in the previous analysis, Figure 4.7 indicates that among univalent partisans, economic preferences are strongly driven by partisanship and are wholly unaffected by personal economic insecurity.[19] Thus, economically insecure (univalent) Republicans

18. Given the small sample size, we dichotomized consistent and conflicting reactions such that 0 indicated no reactions at all, and 1 indicated one *or more* reactions. Univalent partisans in this analysis thus possess one or more consistent reactions and no conflicting reactions. Mixed partisans possess one or more of both types of reactions, and ambivalent partisans possess one or more conflicting, but no consistent reactions.

19. While the coefficient on personal economic insecurity is actually negative for univalent partisans, the effect is statistically indistinguishable from zero.

ignored the policy implications of their pocketbooks and toed the party line in opposing economic redistribution. By contrast, ambivalent partisans updated their preferences on the basis of economic circumstance (the marginal effect is .23 and highly significant), whereas partisanship failed to make any contribution at all.

Finally, as in the 2008 analysis, our triad of competitor engagement variables failed to exert any conditioning influence on either party identification or personal economic security. Most notably, none of these factors heightened respondents' reliance on self-interest. It is especially noteworthy that in both the 1992–1994 and 2008 analyses, political sophisticates—who are best equipped to comprehend the relationship between public policy options and their own private circumstances—are no more likely than ill-informed citizens to hold preferences on economic issues that dovetail with material considerations.

SURVEY-BASED TESTS OF THE MODEL II: POLICY CONSTRAINT

In this last empirical section, we examine the role of partisan ambivalence in conditioning the bases of issue constraint. As we noted at the beginning of the chapter, the question of whether citizens hold organized political beliefs is a long-standing concern in political science (e.g., Converse, 1964; Lane, 1962, 1973; Sniderman et al., 1991). While early reviews concluded that there was little evidence of organization, the public's attitudes have become more tightly aligned after three decades of elite party polarization (Abramowitz, 2010; Levendusky, 2010). While this might seem like a normatively positive development, consistency can arise from multiple processes. Levendusky's (2009) work on sorting indicates that much of this increased alignment is the result of partisan cue-taking. Thus, liberal Republicans have become conservative Republicans, and conservative Democrats have become liberal Democrats. The question we raise here is whether consistency, in and of itself, is a desirable quality, or whether its normative character depends on the process by which it is generated. More specifically, is constraint that derives from adherence to some abstract, superordinate idea(s) about social life, such as limited government or egalitarianism, superior to constraint that derives from partisan cues? We believe the underlying sources matter.

Value-based constraint implies that citizens hold principled ideas about social life and use them to construct broader perspectives on politics. For example, support for affirmative action, a progressive tax system, and a generous welfare state can each be seen as a means to achieving greater equality of opportunity. To the extent that policy preferences reflect broader value-based goals, public opinion provides a genuine signal to elites of the kind of society that citizens would like to live in. Party-based constraint, by contrast, does not require a consideration of desired end states. It may simply reflect the pressures of cognitive consistency, which have most likely increased over time as a result of polarization. Moreover, as Jacobs and Shapiro (2000, 2010) have argued, partisan cue-taking allows polarized elites to move the public in the direction of its own policy goals. This should be more difficult to accomplish among citizens whose policy preferences are anchored in core values.

In this analysis, we examine whether the qualitative basis of policy constraint depends on ambivalence. As we have seen thus far, univalent partisans are content to rely on partisanship as the primary basis of political preference. From the perspective of our model (and the evidence presented thus far), this occurs because they are more likely than their ambivalent peers to reach confident judgments on the basis of party cues. Therefore, they see little reason to think about the political world from other perspectives. Thus, whatever interdependence exists among the policy preferences of univalent partisans is likely to be rooted in common links to partisan attachment. Ambivalent partisans, by contrast, find partisan cues to be unreliable, and this motivates them to think more deeply about their political options, including (perhaps) how different policies foster the same value-based goals (e.g., Feldman, 1988; McClosky & Zaller, 1984; Rokeach, 1973).

To examine whether the substantive basis of constraint depends on ambivalence, we turn to the 2004 ANES. In addition to carrying items necessary to measure all of our standard variables, the 2004 study contains a battery of items tapping core values, including two that we examine here: limited government and moral traditionalism. The former refers to one's view of the proper role and scope of the federal government, whether it should act to alleviate suffering and decrease inequality, or whether the free market should largely dictate economic outcomes. One of the three forced-choice items used to measure support for limited government is "one, we need a strong government to handle today's complex economic problems; or two, the free market can handle these problems without government being involved."[20] Orientations on this

20. The two other items are as follows: (1) one, the main reason government has become bigger over the years is because it has gotten involved in things that people should do for themselves; or two, government has become bigger because the problems we face have become bigger; and (2) one, the less government, the better; or two, there are more things that government should be doing.

value should constrain attitudes on economic policies such as national health insurance and the privatization of Social Security.

Moral traditionalism refers to orientations toward social change: whether citizens should conform to time-honored modes of conduct or whether tolerance should be accorded to nontraditional lifestyles and beliefs. Orientations on this dimension should constrain attitudes on sociocultural issues such as gay rights and abortion. One of the four (agree-disagree) items used to measure attitudes toward moral traditionalism is "the world is always changing and we should adjust our view of moral behavior to those changes."[21] The 2004 study also solicited attitudes toward a battery of economic and sociocultural policy items. The economic items were government spending and services, government-provided health insurance, government-guaranteed jobs and income, and the privatization of Social Security. The sociocultural items were abortion rights in general, the specific procedure of partial birth abortion, gay marriage, and gay adoption.

We used confirmatory factor analysis to test whether the basis of constraint depends on ambivalence. The model treats the covariances among the policy items within a given issue domain (economic or sociocultural) as a function of two superordinate factors: partisan orientation and a domain-relevant value (either limited government or moral traditionalism). We define latent partisanship as a function of three observed indicators: the traditional seven-point ANES party identification scale, and two 101-point "feeling thermometer" scales that measure how warm or cold respondents feel toward each of the party labels. We define latent economic values with three items tapping orientations toward limited government, and latent sociocultural values with four items tapping moral traditionalism. If constraint among policy preferences derives from partisan cue-taking, we should see high factor loadings on the latent partisanship factor. Alternatively, if constraint derives from common values, we should see high factor loadings on the latent value dimensions. The basic structure of the model is displayed in Figure 4.8.[22]

---

21. The other three items are as follows: (1) The newer lifestyles are contributing to the breakdown of our society; (2) We should be more tolerant of people who choose to live according to their own moral standards, even if they are very different from our own, and (3) This country would have many fewer problems if there were more emphasis on traditional family ties.

22. We estimate the models for each policy domain separately and allow the four policy items in each analysis to load on latent partisanship and the relevant latent value (limited government for economic issues and moral traditionalism for sociocultural issues). Moreover, we allow the factor loadings for the issues—but not for the partisanship and values items—to vary across levels of

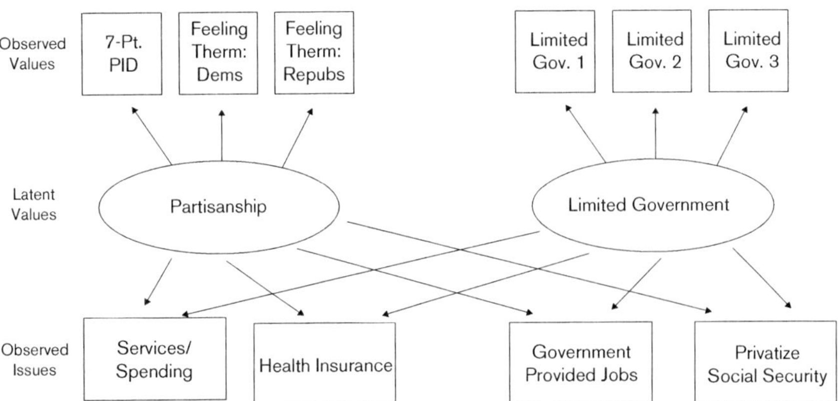

Figure 4.8 Covariance Structure Model for Issue Constraint.

Notes: Figure represents the estimated model for economic issue items. The model for social items is identical in structure but substitutes moral traditionalism for limited government, and substitutes the following social issues for the observed economic issues: abortion, partial birth abortion, gay marriage, and gay adoption. Latent variables are identified by fixing their variances to one.

Before running the models, we extracted the variance in ambivalence contributed by the three engagement variables. We then divided the residualized ambivalence scores into four quartiles and estimated the covariance structure model shown in Figure 4.8 as a multiple-group analysis.[23] We turn first to the results for economic issues, which are displayed graphically in Figure 4.9.[24] It is apparent that the nature of issue constraint is highly contingent on ambivalence.

---

ambivalence. In this way, the substantive content of the two factors is equivalent across levels of ambivalence, but the degree to which each issue item is constrained by the two superordinate factors is allowed to vary.

23. In the economic domain, the model was estimated via weighted least squares with probit link functions for the limited government items. For the sociocultural domain, the estimates were obtained via maximum likelihood. Both models were estimated in MPLUS (Muthén & Muthén, 2007).

24. The factor loadings can be interpreted as beta coefficients in a regression of the respective issue item on the corresponding latent factor. The factors were standardized to have a standard deviation of 1, and the issue items are all measured on seven-point scales. Thus, each loading represents the expected change on the seven-point issue scale for a 1 standard deviation change in the latent factor.

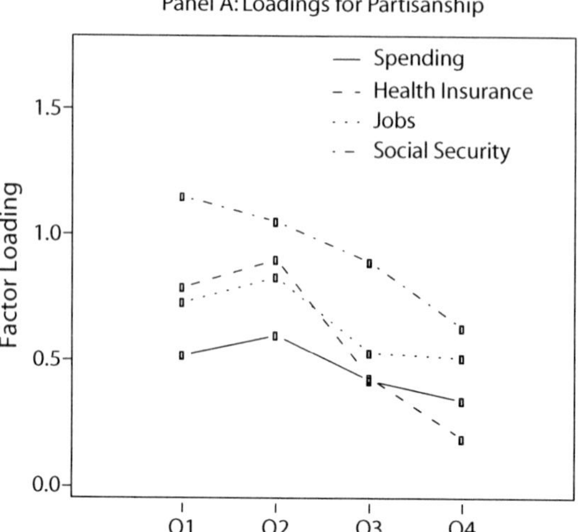

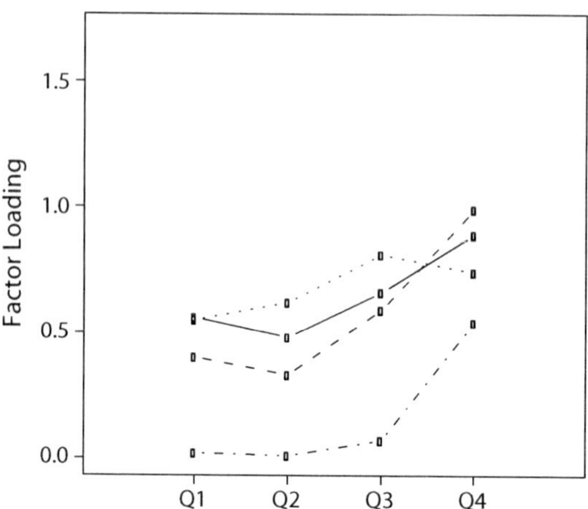

Figure 4.9 Factor Loadings of Economic Issue Preferences on Latent Partisanship and Latent Economic Values Across Ambivalence, 2004 ANES.

Notes: Lines represent the standardized factor loadings of each issue on the latent partisanship (A) and limited government (B) factors, respectively, at each quartile of partisan ambivalence. Partisan ambivalence was first residualized of common variance with partisan strength, political interest, and political sophistication. The model was estimated via weighted least squares with probit link functions for the observed indicators of limited government.

Looking first at Panel A, the factor loadings on the latent partisanship factor show a general downward trend as ambivalence increases. Conversely, Panel B—showing the loadings on the limited government factor—exhibits the opposite pattern: As ambivalence rises, the loadings on the latent value dimension increase. To get a sense of the bottom-line difference, in Figure 4.10 we calculated the ratio of the factor loadings on the limited government factor to the loadings on the partisanship factor. This figure makes clear that as ambivalence rises, the ratio increases dramatically. This means that the substantive nature of attitudinal organization among univalent and ambivalent partisans is quite different, with the latter defined to a much larger extent by ideas than identity.

We turn now to the results for the sociocultural domain, which differ somewhat from those obtained for economic issues.[25] Specifically, when controlling for the influence of moral traditionalism, there was little effect of latent partisan orientation at any level of ambivalence.[26] This makes sense, as abortion and gay rights are prototypically "easy" issues, thus requiring little in the way of elite guidance. By contrast, levels of value-based constraint were strongly affected by ambivalence. As Figure 4.11 shows, the loadings of the four sociocultural items on the latent moral traditionalism factor increase sharply as ambivalence rises. The pattern is most pronounced for the two abortion items, with only a slight increase for the gay rights items.

In sum, these results are largely supportive of our theory. In both economic and sociocultural domains, underlying values become increasingly powerful determinants of policy preferences as ambivalence rises. For univalent

25. The basic model is similar, but the interpretation of the factor loadings differs slightly. Given the nature of the preference items, we placed all four on a 0 to 1 scale prior to estimation. The gay rights items are dichotomous. The factor loadings for these items thus represent the expected change in the probability of a conservative response (e.g., opposition to gay rights) for a 1 standard deviation change in the latent variable. The loadings on the abortion items (both of which were measured on four-point scales) can be interpreted as the expected change on a 0 to 1 scale for a 1 standard deviation change in the latent variable.

26. There was, however, a large and significant influence of latent partisan orientations on attitudes toward partial birth abortion for citizens in the lowest quartile of ambivalence ($B = .30, p < .01$). This result is consistent with our theoretical expectations; it is also consistent with the idea that partial birth abortion is a more difficult issue than the other three sociocultural issues, as it involves a procedure with implications that may not be clear to all citizens.

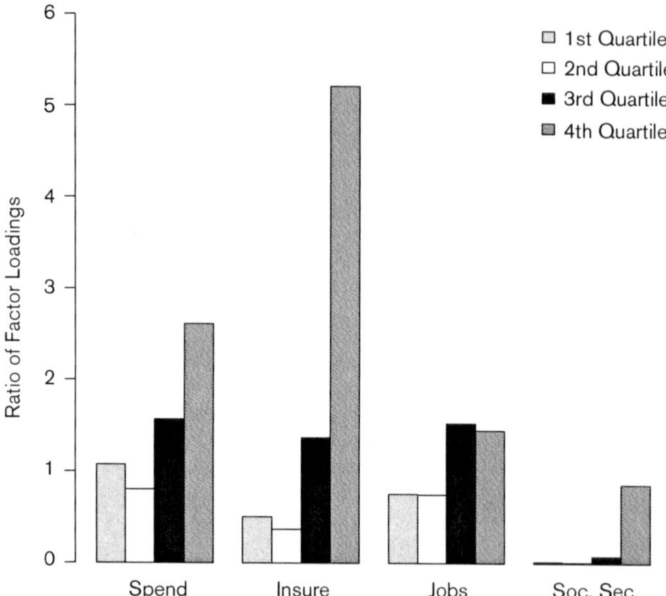

Figure 4.10 Ratio of Limited Government Loadings to Partisanship Loadings in Four Quartiles of Ambivalence, 2004 ANES.

Notes: Bars represent the ratio of the factor loading of each issue on the limited government latent factor to its loading on the partisanship latent factor at each quartile of partisan ambivalence.

partisans, the basis of issue constraint (at least for economic issues) is clearly partisan attachment. This dovetails with Levendusky's (2009) finding that the recent rise in belief system consistency is driven by party-based changes in substantive political beliefs. As elite polarization has clarified where party leaders stand on policy issues, univalent Republicans have shifted their attitudes to the right and univalent Democrats have shifted theirs to the left. This appears to be much less the case among ambivalent partisans, for whom the interdependent links among different policy attitudes is provided by corresponding variation in support for broader societal goals.

SUMMARY AND CONCLUSIONS

In this chapter, we tested our theoretical framework in the realm of preference formation, organization, and change. In two studies, we manipulated partisan ambivalence experimentally to examine its *causal* influence on the preference formation process. We also manipulated the types of information available to participants in forming their attitudes. In the "Party-Over-Policy"

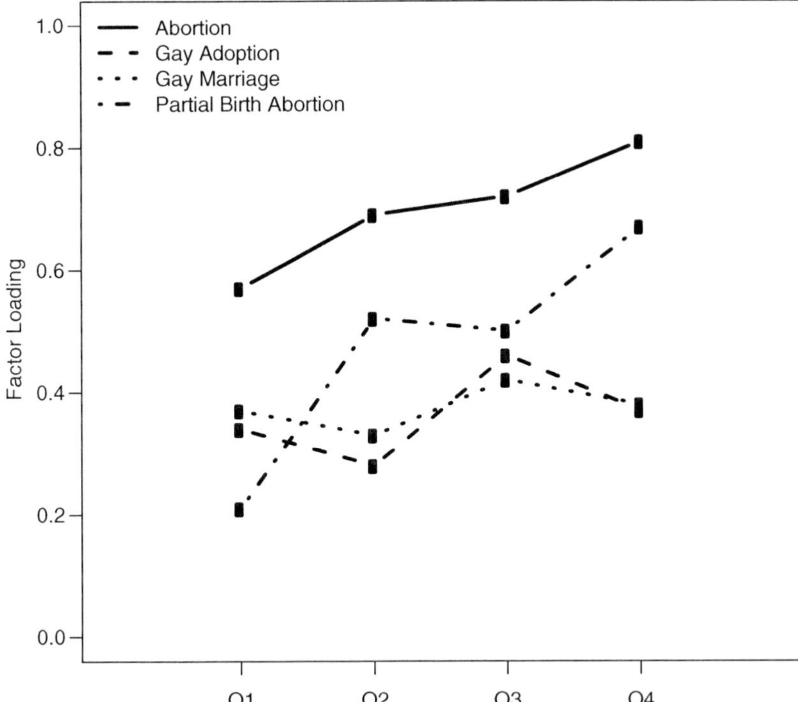

Figure 4.11 Factor Loadings of Sociocultural Items on Latent Moral Traditionalism, 2004 ANES.

Notes: Lines represent the standardized factor loadings of each issue on the latent moral traditionalism factor at each quartile of ambivalence. Ambivalence was first residualized of common variance with partisan strength, political interest, and political sophistication. The model was estimated via maximum likelihood.

experiments, we presented participants with two policy statements—one more liberal than the other—and varied the presence of a counterstereotypic partisan cue. We reasoned that in forming a preference for one policy over the other, participants would choose according to their broader political outlook in the absence of partisan cues, but that univalent partisans would ignore the substance of the policy statements when partisan cues were present. This is precisely what we found. When the perverse cues were provided, participants assigned to the low-ambivalence condition were likely to switch their preference from the ideologically congruent option to the one endorsed by their party. By contrast, participants assigned to the high-ambivalence condition were impervious to the cue and maintained "correct" (i.e., ideologically congruent) policy attitudes throughout.

In our third (and largest) experiment, we directly tested a psychological mechanism by which this ambivalence-moderated effect occurs. As we discussed in Chapter 2, partisan cues should provide univalent partisans with sufficient confidence in the correctness of their judgments, allowing them to ignore the substantive details of a political debate. Ambivalent partisans, by contrast, should derive less confidence in such cues, and this should motivate them to process the details in greater depth. We tested this hypothesis in the Knowledge Networks study by asking participants to recall as many facts as they could about each of the two policies. We found that when partisan cues were present, those assigned to the high-ambivalence condition recalled significantly more policy facts than did those assigned to the low-ambivalence condition.

In the Argument Quality experiment, we tested this mechanism directly by asking participants directly about the degree of judgment confidence they derived from partisan cues. We found a strong effect of ambivalence on perceived cue reliability. Moreover, the latter mediated the influence of ambivalence in conditioning the power of the partisan cue manipulation on policy preferences. In sum, the results of these experiments provide empirical support for our claim that partisan ambivalence heightens citizens' motivation to attend to and use highly diagnostic information in forming their judgments, and that its effect is mediated by concomitant differences in the subjective utility of partisan cues.

In the second empirical section of the chapter, we conceptually replicated the results of our experiments using observational data with large national surveys. In four sets of analyses, we demonstrated that partisan ambivalence strongly conditions the processes by which citizens generate and update their policy opinions. First, drawing on panel data from the 2008 ANES, we showed that opinion changes over the course of a presidential election campaign exhibited a strong pattern of partisan polarization for univalent but not ambivalent partisans. Controlling for precampaign preferences, the October preferences of univalent partisans were strongly determined by partisan attachment, suggesting that these individuals chose to receive and/or accept policy messages only from fellow Democrats or Republicans. Second, the economic policy preferences of univalent partisans were entirely independent of their personal economic positions. Low-income univalent partisans were no more likely than their wealthier peers to prefer economic redistribution, even though they would be its beneficiaries. We replicated this effect using the 1992–1994 ANES panel study, demonstrating that the economic policy preferences of univalent partisans were unrelated to a broad measure of personal economic insecurity.

In line with expectations, we observed the opposite pattern among ambivalent partisans. For these citizens, partisanship played little role in regulating opinion change. Instead, what mattered was objective self-interest, suggesting that ambivalent partisans were less attuned to the identity-related implications of a policy than to the merits of its content. This result is noteworthy for two reasons. First, scholars have struggled to demonstrate the impact of material considerations on policy preferences, finding instead that they are more often a function of symbolic factors (Sears & Funk, 1991). Second, our analysis suggests that the role of self-interest in the political sphere may require more extensive thought, or at least a willingness to break free from the encompassing prism of partisanship.

In our last analysis, we applied the model to heterogeneity in the nature and meaning of issue constraint. Our analysis here suggests that constraint among univalent partisans has precious little to do with superordinate ideas about social life and (for economic issues) everything to do with partisan identity. As Figures 4.9 and 4.10 clearly show, however, the reverse is true—values trump partisanship—among ambivalent partisans. What is important among these more thoughtful citizens is less the positions taken by the parties and more the implications of alternative policy options for the size of government.

Given how polarized elites currently are, it is relatively easy for most citizens to make out the partisan differences in their policy goals. Those citizens who are inclined to limit their political information processing to partisan cue-taking should therefore have little trouble aligning their preferences with their partisan attachments. The trouble with this form of delegation is that it provides elites with an opportunity to subvert the public's will. As Jacobs and Shapiro (2000) forcefully argue in *Politicians Don't Pander*, partisan elites are prone to ignore the preferences of ordinary voters (at least between elections) and to pursue their own policy goals (see also Bartels, 2008). This is feasible, however, only to the extent that citizens are willing to take party-approved positions while ignoring their own values and interests. Given the relatively low correlations between partisanship on one hand and orientations toward limited government and objective self-interest on the other (the former is .35 according to the 2004 ANES and the latter is .20 according to the 2008 ANES), this should lead to a good deal of failed delegation, and ultimately to a downgraded form of political representation.

CHAPTER 5

Ambivalence and the Partisan Perceptual Screen

We do not see things as they are; we see them as we are.
–The Talmud

In the last chapter, we tested some key aspects of the partisan ambivalence model within the confines of highly controlled—some might say *artificial*—experimental contexts. What these sorts of exercises can provide, if all goes according to plan, is an environment within which one's hypotheses can be falsified (Mook, 1983). But even if they pass such empirical tests, as our hypotheses did, it does not mean that they apply in the real political world. The survey-based analyses presented in the last chapter provide some evidence that they do. Chapters 5–7 examine this question more fully. In this chapter, we focus on the normative quality of mass judgment pertaining to a fundamental task of democratic citizenship: becoming informed about central features of the *factual* political landscape.

If individuals are to function as responsible citizens—if they are to form meaningful policy preferences and make informed electoral choices—they should, at minimum, hold accurate perceptions of political reality. Indeed, as preferences often follow from perceptions of facts, the quality of the former depends on the accuracy of the latter. On many issues, however, reliable political information can be difficult to come by, as elected officials and the media often lack the incentive to provide it. Politicians are motivated to move public opinion to their side, not to educate voters about facts. And the content of commercial news is dictated chiefly by the desire to maintain viewer interest. The presentation of political facts is therefore likely to be sporadic, occurring mainly in the service of persuasion and entertainment. As Gaines et al. (2007, p. 962) note in discussing the dearth of factual information on many issues in the media: "people can believe almost whatever they want to believe, because the facts rarely confront them."

In this chapter, we examine whether partisan ambivalence, all else equal, increases the *accuracy* with which citizens perceive key aspects of the political environment. We focus on economic performance (e.g., unemployment, inflation), the policy locations of presidential candidates, the roll-call votes of US Senators, and crime rates. These factors correspond to some of the major short-term "dynamic" forces that shape national elections. If, as our theory suggests, ambivalence undercuts the judgmental confidence that citizens typically derive from partisan cues, they should turn away from these perceptual anchors and pay more attention to the particulars. As a result, they should hold more accurate perceptions of political reality than other citizens, and their policy attitudes and electoral behavior should consequently rest on a more rational foundation (we demonstrated the former in Chapter 4 and will address the latter in Chapter 6).

In their comprehensive study of political sophistication, *What Americans Know about Politics and Why It Matters*, Delli Carpini and Keeter (1996, p. 8) write that "political information is to democratic politics what money is to economics: it is the currency of citizenship." Echoing a central plank of classical democratic theory, they argue that passion and reason will fail to produce decisions that approximate the public interest in the absence of an adequately informed electorate. For example, the rudimentary reward-punishment version of economic voting holds that citizens will re-elect government officials if the economy is doing well; otherwise they will vote to replace them (Erikson, 2009; Lewis-Beck & Stegmaier, 2000). Debates about the government's capacity to control the economy notwithstanding, the rationality of economic voting depends on the president's supporters recognizing economic deterioration and his opponents recognizing improvement.[1] Similarly, if perceptions of candidate policy stands contain large amounts of random or systematic error, the logic of issue voting—and thus popular control over public policy—falls apart. Dispiritingly, repeated soundings over the past half century provide a consistent portrait of citizen *in*competence, in which the public is charged with possession of "too little political information, insufficiently crystallized political attitudes, too-strong partisan attachments, [and] too much political

1. Recent work by Bartels (2008) shows that in the post–World War II era, Democratic and Republican presidents presided over systematically different economic outcomes, with the former associated with greater economic growth, especially for the poor and middle class.

attention deficit disorder...to function as good citizens in a liberal representative democracy" (Borgida, Federico, & Sullivan, 2009, pp. 3–4).[2]

As we will document in this chapter, garden variety political ignorance is not the only impediment to accurate political perception. An arguably more serious problem is motivated perceptual bias (Bartels, 2008; Hochschild, 2000; Kuklinski, Quirk, Jerit, Schwieder, & Rich, 2000). As Hochschild (2000, p. 318) put it, "people's perceptions are [not just] frequently wrong," [but] wrong in particularly patterned ways." Consider the following examples. In 1988, the ANES asked a random sample of adults to assess whether the economy had improved or deteriorated over the 8 years of Ronald Reagan's presidency. Objectively, the economy had shown marked signs of improvement: Inflation fell from 14 percent in 1980—a rate not seen since 1947—to 4.1 percent in 1988, and unemployment fell from nearly 11 percent in December of 1982—the highest since World War II—to 5.3 percent by the end of 1988.[3] Stunningly, these economic facts were lost on Democrats with strong partisan attachments, a majority of whom claimed that both indicators had *worsened* during the Reagan era (Bartels, 2002).[4] In 2006, after several widely disseminated reports to the contrary (e.g., Deulfer, 2004), a majority of Republicans—but

2. The perspective that the public is unprepared to govern itself effectively has been echoed many times over, from the earliest studies of political behavior (e.g., Berelson, Lazarsfeld, & McPhee, 1954; Converse, 1964; Lippman, 1922; Schumpeter, 1942) through more recent accounts (e.g., Bennett, 2005; Neuman, 1986). As Kinder (2006, p. 197) has recently written, "if democracy means rule by the people, then in today's world democracy is widely endorsed in principle but rarely realized in practice."
3. These figures are taken from the Web site of the Bureau of Labor Statistics (US Department of Labor), http://www.bls.gov/bls/proghome.htm. Accessed May 10, 2010.
4. Republicans fared little better in the accuracy of their economic perceptions under Clinton. In 1996, the ANES asked, "Has the size of the yearly budget deficit increased, decreased, or stayed about the same during Clinton's time as president?" According to Bartels (2002), nearly half of Democrats but only about a quarter of Republicans correctly noted that the deficit had decreased. In fact, the plunge in the deficit was dramatic, from $255 billion in 1993 to $22 billion in 1997. Similarly, Republicans were twice as likely as Democrats to respond incorrectly to the question (also asked in the 1996 ANES) "Over the past year, has the nation's economy gotten better, stayed the same, or gotten worse?" In 1996, real disposable income and per capita GDP were up compared to the previous year, and unemployment was down.

few Democrats—continued to believe that Iraq possessed weapons of mass destruction[5] and that Saddam Hussein actively collaborated with Al-Qaeda in the 9/11 terrorist attacks (Gelman et al., 2008; Jacobson, 2010[6]).[7] And according to a *New York Times* poll conducted in April of 2010, Tea Party supporters (largely conservative Republicans) were three times more likely than other citizens to mistakenly believe that the Obama and not the Bush administration was responsible for most of the 2009 $1.6 trillion federal deficit (non–Tea Party supporters were five times more likely than supporters to correctly believe otherwise).[8] These examples illustrate a principal, if normatively undesirable

5. Using multiwave panel data over the period between October 2003 and September 2004, Gaines et al. (2007) argued that Republicans did in fact change their beliefs about the existence of weapons of mass destruction; however, they opted for *interpretations* of those facts that provided a continuing rationale to support the war.
6. Jacobson (2010) also reported that a majority of Republicans either agreed with or answered "not sure" to the following question: "Do you believe that George W. Bush was chosen by God to lead the United States in a global war on terrorism?" Only 1 in 10 Democrats agreed that Bush was God's chosen instrument for this mission.
7. In several surveys taken between 2006 and 2008, Jacobson (2010) also provided compelling—albeit indirect—evidence of partisan bias about the war among Democrats. His surveys asked respondents to recall what their beliefs were about the existence of weapons of mass destruction and whether Saddam Hussein was personally involved in September 11 *prior to* the invasion of Iraq in 2003. By comparing respondents' recollections of their beliefs several years earlier to survey data at the time of the invasion, Jacobson demonstrated a hefty dose of memory bias among Democrats. Specifically, he reported that in eight surveys taken prior to the war, between 57 and 83 percent of Democrats said they thought Iraq possessed weapons of mass destruction; the average was 71 percent. But in the later data, less than half remembered subscribing to this view. The average difference between Democrats' recalled views on weapons of mass destruction and those expressed in the surveys taken before the war was a whopping 38 percentage points. Republicans, by contrast, evidenced no such memory bias: Their beliefs in the later period closely matched those observed in the surveys taken before the war.
8. Complete poll results can be found at http://documents.nytimes.com/new-york-timescbs-news-poll-national-survey-of-tea-party-supporters?ref=politics. This poll included a large oversample of tea party supporters ($N = 881$), making it the most reliable sounding to date of their political perceptions and attitudes. Accessed June 14, 2010.

aspect of mass belief systems: Perceptions of political reality are inextricably intertwined with citizens' political preferences and identities.[9]

These misperceptions are by no means exceptional, nor are they limited to the highly polarized politics of early 21st-century America or to members of one political party or social class. Moreover, unlike plain ignorance, misperception constitutes *systematic* rather than random error, and it is often more prevalent among those scoring high on traditional measures of political engagement (we will demonstrate this assertion shortly). As we argued in Chapter 2, perceptual bias can be understood in light of the *motivated* nature of political reasoning, whereby judgments reflect the competing desires for accuracy and cognitive consistency (Festinger, 1957; Kunda, 1990; Lodge & Taber, 2000). At the extremes, when reasoning about matters that impinge on cherished values and core identities, an individual's goals, needs, and fears—for example, protecting the perceived worth and integrity of the self, achieving constancy and consistency of meaning—may overwhelm the normal constraints of reality.

While motivated perceptual bias may be useful as a mechanism for affective self-regulation (Sherman & Cohen, 2002), it raises deeply troubling questions about political representation and accountability that are so central to democratic politics. If, as many political analysts argue, elections are often blunt instruments for achieving these goals (e.g., Manin, Przeworski, & Stokes, 1999), inaccurate perceptions blunt them even further. For how can an electorate possibly reward or punish an incumbent party if it holds grossly distorted views of political conditions? And how can it elect leaders who will pursue desired policy reform in the face of widespread misperception about where leaders stand and what the central elements and likely consequences of proposed reform are? For example, polls taken during the 2009–2010 health care debate indicated widespread misperception about the provisions of Obama's plan, as well as its social and economic consequences (e.g., "death panels," decreased physician choice, forced entry into a government-run plan).[10] One can certainly argue against placing strong informational demands on average citizens.

9. In his analysis of the dynamics of thought systems, McGuire (1990, p. 505) provides an extensive experimental demonstration that judgments of desirability (i.e., preferences) directly influence judgments of probability (beliefs about reality). He refers to this process as the "autistically gratifying coping mechanism" of *wishful thinking*.

10. For evidence that extreme claims about a policy's expected consequences often succeed in moving public opinion, see Jerit (2009).

People need not be surrogate politicians to be effective in a democratic polity. Nevertheless, widespread systematic misperception of political reality would seem unpalatable even to those who have tried to sketch a more positive image of mass opinion (Erikson et al., 2002; Green et al., 2002; Lupia & McCubbins, 1998; Popkin, 1994).

In recent years, the notion that citizens need to be well informed for democracy to flourish has been challenged from two different directions. At the micro level, political psychologists have argued that citizens can fulfill their role with relatively little knowledge by relying on cognitive shortcuts (e.g., for critical assessments, see Kuklinski & Quirk, 2000; Lau & Redlawsk, 2006; Lupia & McCubbins, 1998; Mondak, 1994). As Sniderman et al. (1991, p. 19) write: "people can be knowledgeable in their reasoning about political choices without necessarily possessing a large body of knowledge about politics." At the same time, scholars in the macro-politics tradition have argued that misperception at the individual level cancels out in the aggregate so that politicians are faced with clear signals from the electorate. As Erikson et al. (2002, p. 5) argue, "One can agree that the average citizen is not particularly informed, not particularly thoughtful, and not particularly attentive, but still find these characteristics emerge in the aggregate."

We are not sanguine about either of these propositions. Regarding the latter, when misperceptions affect a large portion of the electorate, and when they are not distributed evenly (i.e., when errors are systematic), collective opinion may do little more than amplify biases at the individual level (Althaus, 1998; Bartels, 1996; Duch et al., 2000; Kuklinski et al., 2000; for enlightening discussions of this issue, see Caplan, 2007; Taber, 2003). And as we discussed in Chapter 1, cognitive shortcuts are a double-edged sword: Sometimes they allow citizens to make high-quality judgments without purchasing costly information, but at other times they lead to failed delegation and systematic error (Kahneman, 2011; Lupia & McCubbins, 1998; Nisbett & Ross, 1980). In their critical review of the heuristics literature, Kuklinski and Quirk (2000, p. 156) conclude that:

> People indeed do use heuristics, but hardly as rational strategies specifically tailored for each kind of decision. Rather, people take their heuristics off the shelf, use them unknowingly and automatically, and rarely worry about their accuracy.

In line with this pessimistic verdict, we present evidence in this chapter that citizens rely strongly on the heuristic of partisanship in many contexts in which it has no diagnostic value—in which its only effect is to produce perceptual distortion.[11]

If neither heuristics nor aggregation can be counted on to shield citizens from the consequences of their inattention to politics, and if motivated bias systematically warps their perceptions, then the prospects for self-government would seem rather dim. Our foremost concern is not to reach any firm conclusion on this weighty matter. Rather, it is to identify the dispositional and situational factors that shape perceptual bias and environmental responsiveness in a wide range of political settings, and to isolate the role of partisan ambivalence therein. If our empirical findings replicate in one setting after the next, we will be in a strong position to offer some broad conclusions about when and why people are prone to distortions of political reality.

In the empirical work to follow, we gauge the role of partisan ambivalence in contributing to the quality of political perception by pitting it in head-to-head competition with our triad of engagement variables. Specifically, we examine whether all else equal, ambivalent partisans simultaneously rely more on diagnostic signals in the environment (thereby reducing random error) and less on the cue of partisanship when it is inappropriate to do so (thereby reducing systematic error). To test our hypotheses, we rely on three principal data sources: pooled cross-sectional ANES data between 1980 and 2004; the 2008 ANES Panel Study; and the 2006 Cooperative Congressional Election Study (CCES). These data sources allow us to model political perceptions in four domains: (a) economic performance; (b) the policy stands of presidential candidates; (c) the roll-call votes of legislators; and (d) changes in crime rates. By examining perceptions of facts, we avoid confusing better or worse judgments with those based on equally valid but different evaluative criteria (Gerber & Green, 1998, 1999). Determining whether the president is a good leader, for example, or whether he cares about "people like me" is an inherently subjective enterprise. But perceptions on matters with objectively correct answers can be readily judged as being of better or worse quality.

11. Beyond their propensity to create distortion, past work suggests that heuristics work best for (and perhaps only among) political sophisticates—those citizens who are the least in need of simplifying cognitive strategies (Lau & Redlawsk, 2001; Sniderman et al., 1991).

THE FORMATION OF RETROSPECTIVE PERFORMANCE JUDGMENTS

We begin our analysis with an examination of retrospective judgments of economic performance over the course of an incumbent president's term in office. In our first analysis, we harness the temporal breadth of the ANES to determine the processes by which citizens generate their economic perceptions. We demonstrate that ambivalence not only decreases their reliance on partisanship, but that it simultaneously increases reliance on more costly but normatively defensible criteria—namely, actual yearly changes in unemployment and economic growth. We then examine retrospective judgments over the course of the 2008 presidential election and demonstrate that the basic dynamics observed in the pooled cross-sectional analysis replicate within a panel context. Fortunately, the 2008 ANES Panel Study measured respondents' economic perceptions both before and after the collapse in September, thus allowing for an assessment of responsiveness to this exogenous shock. We demonstrate that Republicans, as in-partisans, were prone to downplay the severity of the country's economic predicament, but that this was much less likely to occur among Republicans who were ambivalent. Having demonstrated the moderating role of ambivalence for *process*, we then assess the implications of these dynamics for perceptual *accuracy*. Drawing on several objective items from two ANES studies, we show that ambivalent partisans, all else equal, are more likely than their univalent counterparts to hold accurate retrospective assessments.

Bias and Responsiveness in Economic Perceptions

The ANES allows us to simultaneously examine individual-level predictors of economic perceptions as well as election-year variation in objective economic conditions. By adding a time dimension to the cross-sectional framework, we can determine whether ambivalence—net the influence of the engagement variables—strengthens respondents' reliance on objective conditions in generating subjective assessments. The dependent variable in our analysis is the respondent's perception of economic performance over the previous year. This five-point item (which debuted in 1980) is constructed from the following question: "Over the past year, would you say that the economy has 'gotten much worse,' 'worse,' 'stayed the same,' 'gotten better,' or 'gotten much better?'" coded such that higher values indicate more positive retrospections.[12]

To capture the expectation that partisan supporters of the president (i.e., "in-partisans") hold more optimistic perceptions of the economy than the president's partisan opponents (or "out-partisans"), we created a dummy variable coded "1" for in-partisans and "0" for out-partisans in each presidential election year (we thus expect a positive coefficient of this indicator for all years of the analysis). To assess whether the bases of economic perceptions depend on ambivalence, we interacted the two objective economic indicators—yearly changes in unemployment and gross domestic product (GDP)—as well as the (in- versus out-) partisan dummy with ambivalence.[13] We estimated two models, one using GDP and the other using unemployment.[14] To control for the potentially biasing effects of political engagement, we also included partisan strength, interest in politics, and sophistication in the analysis, both as first-order terms and as interactions with the economic variables and the partisan dummy.[15]

12. The ANES has changed the retrospective evaluation question over the years. Until 1996, the question read: "How about the economy? Would you say that over the past year the nation's economy has gotten better, stayed the same, or gotten worse?" After 1996, the lead into the question changed to: "Now thinking about the economy." In 1990 and 1994 and onwards, the lead-in was: "Now thinking about the economy in the country as a whole." In 1984, the neutral response category was formulated as "about the same."
13. To minimize endogeneity, we rid the analyses of those respondents whose open-ended responses reflected any considerations related to the economy, including those about prosperity, inflation, employment, wages, or references to government spending, the budget, the value of the dollar, or economic policy.
14. The two measures are highly correlated over time ($r = -.90$); thus, including them in the same model would pose estimation problems.
15. For ease of interpretation, all variables (including the dependent variable) were recoded to a 0 to 1 scale. To allow for heterogeneity in perceptions due to context effects unrelated to objective economic performance, we included random intercepts for years and estimated the model via restricted maximum likelihood.

The results of this analysis reveal strong support for our model. Not only does ambivalence inhibit citizens' use of partisan cues in judging economic performance, it also significantly increases their reliance on objective information. The full regression models—which reveal statistically significant and substantively large interactions of partisan ambivalence with both the in-party dummy and the two economic indicators—are shown in the Appendix in Table A5.1. To interpret the estimates, we present the results graphically in Figure 5.1. The x-axis of the graph represents degrees of partisan ambivalence, holding all other variables at their central tendencies. The y-axis represents the (absolute) marginal effect of each independent variable on subjective perceptions. For partisanship, this is simply the expected difference in average perceptions between in- and out-partisans. For the economic indicators, this value represents the absolute expected difference in perceptions between citizens in a good economy (strong growth or declining

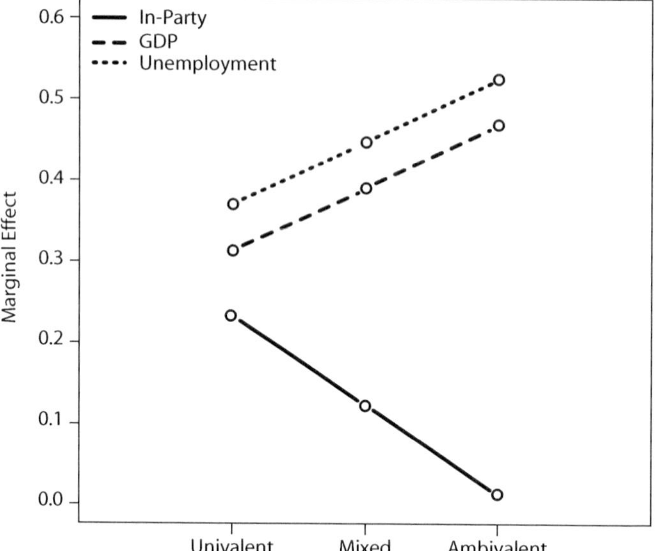

Figure 5.1 The Influence of Partisanship and Changes in Objective Conditions on Economic Retrospections, by Level of Partisan Ambivalence, 1980–2004 ANES.

Notes: The figure displays the marginal effects of partisan identification (labeled "in-party" in the graph), economic growth, and yearly changes in unemployment on retrospective economic perceptions. Higher values of the dependent variable represent more positive retrospections. For clarity of presentation, the line for changes in unemployment represents its absolute value; the true coefficients are negative. GDP, gross domestic product.

unemployment) versus those in a bad economy (negative growth or increasing unemployment).[16]

As Figure 5.1 shows, the effect of being a partisan supporter of the president on economic retrospections declines from .23 among univalent partisans to .02 (effectively zero) among ambivalent partisans. This means that in an average economy, univalent in-partisans were 23 percentage points more optimistic about economic change than univalent out-partisans. Figure 5.1 also shows that ambivalence strongly enhanced the impact of yearly changes in both unemployment and GDP on economic retrospections. Among univalent partisans, the marginal impact of unemployment is –.36 (i.e., higher negative values predict lower evaluations). Specifically, moving from the most severe yearly increase in unemployment (which in our series occurred in 1982) to the steepest decline (in 1984), the change in subjective perceptions among univalent partisans was 36 percent of the range of the economic retrospections scale. For ambivalent partisans, this effect rises to –.52 (a nearly 50 percent increase). The influence of GDP is similarly moderated by ambivalence. For univalent partisans, GDP exerts a 31 percentage point influence on subjective economic perceptions; for ambivalent partisans, the effect rises to 48 percent (in increase of more than 50 percent).

In sum, this analysis reveals that ambivalent citizens are at once less swayed—in fact, they are *unswayed*—by the irrelevant cue of partisanship in judging economic performance, and strongly reliant on information directly applicable to the judgment at hand. Table A5.1 also shows that all three standard engagement factors—interest, sophistication, and partisan strength—*heighten* the perceptual divergence between in- and out-partisans (i.e., they increase bias). For example, moving from apathetic to highly interested citizens entails an increase in the partisan gap of 9 percentage points. However, both interest and sophistication also heightened citizens' reliance on unemployment and GDP, although their effects are smaller than that for ambivalence. Among the least sophisticated, for example, the marginal impact of GDP is 34 percentage points; for the most sophisticated, the effect is 43 points (an increase of 26 percent; the effect for political interest is identical in magnitude). Turning to unemployment, the marginal effect is –.34 for the least sophisticated and –.48 for the most sophisticated (an increase of 41 percent; the effect of interest is about a third of this size).

16. For ease of interpretation, we plot the absolute value of the predicted marginal effect for changes in unemployment. Obviously, these changes are predicted to *decrease* the positivity of economic retrospections.

Let us now consider the *total* effects of partisan cue-taking and economic responsiveness together. First, partisan strength has a *simple* conditioning effect: It heightens partisan bias but has no influence on economic responsiveness. Second, both sophistication and interest have *countervailing* effects: They increase the impact of bias *and* responsiveness to objective information.[17] This means that failure to account simultaneously for the two conditional effects will produce a distorted portrait of whether political engagement has a net salutary or detrimental impact on the accuracy of economic perceptions. Modeling the influence of engagement on bias but ignoring its impact on responsiveness would lead mistakenly to the conclusion that engagement impedes accuracy. Following the opposite course—modeling its impact on responsiveness but ignoring bias—would lead to the conclusion that engagement promotes accuracy. To the extent that the two sets of moderating impacts are offsetting, both conclusions would be wrong. In the present case, the net influence of sophistication on accuracy should be positive, as its impact on economic responsiveness is somewhat larger than its countervailing impact on partisan bias. By contrast, the total effect for political interest should be about zero, as the two offsetting impacts are similar in magnitude.

In contrast to the traditional engagement variables, the effects of ambivalent partisanship are *cumulative*: Ambivalence inhibits partisan bias and at the same time strengthens the individual's reliance on objective conditions (i.e., changes in GDP and unemployment). Together, these processes should powerfully facilitate perceptual accuracy, especially among in-partisans in a deteriorating economy and out-partisans during periods of prosperity. It is under these circumstances that ambivalence is normatively valuable, as it is when partisan expectations are contradicted by economic reality that political accountability is of critical importance.

Perceptions in Flux: The Economic Collapse of 2008

While the foregoing results provide strong support for the ambivalence model, our ability to make causal claims is hampered by the cross-sectional nature of the data. That is, because the variables are all measured at the same time, we cannot entirely rule out the alternative explanation that changes in perceptions lead to changes in ambivalence. For example, Democrats responded to economic deterioration in the late 1970s with negativity toward their own

17. We refer to these effects as "countervailing" because partisan bias and economic responsiveness have opposite downstream consequences for perceptual accuracy.

party, and Republicans responded favorably to positive performance by the out-party during the economic super-boom in the late 1990s (see Lebo & Cassino, 2008). One strategy for determining the causal ordering between variables in a nonexperimental setting is to use a panel design, in which the independent variables of interest can be measured at lagged time points. This would help to ensure that the effects of ambivalence on perceptions are not due to reverse causation. Fortunately, the 2008 ANES panel study allows us to examine individual-level *changes* in perceptions over the course of a campaign in which the economic outlook changed dramatically.

In 2008, the ANES surveyed a random sample of the electorate six times: in January, February, June, September, October, and November. Many items were asked in multiple waves, allowing for an examination of changes in perceptions and preferences over time. Of particular interest here are partisan differences in the recognition of economic deterioration from January to October, which straddled the occurrence of several high-profile economic events, including a plunge in the Dow Jones of more than 5,000 points (a nearly 40 percent drop), the collapse of two major Wall Street financial institutions (Bear Stearns and Lehman Brothers), and dire warnings in late September by the Chairman of the Federal Reserve and the Treasury Secretary (and ultimately the president) of a complete meltdown in the US economy. The primary question for us is whether ambivalence moderated the economic perceptions of Republicans (as in-partisans). Given the salience of the meltdown in late September—during which the two presidential candidates met with President Bush to discuss an immediate trillion dollar bailout of the major banks—we might expect to see a convergence among all citizens in their economic assessments. By controlling for lagged economic perceptions (in January) and measuring the explanatory variables at lagged time points relative to economic perceptions in October, we can be more confident that ambivalence is driving perceptions and not the other way around.[18]

The results, reported in Table A5.2 and graphed in Figure 5.2, dovetail with the cross-sectional analysis. Even in this unique context of economic collapse, partisanship continues to exert a significant influence on economic perceptions. Among univalent partisans, Republicans were 9 percentage points more optimistic than Democrats, a statistically significant difference. Among

18. This is not to say that the causal arrow cannot work in the reverse direction. Indeed, we demonstrated in Chapter 3 that economic events during 2008 played a role in heightening levels of ambivalence among Republicans. In general, as we discuss more fully in Chapter 8, we expect this relationship to be bidirectional.

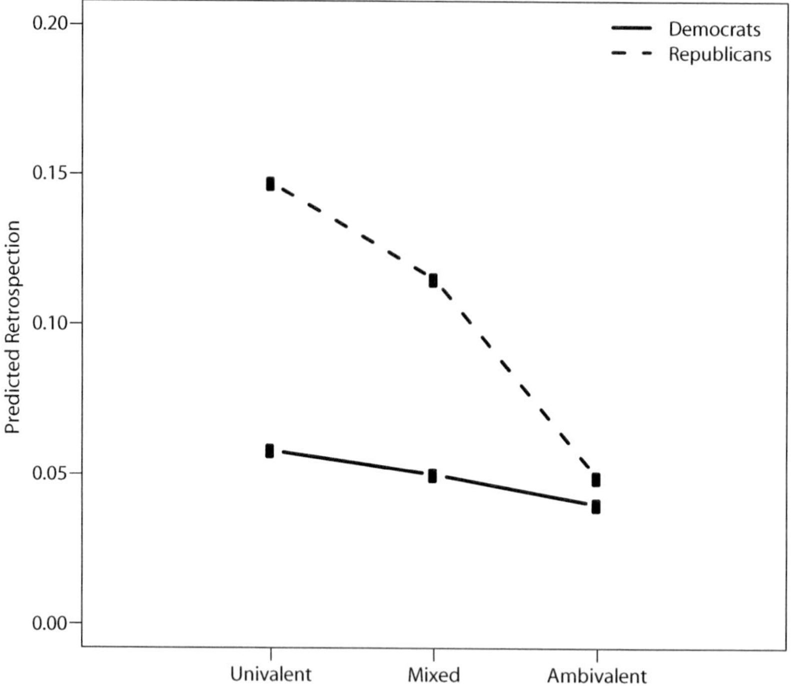

Figure 5.2 The Partisan Gap in Retrospective Economic Perceptions in October of 2008, 2008 ANES.

Notes: The figure displays predicted economic retrospections across level of ambivalence. Higher values on the vertical axis represent more positive perceptions.

ambivalent partisans, however, the partisan gap was eliminated. We find no other moderating effects in this analysis. Indeed, the coefficients on the traditional engagement variables are *positive*, indicating an exacerbation in the partisan gap, not attenuation. Overall, then, our analysis of the 2008 panel study converges with the cross-sectional results reported earlier. Most important, ambivalence was measured in February and economic perceptions were measured in October (adjusting for pre-collapse perceptions in June); thus, any concerns about reverse causation are alleviated by the structure of the model. In sum, partisan ambivalence conditioned the influence of partisan cues in the updating of economic perceptions, even in a context in which one might expect universal agreement on the facts.

Implications for Perceptual Accuracy

To this point, we have demonstrated that the dynamics set in motion by ambivalence and observed in our experimental studies apply in the real world. We now examine their downstream consequences for the *accuracy* of citizens' economic perceptions. If, as we have observed, ambivalence simultaneously decreases motivated perceptual bias and heightens responsiveness to objective information, ambivalent partisans should be especially likely to hold economic assessments in line with reality. For this analysis we need dependent variables with objectively correct answers. Ideally, we need items measuring perceptions of economic performance over a specified period of time that can be coded unambiguously as correct or incorrect.

The 1988 and 2000 ANES surveys contain such items. In 1988, respondents were asked about changes in inflation and employment over the course of Ronald Reagan's presidency, from 1980 to 1988. As we noted earlier, both indicators fell steeply during Reagan's 8 years in office. In 2000, respondents were asked about changes in the budget deficit during the Clinton years, from 1992 to 2000. This too fell steeply, from $255 billion in 1993 to $22 billion in 1997, and into surplus territory through 2000.[19] The 2000 ANES also asked about changes over the same period in the national crime rate. While not a measure of economic activity, it does have a factual answer (crime decreased precipitously over Clinton's presidency); thus, we include responses to this item in our analysis.[20]

In addition to containing all of the measures necessary to isolate the role of ambivalence in contributing to perceptual accuracy, the 1988 and 2000 ANES studies were administered in different political contexts—the first at the end of a Republican administration and the second at the end of a Democratic one. This provides us with the opportunity to examine partisan bias in a situation where Democrats should be motivated to counterargue positive performance information (i.e., 1988), and one where Republicans should be motivated to do so (i.e., 2000).

In the 1988 survey, respondents indicated whether unemployment and inflation had gotten better, worse, or stayed the same over the course of Reagan's presidency. As a first cut at these data, consider Table 5.1. Here we display the raw percentages of Democrats and Republicans falling within each of the three categories (e.g., better, same, worse). The top panel of the table shows massive perceptual gaps between partisan groups. While 75 percent of

19. In the last year of Clinton's presidency, the budget surplus was $200 billion.

20. The national murder rate, for example, dropped from 9.5 per 100,000 inhabitants in 1993 to 5.5 per 100,000 inhabitants in 2000, a decrease of 40 percent. Decreases in other categories of violent crime (assault, rape, armed robbery) were similar. For details, see the FBI's Uniform Crime Reports at http://www.fbi.gov/ucr/ucr.htm. Accessed on July 12, 2010.

TABLE 5.1. RAW PERCENTAGES OF ECONOMIC AND CRIME RETROSPECTIONS ACROSS PARTISAN GROUPS

	Panel A. Reagan Era			
	Unemployment		**Inflation**	
	Dems	**Reps**	**Dems**	**Reps**
Worse	36	9	47	21
Same	25	15	28	22
Better	39	75	25	57
	Panel B. Clinton Era			
	Budget Deficit		**Crime Rate**	
	Dems	**Reps**	**Dems**	**Reps**
Worse	10	22	27	33
Same	23	23	28	35
Better	66	55	45	33

all Republicans correctly reported a decline in unemployment over the previous eight years, only 39 percent of Democrats did so. Moreover, 36 percent of Democrats but only 9 percent of Republicans incorrectly stated that unemployment had actually risen under Reagan. The results for inflation were similar: 57 percent of Republicans correctly noted an improvement, while only 25 percent of Democrats did so. Moreover, a near majority of Democrats (47 percent) believed that inflation had gotten worse over the Reagan administration, whereas the figure for Republicans was only 21 percent. These results are remarkable for two reasons. First, these are not subtle partisan differences, but substantial ones. Second, actual changes in the economy over Reagan's 8 years in office were quite considerable, with both unemployment and inflation dropping by 50 percent or more.

While not as dramatic, partisan differences also emerge in perceptions of Clinton's economic legacy (see Panel B of Table 5.1). With regard to changes in the deficit, Democrats were 11 percentage points more likely than Republicans to correctly report a decline (66 percent to 55 percent), and 12 percentage points less likely than Republicans to state (incorrectly) that the deficit had risen (10 percent to 22 percent). Partisan differences in crime perceptions were similar: Democrats were 12 percentage points more likely than Republicans to correctly note an improvement (45 percent to 33 percent), and 6 percentage points less likely to incorrectly state that crime had gone up (27 percent to 33 percent).

In sum, it is clear that compared to partisan supporters of the president, out-partisans are less likely to notice (or acknowledge) positive changes in economic (and social) reality, changes that disconfirm their partisan expectations and potentially threaten the positivity of their in-group identities. Our interest is in whether, all else equal, ambivalent out-partisans are more likely than their univalent counterparts to correctly perceive these improvements. Given the positive changes over both the Reagan and Clinton presidencies, the benefits of exchanging partisan cues for attention to relevant information should redound more to partisan *opponents* than *supporters* of the president. The simple reason is that in-partisans should reach the same conclusions about positive performance whether they rely on partisanship or acquire the relevant information.[21] For example, while some Republicans reported that inflation had decreased under Reagan because they paid close enough attention to the news, other Republicans might have reached the same conclusion simply as the result of partisan affinity with the president. It is thus exceedingly difficult to trace the salutary perceptual consequences of ambivalence among in-partisans by examining positive presidential legacies. For out-partisans (i.e., Democrats under Reagan and Republicans under Clinton), however, partisan cue-taking and reliance on objective conditions should lead to opposite performance conclusions. The former should lead to biased (and incorrect) perceptions, whereas the latter should promote accuracy.

These considerations lead us to examine the influence of ambivalence on perceptual accuracy separately for in- and out-partisans. We estimated two models for each retrospective item, one for Democrats and one for Republicans. In 1988 we expect that Democrats (as out-partisans during Reagan's presidency) will benefit most from ambivalence, while in 2000 we expect that Republicans (as out-partisans during Clinton's presidency) will benefit most. As always, we include controls for demographics and the traditional engagement variables.[22] The findings for 1988 are shown in Tables A5.3

21. The same is true when out-partisans are asked to judge an aspect of government performance that has objectively gotten worse (e.g., Democrats judging the economic trajectory under Carter).

22. As inflation and unemployment decreased under Reagan and the budget deficit and crime decreased under Clinton, we coded responses of "gotten better" as "2," "stayed the same" as "1," and "gotten worse" as "0" for all four analyses. As the items are all three-category, ordinal variables, we estimate the parameters of the models with ordered probit.

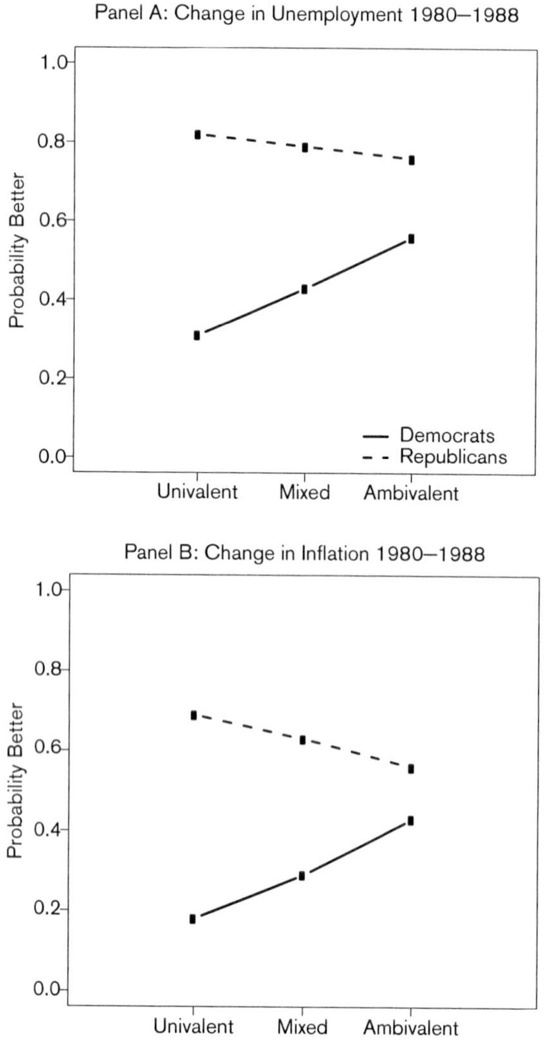

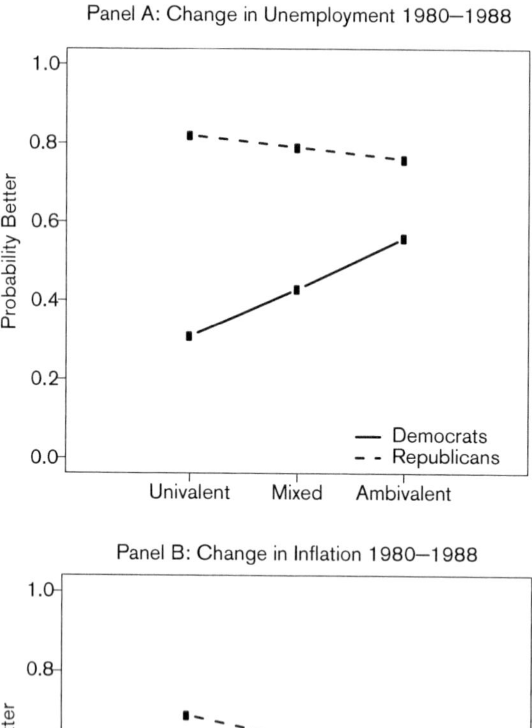

Figure 5.3 The Accuracy of Retrospective Judgments of Reagan's Economic Legacy, 1988 ANES.

Notes: The figures represent the predicted probabilities of rendering an accurate judgment about the economy as a function of partisanship and levels of partisan ambivalence. Since both inflation and employment improved during Reagan's presidency, we consider "gotten better" to be the correct response.

and A5.4 and graphed in Figure 5.3. The top panel displays the results for unemployment and shows that while ambivalence has a minimal influence among Republicans (as in-partisans), it drastically improves accuracy among Democrats (for the latter, the predicted change in accuracy from low to high ambivalence is .25; i.e., .31 to .56). Ambivalent partisanship also substantially improved the accuracy of inflation perceptions among Democrats (the predicted change in accuracy associated with ambivalence is also .25; i.e., .18 to .43; see Panel B of Fig. 5.3). Ambivalent out-partisans are thus considerably more accurate in their beliefs about economic reality than similarly situated univalent out-partisans.

The findings for perceptions of Clinton's legacy—shown in Tables A5.5 and A5.6 and graphed in Figure 5.4—are similar to those in the previous figure, with the expected reversal between Democrats and Republicans (as the latter are now out-partisans). Across the two panels, we see little change for Democrats (as in-partisans) but a substantial change for Republicans. With respect to budget deficit retrospections, univalent Republicans have only a .36 probability of correctly reporting a decline; this probability nearly doubles among ambivalent Republicans. With respect to changes in the crime rate, we see a smaller, yet still significant increase in accuracy from univalent to ambivalent of .29 to .42.

In sum, by simultaneously reducing partisan bias and heightening attention to diagnostic information, partisan ambivalence leads to more accurate perceptions of the economic and social environment. How do our competitor engagement variables fare in promoting (or inhibiting) accuracy? Recall that all of these factors increased partisan bias, and that both sophistication and interest had the countervailing effect of increasing responsiveness to objective conditions. In terms of overall accuracy, there is little evidence that either partisan strength or interest in politics matters one way or the other. The effects for sophistication were mixed. For unemployment and inflation, sophistication among out-partisans heightened accuracy by 23 and 28 percentage points, respectively. For the budget deficit and crime rates, however, sophistication made no difference at all.

PERCEIVING THE PREFERENCES AND BEHAVIOR OF POLITICIANS

In the last section, we examined how ambivalence conditioned perceptions of past party performance. In this section, we examine a prerequisite of *prospective* decision making: whether citizens can accurately place the positions of presidential candidates and recall (or infer) the roll-call votes of their US

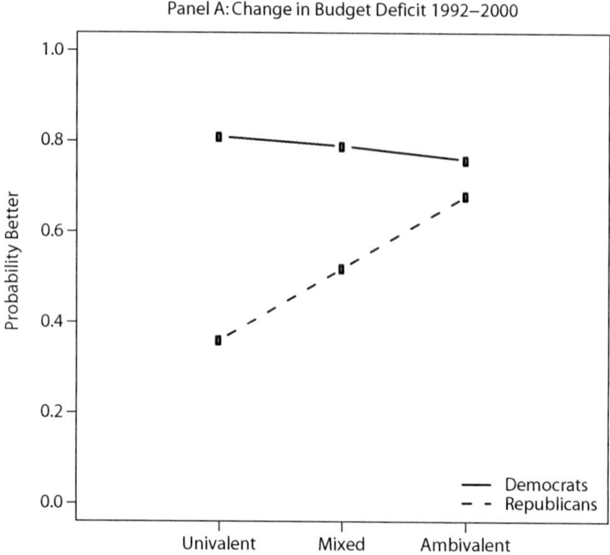

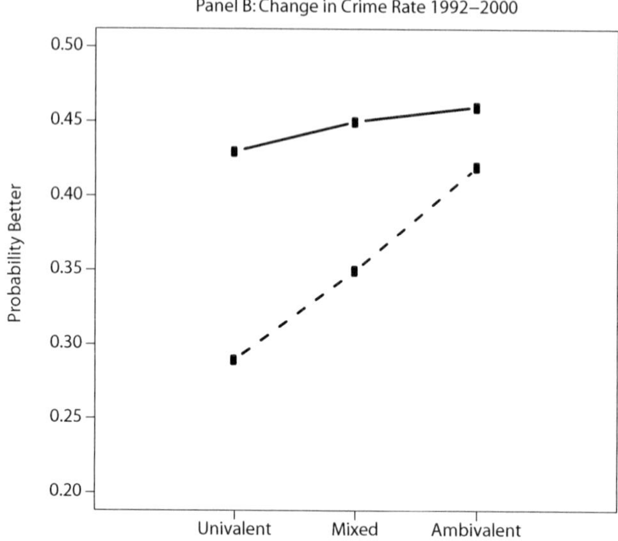

Figure 5.4 The Accuracy of Retrospective Judgments of Clinton's Legacy, 2000 ANES.

Notes: The figures represent the predicted probabilities of rendering an accurate judgment about the budget deficit and crime rate. Since the rates for both variables decreased during the Clinton presidency, we count "gotten better" as the correct response.

Senators on important policy debates. In contrast to retrospective voting, prospective voters examine the issue positions of candidates for office, compare them to their own preferences, and vote on the basis of perceived future utility. The success of this strategy—which is typically seen as the epitome of rational electoral choice—rests on holding accurate perceptions of where the candidates stand on salient policy issues. Similarly, in deciding whether to return their elected representatives to office, voters should examine their behavior, including how they voted on important policy issues. We begin by examining two heuristic processes by which citizens may generate these perceptions, one based on shared versus unshared partisanship between a candidate and a voter, and a second based on inferences about the policy preferences of Democratic and Republican elites. We examine the relative influence of each process across levels of partisan ambivalence and institutional context. Then, as in the last section, we examine the consequences of these processing dynamics for judgmental accuracy.

Processes of Candidate Perception

We focus on two general strategies by which citizens may form their perceptions of the policy stands and voting records of elite political actors: projection and inference. Projection is a low-effort method whereby favored candidates are assumed to share the policy preferences of the voter (Feldman & Conover, 1983; Granberg, 1993).[23] This is a form of partisan bias whereby citizens believe that candidates who share their partisan identity also share their positions on a range of policy issues. We refer to the second strategy of candidate perception as "ideological inference" (see Conover & Feldman, 1986, 1989). According to this strategy, citizens draw on their knowledge of the typical policy preferences of Democratic and Republican elites. So long as one is aware that Republican candidates and officeholders have operated to the right of Democrats over the past several decades, ideological inference should produce more accurate judgments than projection by the simple logic that the policy preferences of elites are more consistent than those of the mass public (Converse, 1964). To the extent that ambivalent partisans derive less judgment confidence on the basis of their own identities, we expect they will either acquire the relevant information directly or rely on ideological inference. Although we cannot distinguish empirically between these two mechanisms, either should lead to more accurate

23. The opposite tendency—whereby disfavored candidates are assumed to hold preferences opposite to the voter—is less likely to occur.

perceptions than projection. As ideological inference is more efficient, we expect it is more prevalent.

To determine whether ambivalence increases ideological inference and decreases partisan projection, we conducted two independent tests. The first examines perceptions of the policy stands of presidential candidates from 1980 to 2004. The ANES has consistently solicited perceptions on seven issues: defense spending, government spending and services, foreign policy orientation toward the USSR/Russia, women's role in society, government-guaranteed jobs and income, government aid to Blacks, and universal government-provided health insurance.[24] The second test draws on the 2006 Cooperative Congressional Election Study (CCES), which solicited responses on six issues which the Senate voted on in 2005–2006: partial birth abortion, stem cell funding, Iraq withdrawal (the Levin amendment), naturalization of illegal immigrants, increasing the minimum wage, and extension of the capital gains tax.[25] After each issue was described, respondents were asked (1) how each of their senators had voted on it and (2) how they themselves would have voted. The CCES data provide an opportunity to assess how ambivalence alters the dynamics of projection and inference in a context in which objective behavior (i.e., roll-call voting) has occurred.

Statistical evidence for projection consists of an association between respondents' own preferences and their (a) perceptions of the candidates' positions (in the ANES study) or (b) perceptions of the roll-call votes of their senators (in the CCES study). These associations should be positive in sign for in-party politicians and negative in sign for out-party politicians. Evidence for ideological inference consists of an association between the party affiliation of the candidate (or senator) and respondents' perceptions of his or her policy preferences (or roll-call votes). Differences in the relative size of these associations can be used to gauge the degree to which subpopulations of respondents engage in projection and inference.

To determine whether ambivalence and the traditional engagement variables condition the magnitude of each process, we interacted the respondent's own position on an issue and the candidate's/senator's party affiliation

24. Not every issue was asked in every year; we rely on all valid responses for a given respondent in a given survey.

25. The CCES is the largest study of congressional elections ever fielded in the United States. The "common content" of the survey is based on an opt-in Internet panel of over 36,000 respondents. For a detailed description, see Vavreck and Rivers (2008).

with partisan ambivalence, partisan strength, interest in politics, and in the ANES only, with sophistication (no suitable measure was included in the common content of the 2006 CCES). Both datasets contain multiple observations for each respondent (typically 14 in the ANES and 12 in the CCES).[26 27] The dependent variable in the ANES model is the respondent's perception of the candidate's policy position on a given issue. The dependent variable in the CCES model is the respondent's perception of his or her senator's roll-call vote on a given issue.

The results for the two models—shown in Tables A5.7 and A5.8 and graphed in the panels of Figure 5.5—provide strong support for our theory.[28] Panel A in the figure displays the results of the ANES study and shows that among univalent partisans the magnitude of the two perceptual strategies is nearly identical. Among ambivalent partisans, however, ideological inference dominates projection by a 10:1 ratio. Among the latter, the marginal effect of projection is .03, meaning that for in-party candidates, respondents with conservative policy attitudes shifted their perceptions of the candidates' stands 3 percentage points to the right of those with liberal policy attitudes (for out-party candidates, the reverse is true). Meanwhile, the marginal effect of ideological inference is .29, indicating that respondents shifted their perceptions of the positions of Republican candidates 29 percentage points to the right of Democratic candidates. As with economic perceptions, then, ambivalence decreased reliance on (comparatively) low-quality information and increased reliance on higher quality information.[29]

---

26. To control for unobserved, individual-level heterogeneity in judgments, the ANES model included random intercepts for respondents and was estimated via restricted maximum likelihood. The model for the CCES was estimated with probit.
27. We include dummy variables for issue and interact these dummies with the party of the political actor being judged (this allows the average judgment to vary across issues).
28. In each analysis, the coefficient for the party of the actor being judged (Democrat or Republican) represents the marginal effect of ideological inference, while the coefficient for the respondent's own issue position represents the marginal effect of projection. As both datasets contained a large number of observations, the estimates are highly efficient.
29. One potential criticism of this analysis is that if the policy preferences of univalent partisans are better sorted than those of ambivalent partisans, the two processes—projection and inference—have less distinctive implications for accuracy among the former. In the strong form of this hypothesis, the results would effectively be a statistical artifact. We address this concern later in the

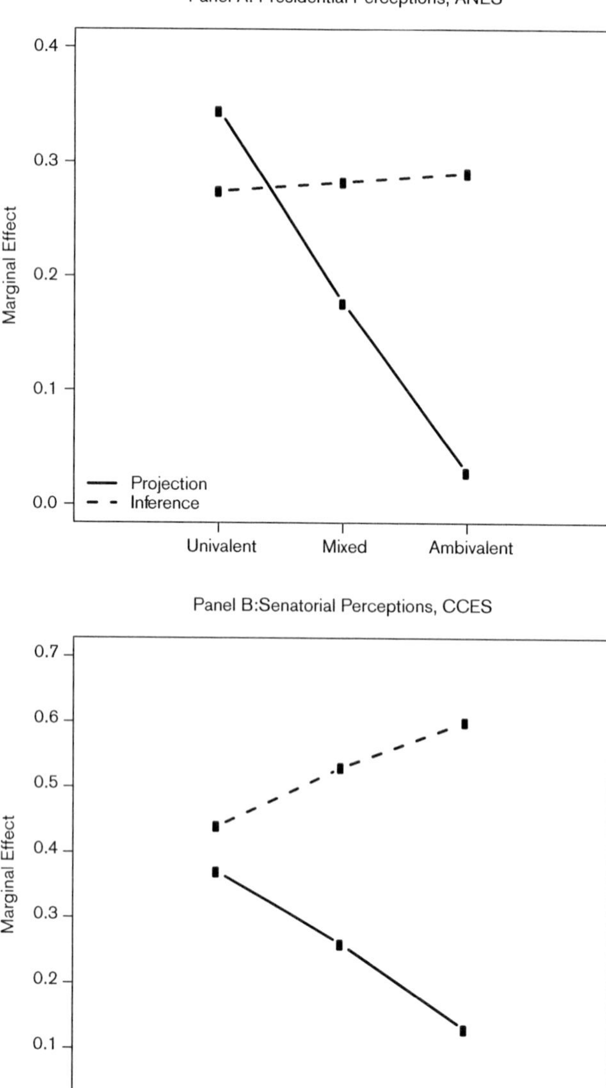

Figure 5.5 The Effects of Projection and Ideological Inference on Perceptions of Political Candidates.

Notes: The figures represent the estimated marginal effects of the respondent's own position on the issue (projection) and the presidential candidate's (or US Senator's) party affiliation (inference).

Our preferred measures of ambivalence were not available in the CCES. As a proxy, we use an item that asked respondents whether their own party was "much too liberal," "slightly too liberal," "about right," "slightly too conservative," or "much too conservative." We folded this variable around the "about right" category to create a measure of ideological divergence between the in-party and the self. Although this is an imperfect proxy, it does capture (albeit narrowly) a disjuncture between partisan identity and party evaluations. On the bright side, the CCES provides an opportunity to replicate our results in a different institutional context with a different dependent variable.

The regression results, shown in Table A5.8, closely replicate the ANES study: Ambivalence inhibits projection and promotes ideological inference. Panel B in Figure 5.5 shows that among univalent partisans, the processes of projection and inference occur in approximately equal measure, at about .40 on the 0 to 1 probability scale. Among ambivalent partisans, however, ideological inference dominates projection by a nearly 5:1 ratio, .60 to .13. With regard to projection, this means that ambivalent partisans with conservative preferences on a given issue are 13 percentage points more likely than those with liberal preferences to perceive co-partisan senators as having cast a conservative vote (and the opposite for those with liberal preferences).[30] With regard to ideological inference, the marginal effect means that Republican senators were about 60 percentage points more likely than Democratic senators to be classified as having voted conservatively. We find the convergence

context of analyses that distinguish between partisans with "matched" and "mismatched" preferences. To further allay these concerns, we examined the connection between ambivalence and the probability of holding a set of preferences fully in line with one's partisan identity. To maintain a reasonable sample size, we coded as "consistent" respondents with either consistently conservative or liberal preferences on three issues: health insurance, government jobs, and government spending. The correlation between this indicator and identity-consistent reactions was .16, while the correlation with identity-conflicting reactions was .04. The probability of consistency at low ambivalence (derived from a fully specified probit model) was .36, while the probability of consistency at high ambivalence was .20. Thus, while univalence *is* associated with consistency, the association is not very strong, and most citizens, regardless of ambivalence, show inconsistency on at least one issue.

30. It also means that they are also 13 percentage points less likely to perceive an out-party senator as having done so.

of the results in the ANES and CCES studies striking, given the variation in political institution (presidency vs. Congress), perceptual task (candidate perception vs. beliefs about legislative roll-call behavior), and in the measure of ambivalence itself.[31] [32]

Ambivalence, Judgment Strategy, and Perceptual Accuracy

To this point, we have demonstrated that in forming perceptions of candidates' policy stands and legislators' roll-call votes, ambivalent partisans rely more on ideological inference and less on projection than other similarly situated individuals. What we have yet to determine is whether ideological inference leads to more *accurate* perceptions than projection. As we described earlier, the logic of this expectation is that contemporary political conflict among elites is well described by a unidimensional ideological continuum such that Republicans almost always operate to the right of Democrats (see Poole & Rosenthal, 1997). Relying on the party labels of elites should thus be highly diagnostic of where they stand on the issues and how they vote in Congress. For projection to work equally well, we must entertain the possibility that the public's issue preferences are also highly structured along ideological lines.

31. The similarities between the two studies extend as well to the moderating effects of the traditional engagement variables. In both studies, partisan strength heightened reliance on projection and decreased reliance on inference. Apparently, strong partisans can achieve sufficient confidence in judging how their senators voted simply on the basis of their own preferences. Interest in politics heightened reliance on both strategies (in both studies), and sophistication had no impact on projection but facilitated reliance on inference.
32. We replicated our results using the 2008 ANES panel study to ensure that perceptions are not driving ambivalence. A subset of respondents participating in the 2008 panel reported their perceptions of Obama and McCain's stands on eight issues in both June and October. We modeled perceptions in October controlling for perceptions in June. We can thus interpret significant coefficients as predicting changes in perception from June to October. This provides a stringent test of our hypotheses, as it represents a relatively short time period over which such changes may occur. As in the economic retrospections analysis described in the last section, the independent variables are measured in January and February. We operationalize all variables as before. The results, shown in Table A5.9, indicate that among univalent partisans, the marginal effects of projection and inference are each .15. For ambivalent partisans, they are –.08 and .15, respectively. We thus find qualified support for our hypotheses: Ambivalence decreases projection, but it does not increase ideological inference in the 2008 study.

Given the evidence to the contrary, we expect that this strategy will often lead to biased perceptions.

Based on this discussion, we examine two hypotheses. First, if ideological inference facilitates accuracy, then ambivalent partisans should hold more accurate perceptions than univalent partisans. Second, a switch in judgment strategy from projection to inference should pay its highest accuracy dividends among citizens with ideologically *unsorted* policy preferences. This is a straightforward implication of the nature of projection. If citizens extrapolate from shared partisanship to shared issue preferences, then a preference *mismatch*—such that the candidate but not the voter toes the party line—will translate into biased perceptions. For example, a Democratic voter would be wrong to assume that Barack Obama supports capital punishment simply because the voter supports the policy and both she and Obama are Democrats. By contrast, when both the respondent and the candidate (or the legislator) toe the party line, projection and ideological inference should be equally likely to result in accurate perceptions.

To test these hypotheses, we return to the ANES and the CCES. To measure perceptual accuracy in the ANES, we simply determine whether the respondent placed the Democratic candidate to the left of the Republican candidate on a given policy issue. Our dependent variable is thus dichotomous.[33] In the CCES we have an objective measure of accuracy—that is, whether the respondent correctly noted how his or her senator voted on a given issue.[34] To determine whether the accuracy benefit in shifting from projection to ideological inference is larger among respondents with unsorted policy preferences, we created a new dichotomous indicator. This variable was coded "1" for unsorted respondents on a given issue and coded "0" for sorted respondents. For example, a person who prefers less government spending was coded "0" if she identified as a Republican and "1" if she identified as a Democrat. We then created interaction terms between the dichotomous sorted/unsorted indicator on one hand, and ambivalence, partisan strength, interest in politics, and sophistication, on the other.

---

33. Specifically, the variable is coded "1" for respondents who placed both candidates on the scale *and* placed the Democrat to the left of the Republican, and coded "0" for respondents who either (a) failed to place one or both candidates; (b) placed the candidates at the same scale point; or (c) placed the Republican to the left of the Democrat.
34. Correct responses were thus coded as "1," and those in which the respondent got the roll-call vote wrong or failed to answer the question were coded as "0."

The results of the two accuracy analyses are shown in Tables A5.10 and A5.11 and graphed in Figure 5.6.[35] As expected, ambivalence substantially increases accuracy among respondents with unsorted issue preferences. For the ANES study (see top panel), moving from univalent to ambivalent partisanship increases the probability of a correct response from .41 to .64.[36] The results for the CCES study (see bottom panel) are largely convergent: Ambivalence heightened accuracy principally among those with unsorted preferences. The dynamics observed in these two analyses are a function of two factors operating together: (a) projection impedes accuracy when preferences are out of step with the in-party's position, and (b) ambivalence decreases reliance on projection as a candidate perception strategy.

In sum, whether in judging the policy stands of presidential candidates or the roll-call votes of members of Congress, partisan ambivalence—all else equal—consistently alters both the processes by which these judgments are made, as well as their normative downstream consequences. Specifically, ambivalent partisans rely less on projection, more on ideological inference, and as a result hold judgments that are more in line with political reality than those of other citizens.

SUMMARY AND CONCLUSIONS

Scholars of voting behavior have identified two broad strategies by which citizens form their voting decisions: *retrospective* evaluations of incumbent performance and *prospective* judgments of relative utility (Downs, 1957; Fiorina, 1981). While these mechanisms do not exhaust the list of possibilities (see Popkin, 1994), they are powerful predictors of electoral choice. For either to contribute to a responsible electorate and a well-functioning democracy, however, citizens must hold accurate perceptions of political reality. To judge whether an incumbent administration deserves to be re-elected on the basis of its past performance, voters must hold accurate perceptions of how conditions have changed over the administration's term in office. Voting on the basis of future policy benefits requires citizens to accurately distinguish between the

35. In the ANES model, we included random intercepts for respondent and fixed effects for issue, and utilized a logit link and restricted maximum likelihood. For the CCES model we utilized a probit link and maximum likelihood with fixed effects for issue.

36. Among sorted respondents, however, there is a slight (but significant) reversal of this effect, such that ambivalence reduces accuracy. This effect is not replicated in the CCES analysis.

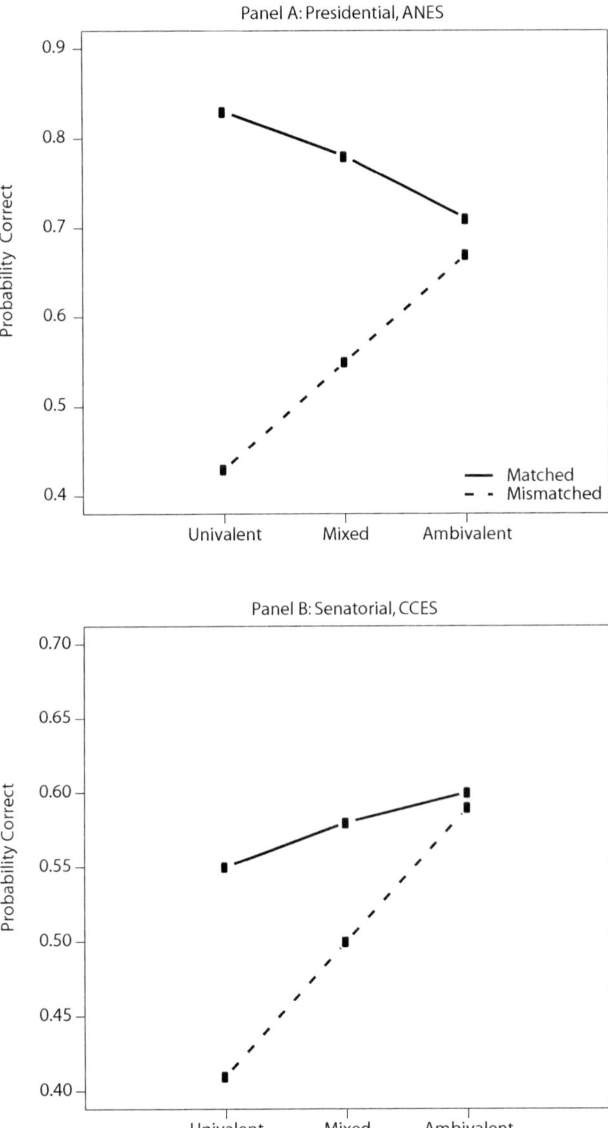

Figure 5.6 The Accuracy of Candidate Placements on Issues.

Notes: The figures represent the probabilities of correct issue placements (Panel A) or correct recognition of roll-call votes (Panel B) as a function of partisan ambivalence and whether a partisan is matched or mismatched with her party on the issue. A mismatch occurs when a partisan takes an issue position that is opposite to that of her party's general ideological orientation.

policy intentions of competing candidates. Unfortunately, prior research has shown that both types of perception are shot through with ignorance and motivated bias, leading scholars to cast doubt on whether ordinary citizens have the capacity or the will to govern themselves effectively.

As we noted at the outset of the chapter, the problem of perceptual inaccuracy has three main sources. The first is environmental: Facts can be hard to come by, as politicians and the media often lack the incentives to provide them. Candidates for political office often have strong incentives to present ambiguous policy positions, and the mass media tend to emphasize nonissue aspects of elections such as candidate image, the "horse race," and campaign strategy. The costs of obtaining political information may thus be prohibitive for many voters. The second source of perceptual inaccuracy is simple ignorance; people have busy lives and their interests lie in domains outside of politics. Much of the public seems more interested in *American Idol* than American foreign policy. And third, people are prone to interpreting the political world in ways that gratify their partisan expectations, leading to motivated errors in perception. As we noted in Chapter 1, partisans expect their representatives to perform better, to produce high-quality candidates, and to take appropriate issue stands. To preserve those beliefs and to protect their partisan identities, people often engage in biased political reasoning as a psychological indulgence.

In this chapter, we examined several questions about the determinants of accuracy in political perception and the cognitive processes that mediate it. According to our theoretical model, citizens would like to see the political world for what it is; however, they are mindful of two additional goals: cognitive efficiency and cognitive consistency. If getting it right takes too much effort, citizens will ignore readily available information and make inferences based largely on partisan cues. If getting it right upsets the individual's other political beliefs, willful distortions of reality may be employed to maintain psychological equanimity. The central questions in our analysis are as follows: When will citizens be willing to devote sufficient cognitive resources to obtain diagnostic information about political reality? Under what conditions will they ignore partisan cues when such cues are normatively irrelevant to the judgment task? And what explains why objectivity and deliberative reasoning are conditional?

Our model makes the following basic prediction: Citizens will minimize the cognitive effort put into acquiring political facts, but they will switch to more effortful strategies when judgment confidence falls too low. Reasoning about political reality on the basis of party identification is particularly attractive because it subjectively maximizes the goals of making it easy, getting it right, and maintaining cognitive consistency. If, however, individuals doubt the efficacy of this strategy, they will turn to other ones, those that are more resource demanding but more likely to lead to accurate perceptions (see Kahneman, 2011).

These dynamics, which we hypothesize to be set in motion by partisan ambivalence, were evident in all three aspects of political perception examined in this chapter. In forming perceptions of economic performance, the policy stands of presidential candidates, and the roll-call votes of US senators, *ambivalence was the only one of four explanatory factors that simultaneously and consistently reduced partisan bias and heightened reliance on diagnostic information.* In judging past economic performance, ambivalent partisans did not reflexively give high or low marks simply because of their status as in- or out-partisans. Instead, they turned away from partisan cues—which provide no diagnostic information about economic reality—and compensated by becoming more responsive to real economic change. Similarly, in judging the policy stands of candidates and the voting behavior of legislators, ambivalent partisans relied less on the simple process of projection (e.g., "co-partisans must believe as I do on the issues") and more on the reliable process of ideological inference (e.g., "Democrats typically endorse liberal policies and Republicans endorse conservative ones"). As a consequence of using better information, ambivalent partisans held more accurate assessments of the economy, the candidates, and the behavior of their representatives.

The findings for the traditional engagement variables were qualitatively different and generally less normatively pleasing. The most consistent effect of both partisan strength and interest in politics was to magnify systematic bias. Strong partisans and those professing an interest in politics were especially likely to avail themselves of judgment strategies that are either demonstrably useless on their face (partisan bias in judging the economy) or highly likely to produce systematic error (projection). Sophistication, by contrast, heightened reliance on changes in objective conditions, but less strongly and less consistently than did ambivalence. We think it is important to point out that the effects of sophistication would have been different, in particular less flattering, had interest in politics been excluded from the models. While it is not uncommon for researchers to study sophistication without controlling for interest, we think this is a mistake. Although the two variables are naturally correlated, they have quite different implications for political information processing and the quality of political judgment. At least with regard to political perception, political knowledge generally has beneficial effects, whereas simply caring about politics does not.

In sum, what seems to matter most, both in terms of relying on good judgment strategies and facilitating good outcomes, is not whether one is a strong or a weak partisan; or whether one professes to be interested in politics, or even how much basic (decontextualized) political knowledge one has. Rather, it is whether an individual has a doubt or two about her own political party, or equally, whether one is willing to acknowledge that the other party is not composed of people who are either malevolent or incompetent. In the next chapter, we examine how the dynamics of ambivalence observed for political perception (and for political preference in Chapter 4) replicate when considering political behavior itself. As these chapters reveal, although judgment strategies are specific to each domain of mass politics, the abstract outcomes are highly replicable: Ambivalence leads citizens to rely on better judgment strategies and leads to better outcomes.

CHAPTER 6

Ambivalent Partisans at the Polls

We learned in Chapter 5 that ambivalent partisans are more likely than their univalent peers to correctly perceive the issue positions of presidential candidates. Do they also rely more on issues at the polls? In this chapter, we demonstrate that they do. In the process, we also show that ambivalence is not a detriment to political participation, for ambivalent partisans are every bit as engaged in political campaigns as other citizens. We then pit our framework against Marcus and colleagues' (2000; MacKuen, Wolak, Keele, & Marcus, 2010) theory of affective intelligence, which provides an alternative explanation of our findings. Marcus et al. hold that voters will switch from heuristic to deliberative thinking when they experience anxiety in response to the political environment. Perhaps, then, the findings presented in previous chapters reflect the operation of anxiety and not ambivalence.

DECISION DIFFICULTY AND PARTICIPATION

Our first task is to disentangle the relationship between ambivalence and political participation. We do this in two steps. First, we show that ambivalent partisans have a more difficult time making up their minds than other citizens. Next, we show that this does not deter them from voting or following campaigns in the media.

Decision Difficulty

Echoing earlier research (Berelson et al., 1954; Lazarsfeld et al., 1948; Mutz, 2006), ambivalent partisans are likely to face a more difficult decision task than other citizens. Their long-term political identities point them in one direction and their contemporary party assessments point them in the other. Decision difficulty can be measured in a number of ways. In their seminal work, Lazarsfeld and colleagues relied heavily on decision timing, and this is a reasonable starting point for our analysis.[1] To the extent that partisanship is

1. See Berelson et al. (1954) and Lazarsfeld et al. (1948).

a reliable cue, as it is for univalent partisans, voters should be able to make up their minds early in the campaign. To the extent that such cues provide little guidance, however, decisions should take longer to crystallize, as more extensive thought should be required to reach them.

In presidential election years, the ANES asks respondents *when* during the campaign they made up their minds. We group together those individuals who formed their voting intentions in the last 2 weeks of the campaign—when election coverage dominates the news—and contrast them with individuals who decided earlier. We predict which type of voter someone is—an early or a late decider—on the basis of ambivalence, the usual controls, and partisanship.[2] The resulting changes in predicted probability are shown in Panel A of Figure 6.1. The graph shows that ambivalent partisans are about 20 percentage points more likely than their univalent peers to delay forming an intention until the final stretch of the campaign (weak partisan loyalty and political apathy have the same effect, while sophistication has no influence).

A second indicator of decision difficulty is "choice set size." In elections with more than two viable candidates, voters rarely consider all of the alternatives. Rather, they apply one or more heuristics to narrow the choice to those who meet some minimum standard of acceptability (Ben-Akiva & Boccara, 1995; Hauser & Wernerfelt, 1990). This first stage may be so effective that the choice set contains only one candidate, obviating the need for further consideration. If, however, heuristics fail to give closure—that is, multiple alternatives remain in the choice set—then decision makers must turn to more effortful decision strategies. The relevance of ambivalence should be clear: Univalent partisans should be more likely to succeed in reducing the choice set to a single alternative using heuristics alone.

Most of the time, researchers do not have direct insight into voters' choice sets, as election surveys rarely ask about all the alternatives that voters considered. In 1992, however, Ross Perot ran an unusually strong third-party campaign, capturing nearly 20 percent of the popular vote. In the 1992 ANES, respondents were asked which candidates they *entertained* voting for. The choice sets included George H. W. Bush only, Bill Clinton only, Ross Perot only, Bush and Clinton, Bush and Perot, Clinton and Perot, or all three candidates. Choice set size can thus range from one to three alternatives, which we model as a function of ambivalence, partisanship, and the usual controls.[3]

2. We estimate a logit model. Detailed estimation results can be found in Table A.6.1.

3. We use a negative binomial count model, although similar results are obtained using ordered logit. Detailed estimation results can be found in Table A.6.2.

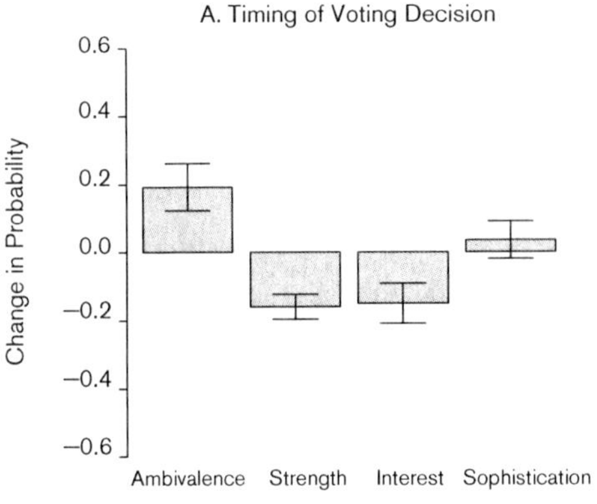

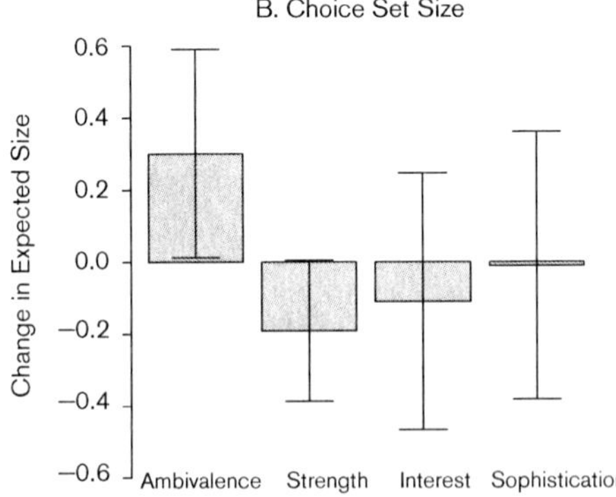

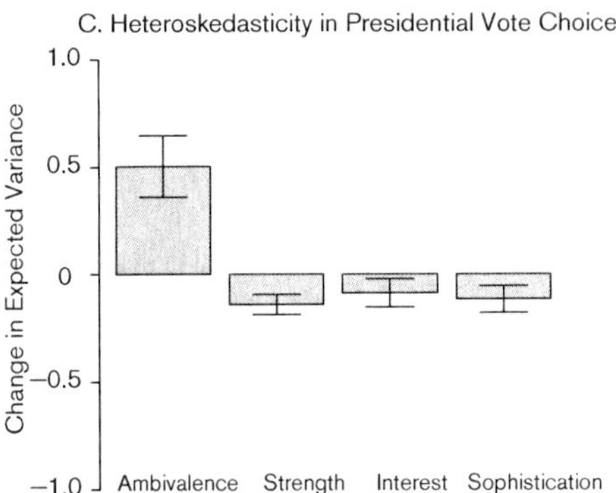

Figure 6.1 Decision Difficulty as a Function of Ambivalence, Interest, Sophistication, and Strength of Identification, 1980–2004 ANES.

Notes: The figures show the expected change in each dependent variable for respective changes in each independent variable. The heights of the bars represent the estimated quantities, whereas the capped lines represent the 95 percent confidence intervals.

The predicted changes in set size, displayed in Panel B of Figure 6.1, indicate that ambivalent partisans entertained significantly more candidates—about a third of a candidate more—than univalent partisans. Moreover, as in the previous analysis, the effect of ambivalence was larger than any of the traditional engagement controls.

As a final indicator of decision difficulty, we examine the degree of individual error variance in vote choice. If the tension between partisan attachment and party evaluations makes for a more complex decision, the choices of ambivalent partisans should be less predictable (i.e., noisier)—reflecting greater *uncertainty*—than those of other citizens. Alvarez and Brehm (1995, 2002) proposed heteroskedastic choice modeling as a way to assess this link empirically. Like other choice models, heteroskedastic models assume that unobserved utilities underlie the choices that voters make. They also allow the variance in the utilities to vary across voters.

To capture errors of prediction in presidential vote choice, we estimate a heteroskedastic probit model using pooled ANES data from 1980 to 2004. The model makes utility a linear function of one set of predictors and the variance an exponential function of another set.[4] As predictors of utility we include partisanship, election year dummies, and demographics. The predictors in the variance model include partisan ambivalence, our triad of engagement variables, and the year dummies. We expect the choices of ambivalent partisans to be more variable, indicating greater uncertainty.[5] The results, shown in Panel C of Figure 6.1, support this expectation. Moreover, as in Panels A and B, this form of uncertainty responds more to ambivalence than to the engagement controls. In sum, the overall picture that emerges is clear: Ambivalent partisans face a more difficult decision task than other citizens. They take longer to decide, they consider more alternatives, and their final decisions reflect greater uncertainty, all else equal.

Political Participation

We now turn to the question of voter turnout. Here, we examine whether ambivalent partisans are less likely than other citizens to cast a vote for president.[6] To find out, we estimate a standard turnout model with age, race, gender, education, and income as key demographic predictors (Wolfinger &

4. The predictors in the choice and variance components of the model may overlap (cf. Harvey, 1976).

5. The heteroskedastic probit results are shown in Table A6.3.

6. We also estimated a turnout model for midterm elections. Since the results are highly similar across the two contexts, we do not report them here.

Rosenstone, 1980). To this we add a party contact variable (to capture party mobilization efforts), internal and external political efficacy (Rosenstone & Hansen, 2002), ambivalence, and the engagement controls.[7]

The results, graphed in Panel A of Figure 6.2, indicate that ambivalent partisans show up at the polls every bit as much as their univalent counterparts. Despite facing a more difficult decision task, they are not turned off to the electoral process. Our initial conclusion, then, is that ambivalence is not a detriment to turnout. We also consider attention to campaign information in the media. As much of what citizens learn about political campaigns comes from mass-mediated sources—TV, the Internet, radio—it is worthwhile to examine whether ambivalent partisans are less (or more) likely to follow campaigns through these channels. Here, the ANES asks respondents whether they watch campaign stories on television, listen to them on the radio, or read about them in newspapers and magazines. We create a dichotomous indicator that takes on a value of 1 if the number of consulted news sources exceeds two, and 0 otherwise.[8 9] The results, shown in Panel B of Figure 6.2, demonstrate that like for turnout, ambivalent and univalent partisans do not significantly differ in their media usage (in fact, the difference is marginally significant in favor of ambivalent partisans).

Overall, then, the analyses indicate that partisan ambivalence is devoid of its potentially deleterious consequences (see Berelson et al., 1954; Campbell et al., 1960). Ambivalent partisans are just as likely to vote as their univalent peers, and they pay attention to campaigns in the media to the same degree (if not slightly more). The importance of these findings cannot be overstated. Had we observed otherwise, our claim that ambivalent partisans are "good citizens" would ring hollow. Although there is precedent in the literature to suspect such a dark side (e.g., Mutz, 2006; see also Berelson et al., 1954; Lazarsfeld et al., 1948), no study (of which we are aware) has examined the form of ambivalence that we consider here (i.e., a disjuncture between partisan identity and party evaluations). In sum, we hope to have convincingly demonstrated that any rumors of the passive ambivalent partisan are false. We now turn to whether and how ambivalence alters the calculus by which citizens make their electoral choices.

7. The estimated model is logit. Detailed estimation results can be found in Table A6.4.

8. This represents a median split of the dependent variable.

9. We estimate a logit model; the results are displayed in Table A6.5.

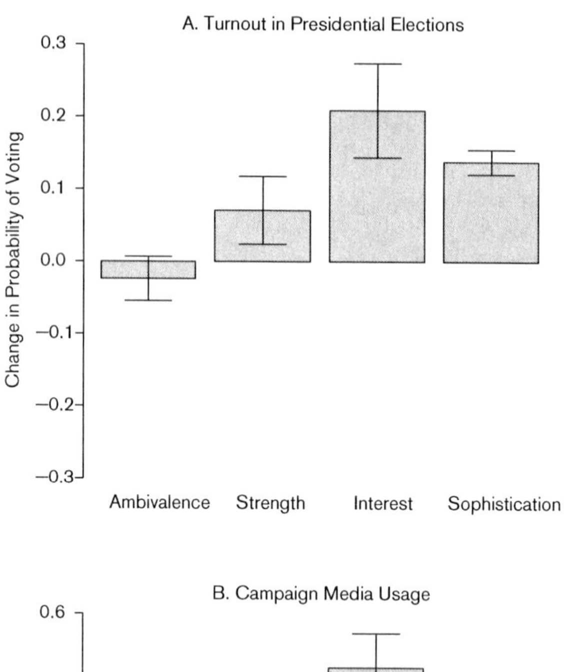

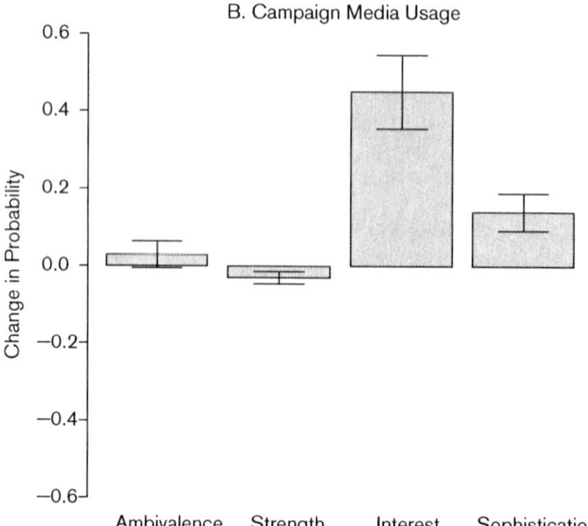

Figure 6.2 Political Participation as a Function of Ambivalence, Interest, Sophistication, and Strength of Identification, 1980–2004 ANES.

Notes: The figures show the expected change in the probability of each behavior for respective changes in each independent variable. The heights of the bars represent the estimated quantities, whereas the capped lines represent the 95 percent confidence intervals.

VOTE CHOICE IN PRESIDENTIAL AND CONGRESSIONAL ELECTIONS

The thrust of our model is that when contemporary party evaluations are out of step with identity-based expectations, citizens are deprived of a powerful yardstick in sorting out their political options. Nowhere should this be of greater consequence than in appraising candidates for the highest office in the land. As we noted in Chapter 1, partisan identification is the single strongest indicator of electoral preference in American presidential elections. It expresses the voter's long-term "standing decision" toward the political world (Key, 1959), and as we demonstrated in Chapter 5, it colors perceptions of candidates' policy stands. The highly polarized state of contemporary American politics only reinforces the "us" versus "them" quality of political competition. Partisanship is also a primary determinant of vote choice in congressional elections (Bartels, 2000; Jacobson, 2001; Kuklinski & West, 1981). Jacobson (2001) has reported that party-line voting in House and Senate elections during the second half of the 20th century hovered around 80 percent.

The question that we address here is how voters pick up the slack in judgmental confidence when ambivalence renders partisan cues unreliable. Do they simply switch from one heuristic to another, such as economic performance or (in congressional elections) incumbency? Or do they engage in deeper, more systematic thought about their political options, and thus rely more on their policy preferences as an electoral guide? If voters' primary concern is with efficiency, they may simply choose to side with incumbents (or incumbent parties in open elections) when the national economy is performing well and to vote them out during hard times (Lewis-Beck & Stegmaier, 2000). If, however, their priority is to boost confidence in the "correctness" of their decisions, they may consider more carefully how well their policy preferences line up with those of the candidates. Or perhaps they split the difference by relying on a combination of low- and high-effort choice strategies.

Presidential Elections

To examine the dynamics of presidential voting, we return to the 1980–2004 ANES and the 2008 ANES panel study. The former provides a time span long enough to capture sufficient variation in economic perceptions (and thus to examine whether their impact hinges on ambivalence), and the latter allows us to harness features of the panel design to make stronger causal inferences. Using the pooled cross-sectional data, we examine whether ambivalent partisanship alters the electoral weight placed on four considerations:

partisanship, policy preferences on economic and social issues, and economic retrospections.

The ANES solicited opinions on the same six issues in at least three of the seven presidential elections between 1980 and 2004, including whether the government should (1) increase or decrease government services and spending; (2) ensure full employment and a decent standard of living for all citizens, and (3) provide health care to all citizens. The survey also asked whether (4) abortion should be legal, (5) gay and lesbians should be protected against discrimination in the workplace, and (6) traditional gender roles should be upheld. From these six issues we created two preference indexes, one for economic issues (issues 1–3) and one for social issues (issues 4–6).[10] As we described in Chapter 5, economic perceptions were measured by asking the following question: "Would you say that over the past year the nation's economy has gotten better, stayed the same, or gotten worse?" To determine whether ambivalence conditioned the electoral impact of partisanship, policy preferences, and economic perceptions, we interacted each of these variables with ambivalence and the usual controls.

The estimates from a probit analysis with fixed effects for election year are shown in Table A6.6 and graphed in Panel A of Figure 6.3. As the figure illustrates, partisan attachment is the dominant influence on the vote choices of univalent partisans. The predicted difference between Republican and Democratic voters in the probability of supporting the Republican candidate is a whopping .97. By contrast, the influence of policy preferences is comparatively small (the difference in predicted probability for those with maximally liberal and conservative preferences is .29 for social issues and –.15 [n.s.] for economic issues). As ambivalence increases, however, the patterns reverse, so that issues matter more and partisanship matters less. Specifically, ambivalent partisans reduce their reliance on party ID by 80 percentage points and increase their reliance on economic issues from an insignificant –.15 to a highly significant .54 (i.e., those with liberal policy preferences are 54 percentage points more likely to vote Democrat than those with conservative preferences).[11] On the basis of this initial analysis, we can state that ambivalent partisans rely much less on party than their univalent peers and considerably more on their beliefs about the role of government in economic matters.

We now turn to two additional questions. First, do ambivalent partisans also place greater weight on their perceptions of economic performance? Second, how do the traditional engagement variables fare in regulating

10. For each index we averaged all available responses.

11. However, the change for social issues is small and insignificant.

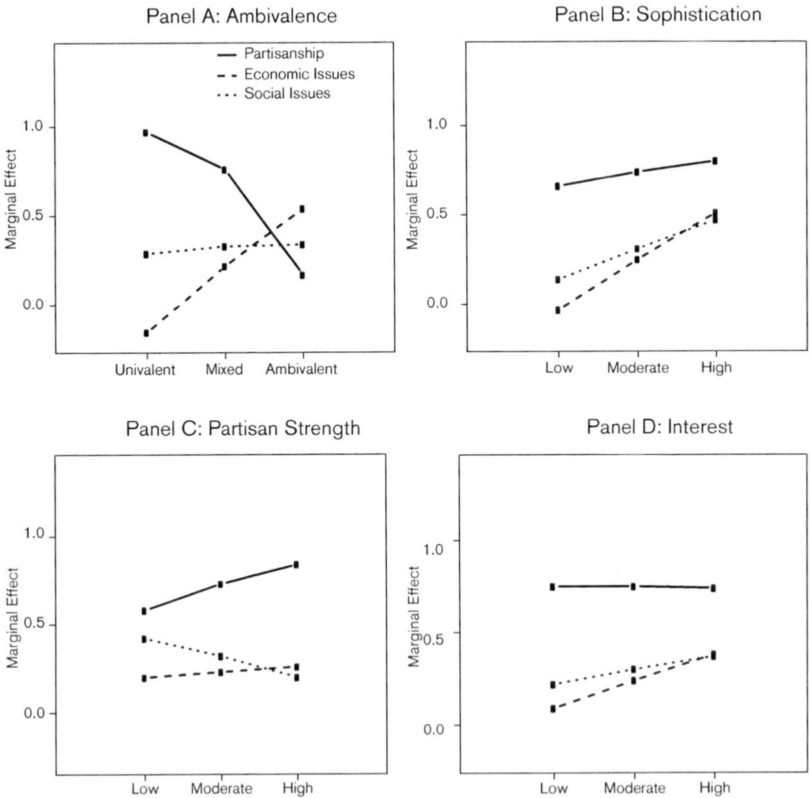

Figure 6.3 The Effects of Partisan Identification and Policy Preferences on Voting in Presidential Elections, 1980–2004 ANES.

Notes: The figures show the estimated marginal effects of partisanship (solid), economic issues (long dash), and social issues (short dash) on the probability of voting for the Republican candidate at different levels of the four key moderators. All variables are coded in the conservative direction.

citizens' choices? The answer to the first question is a flat no; as Table A6.6 indicates, the coefficient on the interaction of economic perceptions and ambivalence is trivial. The answer to the second question is depicted in Panels B–D of Figure 6.3. These panels—which graph the marginal effects of partisanship and policy preferences on vote choice across levels of the engagement variables—indicate the following: Sophistication heightens reliance on economic issues (although not as much as ambivalence does; Panel B); partisan strength heightens reliance on party ID (Panel C), and interest in politics makes no difference in how voters decide (Panel D).

We replicated these results using the 2008 ANES panel study, with comparative candidate evaluation (feelings toward McCain minus feelings toward Obama) as the dependent variable.[12] In this analysis, we use lagged measures of party ID and issue preferences, and a lagged measure of candidate evaluation.[13] By controlling for candidate evaluations in January, we can examine how voters' electoral preferences changed over the course of the campaign

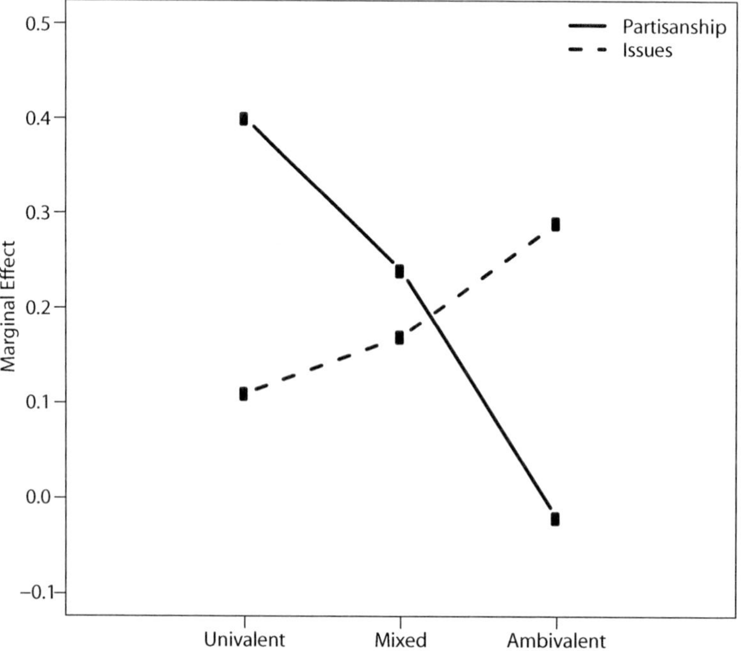

Figure 6.4. The Effects of Partisanship and Policy Preferences Over Levels of Ambivalence in the 2008 Presidential Election, 2008 ANES Panel Study.

Notes: The lines represent the estimated marginal effects of partisanship (solid) and issues (dashed) on respondents' relative preference for McCain over Obama in the 2008 election at each level of partisan ambivalence. Partisanship is coded so that higher values indicate greater Republican identification, and issues are coded in the conservative direction.

---

12. There is no direct measure of vote choice in the panel study (it was asked in the regular postelection time-series study). Thus, we use the 10-point feeling thermometer scales to compute a measure of comparative candidate evaluation.
13. Economic perceptions were excluded from the analysis, as they generally converged across partisan lines on the belief that the economy had gotten "much worse."

TABLE 6.1. CORRELATIONS BETWEEN PARTY IDENTIFICATION AND ISSUE PREFERENCES, 1980–2004 ANES

Issue	Univalent	Ambivalent
Spending	.40	.30
Jobs	.36	.30
Insurance	.36	.28
Economic Issues Scale	*.42*	*.34*
Abortion	.14	.06
Gay discrimination	.25	.20
Women's role	.11	.02
Social Issues Scale	*.16*	*.07*

Notes: Partisan ambivalence was initially residualized of variance associated with partisan strength, political interest, and sophistication.

and whether such changes were driven by partisan cues or policy considerations.[14] The policy variable is an additive scale of all eight items included in the survey (all assessed in January).[15] Table A6.7 and Figure 6.4 display the now familiar dynamic: Univalent partisans make their decisions based on party, whereas ambivalent partisans make theirs based on issues.

14. Moreover, by using a lagged measure of issue preferences, we side-step two causal ambiguities that routinely attend examinations of issue voting: projection and persuasion. Projection, as we discussed in Chapter 5, occurs when voters perceive the issue positions of in-party candidates as closer to their own than they actually are, and persuasion occurs when voters change their positions to match those of in-party candidates. In the former, voters' candidate perceptions are systematically biased; in the latter, voters' policy stands are endogenous to their candidate preferences. By estimating the influence of policy positions measured in January on candidate evaluations measured in October (while controlling for lagged candidate evaluations in June), any connection between the two variables reflects policy voting. This cause-effect relationship is considerably more difficult to establish with cross-sectional data.

15. These are as follows: a constitutional amendment banning gay marriage, increasing taxes on citizens making more than $200,000 per year, government-provided prescription drugs for elderly citizens living on low income, suspension of habeas corpus for suspected terrorists, warrantless wiretapping, temporary work visas for illegal immigrants, a path to citizenship for illegal immigrants, and government-provided health insurance. As there is no clean way of breaking up these items into different ideological dimensions (and moreover, as they are highly intercorrelated, $\alpha = .65$), we simply created a single issue composite by averaging them.

While these results suggest that the two groups of partisans rely on different informational inputs in making their decisions, one might reasonably ask whether party and issues actually provide divergent electoral signals. Perhaps, after decades of partisan sorting, the two factors imply the same choice, at least for most citizens most of the time. For example, in Chapter 4 we showed that univalent (but not ambivalent) partisans update and organize their policy preferences on the basis of partisanship. Perhaps, then, party voting incorporates policy voting among univalent partisans (as Fiorina, [1981, p. 200] noted, "the 'issues' are *in* party identification;" see also Pomper, 1972). If this is correct, we may be distinguishing between cognitive strategies that make no practical difference in actual behavior. The correlations in Table 6.1—which show the relationship between party ID and policy preference on the six issues regularly included in the ANES surveys between 1980 and 2004—suggest that this is unlikely to be the case. Although the average correlation is somewhat higher among univalent than ambivalent partisans (.28 vs. 20, respectively), the relationship is quite weak for both groups. Thus, toeing the party line does little to ensure a choice that reflects one's policy preferences. Moreover, there remains a substantial proportion of outright "unsorted" voters in the electorate, that is, Republican-identifying policy liberals and Democratic-identifying policy conservatives. Among these voters party and issues have *opposing* choice implications. In the next section, we examine how these cross-pressured individuals negotiate the tension between these two factors. First, however, we address whether the empirical dynamic observed for presidential voting holds in the congressional context or whether, given the lower salience of the latter, ambivalent partisans simply switch to other shortcuts in making their decisions.

Congressional Elections

Voters often lack basic information about the candidates and issues in US House elections. To make informed decisions, they rely on cognitive shortcuts such as party, economic conditions, and incumbency (see Herrnson, 2000; Jacobson, 2001). These factors work in conjunction with other national forces and events to shape congressional election outcomes (Abramowitz, Cover, & Norpoth, 1986; Campbell, 1985; Fiorina, 1981; Tufte, 1975). For example, dissatisfaction with President Clinton led to a historic takeover of both houses of Congress by Republicans in the 1994 midterms. Twelve years later, the Democrats took back both chambers in a fit of disfavor with the Iraq War.

We analyze whether partisan ambivalence moderates the impact of these alternative cues. In turning away from party, do ambivalent voters simply switch to incumbency or economic conditions? Or, as we found in the presidential case, do they turn to their issue preferences in deciding how to vote?

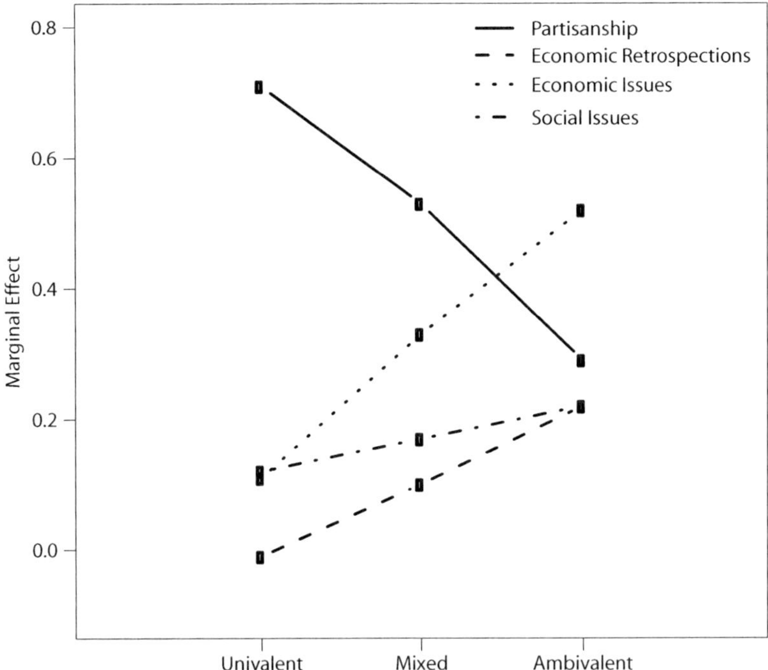

Figure 6.5. Determinants of Voting Behavior in House Elections, 1980–2004 ANES.

Notes: The lines represent the estimated marginal effects of four distinct electoral considerations on respondents' probability of voting Republican at each level of partisan ambivalence. Partisanship is coded so that higher values indicate greater Republican identification, and issues are coded in the conservative direction. Retrospections are coded so that higher values indicate more positive retrospections under the incumbent.

We estimated a model using ANES data to explain the probability of voting for the Republican in US House elections between 1980 and 2004. In addition to partisanship and demographic controls, the model included incumbency, economic perceptions, economic and social policy preferences, and interactions of these variables with ambivalence and our engagement triad.

The results, shown in Table A6.8 and graphed in Figure 6.5, show that ambivalence reduces the effect of party identification while simultaneously increasing voters' reliance on both economic retrospections and economic policy preferences.[16] Among univalent partisans, the probability of supporting the Republican candidate is .70 higher among Republican than Democratic

16. We find little evidence that any factor consistently conditions reliance on incumbency; thus, we do not consider it further.

TABLE 6.2. PERCENTAGE OF REPUBLICANS AND DEMOCRATS WITH "UNSORTED" POLICY PREFERENCES, 1980–2004 ANES

	Democrats	Republicans
Economic issues	20.01	17.04
Social issues	14.92	33.13

voters. Policy preferences, meanwhile, have only a small influence on the vote, and economic perceptions do not matter at all. As ambivalence increases, the trends reverse so that both economic policy preferences and economic retrospections matter more, and partisanship matters less. Moreover, a glance at the interaction coefficients in Table A6.8 indicates that ambivalence is the *only* variable to reliably alter the electoral impact of these factors. Sophistication and interest in politics have no influence on how voters make up their minds, and partisan strength simply increases the impact of partisanship. In sum, looking across the two voting contexts, the role of ambivalence is consistent: ambivalent partisans eschew party as a cue and turn to their policy preferences—and to a lesser degree, their economic perceptions—to pick up the slack in decision confidence. By contrast, univalent partisans rely overwhelmingly on partisan cues in making their electoral decisions while paying scant attention to either their substantive preferences or the nature of the times.

Party Versus Policy Voting Among Cross-Pressured Citizens

To distinguish further between the two primary bases of electoral choice, we focus on voters for whom partisanship and policy preferences point in opposite directions. As Table 6.2 shows, a sizable proportion of the historical electorate consists of Republican-identifying policy liberals and Democratic-identifying policy conservatives.[17] How do these cross-pressured citizens vote? Do they toe the party line and ignore the implications of their substantive preferences?

17. We use separate criteria to define whether a voter is sorted or unsorted on the economic and social policy dimensions. For the economic dimension, we include three items that were asked in a large number of ANES surveys: government spending and services, government-provided health insurance, and government-guaranteed jobs and income. For each item, we consider respondents to be "unsorted" if they placed themselves on the liberal (conservative) side of the issue and identified as Republican (Democrat). We then defined respondents to be unsorted on the economic dimension as a whole if they held unsorted opinions on at least two of the three issues. For the social dimension, we utilize two issues: opposition to abortion and opposition to laws protecting

Or do they do the reverse, or split the difference? Our findings on voting behavior (and our experimental findings from Chapter 4) suggest that univalent partisans will privilege party tribalism and that ambivalent partisans will privilege policy substance.

We examine the probability of voting for the in-party candidate among four cross-pressured groups of citizens: (1) Republicans with economically liberal policy attitudes (17 percent of the 1980–2004 electorate); (2) Democrats with economically conservative policy attitudes (20 percent); (3) Republicans with socially liberal policy attitudes (33 percent); and (4) Democrats with socially conservative policy attitudes (15 percent). To simplify the analysis, we collapse the groups into three categories: those with unsorted opinions in *both* policy domains (e.g., pro-choice Republicans favoring greater taxation on the wealthy), and those with unsorted opinions in one *or* the other domain.[18] As always, we include the standard demographic and political engagement controls. If ambivalence facilitates issue voting, it should lead unsorted voters to choose policy over party when the two point in opposite directions.

Only two variables made any difference in this regard: partisan strength and ambivalence. As Table A6.9 and Figure 6.6 show, the former led voters to prioritize party over policy, whereas the latter moved voters in the other direction. Panel A shows that univalent partisans are virtually assured of ignoring their policy preferences when they conflict with partisan attachment. For example, the probability of party voting among univalent partisans with unsorted preferences on economic issues is .98. This probability drops by more than 50 points (to .43) among similarly situated ambivalent partisans. The bottom panel shows that strong partisans are more likely than partisan "leaners" to vote with the party (.84 vs. .64). Thus, when identity and substantive preferences collide, as they do for about a fifth of the electorate, ambivalent partisans tilt toward issues, univalent partisans swing heavily toward party, and neither sophistication nor interest in politics matters in determining how voters resolve the dilemma.

To conclude, our analyses of heterogeneity in presidential and congressional voting point to a clear verdict: Ambivalent partisans are issue voters. The

homosexuals from job discrimination. Each was coded on a four-point scale, and liberal and conservative preferences were defined as the lower and upper two response categories, respectively. We then defined respondents to be unsorted on the social dimension if they held unsorted opinions on *both* issues.

18. We run one analysis on respondents with sorted preferences on economic but not social issues, and another analysis on respondents with sorted preferences on social but not economic issues.

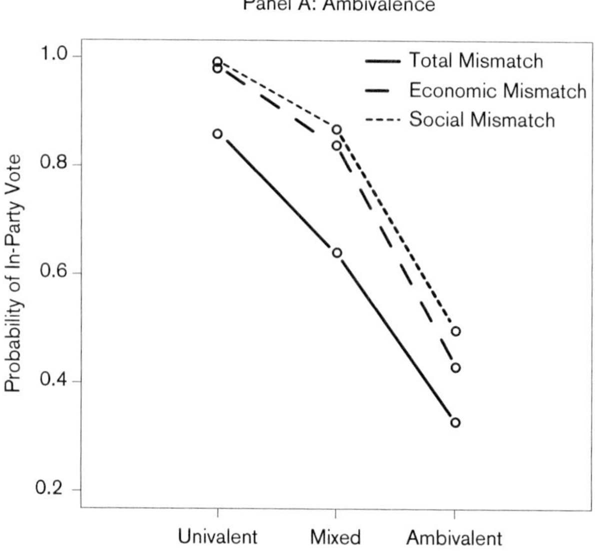

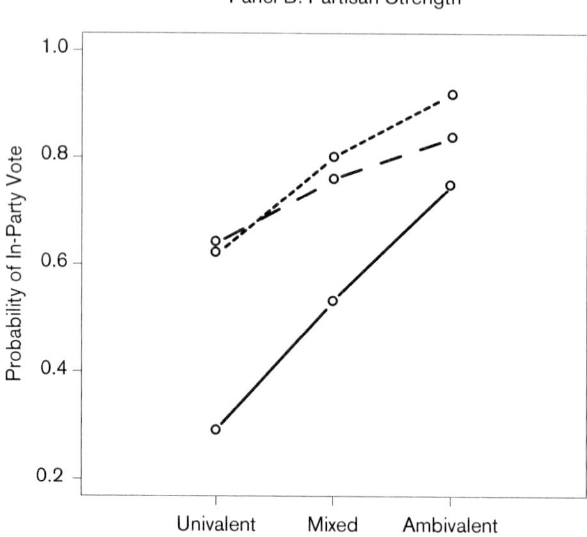

Figure 6.6. Party Versus Policy Voting Among Cross-Pressured Partisans, 1980–2004 ANES.

Notes: Figures show the predicted probabilities of an in-party vote for citizens who are cross-pressured on one or both dimensions of public policy (economic and social).

dynamic is also clear: Ambivalent partisans rely more on issues to compensate for their distrust in the otherwise powerful pull of partisan loyalty. Factors that are often ascribed a primary role in engineering heterogeneity, namely political sophistication, exert weaker, less consistent, and less desirable effects overall. Perhaps most tellingly, when voters hold preferences over policy issues that conflict with their partisan loyalties, sophistication does nothing to sway them to favor the former.[19] Finally, the manner in which ambivalent partisans pick up the slack in judgment confidence depends on electoral context: In presidential elections, they switch from partisanship to economic issues, whereas in congressional elections they switch from partisanship to both economic issues and economic retrospections. Thus, in the lower salience context, ambivalent partisans rely on a mixture of heuristic and deliberative thinking. We now turn to the question of whether ambivalence creates a measure of *volatility* in national elections by encouraging defection, ticket splitting, and third-party voting.

DOES PARTISAN AMBIVALENCE CREATE VOLATILITY IN ELECTIONS?

In *The Persuadable Voter*, Hillygus and Shields (2008) found that defection in presidential elections occurs when voters disagree with their party on an issue of personal importance. Our more general expectation is that defection may result when voters find any reason to be unhappy with their party—whether it is a disagreement on policy, a matter of performance, or a dislikeable candidate—or when they find something to like about the other party. We have already seen that ambivalent partisans have a harder time making up their minds. This makes it a potentially important dynamic force in elections. We test this prediction here by considering three additional aspects of voting behavior: defection, ticket splitting, and third-party voting. Defection occurs when a Democrat votes for the Republican candidate and vice versa; ticket splitting arises when a person casts a vote for different parties for the presidency and the House (or Senate); and third-party voting exists when a voter who identifies with one of the two major parties votes for a third-party candidate.

Defecting Partisans

Let us first consider defection, which may occur in both presidential and congressional elections. The results of our standard modeling procedure are displayed in Table A6.10 and graphed in Panels A and B of Figure 6.7. At the

19. Neither for that matter does interest in politics or partisan strength.

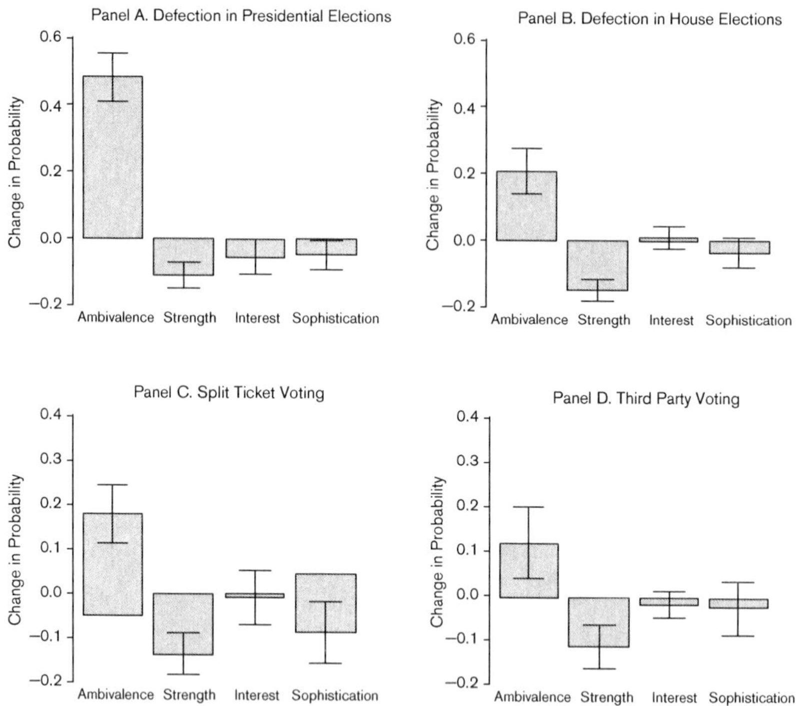

Figure 6.7. Indicators of Electoral Volatility.

Notes: Figures show the estimated marginal effects of each independent variable on the probability of defection, split-ticket voting, and third-party voting. The bar heights give the estimated quantity, whereas the capped lines give the 95 percent confidence intervals.

presidential level ambivalence heightens the probability of defection by .48 points (see Panel A); at the congressional level, the predicted increase is .21 points (see Panel B). Both changes are statistically significant, and in each case, they are substantially larger than those of the traditional engagement variables (all of which inhibit defection).

Ticket Splitting

The voluminous literature on ticket splitting calls attention to several factors, including partisan strength, House incumbency effects, and policy balancing (for a review see Beck, Baum, Clausen, & Smith, 1992; Burden & Kimball, 2004). From a motivational perspective, ticket splitting may also be an effective strategy for resolving the tension between the identity and evaluative components of partisanship. Research on cognitive consistency indicates that disharmony among beliefs causes mental and physiological distress, and that individuals will take steps to restore consistency by changing one or more belief elements (e.g., Abelson, 1959; Cooper, Zanna, & Taves, 1978; Festinger, 1957; Heider, 1958). Occasionally, however, it is possible to let inconsistent beliefs flow into multiple behaviors, each of which is consistent with one key element. While this does not restore consistency, it should alleviate some of the difficulty in deciding which of the two conflicting components of partisanship should take precedence in political behavior. Thus, ticket splitting may be a particularly attractive electoral decision strategy among ambivalent partisans.

To weak partisanship and the visibility of out-party candidates, we add our standard package of variables along with election year dummies.[20] The results, shown in Table A6.10 and graphed in Panel C of Figure 6.7, support standard explanations (i.e., strong partisan loyalty decreases the probability of casting a split ballot and highly visible out-party candidates increase it).[21] Net the influence of these factors, ambivalent partisanship increases the likelihood of casting a split ticket by nearly 20 percent (an effect larger than any of the engagement controls).

Third-Party Voting

Since 1980 there have been three major third-party candidacies: John Anderson in 1980 and Ross Perot in 1992 and 1996.[22] The success of third-party movements in American politics has traditionally been explained in terms of partisan strength and major party failure, mixed together with the quality and visibility of the third-party candidate (e.g., Rosenstone, Behr, & Lazarus, 1996; Zaller & Hunt, 1994, 1995). Both Anderson and Perot met one of these criteria. A successful 10-term member of Congress from Illinois and former chair of the House Republican Caucus, Anderson was among the best-qualified

20. A third standard explanation is that voters split their tickets because they believe divided government to be desirable (Alesina & Rosenthal, 1989; see also Fiorina, 1996). We do not explore this explanation here because the ANES has only occasionally asked respondents to indicate their preferences for divided government.

21. Visibility is measured by whether the voter can recall the name of the other party's candidate. This is a trivial matter in presidential elections, but it has been shown to be important in elections in the House of Representatives (Jacobson, 2005).

22. We use a cutoff of 5 percent of the popular vote to determine whether a candidate is a "major" third-party candidate.

third-party candidates in postwar American politics. As for Perot, although he lacked prior political experience, he made up for it through massive spending on television advertisements (including 30-minute seminars devoted mostly to the issue of deficits), giving him unusually high visibility for a third-party candidate.

Qualification and visibility only go so far in explaining third-party success, however. As Rosenstone et al. (1996) have argued, third-party movements tend to resonate when significant numbers of voters believe that the two major parties are failing. Like with ticket splitting, we expect ambivalent partisans to be attracted to third-party candidates. If giving one vote to one party and another vote to the other party is one way out of the dilemma that ambivalent partisans face, so too is third-party voting. This should be especially true if the insurgent candidate is seen as a reasonable compromise between the major party alternatives.

In our final analysis in this section, we model third-party voting on the basis of major party candidate dislike, a Perot dummy, ambivalence, and all the usual controls. As can be seen in Table A6.10, partisan ambivalence is indeed a significant determinant of third-party voting. Next to major party candidate dislike and partisan strength, it is the most important factor in shaping this form of electoral volatility. As Panel D of Figure 6.7 shows, moving ambivalence in the usual manner increases the predicted probability of a third-party vote by .13 points (a figure similar to that of partisan strength).[23] Both interest and sophistication tend to depress the likelihood of casting a third-party vote, though neither effect is statistically reliable.

In sum, the picture that emerges in all three analyses is that ambivalent partisanship facilitates electoral volatility. Ambivalent partisans are more likely than other voters to defect from their party's candidate in both presidential and congressional elections, to split their tickets, and to vote for third-party presidential candidates. Moreover, as we have seen throughout the book, the effects for ambivalence are substantively large and more consistent than rival explanations. In short, the votes of ambivalent partisans are in play, adding an important dynamic element to American elections.

---

23 The simulation assumes that Perot was the third-party candidate. It also assumes that the voter is a non-Southern, White female of average age and median education and income. The assumed partisanship is Democrat. Partisan strength, political interest, and political knowledge are all set to their mean values. Finally, it is assumed that the voter does *not* dislike both major party candidates (the modal response).

CAN AFFECTIVE INTELLIGENCE THEORY ACCOUNT FOR OUR FINDINGS?

The analyses presented throughout the chapter demonstrate the centrality of ambivalence in regulating how voters decide how to decide. In this last section, we directly pit the predictions of our model against Marcus and colleagues' (2000) theory of affective intelligence. As we noted in Chapters 1 and 2, the two theories bear a strong resemblance to one another. Most important, both perspectives hold that citizens are conditionally willing to set aside partisan habits and think in a more deliberative manner about their political options. Where the theories differ is in the nature and origins of this motivation.

According to affective intelligence theory (AIT), the motivation to engage in effortful information processing hinges specifically on activation of the "surveillance system," a biobehavioral system in the brain that continuously monitors the environment for the presence of threat and danger (see Gray, 1981; Watson & Tellegen, 1985). Activation of the surveillance system results in the emotion of anxiety, which interrupts ongoing habitual action, redirects attention to novel stimuli, and promotes increased thoughtfulness and greater motivation for learning. Applied to the electoral realm, anxiety is expected to lead voters to reduce their reliance on existing predispositions (e.g., party identification) and to pay greater attention to relevant information in the environment (e.g., issue debates). In their research, Marcus and colleagues (1993, 2000) find that anxious voters are indeed more attentive to campaigns and rely less on partisanship and more on policy in forming their candidate evaluations.

Our framework, by contrast, makes the broader claim that effortful and even-handed judgments occur when long-term attachments are out of step with contemporary party assessments, leading voters to lose faith in the utility of partisan cues. The critical difference between the two frameworks is whether anxiety is a necessary and sufficient condition to alter how voters decide. According to AIT, anxiety is both necessary and sufficient. As Marcus and MacKuen (1993, p. 673) argue, "anxiety uniquely contributes to our understanding of political matters," and "anxiety works cooperatively with learning to shift attention to political matters and to diminish reliance on habit in voting decisions" (p. 672). According to our ambivalence model, anxiety may be a sufficient condition (if it is experienced as dissonant with one's partisan identity), but it is not necessary to instigate more careful thinking. Negative in-party evaluations may also result from feelings of anger or resignation, or in more cognitively flavored evaluations.

For example, one might experience disappointment in one's party when it fails to deliver on desired policy change (e.g., health care reform under Clinton) or respond with anger when it proposes legislation at odds with the party's ideology (e.g., increased spending under Bush II). Each of these emotions may result in ambivalence, as each implies an evaluation at odds with one's identity. Ambivalence may also be instigated by feelings of enthusiasm toward the other party when it produces (or presides over) positive conditions. For example, as we noted in Chapter 2, approval of Clinton's job performance among Republicans increased during the economic super-boom in the late 1990s (see Lebo & Cassino, 2008). What matters, then, according to ambivalence theory, is not the specific nature of the emotion, but whether it dovetails or conflicts with one's partisan attachment.

The predictions of the two frameworks in the context of candidate evaluation are depicted in Figure 6.8.[24] According to AIT (see top panel), only feelings of anxiety modulate the degree to which party identification and issue preferences drive candidate evaluations. Enthusiasm, by contrast, is hypothesized to exert a direct influence on electoral preferences. As Marcus and MacKuen (1993) write:

> anxiety and enthusiasm play importantly different roles in the voting decision. In particular, the data indicate that enthusiasm directly affects voting preference (reflecting something very close to the voting decision itself), while anxiety has practically no direct impact on choice. Equally important for our point of view, anxiety appears to give voters pause—to get voters to base their decision on candidate characteristics or campaign information rather than merely stick with their "standing choice."

According to AIT, then, enthusiasm and anxiety exert *functionally* distinct effects on political judgment.

According to ambivalence theory (see bottom panel of Fig. 6.8), the political effects of enthusiasm and anxiety depend entirely on whether they represent identity *conflicting* or *consistent* emotions. Anxiety experienced in relation to the in-party and enthusiasm experienced in relation to the out-party—hereafter "in-candidate anxiety" and "out-candidate enthusiasm"—should each arouse ambivalence, as both emotions (so directed) conflict with party loyalty. In-candidate enthusiasm and out-candidate anxiety, however, reinforce identity and should thus heighten confidence in standing (partisan) decisions.

In sum, AIT predicts that partisan cues will be abandoned in favor of policy voting when anxiety signals that one's standing decision should be reexamined in light of new information. Ambivalence theory, by contrast, predicts that the switch from party to issues depends more broadly on the pattern of identity conflicting and consistent evaluations, regardless of whether

24. The illustrations are inspired by Ladd and Lenz (2008).

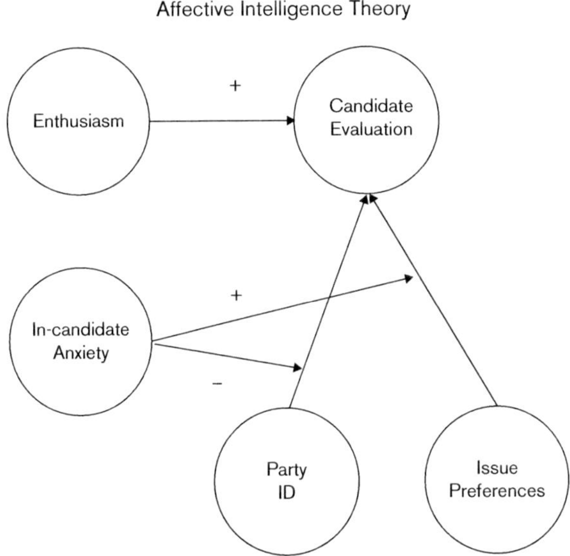

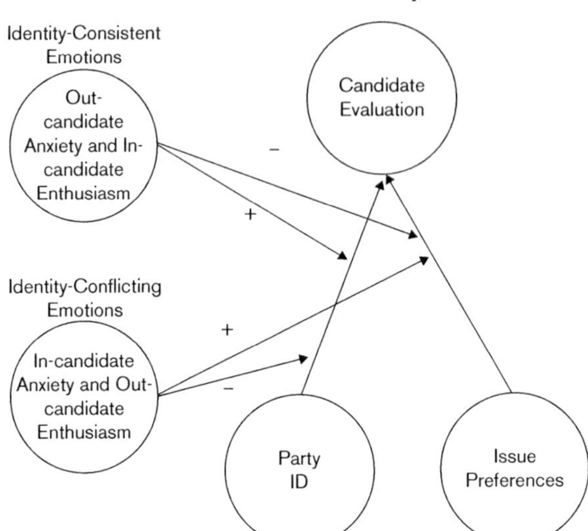

Figure 6.8. Two Models of Emotion-Based Voter Choice.

anxiety is involved. Fortunately, the ANES regularly carries items to allow a straightforward test of the two theories. Beginning in 1980, the survey has solicited emotional reactions toward the two major party presidential candidates. The relevant question asks: "Has [candidate name], because of the kind of person he is or because of something he has done, ever made you feel _______?" Respondents are asked about four emotions: afraid, angry, hopeful, and proud. We combine the "proud" and "hopeful" items for each candidate as a measure of candidate-specific enthusiasm, and we use the "afraid" item to measure candidate-specific anxiety.[25]

To compare the two theories, we estimate models similar to those in Table A6.7 and A6.8, except that for comparability to Marcus and colleagues we include only two sets of interactions: (1) partisanship x each emotion term (i.e., in-candidate anxiety and enthusiasm and out-candidate anxiety and enthusiasm); and (2) issue preferences x each emotion term.[26] [27] [28] If AIT is right, the presence of anxiety should decrease party voting and increase issue voting, whereas enthusiasm should not exert any conditional effects. If ambivalence theory is right, the identity-conflicting emotions (in-candidate anxiety and out-candidate enthusiasm) should create partisan ambivalence, thus elevating *policy over party*. By contrast, the identity-consistent emotions (out-candidate anxiety and in-candidate enthusiasm) should reduce ambivalence, thereby producing the opposite pattern of *party over policy*.

The ordered probit results for the pooled cross-sectional analysis (1980–2004) are presented in Table A6.11 and graphed in Panels A and B of

---

25. While Marcus and colleagues (1993, 2000) originally measured candidate anxiety with both the "afraid" and "angry" items, they have recently reconceptualized the latter as "aversion" (Marcus, 2002; Marcus, MacKuen, & Neuman, 2009; Marcus, MacKuen, Wolak, & Keele, 2003). As our core interest lies in assessing the effects of anxiety per se, we exclude the anger item from the measure.

26. A more critical test of the two theories would involve the examination of emotions directed at the party labels rather than the candidates. Although such items are available in the 2008 ANES panel study, they are measured only in the November wave of the study—that is, after the election—and are therefore unusable for this purpose.

27. To maximize comparability, we use Marcus et al.'s (2000) operationalization of issue preferences, which is constructed as the average relative perceived distance of each respondent to the candidates on the issues available within each year of the ANES.

28. We rely on vote intention than self-reported vote, as this is how Marcus et al. (2000) operationalized candidate preference.

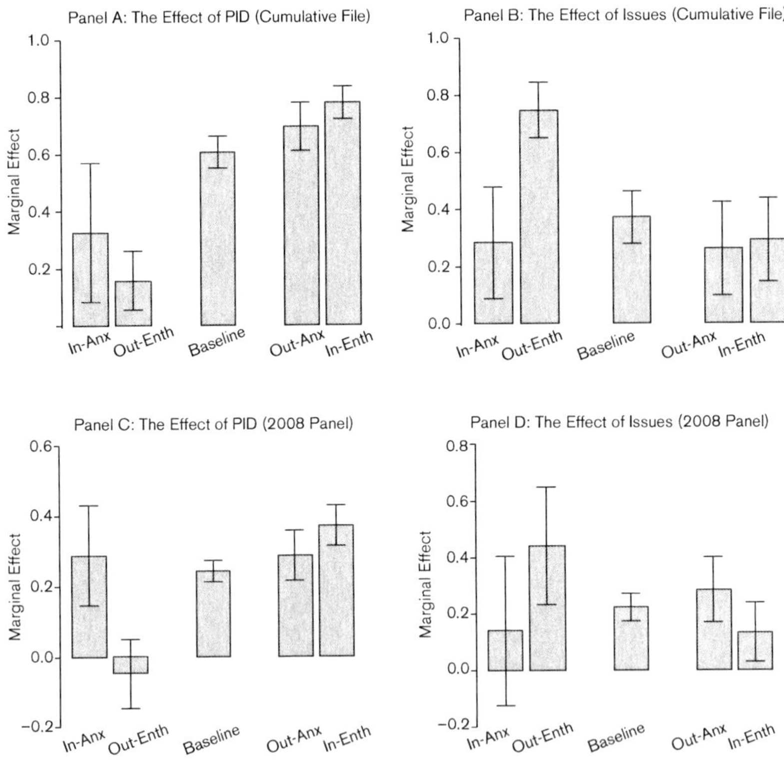

Figure 6.9. Marginal Effects of Party Identification and Issue Preferences, by Anxiety and Enthusiasm, on Vote Intention, 1980–2004 ANES. PID, party identification.

Notes:Figures show the estimated marginal effects of partisanship and issues positions across different levels of expressed emotions toward the candidates. "Baseline" estimates hold all emotions at their means, while each respective bar raises an emotion to its maximum value, holding constant the other three. The bar heights give the estimated quantity, whereas the capped lines give the 95 percent confidence intervals.

Figure 6.9.[29] The "baseline" bars represent the marginal effects of party and issues holding all emotion terms at their central tendencies. The other bars represent the marginal effects when each emotion term is moved to its maximum value. As the panels show, the conditional effects depend not on anxiety alone but on the broader pattern of identity conflicting and consistent emotions. As it turns out, it is *enthusiasm* and not *anxiety* that most strongly determines how voters make up their minds. Perhaps most tellingly, AIT's signature effect—that in-candidate anxiety bolsters issue voting—fails to obtain. Rather, Panel A indicates that

29. We are grateful to Benjamin Woodson for his work in estimating these models.

feeling enthusiastic about the in-party candidate heightens the role of party, whereas feeling enthusiastic about the opposition decreases it. Panel B illustrates the compensatory dynamic: Feeling enthusiastic about the out-party candidate heightens the role of issues, whereas feeling enthusiastic about the in-party candidate diminishes the role of issues. None of these findings follow from AIT; however, they are consistent with ambivalence theory. As voters experience more identity-conflicting feelings, they rely less on party and more on issues; as they experience more identity-consistent feelings, the opposite occurs.

As a check on robustness, we replicated the analysis using the 2008 ANES panel study with lagged right-side emotion variables and a lagged measure of comparative candidate evaluation (i.e., the dependent variable). These findings are reported in Table A6.12 and graphed in Panels C and D of Figure 6.9. While the overall results are weaker, they closely replicate the primacy of enthusiasm over anxiety. As in the pooled cross-sectional analysis, out-party enthusiasm heightens issue voting and decreases party voting, whereas in-party enthusiasm has the opposite effects. Anxiety, by contrast, whether experienced in relation to the in-party or the out-party, has no effect on party voting; moreover, as before, in-candidate anxiety fails to condition the magnitude of issue voting. There is one result, however, that ambivalence theory cannot explain but that AIT can: Anxiety toward the out-party candidate heightened—rather than reduced—the role of issues on candidate choice.

Taken as a whole, the findings do not fit the pattern proposed by AIT, which holds that anxiety—but not enthusiasm—leads voters to back away from their standing (partisan) decisions and judge the candidates in terms of policy agreement. In fact, AIT was supported in only one of many cases in which the two perspectives made divergent predictions. We take these findings as evidence that the emotion terms tapped in ANES surveys function as *evaluations* that either dovetail or conflict with one's partisan attachment, with judgmental implications best fitting the framework of partisan ambivalence.

SUMMARY AND CONCLUSIONS

In this chapter we examined the role of ambivalence on electoral behavior. We first sought to determine how ambivalent partisans stack up against other citizens in their participatory habits. While the evidence suggests they face a more difficult decision task (e.g., they take longer to decide, their decisions reflect greater uncertainty), we find no evidence that ambivalent partisans are apathetic citizens. Rather, they vote every bit as much as their univalent counterparts in both presidential and congressional elections. However, the nature and quality of their political behavior are distinct. Rehearsing the refrains of Chapters 4 and 5, univalent partisans rely heavily on their partisan attachments. Chapter 4 showed that they anchor policy preferences and Chapter 5 showed that they drive subjective perceptions of political reality. In this chapter, we showed that partisan attachments also dominate the voting choices of univalent partisans. Ambivalent partisans, by contrast, are issue voters. It is tempting to argue, especially in light of decades' worth of partisan sorting, that the two forms of voting are highly redundant. However, this is not the case. While the correlation between party identification and ideological self-identification has skyrocketed into the .70s over the past three decades—especially among politically active citizens (see Abramowitz, 2010)—the correlation between party ID and policy preferences is much weaker. As we demonstrated in Table 6.2, while most citizens are now "sorted," many are not.

As the panels of Figure 6.6 show, whether such cross-pressured voters turn to party loyalty or their issue preferences in casting votes depends strongly on ambivalence. Univalent partisans—whether they are Republicans with liberal issue positions or Democrats with conservative ones—betray their policy preferences and vote their partisan loyalty. Ambivalent partisans, by contrast, do the opposite (although to a lesser degree). This is consistent with the results of our experiments in Chapter 4, in which univalent partisans privileged party over policy when we created a mismatch between the two, whereas ambivalent partisans privileged policy over party. We should also note that two of our three competitor engagement variables—sophistication and interest—failed to create heterogeneity in how cross-pressured voters negotiated the trade-off, and strong partisanship only served to move them toward party and away from issues. In sum, as we have seen throughout the book, the political consequences of ambivalence are consistent and normatively desirable, whereas those of the standard engagement factors often are not.

One potential criticism of the ambivalence model is that its predictions overlap with affective intelligence theory. We empirically investigated the viability of this alternative explanation and found it wanting. The evidence suggests that it is not the discrete emotion of anxiety that matters in regulating how voters decide, but the broader pattern of emotions that dovetail or conflict with their partisan loyalties. In all, these results, along with the propensity of ambivalent partisans to defect, split their tickets, and vote for third parties, indicate that the votes of ambivalent partisans are in play. In this way, they add fluidity to elections, which outside of major realignments is what gives them their dynamic quality. Not all fluidity is good for democracy, however. One would worry if the changing tides were driven mainly by ignorant voters who are easily manipulated. Fortunately, ambivalent partisans do not fit this description. If we consider the results from the last three chapters, it appears that ambivalent partisans perceive the world accurately, form their preferences in a principled manner, and communicate those preferences by making issues an important component of their electoral decisions. In this manner, they manage to communicate policy ideas and to act on accurate beliefs about political reality. All of this is no small feat, for ambivalent partisans do not face the easiest of decision tasks (we have uncovered plenty of evidence to the contrary). The important point, in the end, is that they *do* come to a decision, and do so in a manner that we think democratic theorists would applaud.

CHAPTER 7

Unmoved Mover or Running Tally?

Ambivalence and the Dynamic Nature of Partisanship

Over the last three chapters, we took a person's loyalty as given and proceeded to examine the judgmental consequences of holding partisan evaluations that either meshed or conflicted with this group attachment. In this chapter we adopt a *dynamic* view of partisanship. In particular, we ask whether ambivalence causes individuals to change their partisan loyalties, and whether it increases the responsiveness of such loyalties to an individual's policy preferences. By doing so, we step into one of the liveliest debates in political science. This debate is concerned with fundamental questions about the nature of partisan politics: How stable are partisan identities? Are they endogenous to the policy preferences of the individual? We begin by reviewing the relevant literature in this debate. We then focus on the conditions that determine the nature of sorting or "dynamic constraint"—that is, the bidirectional influence of partisan loyalty and issue preference on one another. We then lay out some considerations that emerge from our own theory, as described in Chapter 2. Finally, we let the empirical light shine on the relationship between ambivalence, partisan stability, and dynamic constraint.

PARTISAN DYNAMICS: NATURE AND CAUSES

The Traditional View

As we have done so frequently in this book, we begin our exploration of partisan dynamics with a consideration of *The American Voter*. In this seminal work, Campbell and his colleagues laid out a theory of party identification that long dominated the literature and that continues to have strong advocates. Party identification, so it was argued, is a long-term psychological attachment to a political party as a cohesive social entity. Shaped by the influence of one's parents and social environment (Jennings & Niemi, 1981), partisanship is believed to be resistant to change throughout the life span. As such, Campbell et al. (1960) expected it to be highly stable and immune—indeed, exogenous—to short-term shocks to the political environment. So convinced were the authors of *The American Voter* of the "unmoved mover" status of party ID, they developed what came to be known as the "normal vote," in which electoral outcomes are predicated on the basis of party identification alone. Short-term influences, including the specifics of issues, candidates, and the nature of the times are explicitly removed from the analysis (e.g., Converse, 1966). Such a prediction is only meaningful, however, if one considers party identification to be stable and exogenous. If it were labile, normal vote predictions would not be particularly compelling, especially when they are made well in advance of an election with ample time for circumstances to change. Furthermore, should partisanship prove to be endogenous, it could not serve the purpose of producing a vote prediction that is stripped of short-term influences. After all, it might itself be a product of those influences.

Strong evidence for the stability of partisanship comes from a variety of sources. Converse's (1964) analysis of the 1956–68–60 ANES panel study showed that party identification is the most stable of political preferences, easily surpassing those on specific policy issues (including those on "hot button" issues such as race; see also Alwin & Krosnick, 1991; Bartels et al., 2011; Feldman, 1989; Goren, 2005; Green & Palmquist, 1990; Green et al., 2002; Krosnick, 1991). The evidence for stability is particularly strong when measurement error is taken into account (e.g., Green, 1990; Green & Palmquist, 1990). Moreover, it emerges strongly over relatively short time intervals (e.g., over the course of a presidential election campaign, from one election to another), and in panel studies in which the waves are scheduled many years apart, such as the 1965–1982 Youth-Parent Socialization Panel Study (Jennings, Markus, & Niemi, 1991). Overall, then, it seems that partisan instability is a rather rare phenomenon.

The Revisionist View

As much evidence as there is in favor of the stability thesis, there is also a sizable literature—sometimes based on the same data—that points in the other direction, that is, to partisan *instability*. The idea that partisanship does not empirically live up to its unmoved mover reputation has always lurked below the surface of the conventional wisdom. It gained considerable momentum with a series of individual-level studies in the late 1970s and early 1980s demonstrating that partisan loyalty is not immune to presidential candidate evaluations (Page & Jones, 1979); that loyalty drops off among members of the incumbent party during economic downturns (Fiorina, 1981); and that it is responsive to an individual's policy preferences (Franklin & Jackson, 1983). These studies reversed the causal logic of *The American Voter*, which had argued that partisanship is the principal driver of political perception and evaluation. In these studies partisanship was found to respond to—rather than cause—changes in all of these factors. In this view, then, partisanship turns out to be quite amenable to change (see also Clarke & McCutcheon, 2009).

The stability thesis came under further attack when political scientists began to analyze aggregate partisanship data over long time spans. Through the 1980s, the evidence for stability had come mostly from individual-level panel data, which in most cases were limited to relatively short time intervals (typically three election cycles). The literature on *macropartisanship* focused on changes in the partisan balance in the electorate over long swaths of time. Researchers in this tradition found that the abiding characteristic of aggregate partisanship is lability. Americans shift their partisan allegiances continuously and do so in response to economic performance and presidential popularity. Moreover, it appears that exogenous shocks to the political system (e.g., war, scandal) decay slowly over time, thus displaying a long "memory" (Erikson, MacKuen, & Stimson, 1998, 2002; MacKuen, Erikson, & Stimson, 1989). In these aggregate-level analyses, partisanship emerges not as the unmoved mover of political behavior but as an endogenous and ephemeral quality (see also Box-Steffensmeier & Smith, 1996).

Those who believe partisanship to be unstable also believe that it should be. They argue that Americans are rational beings who do not sell their souls to one or the other party but express partisan loyalties on the basis of performance in office (e.g., Erikson et al., 2002). Partisanship thus loses its quality as a psychological attachment and takes on the guise of a rationally informed—and contextually contingent—evaluation (Downs, 1957). The debate over the stability of partisanship is by no means over. Where some observe stability, others see change. Where some attribute change to rational reflection, others deny such a pattern. Our goal in this chapter is not to act as arbiter in this debate. Rather, we seek to insert a new perspective, namely that it is essential to consider voter heterogeneity and that one key component thereof is partisan ambivalence.[1]

PARTISAN AMBIVALENCE AND PARTISAN CHANGE

When should we expect citizens to switch allegiances? Is the process of partisan change triggered by the desire to accommodate one's policy preferences? These are the central questions that we seek to answer in this chapter. Our theoretical argument has drawn a sharp distinction between long-standing

1. Other scholars have found evidence for the heterogeneity hypothesis, though none have examined the role of partisan ambivalence (see Box-Steffensmeier & Smith, 1996, 1997; Carsey & Layman, 2006; Dancy & Goren, 2010).

partisan identities and temporally specific party evaluations. We have implied that it is rational to identify with a party and yet at times hold feelings and beliefs that directly contradict this attachment. As we noted in Chapters 1 and 3, this disjuncture is not uncommon and does not ordinarily provoke an identity crisis or lead to fundamental belief change. What it does do, as we have shown, is lead citizens to turn away from partisan cues as informational crutches and to pick up the slack in judgment confidence by seeking out other (usually better) information.

However, this initial resistance to toeing the party line has the potential to lead to more drastic change. In particular, the deliberative thinking that characterizes the ambivalent partisan can operate as a positive feedback system. Persistently unfavorable evaluations of the in-party (or favorable ones of the out-party) can instigate a reconsideration of identity itself, so that citizens begin to actively reevaluate the "fit" between their long-standing attachments and their substantive beliefs and preferences. Persistent ambivalence may thus result in a specific—and apparently unusual—pattern of sorting, one of *issue-based partisan change*, that largely eluded detection in earlier work (Carsey & Layman, 2006; Franklin & Jackson, 1983; Levendusky, 2009). For example, racial animus among Whites played a central role in engineering partisan realignment in the South (Valentino & Sears, 2005). Perhaps, then, we can move toward a resolution of the debate over the stability and endogeneity of partisanship by appealing to the heterogeneous nature of the American electorate. Partisanship may indeed be responsive to party performance and citizens' substantive preferences, but only for some people some of the time.

We test these arguments in two steps. First, we operationalize the notion of positive feedback with a dynamic model of partisanship. Specifically, we examine heterogeneity in the tendency of "shocks" in the environment to cause persistent change in the individual's party identification. For univalent partisans, we expect such shocks to be ephemeral, that is, to quickly decay, and to bring about a return to the partisan status quo ante. For ambivalent partisans, by contrast, we expect such shocks to persist longer, creating the potential for sustained partisan change. Second, we examine whether the propensity to engage in partisan change to accommodate one's policy preferences depends, all else equal, on ambivalence. Using panel data, we hypothesize that issue-based partisan change will occur only when the following three conditions are met: partisanship is of the ambivalent variety; the issue is widely discussed in the media during the period in question (thus being salient in citizens' minds);

and the individual's policy preferences at time $t-1$ are unsorted with respect to party identification.

AMBIVALENCE AND THE STABILITY OF PARTISANSHIP

We assess the individual-level stability of partisan identification using ANES panel data. Relying on the dynamic panel model specified by Green, Palmquist, and Schickler (2002; see also Green & Yoon, 2002), we assume current partisanship to be a function of an individual baseline value, lagged partisanship, and a random component. Thus, our model is as follows:

$$pid_{t,i} = \alpha_i + \beta pid_{t-1,i} + \varepsilon_{t,i} \quad (1)$$

where t denotes the year and i the individual. The parameter α is the individual's partisan baseline value, ε is a random shock at time t for individual i, and β is an autoregressive parameter that controls the rate of decay of any random shocks to partisan identification.[2] In keeping with most of the literature, we treat partisanship (*pid*) as continuous (e.g., Green et al., 2002; but see Clarke & McCutcheon, 2009).

For our purposes, the autoregressive parameter is of greatest interest. When this parameter equals 0, random shocks have no staying power and partisanship returns immediately to its baseline value. By contrast, a parameter of 1, that is, a unit root, generates a "random walk," in which perturbations to the partisan baseline live on forever. As a result, the path of partisanship over time shows no tendency toward recalibration. Intermediate values reflect patterns of decay that last for some time but not in perpetuity.

To illustrate these points, consider Figure 7.1, which simulates an individual whose baseline partisanship (α) is zero, which corresponds, say, to being a strong Democrat. Up until $t = 0$, partisanship is stable, but at this

2. In the context of the model, ε is an error term representing everything not accounted for on the basis of the observed predictors. As the specified model is sparse, including only baseline partisan identity and its lagged value at time $t-1$, the error term represents all events in the environment and in the minds of voters at time t. In effect, it is the difference between the value of party ID at time t and what would be predicted on the basis of the baseline value and the portion due to time $t-1$. This residual carries through to the next period to the extent that the lagged value of party ID has an influence on the contemporaneous value.

point in time a random shock (ε) is introduced that pushes the individual in a Republican direction. The shock might be a major scandal or the fumbling of a crisis in a Democratic administration, but any other piece of negative news about the Democrats (or positive news about the Republicans) could have the same effect. The key question is how quickly the shock decays (or alternatively, how long it lasts). To simplify things, we assume that no new shocks are introduced after $t = 0$. The solid and dashed lines at the top of the graph illustrate the two extreme cases. The solid line corresponds to an autoregressive parameter (β) of zero. At this value, the shock dies out immediately and partisanship returns to the baseline by $t = 1$. The dashed line reflects a parameter value of 1. Here, the shock is perpetuated at its full strength for eternity, meaning that partisanship is permanently displaced from its baseline. Our strong Democrat has become, say, a weak Democrat, and will never again reclaim strong allegiance to the party. Intermediate values of the dynamic parameter illustrate various patterns of decay whereby the partisan baseline is regained after some length of time, but not immediately. As an illustration, we compare the decay curves for $\beta = .25$ and $\beta = .75$. In the former case, Figure 7.1 shows that only 25 percent of the shock remains after one period, only 6 percent after two periods, and so on. In the latter case, we observe that 75 percent of the shock remains after one period, 56 percent after two periods, and the return to baseline occurs only after 15 periods (assuming no further shocks). Decay is slower, thus implying greater instability.

In discussing partisan instability, Box-Steffensmeier and Smith (1996, 1997) make a persuasive argument that scholars should consider heterogeneity in the dynamic parameter. This is consistent with (a) aggregate-level evidence of long "memory" in time series of partisanship (Erikson et al., 2002); (b) individual-level differences in stability across levels of age and political involvement (Miller, 2000); and (c) work on motivated reasoning showing that partisan bias occurs more strongly among political sophisticates and those with strong prior attitudes (Bartels, 2008; Taber & Lodge, 2006).[3] As much as we appreciate the work of Green and his colleagues—who hold that citizens respond *uniformly* to political news—we have repeatedly stated that we believe the American populace to be a heterogeneous lot. We

3. Specifically, Box-Steffensmeier and Smith (1996) assume that the dynamic parameters are drawn from a beta-distribution. With this assumption, the sum of the individual partisanship scores forms a fractionally integrated series, displaying long memory.

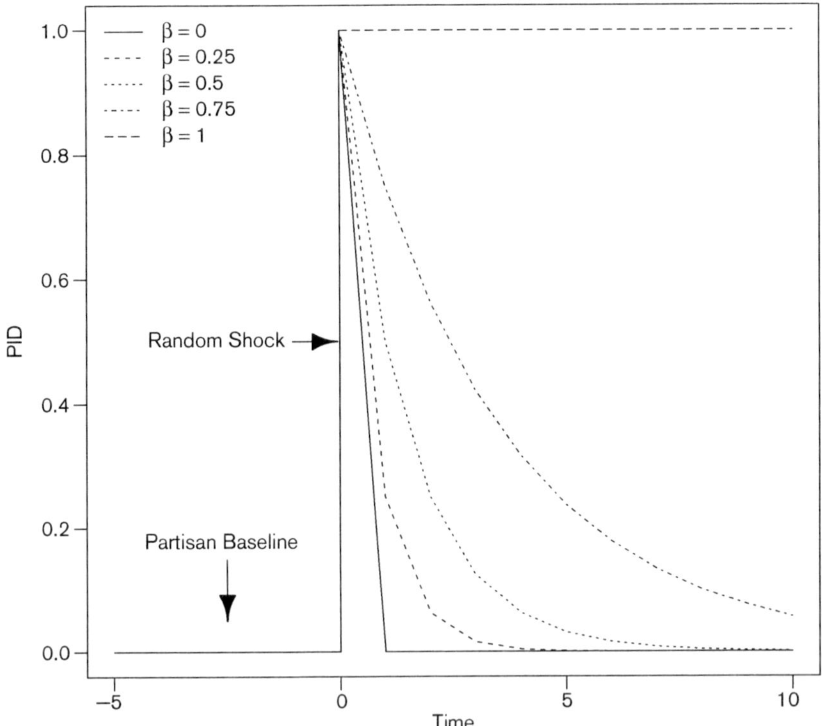

Figure 7.1 Patterns of Decay From Random Shocks to Partisanship.

Notes: The graph shows an individual with a baseline partisanship value of zero. It is assumed that this baseline prevails up until $t = 0$, at which time a random shock of size one is introduced. After this point in time, no new shocks are introduced. The patterns from $t = 1$ to $t = 10$ show how the random shock decays over time as a function of the dynamic parameter β. Decay is immediate when $\beta = 0$ and does not occur at all when $\beta = 1$. For intermediate values, the decay process will take several time periods, with higher values of β being associated with slower decay.

have shown that partisanship, when it is univalent, produces biased perceptions and inattention to valuable political information. We have also shown that ambivalence can overcome these limitations. In our view, then, perceptions of political events are bound to be heterogeneous, and this is likely to translate into heterogeneity in the autoregressive parameter. We assess this hypothesis using two panel studies from the ANES series, the 1992–94–96 and 1956–58–60 panels. In each case, we stratify the analysis by ambivalence in

TABLE 7.1 *STABILITY OF PARTISAN LOYALTY AMONG UNIVALENT AND AMBIVALENT PARTISANS IN SELECTED ANES PANELS*

	Univalent Partisans			Ambivalent Partisans		
Panel Study	**B**	**SE**	**N**	**B**	**SE**	**N**
56–58–60	.123	.172	376	.324	.233	463
92–94–96	–.033	.377	157	.890	.663	248

Notes: Table entries are autoregressive parameter estimates and their estimated standard errors. Values closer to zero reflect greater partisan stability.

the first wave.[4] We thus assess how an initial state of ambivalence affects the dynamics of partisan identifications.

Estimates of the dynamic parameter for each panel study are shown in Table 7.1, and they strongly support our ambivalence-induced heterogeneity hypothesis.[5] The autoregressive parameter for persistently univalent partisans is close to zero in both panel studies, reflecting a high degree of partisan stability. By comparison, the parameter for ambivalent partisans is much larger, reaching a value of just below .90 in the 1990s panel study and around .30 in the 1950s panel. Thus, whereas shocks die out quickly for univalent partisans,

4. In these analyses, we define ambivalence as holding at least one identity-conflicting partisan reaction, while also holding at least one identity-consistent reaction. Univalent partisanship, then, amounts to holding at least one consistent evaluation and no conflicting considerations. The decision to require at least one consistent reaction is not critical; without it the pattern of results looks much the same.
5. The estimation was patterned after Green et al. (2002) and uses the procedure of Anderson and Hsiao (1982). It has two components, namely the elimination of unidentified parameters and the removal of bias associated with using a lagged dependent variable. In equation (1), the alphas are not identified, as there is not enough data to estimate them (they are so-called incidental parameters). They are eliminated by taking the first difference of equation (1), that is, by estimating

$$pid_{t,i} - pid_{t-1,i} = \beta(pid_{t-1,i} - pid_{t-2,i}) + (\varepsilon_{t,i} - \varepsilon_{t-1,i})$$

To remove the bias associated with using lagged dependent variables in the model, Anderson and Hsiao propose, among other things, using pid_{t-2} as an instrumental variable. Doing this allows one to estimate the model with a minimum of three panel waves, the typical time span of ANES panel studies.

they show considerable staying power for ambivalent partisans.[6] In sum, the evidence is consistent with the idea that bouts of ambivalence may cause partisans to change their loyalties. We turn now to the question of *how* such changes occur.

POLITICAL ISSUES AND PARTISAN DYNAMICS

When elites debate public policies, partisan attachments become activated, and these attachments constrain the policy choices that individuals make (Zaller, 1992). In Chapter 4, we demonstrated that this is especially true among univalent partisans. Using panel data from the 2008 presidential election, we showed that over the course of the campaign, univalent Democrats shifted their preferences to the left and univalent Republicans shifted theirs to the right. This form of mass polarization is consistent with Zaller's (1992) elite-driven model of public opinion and with theories of motivated reasoning proposed by social and political psychologists (Lord et al., 1979; Redlawsk, 2002; Taber & Lodge, 2006). It is also consistent with several studies demonstrating that when citizens dynamically adjust their policy preferences and party identifications to achieve greater consistency, they are more likely to bring the former into line with the latter than vice versa (Carsey & Layman, 2006; Dancey & Goren, 2010; Layman & Carsey, 2002; Lenz, 2009; Levendusky, 2009; cf. Abramowitz & Saunders, 1998; Putz, 2002). Our experimental studies in Chapter 4 reinforce this finding and suggest that univalent partisans may alter their policy preferences in a rather reflexive manner (a finding not out of line with the traditional view of partisan identification; e.g., Campbell et al., 1960).

Despite its strong empirical basis, the unmoved mover thesis is subject to two important constraints. First, the occurrence of dynamic updating depends on the presence of elite debate about an issue. Dancey and Goren (2010) measured the amount of media attention devoted to several issues during President Clinton's first term in office. They report that health care reform, which was the dominant policy emphasis during Clinton's first 2 years, was subject to more than 500 stories on network television during

6. For the 1990s panel, we also looked at the effects of political interest and sophistication on the autoregressive parameter. Performing a median split on interest produces parameter estimates of .38 for the low-interest group and .10 for the high-interest group. For political sophistication, a median split produces a more dramatic contrast: an estimate of .89 for the low-knowledge group and of .10 for the high-knowledge group.

1993–1994, but to only 10 stories during 1995–1996 (after Congress failed to pass a health care bill). Affirmative action, by contrast, received almost no media coverage in 1993–1994 but spiked in 1995–1996 as a result of relevant Supreme Court rulings and Clinton's "mend it don't end it" response. Dancey and Goren documented the occurrence of dynamic updating (i.e., reciprocal causation) between party ID and policy preferences on health care reform from 1993 to 1994, but not between 1995 and 1996 (i.e., once the issue was settled in Congress and the media ceased reporting on it). Specifically, during the former period, Republican partisanship led to opposition to the Clinton reforms, and this opposition reinforced Republican partisanship. Updating occurred on affirmative action as well, but only in the latter part of Clinton's first term (when it was extensively covered in the media). Dynamic adjustments in political beliefs and partisan attachments are thus made only when such inconsistencies are salient in people's minds, a finding in line with decades of work in psychology on "cognitive accessibility" (e.g., Fazio, 1995).

A second boundary condition to the unmoved mover thesis is that the updating process involves *mutual* influence, such that "partisanship and issue attitudes both cause and change each other" (Carsey & Layman, 2006, p. 465; Carmines, McIver, & Stimson 1987; Dancy & Goren, 2010; Franklin & Jackson, 1983; Johnston, 2006; Page & Jones, 1979). In line with the unmoved mover thesis, party-based changes in policy preference are more frequent than policy-based changes in party ID. That is, when party and issues collide, the latter are typically adjusted to accommodate the former (Levendusky, 2009). However, the reverse causal process—reflecting the impact of issues on party—occurs among citizens for whom a given policy issue is personally important and who are aware of party differences on that issue (Carsey & Layman, 2006). Thus, among policy-specific activists, issue positions are more stable than party attachments.

Both age and general political involvement also moderate the direction of causal influence between party ID and policy preferences. Consistent with evidence that party ID strengthens with age (e.g., Converse, 1966), Miller (2000) demonstrated that the parental and offspring cohorts in the Youth-Parent Socialization Panel Study exhibited contrasting patterns of dynamic updating. On the issue of whether the federal government should assure the availability of jobs and a good standard of living, the direction of influence favored partisan loyalty as a "cause" by a 2:1 ratio among parents; by contrast, the ratio in the offspring cohort was close to 1:1. More dramatic age-related differences were observed on the Vietnam War issue. As before, party dominated preferences among the parents; in the offspring cohort, however, attitudes on Vietnam dominated party ID by a nearly 2:1 ratio. Miller also finds that party constrains policy preferences among habitual voters, but that in many instances—in particular on cultural issues such as civil rights—policy preferences are more likely to drive changes in party ID among *nonvoters*. Miller (2000, p. 130) concluded that "whichever analytic ordering we might choose would be inappropriate for some people at least some of the time. This underlies the crucial recognition that any optimal ordering will, as with virtually all models, only be the best 'average' fit for a heterogeneous population."

In this last section of the chapter, we examine whether partisan ambivalence, ceteris paribus, is a determinant of heterogeneity in causal processes. Specifically, our model predicts that among univalent partisans, discrepancies at time $t - 1$ between party identification and policy preferences should be resolved at time t by changes in the latter (i.e., policy positions should be brought into line with prior partisan attachments). By contrast, we expect that among ambivalent partisans, discrepancies between substantive preferences and party ID will be resolved by changes to the latter. These expectations are grounded in the empirical work presented throughout this book, especially in the finding from Chapter 4 that preference updating among univalent partisans is driven largely by partisan identity.

In keeping with the idea that dynamic updating is most likely to occur when a political issue is debated by partisan elites and given widespread coverage in the media, we focus our investigation on two political "issues" that were salient in national politics in 1992: health care reform and the general value of moral traditionalism. As we noted earlier, reform of the health care system was Bill Clinton's top legislative priority during his first 2 years in office, and the issue received extensive media attention (Dancey & Goren, 2010). At the same time, the partisan system had been undergoing a "secular realignment"—focused first on race but branching out in the 1980s and 1990s to include a variety of cultural domains—in which changes in the policy positions of the parties gradually led to changes in the basis and distribution of partisan loyalties in the electorate (Abramowitz & Saunders, 1998). As Hetherington and Weiler (2009) argue in their book *Authoritarianism and Polarization in American Politics*, the Republicans, in an effort to reshape electoral competition dominated by the Democrats since the 1930s, adopted a number of emotionally laden symbolic concerns, including those related to race and ethnicity, crime, law and order, religion, feminism, and family structure (for highly readable discussions of the origins of this realignment, see Perlstein 2001, 2008).

The Republican Party cultivated a set of appeals on these issues that resonated with voters who at the time were disproportionately Democrats, setting in motion the rise of moral traditionalism as a defining basis of partisan conflict. Pat Buchanan's speech at the 1992 Republican National Convention in Houston crisply laid out the competing sides in the "culture war." He declared:

> we stand with [President Bush] for the freedom to choose religious schools, and we stand with him against the amoral idea that gay and lesbian couples should have the same standing in law as married men and women. We stand with President Bush for right-to-life and for voluntary prayer in the public schools. And we stand against putting our wives and daughters and sisters into combat units of the United States Army. And we stand, my friends, with President Bush in favor of the right of small towns and communities to control the raw sewage of pornography that so terribly pollutes our popular culture... Friends, this election is about more than who gets what. It is about who we are. It is about what we believe and what we stand for as Americans. There is a *religious war* going on in this country. It is a *cultural war*, as critical to the kind of nation we shall be as the Cold War itself. For this war is for the soul of America (emphasis added).

Buchanan's speech made it clear that the Republican Party stood for traditional morals and that the Democrats were the party of secularism and tolerance. This division also helped the Republicans to define Bill Clinton himself, who protested the Vietnam War, smoked pot, and admitted on national television to having extramarital affairs. In her convention speech, Marilyn Quayle, the vice-president's wife, amplified this view of Clinton by quipping that "not everyone demonstrated, dropped out, took drugs, joined in the sexual revolution, or dodged the draft." Hillary Clinton also failed to fit the traditional mold of First Lady. She took her husband's last name only after he was elected president, and she was the only First Lady to maintain her own professional career up until the Clintons entered the White House. She also made a number of inflammatory remarks about traditional marriage during the campaign, stating on television that "I suppose I could have stayed home and baked cookies and had teas, but what I decided to do was fulfill my profession." In touting his wife's abilities—and signaling his own view of the changing role of women—Bill Clinton stated that in electing him, the nation would be getting "two for the price of one," indicating that Hillary would be, as her critics charged, "co-president." In sum, as the parties and candidates cultivated distinct cultural images and staked out different positions on gay rights, abortion, and the role of women, the public began to view party differences along the dimension of moral traditionalism.[7]

If 1992 thus represented a defining moment for culture-based partisan politics, citizens during this period are likely to have adjusted their cultural preferences and/or partisan attachments to reduce the inconsistency between them. Our interest is in whether any such sorting produced greater instability in party identification among ambivalent than univalent partisans. Specifically, we expected that *unsorted* ambivalent partisans—that is, those for whom long-term loyalties were out of sync with preferences on the contemporary issues of health care reform and moral traditionalism—would engage in dynamic updating by altering their partisan loyalties to accommodate their substantive opinions.

Figure 7.2 displays the percentage of Republican and Democratic respondents in the 1992–94–96 ANES panel study with unsorted preferences in 1992 on the two focal issues. Unsorted respondents are Democrats who opposed health care reform or supported moral traditionalism, and Republicans who supported health care reform or opposed moral traditionalism.[8] As the graph illustrates, about a quarter of the public held out-of-sync preferences on health care reform, and about a third held out-of-sync preferences on moral traditionalism. Democrats were better sorted on both issues, though the differences are small.

To test the hypothesis that issue-based partisan change is most likely to occur among ambivalent partisans with unsorted preferences at time $t-1$ (i.e., in 1992), we created a measure of instability in partisan loyalty from

7. In a clever experimental test of this proposition, Hetherington and Weiler (2009) made either cultural politics (i.e., gay rights) or New Deal issues (i.e., government spending) salient prior to having respondents report their perceptions of ideological differences between the parties. They found that the public perceived the parties as substantially more polarized when gay rights was salient than when government spending was salient.

8. Orientations on moral traditionalism were measured by four items included in most ANES surveys since 1986 (e.g. "Newer lifestyles contribute to society's breakdown"). Attitudes toward health insurance reform were measured with a single item asking about the desirability of public versus private health insurance. To operationalize sorted and unsorted citizens, we took the median split on moral traditionalism and categorized above the median scores as conservative and below the median scores as liberal. For health insurance, we divided the seven-point scale into three categories with the middle value indicating moderate preferences, and the upper and lower three values indicating conservative and liberal preferences, respectively.

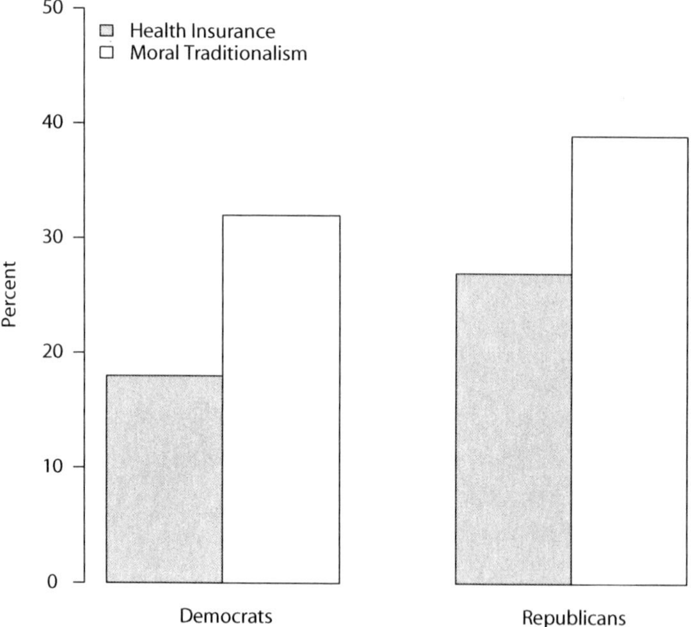

Figure 7.2 Proportion of Unsorted Partisans on Health Care Reform and Moral Traditionalism, 1992 ANES.

1992 to 1994 such that no change = 0 and change from one party category to either Independent or (less frequently) the opposite party = 1. We modeled this dichotomous indicator on the basis of partisan ambivalence and our standard package of controls. The three panels of Figure 7.3 show the predicted probability of partisan change from 1992 to 1994 based on the probit models in Table A7.1. Panel A presents the results for univalent and ambivalent partisans on both issues, separately for those with sorted and unsorted preferences in 1992. As one would expect, the partisan loyalties of sorted respondents changed very little over the 2-year period. Even among ambivalent partisans, sorted respondents exhibited a great deal of partisan stability (about 90 percent across the two time periods). Similarly, univalent partisans with unsorted preferences (on either issue) exhibited very little partisan change (below 5 percent).

As expected, it is ambivalent partisans with unsorted preferences that changed the most. For example, the probability of partisan change among ambivalent partisans with unsorted health care preferences in 1992 was .34; this figure dwarfs the corresponding change likelihoods for sorted ambivalent partisans (.11), unsorted univalent partisans (.02), and sorted univalent partisans (.05).[9] The results are the same for moral traditionalism, where the likelihood that unsorted ambivalent partisans updated their partisan identities is .21. This is more than twice the rate of predicted change for sorted ambivalent partisans (.08); more than four times the rate for unsorted univalent partisans (.05); and ten times that for sorted univalent partisans (.02; all differences between unsorted ambivalent partisans and the other groups are highly reliable, *ps* < .01). In sum, for ambivalent but not univalent partisans, change in partisan loyalty occurs in the service of accommodating salient policy preferences.

How did the traditional explanatory variables fare in conditioning partisan change? Panels B and C of Figure 7.3 present the predicted change probabilities based on unsorted/sorted preferences on health care reform (Panel B) and moral traditionalism (Panel C). Looking first at Panel B, we can see that partisan change was considerably more likely among partisan leaners, the ill informed, and those professing little interest in politics. However, the effects were considerably smaller than that for ambivalence. For example, the difference in the predicted likelihood of partisan change between ill-informed and sophisticated respondents with unsorted preferences on health care reform is .09 (the comparable effect for ambivalence is .34). The partisan change likelihoods for moral traditionalism, depicted in Panel C of Figure 7.3, show the same pattern. In this case, however, the effect sizes for the traditional engagement variables are comparable to those for ambivalence.

Taking these results together with our findings on party-based change in policy preferences from Chapter 4, we conclude that the nature of dynamic updating (or sorting) depends strongly on partisan ambivalence. Among univalent partisans, discrepancies between party ID and policy preferences are resolved such that the latter are adjusted to accommodate the former. Among ambivalent partisans, causal influence works in the other direction: Partisan loyalty is adjusted to accommodate salient policy preferences. Combined with other evidence presented in the preceding chapters, it appears that partisanship plays a more peripheral role in the belief systems of ambivalent partisans.

SUMMARY AND CONCLUSIONS

There has been a long-standing debate about whether partisanship is a stable quality or something that changes with the political tides. The exchange has sometimes generated caricatures of the American public, such that everyone is

9. All differences between unsorted ambivalent partisans and the other groups are highly reliable (*ps* < .001).

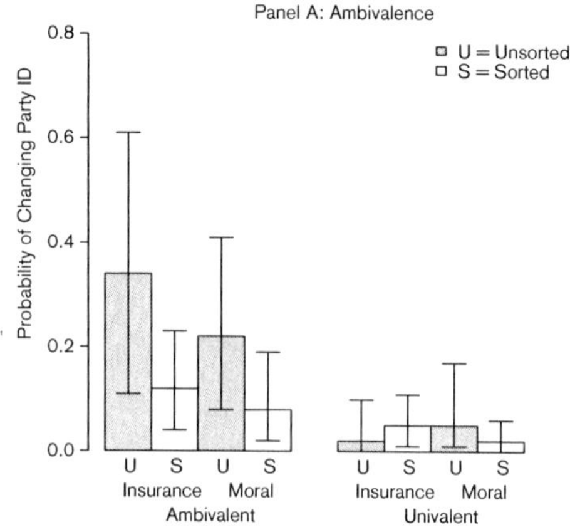

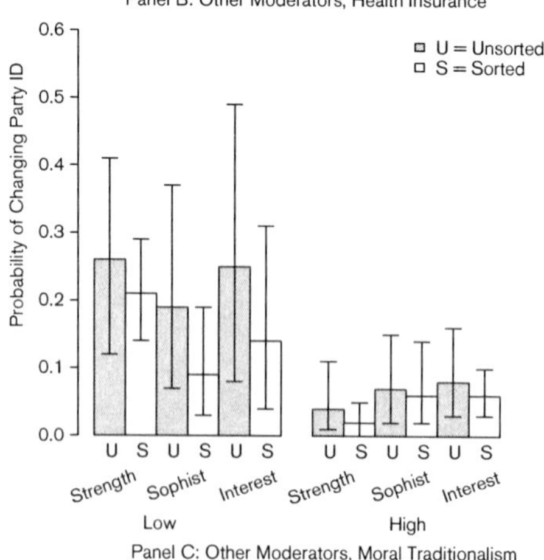

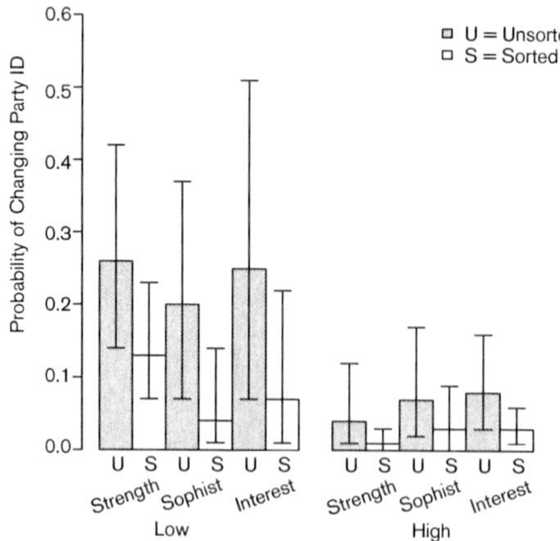

Figure 7.3 Change in Party ID from 1992 to 1994 Among Sorted and Unsorted Partisans on Health Care Reform and Moral Traditionalism, 1992–1994 ANES.

Notes: Figures show the probability of changing one's party identification (either to Independent or the out-party) from 1992 to 1994 as a function of ambivalence, sorted/unsorted status, and the traditional engagement factors.

assumed to be stable or everyone is assumed to change sides now and again. We deem it more plausible that American partisans are a heterogeneous lot. Some are immune to change while others are willing to update their loyalties when events (see Table 7.1) and policy preferences (see Fig. 7.3) dictate that change may be appropriate. Treating the American public as heterogeneous in the manner of its political belief systems is not new (e.g., Box-Steffensmeier & Smith, 1996). What is new is the way in which we fill in the idea of heterogeneity. Rather than focusing on cognitive ability (Sniderman et al., 1991; Zaller, 1992) or the personal importance attached to a given issue (Carsey & Layman, 2006; Hillygus & Shields, 2008), we treat instability as a function of ambivalence. From a normative perspective, party switching is to be applauded only if it has some rational basis. Our analysis indicates that instability occurs when ambivalent partisans hold unsorted preferences on salient dimensions of public policy. Unlike univalent partisans, who as we demonstrated in Chapter 4 exhibit the classic pattern of party-based change in substantive preferences, ambivalent partisans treat their identities as an instrumental means of expressing their policy goals.

Our analysis has two implications for understanding the relationship between party identification and policy orientations. First, it suggests that the main conclusion drawn from prior work on dynamic constraint—in which citizens are hypothesized to simultaneously adjust *both* their identities and their preferences to achieve greater consistency—may be incorrect. In particular, while some scholars have assumed an individual-level process of bidirectional recalibration over time, this need not be the case. Moreover, it cannot be inferred on the basis of results derived from cross-lagged regressions. As with any regression analysis, the cross-lagged coefficients correspond to *average* differences in each model. To infer that the model captures a bidirectional adjustment process at the individual level is an ecological fallacy. Instead, as our results suggest, such findings likely reflect a heterogeneous citizenry characterized by qualitatively distinct processes. This distinction is important because it implies very different models of political cognition with downstream consequences for the normative quality of democratic citizenship. The dynamic constraint model, when interpreted as a model of individual-level cognition, implies a citizenry that is both homogeneous and rational (i.e., party and issues bend toward one another). By contrast, our heterogeneity perspective implies that there are two distinct types of citizens, those for whom partisanship is the driving force and those for whom issues are paramount. Thus, at any given time, the electorate is composed of a majority of blind partisans and a minority of responsive ones.

More broadly, our perspective leads to a novel understanding of the nature of partisan change, as well as when and how it occurs. First, given the status of partisanship as an *identity*, change is unlikely to be a linear, incremental process as the Bayesian revisionist perspective implies. Rather, the potential for change should occur as a discrete window of opportunity, opened temporarily in response to the experience of identity-conflicting evaluation. This critical period allows for open-minded reassessment of the fit between one's identity and substantive preferences, providing the potential for change in the former. However, once this window closes (i.e., when uncongenial partisan evaluations fade), the system returns to equilibrium, and the partisan perceptual screen is reinstated.[10] In the normal state of things (i.e., periods of political quiescence) the system is stable, but large or persistent shocks have the capacity to shift the system to a new partisan equilibrium. Once this occurs, we expect a subsequent reassessment of other belief elements in response to its new gravitational center (i.e., identity).

10. Our model displays a striking similarity to nonlinear models of attitude change proposed in social psychology (e.g., Nowak & Vallacher, 1998), in which persuasion occurs when a threshold of counterattitudinal information is met.

CHAPTER 8

Partisan Ambivalence, Citizen Competence, and American Democracy

Over the past half-century, two broad questions have dominated the study of mass political behavior. First, *how*—by what reasoning processes—do ordinary citizens form their political perceptions, preferences, and choices? And second, how "good" are those judgments from a normative perspective? In pursuing answers to these questions, scholars have learned that most Americans know and care very little about politics (Converse, 1964; Delli Carpini & Keeter, 1996; Neuman, 1986). Quiz a person standing in line to vote, Caplan (2007) writes in *The Myth of the Rational Voter*, and "you are almost sure to conclude, with alarm, that he has no idea what he is doing." In summarizing their work on political information processing, Lau and Redlawsk (2006, p. 13) write that "most decisions are better understood as semiautomatic responses to frequently encountered situations than as carefully weighed probabilistic calculations of the consequences associated with the different alternatives." It seems hard to deny that many citizens make up their political minds on a thin reed of knowledge. Worse, the most crucial pieces of information often elude them. If, as Lupia and McCubbins (1998, p. 2) argue, citizens must "substitute the advice of others for the information they lack," the key normative question becomes whether that advice tends to produce judgments that are in some sense "rational" (e.g., in line with one's values, interests, and relevant facts).[1]

In his book *The Good Citizen*, Schudson (1998, p. 193) argues that "where people necessarily depend on information they cannot authenticate from everyday knowledge, the citizen's capacity for being misled is unbounded." We imagine that few political observers would disagree that politicians and partisan-oriented news jocks slant the political world to their advantage, and in doing so disseminate information of doubtful veracity.[2] Nevertheless, there

1. Or, using Lupia and McCubbins' (1998) own definition, whether citizens understand the implications of their judgments.
2. For a representative smattering of statements by politicians and others deemed untruthful by a nonpartisan watchdog organization, see http://www.politifact.com. Accessed July 1, 2011.

would seem to be a good deal of enthusiasm among political scientists for the claim that ordinary citizens can act more or less rationally while knowing next to nothing about politics. This is said to be made possible by the human mind's adaptive ability to pick out simple cues in the environment (e.g., the advice of others) that substitute effectively for more costly information. It was not our intention to render a firm conclusion on the general claim of "low information rationality" in mass politics (Popkin, 1994). Rather, we sought to formulate and test a motivational theory of adaptive judgment centered on the idea that good citizenship requires critical partisan loyalty.

We acknowledge that voters can and do use a wide range of informational shortcuts in deciding what policy options to support and what electoral choices provide the most attractive outcomes. In many and probably most political judgment contexts, however, we also believe—as we think most political scientists do—that the divide of party identification, Democrats versus Republicans, is the primary perceptual and evaluative yardstick at the public's disposal (Bartels, 2000; Campbell et al., 1960; Goren et al., 2009; Sniderman, 2000). As we noted early and often in the book, partisan loyalty serves as an *anchor* from which adjustments, almost always insufficient ones, are made in judging the political landscape. Whether because partisanship is a product of early affective socialization (Campbell et al., 1960); because the party system constrains the public's menu of choices and attaches well-known, easily identifiable brand names to the competing options (Jackman & Sniderman, 2002); or, as we argue, because citizens simultaneously attempt to make it easy, get it right, and maintain cognitive consistency when forming judgments, partisanship as a heuristic cue stands out in terms of its breadth, inferential power, and cognitive efficiency. For us, then, the key question is whether reliance on partisanship allows citizens to transcend their limited understanding of politics and make judgments in line with their values, interests, and relevant facts.

The evidence amassed in this book indicates that partisan loyalty per se is not a sufficient condition for responsible democratic citizenship. As others have pointed out, without partisanship there is little political involvement, at least not enough to facilitate the discovery of valid decision cues. Thus, without partisanship, attention to politics is lacking, and judgments are perforce suboptimal (Campbell et al., 1960; Pierce & Hagner, 1982). But partisanship seems to ensure that people will view the political world through a crooked lens, leading to a different but equally negative outcome. Accordingly, then, it would appear that people either tune out politics altogether, or they interpret information in a biased manner due to their virtually unbounded proclivity to yield to the pronouncements of copartisan elites. As our chapter-by-chapter review of the evidence will suggest, this is an accurate description of how partisanship typically functions in mass politics. However, our research also suggests that a nontrivial portion of the electorate manages to escape the vicissitudes of apathy or wanton bias, and it is these citizens—these *ambivalent partisans*—that reliably approximate a more desirable standard of citizenship.

In the next section, we review the evidence presented in Chapters 4–7 and render an assessment of the normative utility of partisanship as an informational shortcut. The evidence affirms the major premise of the book: Partisanship comes in qualitatively different forms, with distinct political consequences. Blind partisan loyalty, as the pejorative label implies, facilitates bias and reduces attention to valuable information. Critical loyalty, by doing the opposite, outperforms standard measures of political engagement in leading to good judgments. We will conclude that breaking out of the apathy-versus-bias prison requires critical involvement, and that critical involvement requires *critical partisan loyalty*.

We then entertain a variety of potential objections to our work pertaining to theory, method, and interpretation. Next, we take up the question of why partisan ambivalence is not more prevalent. To preview our argument here, we believe that political institutions tend to incentivize blind rather than critical loyalty by failing to provide citizens with much of a stake in the "correctness" of their judgments. As Caplan (2007) argues, this encourages citizens to gratify their gut (partisan) feelings rather than seek out the truth, as the latter is a costly pursuit with little prospect of affecting political outcomes (see also Downs, 1957). We also believe that the expressive—as opposed to utilitarian—nature of partisan identification leads to a group-centric mindset, facilitating intergroup conflict and activating the need for "positive distinctiveness" (Tajfel & Turner, 1979). These two factors create ideal conditions for what Jacobs and Shapiro (2000, p. iv) call *simulated responsiveness*, in which partisan elites craft particular phrases and presentations to "change public opinion and create the appearance of responsiveness as they pursue their [own] desired policy goals." Among the most important conclusions that we reach in the book is that critical loyalty in the form of ambivalent partisanship—and not individual differences in political knowledge per se—stands as a bulwark against this insidious form of cooptation.

DOES AMBIVALENT PARTISANSHIP PROMOTE GOOD CITIZENSHIP? A REVIEW OF THE EVIDENCE

Our empirical investigation in Chapters 4–7 was motivated by three tasks vital to democratic citizenship: forming preferences about public policy issues, selecting candidates to political office, and holding accurate perceptions of political reality. We will begin with a review of how partisanship—in its distinctive blind and critical forms—influences the accuracy with which citizens perceive key aspects of the *factual* political environment.

Perceptions of Political Reality

As we noted in Chapter 2, bias can be difficult to distinguish from rational differences in the credibility of information (Gerber & Green, 1998, 1999). The problem is that many political perceptions are subjective, allowing for no simple right and wrong answers. Therefore, we examined the extent to which Republicans and Democrats held divergent perceptions of the same set of facts. We focused on economic performance, candidate placements on policy issues, roll-call voting in the US Senate, and changes in crime rates. We chose these factors for three reasons: They have clear factual referents, they are important short-term "dynamic" factors in elections, and relevant items are available in several national surveys.

Beyond easing the determination of accuracy, analyzing perceptions of facts allows us to clearly specify the role that partisanship *should* play in making them: namely, none. The economy does not perform better—and crime rates are not lower—simply because a copartisan happens to occupy the White House. Perceptual differences owing to individuals' partisan identities reflect either flawed reasoning or simple wishful thinking. Nevertheless, in Chapter 5 we found that univalent partisans relied on their status as in- or out-partisans in judging multiple aspects of political reality. In judging economic performance, they relied nearly as much on partisan loyalty as on objective information (i.e., unemployment, gross domestic product [GDP]). Ambivalent partisans, by contrast, relied nearly *ten* times more on the latter than the former. In judging the policy stands of presidential candidates, univalent partisans relied more on the comparatively fallible cue of their own partisan identities than on those of the candidates (i.e., "partisan projection" vs. "ideological inference"). Ambivalent partisans, by contrast, relied 15 times more on the latter. And finally, in making inferences about how their senators voted on key issues, univalent partisans relied equally on projection and ideological inference, whereas ambivalent partisans relied six times more on the latter. In sum, ambivalence led citizens to rely more on valuable information and less on the cue of partisanship when it was inappropriate to do so. The evidence thus paints a picture that blind and critical partisans decipher political reality in strikingly different ways, with clear normative implications.

Preference Formation and Change

The findings for perceptual accuracy were conceptually replicated in our analysis of preference formation and change. Here, we found that while ambivalent partisans formed and updated their policy preferences on the basis of self-interest and values, univalent partisans hued blindly to party cues. For example, the pattern of preference updating among univalent partisans during the 2008 presidential election was one of unadulterated partisan polarization: Univalent Democrats moved to the left on policy issues over the course of the campaign, and univalent Republicans moved to the right. Ambivalent partisans, by contrast, updated their preferences on the basis of economic self-interest: Low-income ambivalent Republicans and Democrats moved to the left on taxes, health care, and prescription drugs, whereas high-income ambivalent Republicans and Democrats moved to the right.[3] It is notable that none of the traditional engagement variables heightened reliance on self-interest (e.g., well-informed citizens were no more likely than the ill informed to update their preferences on the basis of personal economic predicaments).

Our policy experiments provided causal evidence that univalent partisans ignore valuable information when partisan cues are present. When respondents were provided with two policy options without partisan cues, they chose appropriately: Democrats preferred the liberal policy, and Republicans preferred the conservative one. However, when the perverse cues were provided—that is, when Republicans in Congress were said to endorse the liberal policy and the Democrats the conservative policy—respondents assigned to the low-ambivalence condition shifted their support to the policy endorsed by the in-party. By contrast, those assigned to the high-ambivalence condition ignored the inappropriate cues and maintained support for the policy closer to their overall political outlooks.[4]

These results extended to differences in how policy preferences are organized. Among univalent partisans, the covariances among economic

3. We replicated this finding using the 1992–1994 ANES panel study with a broad indicator of personal economic security.

4. According to our theory, this conditional finding can be explained by the belief among ambivalent partisans that such cues are unreliable judgment guides, thereby motivating greater scrutiny of the substantive details. Two additional findings from these studies provide direct support for this interpretation. First, we found that ambivalent partisans derive less judgment confidence from party cues than do univalent partisans. Second, in a surprise recall task, we found that ambivalent partisanship heightened recall for policy facts when party cues were present.

preferences were better accounted for by party attachment than by orientations toward limited government; for ambivalent partisans, the reverse was true. What should we make of this difference in the basis of constraint? In line with other evidence presented in the book, we believe it suggests that the policy preferences of univalent partisans are less a reflection of systematic thought about desired end states (or means) than reflexive accommodations to socialized partisan attachments. As we wrote in Chapter 4, rather than reasoning that "I favor a progressive tax system because I value social equality," univalent partisans seem to reason that "I favor a progressive tax system because I am a Democrat and that's what Democrats favor." While some might hold the latter to be sufficient, when partisan cue-taking becomes wholly detached from social values—and, as we have shown, from material interests and basic facts—it verges on being *politically* vacuous, reflecting little more than the psychological need for positive social identity (see Tajfel & Turner, 1979). While this may facilitate emotional self-regulation, it inevitably leads to the relinquishing of popular control over public policy.

Political Behavior

Beyond the domains of preference and perception, ambivalence alters how voters make their electoral decisions. We learned first that ambivalent partisans have a more difficult time reaching these decisions: They take longer to make up their minds and their choices reflect greater uncertainty. We might expect this complexity to discourage them from participating at all. However, this is not the case: Ambivalent partisans go to the polls just as much as other (attached) citizens. Third, given their lack of faith in the partisan divide as an informational shortcut, the votes of ambivalent partisans are largely a reflection of their policy preferences. This is considerably less true for univalent partisans, for whom party ID is the dominant factor. Rather than switching from party to issues in making their choices, ambivalent partisans could have simply switched from one low-effort cue to another. That is, they could have picked up the judgmental slack by turning to other shortcuts such as retrospective performance evaluations or (in congressional elections) incumbency. While there was some evidence that this was the case in the congressional context, the primary recourse of ambivalent partisans was to vote in line with their policy preferences. As we noted in Chapters 6 and 7, many voters continue to hold policy preferences that do not line up with their partisan attachments (e.g., pro-life Democrats; Republicans who support national health insurance). How do these cross-pressured individuals vote? Do they toe the party line and ignore their policy preferences? Or do they abandon their identities, or split the difference? Our results are interesting in two respects: (a) ambivalence stratified how voters negotiated this conflict; for univalent partisans, party trumped policy; for ambivalent partisans, the reverse obtained, and (b) none of the traditional engagement variables had any influence in moving voters to weigh party less and issues more.

Partisan Change

In our last empirical effort, we demonstrated that ambivalence promotes the staying power of exogenous shocks to one's partisan loyalty. We also demonstrated that it induces heterogeneity in dynamic constraint, the process by which people adjust their policy preferences and party identification to achieve greater mutual consistency. Reflecting the centrality of partisanship in mass belief systems, prior work indicates that such adjustments typically involve changes in substantive preferences to accommodate long-term identities (Carsey & Layman, 2006; Levendusky, 2009). In Chapter 7, we argued that constraint should occur in the other direction—that is, through changes in partisan identity to fit with substantive preferences—when the following criteria were met: Partisanship is of the ambivalent variety; the issue is widely discussed in the media during the period in question (thus being salient in citizens' minds); and policy preferences at time $t - 1$ are unsorted with respect to party identification. Our results indicate that substantial partisan updating occurred under precisely these circumstances and otherwise very little at all. Taking these results together with those on party-based preference change in Chapter 4, we come to the conclusion that the nature of partisanship—social identity versus rational updating—must be understood as fundamentally heterogeneous. The distinction is also highly fluid. As we discuss later, these two groups do not constitute unwavering differences in behavioral scripts; rather, their status is determined dynamically on the basis of a changing political environment and personal experiences of a situational nature (e.g., being unemployed).

OBJECTIONS TO THE MODEL AND THE ANALYSIS

Until now, we have been advocates for our theoretical framework of political judgment. We would like now to raise several potential objections to our work pertaining to matters of theory, method, and interpretation. We first take up the question of whether our measures of ambivalence can be viewed in terms of political sophistication (traditionally defined). If our empirical work can be understood within the context of cognitive ability—rather than, as we believe, on *motivation*—our conceptual edifice falls apart. We then consider (again) the argument that partisan ambivalence is nothing more than the strength of partisan attachment. Next, we discuss the possibility that our general empirical dynamic can be explained by Marcus and colleagues' (2000) theory of affective intelligence. As we noted in Chapters 1–2 and 6, perhaps it is anxiety and not ambivalence that lies at the heart of our results. We next consider the question of political Independents, whom we have excluded throughout the book. Finally, we discuss the problem of circular reasoning in our model. We have argued that attentiveness and objectivity follow from ambivalence, and that people *become* ambivalent in the first place by paying attention to and objectively perceiving party performance.

Are We Measuring Political Sophistication?

As we have stated a number of times in the book, political sophistication has been widely embraced by political scientists as the key moderator of political behavior (Converse, 2000; Delli Carpini & Keeter, 1996; Lau & Redlawsk, 2001; Sniderman et al., 1991). Despite some variability in what different measures capture—for example, "levels of conceptualization," "strata of knowledge and understanding," years of formal education—the standard view is that a small number of *able* citizens are more likely than the ill-informed masses to form their political judgments using complex decision rules that focus on the most diagnostic information. Perhaps, then, our measures of ambivalence are simply (or largely) capturing variation in cognitive ability and general political knowledge. We see two reasons to consider this a serious possibility. First, and most directly, the correlations between political sophistication and our two count measures of ambivalence are not inconsiderable: $r = .31$ for the number of identity-conflicting reactions and $r = .37$ for the number of identity-consistent reactions.[5] Second, some scholars have interpreted the sheer number of open-ended responses to the likes/dislikes questions—rather than their specific content—as an indicator of political sophistication (Smith, 1989).

However, there are four observations suggesting that this is probably not a serious worry. First, in all of our findings using observational methods, we controlled for interest in politics, partisan strength, and political knowledge itself. Second, our measures of ambivalence included in the 2008 ANES panel study produced the same results (as the count measures) but were not as strongly correlated with sophistication ($r = .16$ for both ambivalence components). Third, if our results reflected sophistication, the sign on the coefficients for identity conflicting and consistent reactions in our statistical models

5. Recall that the number of identity-conflicting reactions is the sum of the number of dislikes toward the in-party and the number of likes toward the out-party. The number of identity-consistent reactions is the sum of the number of likes toward the in-party and the number of dislikes toward the out-party.

would be the same (as the two ambivalence components are both positively correlated with sophistication). However, this is rarely the case; as our theory expects, these coefficients are routinely of opposite sign (i.e., a large number of identity-conflicting reactions indicates *high* ambivalence, whereas a large number of identity-consistent reactions indicates *low* ambivalence).[6] Last, in two policy studies in Chapter 4, we experimentally manipulated ambivalence, and the results replicated the main empirical dynamic observed in the observational data. In sum, the evidence does not comport with the argument that our findings reflect political sophistication.

Are We Measuring Partisan Strength?

Perhaps, however, our ambivalence measures are picking up on something else. The results in Chapter 5 indicate that partisans with the strongest attachments engage in the most perceptual distortion. They should therefore be less likely than other partisans to hold uncongenial party evaluations. The data support this hypothesis, but only weakly. The correlations between the standard (folded-over) measure of partisan strength and our conflicting and consistent components of ambivalence are –.09 and .22, respectively. Strong partisans are therefore not immune from finding fault with their own party (or crediting the other party when it is deserving). Ambivalence and strength were also consistently associated with different empirical patterns: While both influenced levels of bias (ambivalence negatively and strength positively), only ambivalence was associated with deliberative political thinking.

What if, however, the political consequences of ambivalence are limited to those with weak partisan attachments (and fade out as partisan strength increases)? This would damage our argument about the centrality of ambivalence in American politics. To determine whether the strongly attached are immune from the consequences of ambivalence, we re-estimated two models, one for economic perceptions (from Chapter 5) and the other for voting in presidential elections (from Chapter 6).[7] The results of the perception analysis, shown in the panels of Figure 8.1, reflect the inclusion of two three-way interactions: GDP growth x partisan strength x ambivalence, and party identification x partisan strength x ambivalence (all lower order interactions were also included). As Panel A shows, ambivalence reduced the impact of party ID on economic retrospections *equally* across the three levels of partisan strength. This was not the case, however, for reliance on changes in GDP: Here, as

6. All tabular results are provided in the Appendix.

7. Both analyses were conducted on pooled data from the 1980–2004 ANES.

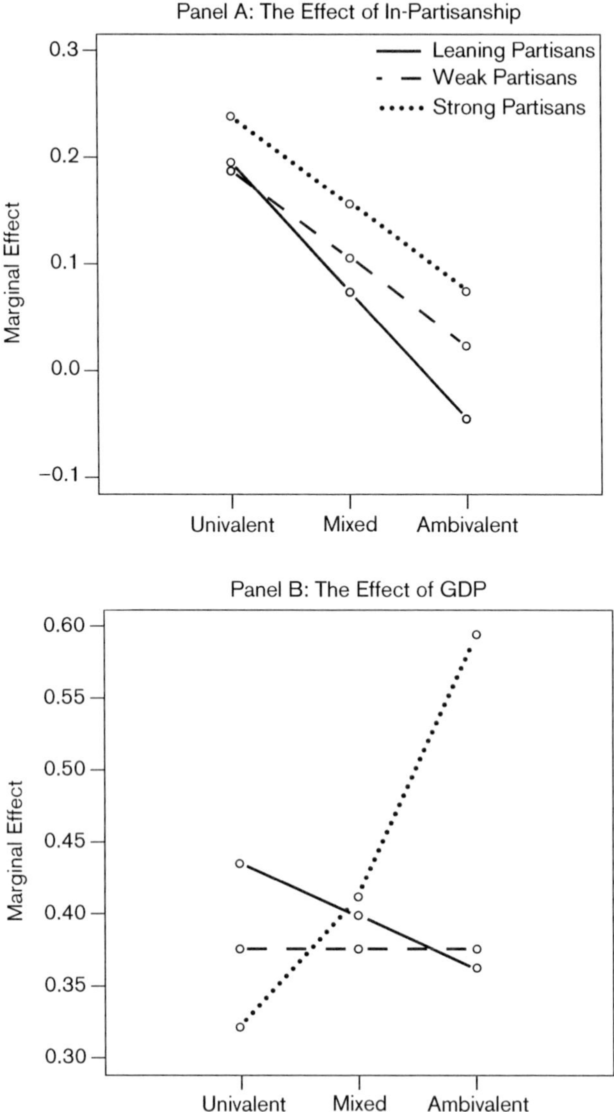

Figure 8.1 Marginal Effects of Party Identification and GDP Growth on Economic Retrospections, by Partisan Ambivalence and Partisan Strength, 1980–2004 ANES.

Notes: Figures show the estimated marginal effects of partisanship and economic changes on economic retrospections across levels of partisan ambivalence, for each level of partisan strength. GDP, gross domestic product.

Panel B demonstrates, it was *strong* partisans who were most—not the least—affected by ambivalence.

The vote choice models are shown in the three panels of Figure 8.2. Here, we examined whether the role of ambivalence in depressing party voting and facilitating issue voting depends on partisan strength. Panel A shows that ambivalence weakens the influence of partisanship among all three groups. Even among strong partisans, the marginal impact of party ID declines from nearly 1.0 to .60. Moreover, like in the perception analysis, Panels B and C indicate that ambivalence promotes issue voting more among strong (vs. weak or lean) partisans. In sum, there is little evidence that the political consequences of ambivalence are limited to weaker partisans. Its effect on

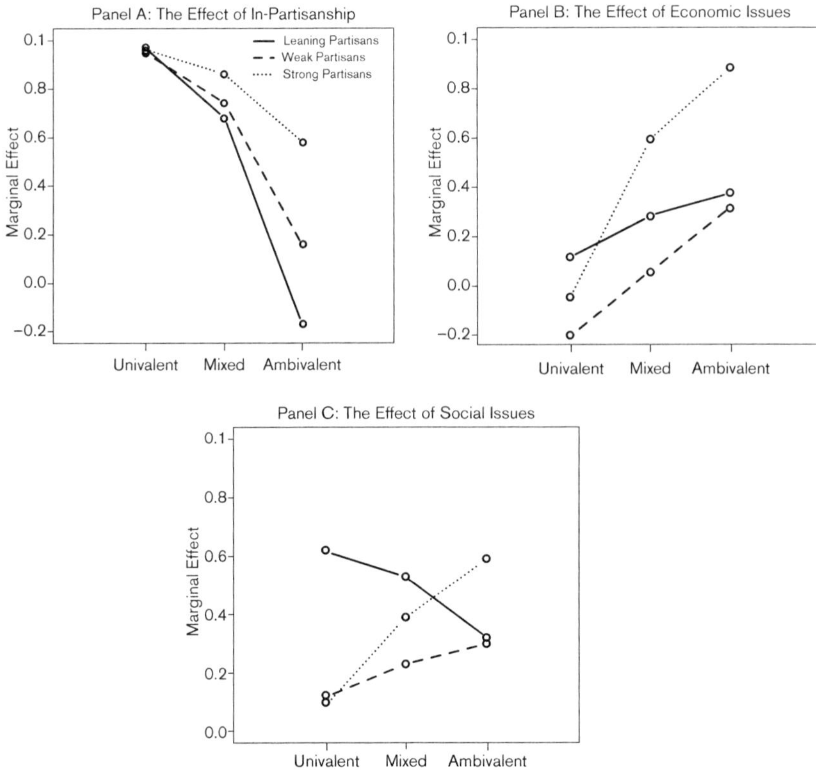

Figure 8.2 Effects of Party Identification and Policy Issues on Presidential Evaluations, by Partisan Strength and Partisan Ambivalence, 1980–2004 ANES.

Notes: Figures show the estimated marginal effects of partisanship, economic, and social issues on the probability of a Republican vote across levels of partisan ambivalence, for each level of partisan strength.

party ID as a heuristic cue is roughly evenly distributed in the partisan electorate, and its compensating dynamic—that is, shifting judgmental weight onto more diagnostic considerations—is, if anything, most powerful among strongly attached citizens. An in-depth exploration of this question is beyond the scope of the book. However, given their fervent loyalty, it makes sense that strong partisans experience the most psychological conflict as a result of holding identity-conflicting evaluations.

Are We Measuring Anxiety?

Our theory is not the only one featuring *motivation* (rather than ability) as the primary driver of deliberative political thinking. Marcus and colleagues' affective intelligence theory (AIT; 1988, 1993, 2000, 2010) holds that voters will think more carefully about their political options when they experience anxiety. In the realm of electoral decision making (the turf on which the theory was developed and has mostly been applied), AIT predicts that citizens will abandon party as the basis of vote choice in favor of policy preferences and other contemporary information when anxiety signals that one's "standing decision" should be reexamined. In Chapter 6, we empirically contrasted this anxiety-focused expectation with our hypothesis that issue voting depends more broadly on the pattern of identity conflicting and consistent evaluations.

As we reported, the results favored ambivalence theory. The experience of identity-conflicting emotion led to a shift from party to issues as the basis of vote choice, whereas identity-consistent emotion shifted the balance in the other direction. What seems to matter is not whether voters experience one particular discrete emotion (e.g., anxiety), but whether their emotional (and cognitive) reactions to the parties dovetail or clash with their partisan identities. For AIT to account for the findings reported in Chapter 6, one would have to believe that identity-conflicting emotions of any discrete type, including enthusiasm toward the other party, activate the surveillance system. Given that past work on AIT has consistently featured only anxiety in this regard, we think it would be a reach to claim that any identity-conflicting emotion can function in this way.

Where does this leave AIT? Despite the fact that our critical tests seem to disconfirm its validity, we believe this is an unwarranted conclusion. In particular, both theories may be "correct" but under different circumstances. AIT may provide a better explanation of heterogeneity in the moments when anxiety is experienced as a full-throttle, physiological event (as opposed to indicating in a survey whether a candidate has "ever made you anxious"). When in the active throws of anxiety, it is adaptive to set aside habit and focus on the most important information (e.g., Kahneman, 2011). Over time, however, the urgency of an emotional reaction decays, leaving a residual *evaluative* response. If this evaluative response is out of step with one's partisan attachment, it should engender ambivalence, and thereby instigate a change in the processes by which politics is perceived and evaluated. Under these circumstances, and all of those in which anxiety is irrelevant, we believe that the ambivalence model provides the better explanation.

What About Independents?

Throughout the book, we have ignored the fact that the American public consists of more than partisans alone. Some Americans—about 10 percent if one considers as partisans those who "lean" toward one party or the other, as we did—do not feel that they belong to either political party.[8] For two reasons, we excluded "true" Independents from our analyses in Chapters 4–6. First, we wanted to highlight the contrast between univalent and ambivalent partisans, while simultaneously reporting on the effects of the traditional engagement variables. This was a complicated enough task without introducing another dimension to the discussion. Second, as partisan ambivalence is technically undefined for Independents, including them would have further complicated our statistical models. It is appropriate, however, to consider the (remote) possibility that Independents epitomize the ideal citizen to an even greater degree than ambivalent partisans, or more realistically, to determine whether their judgments compare favorably to those of univalent partisans.

---

8. How large the segment of Independents looms depends to a considerable extent on how one defines them. Some scholars include Independents that "lean" toward either the Democrats or Republicans, while others include only those who admit to having no major party attachment whatsoever (i.e., "true" Independents). When defined in the more restrictive manner, evidence from the ANES suggests that the share of Independents grew only modestly between 1952 and 2008, from 6 to 11 percent. When the definition includes "leaners," the share of Independents increased from 23 to 39 percent, a more significant shift. There are good reasons, however, to exclude leaning partisans from the Independent category. As Petrocik (1974) has convincingly demonstrated, these individuals often turn out to behave in a more partisan fashion than so-called weak partisans (e.g., they are more inclined to vote a straight ticket). For this reason, we have consistently removed leaners from our definition of Independents and included them as partisans.

Some scholars see Independents as relatively sophisticated individuals who, unburdened by partisan loyalties, can act as fully emancipated citizens (e.g., Burnham, 1970; Dalton & Wattenberg, 2002; Ladd & Hadley, 1975; Sorauf, 1975). The dominant view, however, is that they are a relatively uninformed and unengaged bunch, hardly the kind of citizen that one would consider "virtuous" (e.g., Campbell et al., 1960, Green et al., 2002; Keith, Magleby, Nelson, Orr, & Westleye, 1992). We had little faith that true Independents would outshine ambivalent partisans in the quality of their perceptions, preferences, and behaviors. Indeed, the evidence—indirect as it is—runs squarely in the opposite direction. However, as our findings in Chapters 4–6 indicate, univalent partisans are not the beacons of good citizenship either, and it is unclear (save for political participation) how well they stack up against unattached citizens. This is an important question, for it allows us to put a finer point on the normative utility of the most prevalent form of partisan attachment in American politics. In Appendix C, we present an extensive empirical analysis comparing the judgments of Independents to those of univalent and ambivalent partisans. The upshot is that, on average, univalent partisans fare no better than Independents on most political judgment tasks. In fact, compared to univalent partisans, we find that Independents are more likely to (1) hold accurate economic perceptions, especially when accountability matters most (i.e., when reality disconfirms partisan expectations); (2) hold accurate perceptions of the policy locations of presidential candidates; and (3) rely more on (social) policy preferences in casting their votes for president. On this basis, limited as it is, it appears that true Independents are in a better position than univalent partisans—or at the least in an equally good one—to send policy signals to elected officials and to hold them accountable for their performance in office.

Circular Reasoning

Measurement problems aside, one might strike a deeper blow by reading into our conceptual framework a simple circularity: Accurate perceptions of performance give rise to ambivalence, and ambivalence instigates accurate perceptions. We do not disagree with this characterization because we believe the reality is one in which ambivalence is both a cause and a consequence of normatively desirable political judgment. Conflict is unpleasant; we thus expect people to seek an equilibrium of correspondence between their partisan identities and party evaluations. Attaining this equilibrium is straightforward if the political environment favors one's own party. What happens, however, when the tide has turned in the other direction? While the most likely response may be to call the perceptual screen into service, motivated reasoning is not unbounded. When a party is plagued by a long stretch of difficulties, efforts to maintain this equilibrium become untenable. At some point even the most resistant of individuals will succumb, turning partisanship into ambivalent partisanship.

We expect that individuals will initially perceive the world through a partisan lens, distorting reality to maintain a good fit between identity and evaluations. Sometimes, however, the political environment will create "facts" that are so formidable that not even the strongest perceptual screen can distort them. If these facts speak against one's own party, the seed of ambivalence may be planted. Once this occurs, partisans will begin to view the political world in a more circumspect way, driven by inchoate doubt that partisan cues provide a reliable guide to understanding political reality. As individuals become further dislodged from this framework, they should look for alternative judgment strategies. If the political environment continues to be fertile ground for ambivalence (e.g., if the in-party fails to turn things around), identity-conflicting reactions should strengthen and crystallize.

The process is much like that of a snowball rolling down a hill. As it rolls, it picks up more and more snow. In a similar manner, ambivalence tends to beget ambivalence. The snowball ceases to pick up snow when it comes to rest against an obstacle; the snowballing nature of ambivalence terminates when the political environment changes. If one's own party starts to perform well, it is precisely because ambivalence fosters veridical perception that partisans will quickly note the improvement and come to a new (univalent) equilibrium.

All that said, the astute methodologist might argue that ambivalence is simply endogenous to some of the outcomes we have sought to model—rendering our estimates biased and untrustworthy. Nowhere does this potential problem loom larger than in Chapter 5, where one could object that the very perceptions we seek to predict on the basis of ambivalence are causally antecedent to it. For instance, consider economic retrospections. We have argued that ambivalent partisans see economic reality for what it is, even if that reality is unflattering to their group attachments. But is it not just as plausible that accurate perceptions cause partisans to become ambivalent in the first place? Which way does the causal arrow run?

Problems of endogeneity are notoriously difficult to resolve; however, we believe there may be a way around the problem. Our strategy is to rid the analyses of those respondents whose ambivalence—as measured by the open-ended likes/dislikes questions—reflects considerations close to the perceptions that we seek to explain. For example, in our analysis of economic retrospections, we set aside all individuals whose ambivalence was rooted in the economy. This meant removing any individual who commented on the state of the economy (prosperity, inflation, employment, wages), who made references to government spending, the budget, the value of the dollar, or economic policy.[9] The resulting subsample should consist of individuals for whom the balance between dominant and conflicting considerations is exogenous to the outcome of interest (i.e., economic retrospections). This should remove the worst of the endogeneity in our ambivalence measures vis-à-vis dependent variables related to economic judgments.

The question is whether this procedure changes our results. Figure 8.3 presents two graphs side by side: the analysis from Figure 5.1, in which the open-ended responses were purged of economy-oriented comments (see left panel), and an analysis in which economic comments are not purged (see right panel). As the figure shows, the results are virtually identical: In both cases, ambivalence decreases the role of party and heightens the role of unemployment and GDP growth on economic perceptions. We consider this strong evidence that the circularity built into our conceptual framework does not distort our empirical findings. Of course, Figure 8.3 speaks to only one of the many analyses in the book. However, given the prominence of open-ended comments about the economy (see Table 3.3), we expect endogeneity problems to be particularly severe in modeling economic perceptions. That our results do not materially change across the two panels should help to inspire confidence in our other findings.

Finally, we supplemented our analyses of cross-sectional data with both experiments (which eliminate endogeneity through random assignment) and panel studies (which alleviate endogeneity concerns through the use of lagged variables). In Chapter 4, we demonstrated that *manipulated* ambivalence had the same effects on preference formation as *measured* ambivalence. In Chapters 4, 5, and 6 we replicated our cross-sectional findings with panel data from the 1992–1994 and 2008 ANES. In these analyses, partisan ambivalence was measured *before* relevant dependent variables in time (typically by 6–9 months), thus eliminating the possibility that the latter influenced the former. That our results coincided across diverse methodological approaches speaks to the robust nature of the partisan ambivalence dynamic.

IMPLICATIONS FOR CITIZEN COMPETENCE AND AMERICAN DEMOCRACY

What do our findings imply about citizen competence and the prospects of responsible self-government? We believe they present a mixture of good and bad news. The bad news is that univalent partisanship is by nearly any

9. To be precise, we counted the following ANES master codes as economic references: 601–602, 605–606, 627, 901–904, 926–956, 1046, and 1080.

standard unhealthy for democracy. As we have documented, it facilitates severe biases in the perception of political reality (Chapter 5); it leads citizens to ignore their material interests and values in forming, updating, and organizing their policy preferences (Chapter 4); and it leads them to privilege partisan attachment over substantive preferences in the voting booth, especially when the two factors conflict (Chapter 6). An electorate composed of such individuals is incapable of sending meaningful policy signals to elites or holding them accountable for their performance in office. The good news is that ambivalent partisans approximate the type of critical, systematic, and open-minded thought praised by democratic theorists (e.g., Dewey, 1933/1997; Mill, 1859/1998). Another piece of good news is that contrary to conventional wisdom, poor citizen performance is not inextricably linked to a lack of formal education or political knowledge. In fact, our results quite clearly indicate that cognitive capability is not the primary problem.

Rational Ignorance and Hedonic Goals

Instead, what is at issue is *motivation*. As Downs (1957) argued, once a person comes to a confident decision, there is little practical reason to devote further effort to the task. The main problem, as we see it, is that a majority of citizens are able to come to confident political decisions on the basis of partisan cues, even when those cues have no logical value, or when they contradict the individual's values and interests. Why should this be the case? The answer at one level is that by toeing the party line, citizens can subjectively maximize the three primary goals of political judgment: making it easy, getting it right, and maintaining cognitive consistency—a feat not otherwise readily accomplished. At a deeper level, we believe the answer lies in the conjunction of the logic of rational ignorance and individuals' *hedonic goals*.

The concept of rational ignorance holds that people balance the costs and benefits of acquiring political information (Downs, 1957). As the instrumental benefit of casting a well-informed vote is essentially zero (elections almost never turn on the decision of any one voter), it makes sense to remain ignorant and to form one's political beliefs on the basis of other motives, such as their hedonic implications. In particular, if people pay no real cost for engaging in delusional thinking, they are free to gravitate to those beliefs that provide attractive *psychological* benefits, such as those linked to siding with the partisan in-group (see Herek, 1986; Katz, 1960; Smith, Bruner, & White, 1956). As Caplan (2007, p. 132) argues, "when a person puts on his voting hat, he does not have to give up practical efficacy in exchange for self-image, because he has no practical efficacy to give up in the first place."

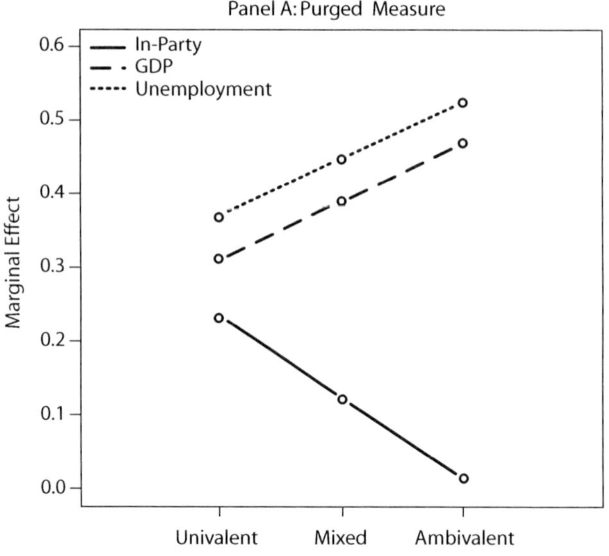

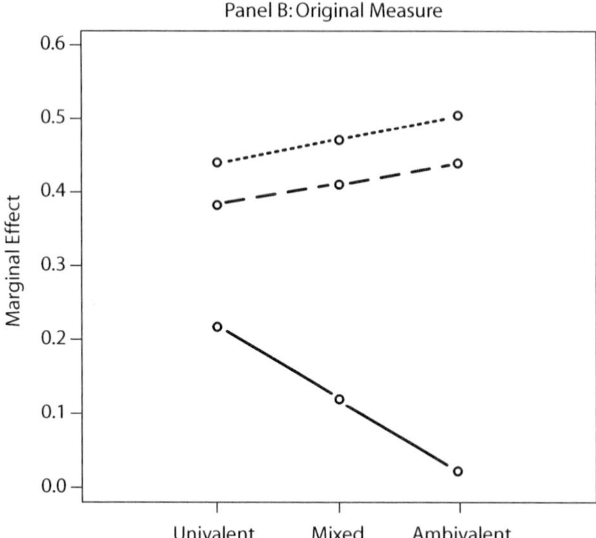

Figure 8.3 The Influence of Partisanship and Economic Change Across Levels of Partisan Ambivalence, 1980–2004 ANES.

Notes: Figures show the estimated marginal effects of partisanship and economic changes on economic retrospections across partisan ambivalence using two operationalizations of the latter: the first where all economic responses were purged, and the second where they were not purged.

We do not believe that people consciously privilege the hedonic implications of their beliefs over or apart from their perceived truth value. With Kunda (1990), we do not believe that people feel at liberty to believe something simply because they wish to believe it. Rather, we suspect that people would like to believe that they are being rational when making political judgments, and that the justifications they give would persuade a dispassionate observer. Lurking just under the surface, however, are people's hedonic needs. Psychologists have found that people derive "expressive" rewards from their attitudes, beliefs, and attachments (Herek, 1986; Katz, 1960; Lavine & Snyder, 1996; Smith et al., 1956). Our interest centers on the psychological benefit that people might derive from holding beliefs that gratify their partisan attachments. That principal benefit, according to social identity theory, is positive self-regard, brought about by the motivated perception of *positive distinctiveness*—the belief that the in-group is different from and better than relevant outgroups (Tajfel & Turner, 1979). According to the theory, intergroup differentiation favoring the in-group enhances self-esteem, while depressed or threatened self-esteem motives people to engage in biased intergroup differentiation (Rubin & Hewstone, 1998, p. 41).[10]

Can this dynamic apply when the groups are defined in a partisan political context? A study by Kelly (1988), in which intergroup differentiation was measured among supporters of various political parties in Britain, suggests so. Kelly demonstrated that partisans whose perceptions and evaluations strongly favored the in-party scored higher on a standard measure of self-esteem than those who exhibited greater balance. Taken to its extreme, this work suggests

10. There is a body of experimental evidence in psychology that being categorized as a group member leads to higher self-esteem among those who are given the chance to engage in intergroup differentiation (i.e., some form of in-group favoritism; for a review see Rubin & Hewstone, 1998). In many of these studies, groups are created on some minimal basis, such as whether a person prefers the paintings of one artist or another, or whether a person under- or overestimates the number of jellybeans in a jar. Once the groups are created, participants in an experimental condition complete an intergroup task (e.g., they assign points to in- and out-group members), whereas those assigned to a control condition perform a non-intergroup task (e.g., they read a newspaper article about an irrelevant topic; e.g., Oakes & Turner, 1980). The typical result is that those assigned to the experimental condition (who reliably engage in in-group favoritism) score higher on standard measures of self-esteem than those assigned to the control condition. Consistent with the theory, this effect does not obtain if the discrimination task occurs on an *interpersonal* rather than an *intergroup* basis (see Lemyre & Smith, 1985).

a purely psychological motive, namely self-aggrandizement, for believing that "our side" is superior—its goals nobler, its policies sounder, and its leaders more honest and capable. At best, this is a mixed blessing. On one hand, it invites greater interest and involvement in politics. On the other, it warps people's perceptions of political reality and can lead to judgments that are dislodged from one's values, interests, and objective facts.[11] In sum, to the extent that partisan competition activates the self-concept, political judgments can easily become obeisant to *symbolic* egoistic needs, which can diminish the quality of democratic citizenship.

None of this is to say that partisan identification or political parties are inherently unhealthy for democracy. They are an inevitable consequence of the clash of interests among individuals and groups striving for power. For the reasons we have just laid out, though, partisanship of an unyielding variety, a partisanship that admits no uncomfortable facts can diminish the responsiveness of elites to the public's policy wishes. In *Politicians Don't Pander*, Jacobs and Shapiro (2000; see also Jacobs & Shapiro, 2010) argue that the causal relationship between public opinion and policy making in contemporary American politics is widely misunderstood: Rather than tailoring policy to centrist public opinion (i.e., the median voter), partisan elites—along with powerful interest groups and partisan activists—have come to dominate policymaking to suit their own (noncentrist) ideological agendas.

Ever mindful of electoral backlash, Jacobs and Shapiro show how politicians conduct extensive public opinion polling and focus groups to identify the most powerful "language, arguments, and symbols" to persuade the public to support its extremist policy goals (see also Luntz, 2007). They (2010, p. 5) write that "competing efforts to tip public evaluations of policy proposals transformed 'public opinion' from an autonomous, external influence into a product of an endogenous process." Using Clinton's effort to reform health care and the Republicans' "Contract with America" as case studies, Jacobs and Shapiro show how political elites use "crafted talk" to attract favorable press coverage and change public sentiment while at the same time minimizing the risks of electoral punishment by centrist voters. What interests us in all this is whether attempts to simulate responsiveness are likely to meet with greater success among univalent than ambivalent partisans. To the extent that the former are more motivated to toe the party line, we believe the answer is yes. Specifically, by failing to think carefully about the actual content of policy contests, blind partisans reinforce the belief that the public is incapable of

11. The self-aggrandizement motive can also lead to intolerance (Tajfel & Turner, 1979).

providing its representatives with sound guidance for government decisions. This, in turn, allows elites to ignore their wishes and pursue policies that represent narrow ideological goals.

Good Citizenship Depends More on Ambivalence Than "Sophistication"

We have argued at several points in the book that political sophistication (qua information holding) is not isomorphic with good citizenship. While it reliably promotes such desirable qualities as political tolerance and participation (see Delli Carpini & Keeter, 1996), scholars have catalogued a number of deficiencies that seem to be especially prevalent among the well informed. For one thing, they are less likely than other citizens to discuss politics with those holding opposing views (Mutz, 2006). Theorists of deliberative democracy argue that communication across lines of political difference produces a variety of positive democratic outcomes, including more informed policy preferences, a more empathic view of others, and a broader understanding of one's own interests (Fishkin, 1991; Habermas, 1989; Mendelberg, 2002; Page, 1996). Mutz (2006), for example, has shown that citizens in politically heterogeneous social networks are better able to understand the rationale and legitimacy of those with whom they disagree.

Political sophisticates are also less likely than other citizens to adjust their voting behavior to national conditions. In analyzing 50 years of presidential elections, Zaller, (2004) finds that well-informed voters are the least likely to reward or punish incumbents for their performance in office and to reject noncentrist presidential candidates (e.g., Goldwater, McGovern). Several studies have also documented that sophisticates are especially prone to holding biased perceptions of political reality (Bartels, 2008; Jacobson, 2010; Kuklinski et al., 2008; Taber & Lodge, 2006; Zaller, 2003). As Bartels (2008, p. 157) writes, "rather than contributing to accurate apprehension...political awareness seems mostly to have taught people how the political elites who share their ideological commitments would *like* them to see the world." Thus, it seems that political sophistication has complex normative implications: It increases citizens' responsiveness to diagnostic information, but it also makes it easier to defend their beliefs through motivated bias.

Among the most touted benefits of sophistication is that it helps citizens to discern their material interests and to project them into the public sphere. For example, Gomez and Wilson (2001) found that the well informed were more likely than other citizens to engage in pocketbook voting, and Delli Carpini and Keeter (1996) found that sophistication strengthened the relationship between citizens' personal economic predicaments and their preferences on government welfare programs. Using a panel design and more stringent controls, we found no evidence for the latter. Moreover, in our analysis of vote choice in House elections in Chapter 6, we found no evidence that policy preferences on economic issues mattered more for sophisticated than poorly informed voters. On the basis of these tests, we are inclined to doubt that political sophistication (qua knowledge) plays a primary role in determining the political relevance of citizens' economic interests.

The normative implications of partisan ambivalence are hands down more attractive. Ambivalent partisans engage in political discussion with their partisan opponents (Chapter 3); they ignore partisan cues when they are contradicted by more diagnostic information, including material interest, values, and facts (Chapters 4 and 5); their perceptions of reality are remarkably free of partisan bias (Chapter 5); they vote on the basis of policy more than do other citizens (Chapter 6); and ambivalent partisans with unsorted policy preferences are especially likely to exhibit partisan change (Chapter 7). These are all "behaviors" that reflect responsible democratic citizenship. Therefore, it would appear to be ambivalent partisanship—not decontextualized information holding per se—that promotes open-mindedness, doubt, and a willingness to think through the implications of alternative courses of action. As we have argued, this reflects the primacy of motivation over ability in producing heterogeneity in political judgment. Accordingly, we propose that the term "sophistication" not be used to describe chronic individual differences in political information holding (as is standard practice in political science) but to describe actual behavior itself: bias versus objectivity, reliance on diagnostic versus low-grade information, deep versus shallow thinking, and so on. Conceived in this way, ambivalent partisans *are* the "sophisticated" citizens in American politics.

Good Citizenship Is Situational

Throughout much of the book, we have described univalent and ambivalent partisans as if they were *dispositionally* distinct breeds of voters. The reality, however, is that the disjuncture between long-term partisan identities and contemporary partisan evaluations responds to the political environment in the form of party behavior and exogenous events, filtered through the individual's chronic priorities and predicaments of a temporary nature. To be sure, there are individuals who are inherently inclined toward ambivalence, as well as those who are unlikely to ever experience doubt, no matter what the circumstances. For most people, however, ambivalence is endogenous to the ebb and flow of party fortunes and to personal experiences. Poor performance in office, scandals, unpopular policies, and individual setbacks can transform a blind partisan into a critical one. Similarly, policy disagreements with the in-party on salient issues that tap into citizens' core values or group identities may create a temporary disjuncture between identity and evaluations (Hillygus & Shields, 2009). It is conceivable that ambivalent partisans remain in this disjunctive state for a prolonged period of time, thereby increasing the likelihood of partisan change. It is more likely, however, that as the environment adjusts, self-criticism dissipates and gives way to a return to homeostasis. The upshot is that contrary to previous trait-based conceptions of "the good citizen," our perspective emphasizes its contextual, dynamic roots.

This sketch supports a dichotomy—or more accurately, a continuum—of citizenship. It also supports the conclusion that the blind variety is an intractable scourge on the body politic. Despite the availability of a wide array of decision aids, partisan cues dominate if not entirely engulf the field. They frame discussions in the media; they structure the options that the public may choose between; and perhaps most important (for both better and worse), they activate our desire for positive social identity. Perhaps, however, this is an exaggeration. Perhaps institutional constraints—such as penalties for lying—prevent citizens from supporting options that they would not otherwise favor (Lupia & McCubbins, 1998). We question whether such penalties truly exist in the highly polarized environment of contemporary American politics. It seems to us that politicians routinely exploit citizens' ignorance of consensual expert opinion to make all manner of dubious claims, with little or no electoral backlash. Here are some examples from contemporary partisan debate:

- "With all of the hysteria, all of the fear, all of the phony science, could it be that man-made global warming is the greatest hoax ever perpetrated on the American people? It sure sounds like it" (Republican Senator James Inhofe, July 28, 2003).[12]
- "In the first year of the Obama administration, more jobs were created in the private-sector than in the 8 years of the Bush administration, with all of the tax cuts that President Bush had" (Democratic Speaker of the House, Nancy Pelosi, May 16, 2011).[13]
- The Medicare proposal by Representative Paul Ryan (Republican of Wisconsin) would propose changes for those under age 55 so that they will "participate in the same kind of health plan that members of Congress do" (Mike Pence, Republican Congressman from Indiana, April 10, 2011).[14]

12. Quote from a speech on the Senate floor, July 28, 2003.
13. Quote from a Bloomsburg News interview, May 16, 2011.
14. Quote from an April 10, 2011 television appearance on ABS's *This Week With Christiane Amanpour.*

- The Medicare proposal by Representative Paul Ryan (Republican of Wisconsin) would "allow insurance companies to deny you coverage and drop you for preexisting conditions" (Wendy Wasserman-Schultz, Democratic Congresswoman from Florida, and Chairwoman of the Democratic National Committee, May 29, 2011).[15]
- "We should not have a government program that determines if you're going to pull the plug on grandma" (Republican Senator Charles Grassley of Iowa, August 12, 2009).[16]
- Republican Florida Governor Rick Scott "has destroyed over 100,000 jobs" (Florida Democratic Party Chairman, June 28, 2011).[17]

None of these statements is true. Each one was classified as "false" (save for the one by Mike Pence, which was deemed "barely true") by Politifact.com, a Pulitzer Prize–winning service of the *St. Petersburg Times*.[18] However, each statement was widely disseminated by a member of Congress (or in the last example, by a state Democratic Party chairman) to influence voters on an important issue or to alter their perceptions of the performance of a sitting president or governor. We do not know whether such statements influence public opinion, or whether they are exceptions in a sea of earnestness and honesty. However, Politifact.com has classified hundreds of statements as either "false" or "pants on fire" in the last few years. Many of these statements are surely repeated by the media, not as lies, but as claims left for the public to adjudicate for itself (Alterman, 2003). Our findings imply that univalent partisans eagerly accept such statements as fact when they are disseminated by co-partisan elites, and update their opinions accordingly (Nyhan & Reifler, 2010).

What Can Be Done to Promote Better Citizen Performance?

The central message of our book is that ambivalent partisanship is a key component of responsible democratic citizenship. Perhaps, then, there is some way to prompt citizens to experience ambivalence more frequently, or more intensely, and to thereby make better political judgments on a more regular basis. Unfortunately, we do not see how in practice this can be done. If, as we have found, ambivalence is largely a product of party performance, exogenous

15. Quote from a May 29, 2011 television appearance on CBS's *Face the Nation*.
16. Quote from a town hall meeting, August 12, 2009.
17. Quote from a mass e-mail from the chairman of the Florida Democratic Party, June 28, 2011.
18. The Web site is often used by mainstream political news outlets (e.g., *This Week With Christiane Amanpour*) to adjudicate disputes of fact. Accessed July 5, 2011.

events, and citizens' priorities and circumstances, it is difficult to imagine how any realizable form of institutional or cultural change could alter this equation. Nevertheless, we will close the book with one modest thought on the matter. It seems to us that the extreme party tribalism now prevalent in American society is a function of the substantive nature of contemporary party conflict, and that its intensity may wane as the locus of such conflict changes. Specifically, the rise of racial conflict in the 1960s, the emergence of cultural and religious conflict in the early 1990s (Adams, 1997; Layman, 2001), and national security concerns in the post-9/11 era are all dimensions that divide citizens on a very basic level. These issues are rooted in core psychological dispositions related to the fundamental needs of existential security and epistemic certainty (e.g., Jost et al., 2003; Jost, Federico, & Napier, 2009), and they lead to differences in end-state values (Goren, 2012).

Hetherington and Weiler (2009, p. 17) argue that a moral worldview divide of this nature now constitutes the dominant cleavage between Democrats and Republicans, and underlies much of the vitriol observed in American politics in the 21st century. As they state, "people come to perceive that their views of right and wrong and good and bad are diametrically opposed to those of their opponents, making it difficult to understand (or perhaps even respect) the worldview that makes those preferences possible." In such a context, it is little surprise that citizens often choose to insulate themselves within partisan echo chambers. However, this "culture war," at least in its present form, cannot last forever. It is possible that as conflict over issues such as gay rights and terrorism recedes, the psychological roots of partisanship will also become less important. This should either make ambivalent partisanship an easier state to attain, or more optimistically, render it unnecessary as a prerequisite for good citizenship.

If the current roots of partisan extremism are truly "cultural," then succeeding generations, finding such divisions anachronistic, may emphasize other, less "hot" forms of partisan competition, and thereby foster less vitriol, fear, and uncertainty. This is, perhaps, overly optimistic. If so, we see few alternative solutions to the problem of responsible citizenship beyond fundamental changes in our formal institutions of democracy, ones that better align the incentives of the participating class with the interests of the larger public. Only time will tell.

Appendix A: Statistical Model Estimates

CHAPTER 3

TABLE A3.1. *INDIVIDUAL-LEVEL ANTECEDENTS OF PARTISAN AMBIVALENCE*

	Conflicting Evaluations			Consistent Evaluations		
	% Change	Lower	Upper	% Change	Lower	Upper
Unemployed	26.14	9.09	44.99	–7.91	–15.93	0.23
Contact w/parties	3.08	–5.23	12.24	2.00	–2.66	6.91
Group feelings	90.62	78.34	101.74	–26.78	–29.13	–24.27
Moral traditionalism	20.15	10.71	30.67	–6.77	–10.81	–2.92
Egalitarianism	39.12	24.53	55.34	–25.19	–29.73	–20.17
Worried job	–5.10	–9.94	0.07	3.64	0.58	6.91
House contact	6.74	–1.47	16.09	1.14	–3.47	5.85
Discuss politics	11.36	–0.19	23.92	3.43	–2.67	9.53
Keep up with costs	26.84	13.95	41.82	–11.57	–16.90	–6.02

Notes. ANES Cumulative File, 1980–2004. Entries are negative binomial estimates of the percent change in each component of partisan ambivalence, with confidence bounds, for a change in the respective variable from its 5th to its 95th percentile. This table is constructed from multiple models. See the text for more details on the procedure.

CHAPTER 4

TABLE A4.1. *POLICY PREFERENCES AS A FUNCTION OF PARTISANSHIP, 2008 ANES PANEL STUDY*

Variable	*B*	*SE*	*p*
Lagged preference	.52	.01	.00
Age	–.01	.03	.65
Male	.02	.01	.08
Black	–.05	.03	.07
Education	–.01	.02	.59
Income	.03	.03	.28
Unemployed	–.01	.02	.47
Republican	–.15	.05	.00
Strength	–.01	.02	.49
Interest	–.05	.04	.13
Sophistication	–.10	.04	.01
Consistent	–.05	.03	.12
Conflicting	.05	.05	.34
Rep × Strength	.06	.03	.06
Rep × Interest	.12	.05	.01
Rep × Sophistication	.13	.05	.01
Rep × Consistent	.17	.05	.00
Rep × Conflicting	–.06	.06	.32
Constant	.27	.04	.00
SD (Constant)	.07	.01	
N		4,159	
Respondents		520	

Notes. ANES 2008 panel. Entries are restricted maximum likelihood coefficients and standard errors. The intercept is modeled as a random variable that varies by respondent. The dependent variable is measured in October, and lagged preferences are measured in January. Partisan identification, strength, and political interest are measured in January, while ambivalence and sophistication are measured in February. Model also includes fixed effects for issue (not shown).

TABLE A4.2. *ECONOMIC PREFERENCES AS A FUNCTION OF PARTISANSHIP AND INCOME, 2008 ANES PANEL STUDY*

Variable	*B*	*SE*	*p*
Lagged preference	.58	.02	.00
Age	–.01	.04	.78
Male	.03	.02	.04
Black	–.01	.04	.85
Education	.04	.03	.16
Income	.34	.14	.02
Unemployed	.01	.03	.74
Republican	–.15	.06	.02
Strength	–.08	.07	.24
Interest	.00	.10	.98
Sophistication	–.07	.11	.53
Consistent	.11	.09	.26
Conflicting	.18	.14	.21
Rep x Strength	.04	.04	.38
Rep x Interest	.14	.07	.04
Rep x Sophistication	.07	.07	.30
Rep x Consistent	.27	.07	.00
Rep x Conflicting	–.02	.09	.80
Income x Strength	.12	.10	.22
Income x Interest	–.13	.15	.37
Income x Sophistication	.01	.16	.97
Income x Consistent	–.33	.15	.02
Income x Conflicting	–.14	.21	.50
Constant	.00	.10	1.00
SD (Constant)	.10	.01	
N		1,559	
Respondents		520	

Notes. ANES 2008 panel. Entries are restricted maximum likelihood coefficients and standard errors. The intercept is modeled as a random variable that varies by respondent. The dependent variable is measured in October, and lagged preferences are measured in January. Partisan identification, strength, and political interest are measured in January, while ambivalence and sophistication are measured in February. Model also includes fixed effects for issue (not shown).

TABLE A4.3. *ECONOMIC PREFERENCES AS A FUNCTION OF PARTISANSHIP AND PERSONAL ECONOMIC CIRCUMSTANCES, 1992–1994 ANES PANEL STUDY*

Variable	*B*	*SE*	*p*
Lagged preferences	.33	.06	.00
Age	–.03	.04	.47
Male	.03	.02	.19
Black	–.10	.03	.00
Education	–.06	.04	.08
Income	.10	.04	.01
Republican	.01	.06	.93
Personal economic	.05	.14	.71
Strength	–.02	.06	.67
Interest	.06	.08	.51
Sophistication	–.04	.09	.69
Consistent	.07	.07	.32
Conflicting	–.07	.05	.18
Rep x Strength	.10	.05	.03
Rep x Interest	–.03	.06	.62
Rep x Sophistication	.07	.07	.35
Rep x Consistent	.11	.05	.04
Rep x Conflicting	–.09	.04	.03
Personal Ec. x Strength	.00	.10	.99
Personal Ec. x Interest	.00	.14	.98
Personal Ec. x Sophistication	–.03	.14	.84
Personal Ec. x Consistent	–.11	.10	.29
Personal Ec. x Conflicting	.20	.08	.02
Constant	.29	.09	.00
R^2		.43	
N		434	

Notes. ANES 1992–1994 panel. Entries are OLS coefficients and robust standard errors. Dependent variable is measured in 1994. All independent variables are measured in 1992.

CHAPTER 5

TABLE A5.1. *BIAS AND RESPONSIVENESS IN ECONOMIC RETROSPECTIONS, 1980–2004*

	Δ in Unemployment			GDP Growth		
Variable	*B*	*SE*	*p*	*B*	*SE*	*p*
Age	.00	.01	.73	.00	.01	.74
Female	–.04	.01	.00	–.04	.01	.00
Black	–.04	.01	.00	–.04	.01	.00
Education	.05	.01	.00	.05	.01	.00
Income	.02	.01	.12	.02	.01	.12
Unemployed	–.03	.01	.01	–.03	.01	.01
Partisan strength	–.03	.01	.00	–.04	.01	.00
Interest	–.04	.01	.01	–.05	.02	.01
Sophistication	–.01	.01	.52	–.06	.02	.00
Conflicting	.11	.03	.00	.01	.04	.81
Consistent	–.12	.02	.00	–.09	.03	.00
In-Party	–.02	.01	.09	–.02	.01	.08
In-Party x Strength	.08	.01	.00	.08	.01	.00
In-Party x Interest	.07	.02	.00	.07	.02	.00
In-Party x Sophistication	.03	.02	.08	.03	.02	.07
In-Party x Conflicting	–.29	.05	.00	–.29	.04	.00
In-Party x Consistent	.26	.03	.00	.25	.03	.00
Change in Economy	–.06	.02	.01	.03	.01	.01
Change x Strength	–.01	.01	.30	.00	.00	.27
Change x Interest	–.01	.01	.29	.00	.00	.33
Change x Sophistication	–.04	.01	.00	.02	.00	.00
Change x Conflicting	–.07	.02	.00	.03	.01	.00
Change x Consistent	.02	.01	.16	–.01	.01	.10
Constant	.40	.03	.00	.32	.04	.00
SD intercept	.08	.02	.00	.08	.02	.00
SD residuals	.23	.00	.00	.23	.00	.00
N		8,159			8,159	
Years		11			11	

Notes. Data from the ANES cumulative file, 1980–2004; dependent variable is economic retrospections (higher values = "better"); models include random intercepts for year and are estimated with a normal link function.

TABLE A5.2. *ECONOMIC RETROSPECTIONS IN THE 2008 PRESIDENTIAL ELECTION*

Variable	*B*	*SE*	*p*
Lagged retrospection	.24	.02	.00
Age	.01	.02	.50
Male	.00	.01	.89
Black	–.01	.02	.66
Education	–.03	.02	.16
Income	.00	.02	.82
Republican	.01	.04	.74
Strength	.01	.02	.71
Interest	–.01	.03	.67
Sophistication	–.01	.03	.71
Consistent	.02	.03	.46
Conflicting	.00	.04	.94
Rep x Strength	–.01	.02	.83
Rep x Interest	.05	.04	.23
Rep x Sophistication	.04	.04	.37
Rep x Consistent	.03	.04	.46
Rep x Conflicting	–.11	.05	.03
Constant	–.01	.03	.81
R^2		.21	
N		981	

Notes. ANES 2008 panel. Entries are OLS coefficients and robust standard errors. Dependent variable is measured in October (higher values = "gotten better"). Lagged retrospections are measured in January. Partisan identification, strength, and political interest are measured in January, while ambivalence and sophistication are measured in February.

TABLE A5.3. *ACCURACY OF UNEMPLOYMENT RETROSPECTIONS DURING REAGAN'S PRESIDENCY*

	Democrats			Republicans		
Variable	*B*	*SE*	*p*	*B*	*SE*	*p*
Age	–.39	.25	.12	–.22	.32	.48
Male	.05	.10	.65	.47	.13	.00
Black	–.21	.12	.08	–.40	.28	.16
Education	.41	.21	.06	.21	.29	.46
Income	.22	.19	.26	.45	.26	.08
Unemployed	–.29	.19	.13	–.07	.33	.82
Strength	–.11	.12	.36	.37	.16	.02
Interest	–.14	.14	.32	.11	.19	.58
Sophistication	.61	.23	.01	.79	.31	.01
Consistent	–.48	.19	.01	.23	.30	.45
Conflicting	1.14	.36	.00	–.35	.32	.28
Cut 1	–.23	.17		–.30	.22	
Cut 2	.45	.17		.41	.22	
Pseudo-R^2		.05			.10	
N		646			549	

Notes. 1988 ANES. Entries are ordered probit coefficients and standard errors. Higher values of dependent variable indicate more positive retrospections.

TABLE A5.4. *ACCURACY OF INFLATION RETROSPECTIONS DURING REAGAN'S PRESIDENCY*

	Democrats			Republicans		
Variable	*B*	*SE*	*p*	*B*	*SE*	*p*
Age	.21	.25	.40	–.63	.29	.03
Male	.28	.10	.01	.42	.11	.00
Black	.10	.12	.39	.20	.28	.48
Education	.55	.21	.01	.28	.26	.27
Income	.09	.19	.64	.25	.22	.26
Unemployed	–.29	.20	.14	–.23	.31	.47
Strength	–.10	.12	.40	.13	.14	.37
Interest	–.27	.14	.06	–.07	.18	.71
Sophistication	.86	.23	.00	1.26	.28	.00
Consistent	–.37	.20	.06	.87	.27	.00
Conflicting	1.51	.35	.00	–.01	.29	.96
Cut 1	.53	.17		.24	.20	
Cut 2	1.35	.18		1.01	.20	
Pseudo-R^2		.08			.13	
N		653			548	

Notes. 1988 ANES. Entries are ordered probit coefficients and standard errors. Higher values of dependent variable indicate more positive retrospections.

TABLE A5.5. *ACCURACY OF DEFICIT RETROSPECTIONS DURING CLINTON'S PRESIDENCY*

	Democrats			Republicans		
Variable	*B*	*SE*	*p*	*B*	*SE*	*p*
Age	.87	.48	.07	.25	.48	.60
Male	.00	.17	1.00	–.01	.17	.95
Black	–.25	.20	.23	–.08	.52	.88
Education	.45	.39	.24	.95	.36	.01
Income	1.60	.61	.01	.01	.51	.98
Strength	–.01	.21	.96	.40	.21	.06
Interest	.34	.25	.17	–.04	.28	.89
Sophistication	.94	.41	.02	.43	.41	.30
Consistent	1.03	.39	.01	–1.05	.37	.00
Conflicting	.63	.54	.24	.96	.45	.03
Cut 1	.53	.36		.13	.36	
Cut 2	1.42	.36		.83	.36	
Pseudo-R^2		.15			.05	
N		301			220	

Notes. 2000 ANES. Entries are ordered probit coefficients and standard errors. Higher values of dependent variable indicate more positive retrospections.

TABLE A5.6. *ACCURACY OF CRIME RETROSPECTIONS DURING CLINTON'S PRESIDENCY*

	Democrats			Republicans		
Variable	*B*	*SE*	*p*	*B*	*SE*	*p*
Age	–.34	.42	.42	.93	.44	.04
Male	.29	.14	.04	.28	.16	.09
Black	–.36	.19	.05	–.02	.49	.97
Education	.58	.31	.06	.31	.34	.36
Income	.41	.43	.34	.24	.47	.61
Strength	.20	.18	.28	.08	.20	.68
Interest	.19	.21	.36	.28	.26	.29
Sophistication	1.01	.33	.00	.41	.38	.28
Consistent	.18	.32	.57	–.11	.35	.74
Conflicting	.39	.41	.34	.83	.43	.05
Cut 1	.41	.30		.82	.34	
Cut 2	1.27	.31		1.80	.35	
Pseudo-R^2		.09			.06	
N		311			234	

Notes. 2000 ANES. Entries are ordered probit coefficients and standard errors. Higher values of dependent variable indicate more positive retrospections.

TABLE A5.7. *PROJECTION AND INFERENCE IN PERCEPTIONS OF PRESIDENTIAL CANDIDATES' POLICY POSITIONS, 1980–2004*

Variable	*B*	*SE*	*p*
Age	–.01	.01	.19
Female	.01	.00	.00
Black	.05	.00	.00
Education	–.01	.00	.01
Income	–.02	.01	.00
Candidate party	.11	.01	.00
R's preference	.06	.01	.00
Strength	–.05	.01	.00
Interest	–.08	.01	.00
Sophistication	–.07	.01	.00
Consistent	–.17	.01	.00
Conflicting	.14	.01	.00
Party x Strength	–.01	.00	.06
Party x Interest	.06	.01	.00
Party x Sophistication	.14	.01	.00
Party x Consistent	.10	.01	.00
Party x Conflicting	.14	.01	.00
Pref. x Strength	.09	.01	.00
Pref. x Interest	.10	.01	.00
Pref. x Sophistication	–.02	.01	.07
Pref. x Consistent	.29	.01	.00
Pref. x Conflicting	–.45	.02	.00
Constant	.50	.01	.00
SD (constant)	.07	.00	
N		57,215	
Respondents		6,725	

Notes. ANES Cumulative File, 1980–2004. Entries are restricted maximum likelihood coefficients and standard errors. "Candidate Party" represents processes of ideological inference; "R's preference" represents projection. The intercept is modeled as a random variable which varies by respondent. Model includes fixed effects for issue, which vary by the party of the candidate being judged (not shown).

TABLE A5.8. *PROJECTION AND INFERENCE IN PERCEPTIONS OF SENATORS' ROLL-CALL VOTES, 2006*

Variable	*B*	*SE*	*p*
Age	–.11	.04	.00
Male	–.01	.01	.51
Black	.06	.03	.02
Education	.00	.03	.99
Income	–.05	.03	.11
Senator's party	.39	.06	.00
R's policy position	.66	.06	.00
Partisan strength	–.09	.03	.00
Interest	–.71	.04	.00
Ambivalence	.00	.04	.98
Party x Strength	–.16	.04	.00
Party x Interest	1.14	.05	.00
Party x Ambivalence	.55	.05	.00
Position x Strength	.24	.04	.00
Position x Interest	.23	.06	.00
Position x Ambivalence	–.65	.05	.00
Constant	–.12	.05	.01
Pseudo-R^2		.44	
N		123,786	

Notes. 2006 CCES. Entries are probit coefficients and standard errors. "Senator's party" represents processes of ideological inference; "R's policy position" represents projection. Model includes fixed effects for issue, which vary by the party of the candidate being judged (not shown).

TABLE A5.9. *PROJECTION AND INFERENCE IN PERCEPTIONS OF PRESIDENTIAL CANDIDATES' POLICY POSITIONS, 2008*

Variable	*B*	*SE*	*p*
Lagged perception	.32	.01	.00
Age	.00	.02	.92
Male	–.02	.01	.00
Black	.03	.02	.14
Education	.02	.02	.27
Income	–.02	.02	.48
R's position on issue	–.09	.04	.03
Party of candidate	–.02	.04	.54
Strength	–.01	.03	.61
Interest	–.09	.03	.01
Sophistication	–.07	.03	.03
Consistent	–.12	.03	.00
Conflicting	–.05	.04	.25
R's x Strength	.05	.04	.16
R's x Interest	–.02	.04	.60
R's x Sophistication	.07	.04	.11
R's x Consistent	.20	.04	.00
R's x Conflicting	–.10	.05	.05
Party x Strength	–.03	.03	.29
Party x Interest	.11	.03	.00
Party x Sophistication	.09	.03	.01
Party x Consistent	.07	.03	.02
Party x Conflicting	.11	.04	.01
Constant	.43	.04	.00
SD (constant)	.05	.01	
N		6,796	
Respondents		475	

Notes. 2008 ANES panel. Entries are restricted maximum likelihood coefficients and standard errors. The intercept is modeled as a random variable that varies by respondent. Dependent variable is respondent's placement of the candidate in the October wave. Lagged perceptions are measured in June. Partisan identification, strength, and political interest are measured in January, while ambivalence and sophistication are measured in February. Model includes fixed effects for issue, which vary by the party of the candidate being judged (not shown).

TABLE A5.10. *ACCURACY OF PRESIDENTIAL PERCEPTIONS, 1980–2004*

Variable	*B*	*SE*	*p*
Age	-1.51	.11	.00
Female	–.30	.05	.00
Black	.32	.07	.00
Education	.59	.09	.00
Income	.26	.09	.00
Mismatched	–.19	.10	.06
Strength	.15	.07	.02
Interest	1.13	.10	.00
Sophistication	1.32	.10	.00
Consistent	2.17	.12	.00
Conflicting	.40	.18	.02
Strength x Mismatch	–.45	.09	.00
Interest x Mismatch	–.59	.14	.00
Sophistication x Mismatch	–.02	.13	.88
Consistent x Mismatch	–2.02	.17	.00
Conflicting x Mismatch	2.09	.23	.00
Constant	–.69	.10	.00
N		32,400	
Respondents		6,935	

Notes. ANES Cumulative File, 1980–2004. Entries are restricted maximum likelihood coefficients and standard errors. The intercept is modeled as a random variable that varies by respondent. Dependent variable is coded "1" for correctly placing the Democratic candidate to the left of the Republican. "Mismatched" is coded "1" for citizens whose own position on the issue conflicts with their party's position. Model includes fixed effects for issue.

TABLE A5.11. *ACCURACY OF SENATORIAL PERCEPTIONS, 2006*

Variable	B	SE	P
Age	.23	.03	.00
Male	.23	.01	.00
Black	–.05	.02	.03
Education	.25	.02	.00
Income	.27	.03	.00
Mismatch	–.28	.04	.00
Strength	.14	.02	.00
Interest	1.03	.03	.00
Ambivalence	.14	.02	.00
Strength x Mismatch	–.17	.03	.00
Interest x Mismatch	–.33	.04	.00
Ambivalence x Mismatch	.32	.03	.00
Constant	–1.12	.03	.00
Pseudo-R^2		.10	
N		174,789	

Notes. 2006 CCES. Entries are probit coefficients and standard errors. Dependent variable is coded "1" for a correct placement of the Senator on the roll-call vote. "Mismatch" is coded "1" for citizens whose own position on the issue conflicts with their party's. Model includes fixed effects for issue.

CHAPTER 6

TABLE A6.1. *TIMING OF VOTE CHOICE, 1980–2004*

Variable	B	SE	p
Age	–.01	.00	.04
Male	–.06	.10	.53
White	.64	.22	.00
Education	.03	.03	.30
Income	–.03	.07	.61
Democrat	.38	.13	.00
Partisan strength	–.92	.08	.00
Interest	–.83	.18	.00
Sophistication	.21	.17	.21
Consistent	–1.34	.25	.00
Conflicting	1.41	.34	.00
Constant	–1.02	.28	.00
N		6,132	

Notes. ANES cumulative file, 1980–2004. Entries are maximum likelihood logit estimates with estimated standard errors.

TABLE A6.2. *CHOICE SET SIZE, 1992*

Variable	*B*	*SE*	*p*
Age	.00	.00	.05
Male	–.01	.05	.86
White	.16	.09	.08
Education	–.02	.02	.40
Income	.04	.03	.17
Democrat	.03	.05	.55
Strength	–.12	.06	.06
Interest	–.07	.11	.54
Sophistication	–.01	.12	.96
Consistent	–.19	.11	.09
Conflicting	.29	.17	.08
Constant	.50	.17	.00
N		1,099	

Notes. 1992 ANES. Entries are maximum likelihood ordered logit estimates with estimated standard errors.

TABLE A6.3. *UNCERTAINTY IN VOTE CHOICE, 1980–2004*

	Presidential			House		
Variable	*B*	*SE*	*p*	*B*	*SE*	*p*
Panel A. Utility Model						
Age	.00	.00	.30	.00	.00	.44
Male	–.01	.02	.58	.02	.02	.31
White	–.29	.05	.00	–.25	.05	.00
Education	.01	.01	.04	–.01	.01	.27
Income	–.02	.01	.07	–.03	.01	.01
Democrat	.90	.10	.00	.71	.09	.00
Constant	–.40	.08	.00	.06	.09	.52
Panel B. Variance Model						
Strength	–.46	.07	.00	–.57	.07	.00
Interest	–.28	.11	.01	.06	.11	.58
Sophistication	–.35	.10	.00	–.18	.09	.04
Consistent	–1.74	.12	.00	–.69	.10	.00
Conflicting	1.95	.18	.00	.63	.16	.00
N		5,014			6,512	

Notes. ANES cumulative file, 1980–2004. Entries are maximum likelihood heteroskedastic probit estimates with estimated standard errors. The standard errors for vote choice in presidential elections are clustered by state; those for vote choice in House elections are clustered by district. The election years 1998 and 2002 drop out due to the absence of a measure of partisan ambivalence. Year dummies are not shown.

TABLE A6.4. *VOTER TURNOUT, 1980–2004*

	Presidential			House		
Variable	*B*	*SE*	*p*	*B*	*SE*	*p*
Age (in decades)	.71	.13	.00	–.29	.48	.55
Age squared	–.05	.01	.00	.03	.03	.28
Male	–.33	.06	.00	–.05	.09	.61
White	–.14	.11	.19	.04	.04	.34
Education	.26	.03	.00	.04	.05	.47
Income	.27	.04	.00	.05	.17	.75
Internal efficacy	.00	.02	.95	.05	.08	.52
External efficacy	.13	.03	.00	.02	.05	.71
Contact	.73	.07	.00	.49	.70	.48
Strength	.64	.17	.00	.05	.32	.88
Interest	1.68	.15	.00	.31	1.51	.84
Sophistication	1.21	.13	.00	.75	1.05	.48
Consistent	.46	.19	.02	.13	.08	.09
Conflicting	–.10	.27	.70	–.06	.23	.80
Constant	–4.59	.33	.00	–.32	3.91	.93
N		6,032			1,904	

Notes. ANES cumulative file, 1980–2004. Table entries are maximum likelihood logit estimates with cluster-corrected standard errors (clustering by year).

TABLE A6.5. *MEDIA USAGE, 1980–2004*

Variable	*B*	*SE*	*p*
Age	.01	.00	.00
Male	.10	.08	.23
White	–.07	.10	.47
Education	.13	.02	.00
Income	.10	.04	.01
Internal efficacy	.03	.03	.35
External efficacy	.07	.03	.03
Contact	.33	.10	.00
Strength	–.12	.03	.00
Interest	2.07	.18	.00
Sophistication	.69	.14	.00
Consistent	.46	.05	.00
Conflicting	.75	.17	.00
Constant	–3.30	.22	.00
N		6,342	

Notes. ANES cumulative file, 1980–2004. Table entries are maximum likelihood logit estimates with cluster-corrected standard errors (clustering by year).

TABLE A6.6. *VOTING BEHAVIOR IN PRESIDENTIAL ELECTIONS, 1984–2004*

Variable	*B*	*SE*	*p*
Age	–.05	.14	.73
Female	–.03	.06	.56
Black	–.85	.10	.00
Education	.18	.11	.08
Income	.28	.12	.02
Unemployed	–.07	.17	.69
Econ. retrospections	.82	.31	.01
Republican	.54	.17	.00
Economic preferences	.01	.42	.98
Social preferences	.50	.32	.12
Partisan strength	–.39	.25	.11
Interest	–.71	.39	.07
Sophistication	–1.65	.35	.00
Consistent	–.96	.52	.07
Conflicting	1.61	.62	.01
Rep x Strength	1.19	.15	.00
Rep x Interest	–.06	.23	.78
Rep x Sophistication	.58	.21	.01
Rep x Consistent	4.78	.33	.00
Rep x Conflicting	–4.96	.35	.00
Retros x Strength	.03	.26	.90
Retros x Interest	.37	.40	.37
Retros x Sophistication	.31	.38	.41
Retros x Consistent	–.36	.57	.53
Retros x Conflicting	–.31	.63	.62
Econ x Strength	.17	.38	.66
Econ x Interest	.76	.57	.18
Econ x Sophistication	1.46	.51	.01
Econ x Consistent	–2.91	.84	.00
Econ x Conflicting	2.00	.94	.03
Social x Strength	–.63	.28	.03
Social x Interest	.40	.42	.35
Social x Sophistication	.89	.39	.02
Social x Consistent	–.10	.62	.87
Social x Conflicting	.34	.68	.62
Constant	–.65	.30	.03
Pseudo-R^2		.60	
N		5,289	

Notes. ANES cumulative file, 1980–2004. Entries are probit coefficients and standard errors. Year dummies are not shown.

TABLE A6.7. *VOTING BEHAVIOR IN THE 2008 PRESIDENTIAL ELECTION, 2008*

Variable	*B*	*SE*	*p*
Lagged evaluations	.48	.03	.00
Age	–.02	.03	.55
Male	–.01	.01	.64
Black	–.07	.02	.00
Education	–.03	.02	.13
Income	–.05	.03	.10
Economic retrospections	.08	.03	.01
Republican	–.04	.06	.51
Issues	.05	.15	.71
Partisan strength	.00	.03	.94
Interest	–.09	.06	.16
Sophistication	–.19	.06	.00
Consistent	–.13	.07	.05
Conflicting	.08	.09	.36
Rep x Strength	.14	.04	.00
Rep x Interest	.12	.06	.03
Rep x Sophistication	–.01	.06	.93
Rep x Consistent	.32	.06	.00
Rep x Conflicting	–.29	.08	.00
Issues x Strength	–.12	.09	.17
Issues x Interest	.04	.14	.77
Issues x Sophistication	.27	.14	.06
Issues x Consistent	–.09	.15	.56
Issues x Conflicting	.19	.20	.32
Constant	.35	.07	.00
R^2		.73	
N		985	

Notes. 2008 ANES Panel. Entries are OLS coefficients and standard errors. All variables scaled from 0 to 1.

TABLE A6.8. *VOTING BEHAVIOR IN US HOUSE ELECTIONS, 1984–2004*

Variable	*B*	*SE*	*p*
Age	.00	.11	1.00
Female	.06	.04	.14
Black	–.39	.09	.00
Education	.15	.08	.05
Income	.16	.09	.08
Unemployed	.18	.14	.18
Economic retrospections	.46	.25	.07
Republican incumbent	1.07	.21	.00
Democratic incumbent	–.73	.20	.00
Republican	.58	.14	.00
Economic preferences	.56	.35	.11
Social preferences	.11	.25	.65
Partisan strength	–.82	.21	.00
Interest	–.01	.35	.98
Sophistication	.31	.32	.33
Consistent	–.33	.36	.36
Conflicting	–.53	.49	.28
Rep. Inc. × Strength	.12	.17	.47
Rep. Inc. x Interest	–.06	.27	.83
Rep. Inc. x Sophistication	–.52	.25	.04
Rep. Inc. x Consistent	.12	.28	.66
Rep. Inc. x Conflicting	–.37	.37	.31
Dem. Inc. x Strength	.04	.16	.80
Dem. Inc. x Interest	–.06	.26	.82
Dem. Inc. x Sophistication	–.29	.24	.23
Dem. Inc. x Consistent	.29	.27	.29
Dem. Inc. x Conflicting	–.21	.36	.55
Retros x Strength	.14	.19	.44
Retros x Interest	.32	.30	.29
Retros x Sophistication	–.40	.29	.16
Retros x Consistent	–.87	.33	.01
Retros x Conflicting	.63	.43	.14
Rep. x Strength	.96	.12	.00
Rep x Interest	.00	.18	1.00
Rep x Sophistication	.04	.17	.80
Rep x Consistent	1.80	.21	.00
Rep x Conflicting	–1.72	.25	.00
Econ x Strength	.53	.29	.06
Econ x Interest	–.21	.45	.64
Econ x Sophistication	.19	.41	.64
Econ x Consistent	–.88	.49	.07
Econ x Conflicting	2.04	.65	.00
Social x Strength	–.07	.20	.72
Social x Interest	.01	.31	.97
Social x Sophistication	.38	.29	.19
Social x Consistent	.05	.34	.89
Social x Conflicting	.66	.45	.14
Constant	–1.07	.29	.00
Pseudo-R^2		.46	
N		7,003	

Notes. ANES cumulative file, 1980–2004. Entries are probit coefficients and standard errors. Year dummies are not shown.

TABLE A6.9. *DEFECTION AMONG UNSORTED PARTISANS, 1980–2004*

	Unsorted Economic			Unsorted Social			Unsorted on Both		
Variable	*B*	*SE*	*p*	*B*	*SE*	*p*	*B*	*SE*	*p*
1988	.30	.22	.17	—	—	—	—	—	—
1992	.80	.28	.00	–.16	.18	.38	.24	.49	.62
1996	.21	.28	.46	–.26	.20	.19	–.05	.48	.91
2000	.58	.28	.03	–.12	.17	.49	–.08	.55	.89
2004	–.39	.23	.09	–.52	.16	.00	–1.04	.40	.01
Age	–.33	.35	.34	.05	.29	.87	.43	.83	.60
Female	.00	.14	.98	–.09	.12	.43	–.14	.29	.62
Black	.22	.26	.38	.14	.22	.51	.27	.50	.59
Education	.62	.26	.02	.15	.22	.50	.93	.56	.10
Income	–.37	.29	.20	–.09	.24	.73	.78	.61	.20
Strength	.64	.19	.00	1.08	.16	.00	1.26	.47	.01
Interest	.00	.28	.99	–.08	.24	.75	.38	.65	.56
Sophistication	–.13	.25	.61	.07	.23	.76	–.98	.60	.10
Consistent	3.13	.43	.00	2.87	.34	.00	2.01	.95	.04
Conflicting	–2.84	.39	.00	–2.78	.32	.00	–2.07	.68	.00
Constant	–.14	.34	.69	.17	.26	.52	–.67	.67	.32
Pseudo-R^2		.33			.32			.41	
N		561			831			137	

Notes. ANES cumulative file, 1980–2004. Entries are probit coefficients and standard errors. Dependent variable is coded "1" if respondent voted for the in-party, and zero if he or she voted for the out-party. Economically unsorted respondents were unsorted on two of the three issues examined, while socially unsorted respondents were unsorted on both of two issues examined.

TABLE A6.10. *PARTISAN AMBIVALENCE, DEFECTION, SPLIT-TICKET, AND THIRD-PARTY VOTING*

	Defect Pres.			Defect House			Split-Ticket			Third-Party		
Variable	*B*	*SE*	*p*	*B*	*SE*	*p*	*B*	*SE*	*p*	*B*	*SE*	*p*
Age	.00	.00	.75	.00	.00	.08	.00	.00	.25	–.03	.01	.00
Male	–.09	.10	.36	–.06	.08	.42	–.06	.09	.47	.41	.16	.01
White	1.00	.18	.00	.83	.17	.00	.66	.22	.00	2.05	.53	.00
Education	–.05	.04	.17	–.01	.02	.63	.01	.03	.82	–.09	.06	.12
Income	.01	.05	.91	.00	.03	.89	.04	.05	.37	.13	.09	.13
Democrat	1.09	.10	.00	–.09	.18	.60	–.05	.13	.70	.18	.16	.27
Out-party familiarity	—	—	—	—	—	—	1.17	.13	.00	—	—	—
Major candidate dislike	—	—	—	—	—	—	—	—	—	2.30	.29	.00
Strength	–.89	.13	.00	–.78	.08	.00	–.65	.11	.00	–1.15	.22	.00
Interest	–.43	.20	.03	.07	.11	.54	–.04	.18	.81	–.35	.34	.31
Sophistication	–.44	.19	.02	–.21	.13	.12	–.45	.18	.01	–.10	.35	.79
Consistent	–4.73	.32	.00	–1.39	.21	.00	–1.10	.20	.00	–1.38	.42	.00
Conflicting	4.53	.10	.00	1.40	.28	.00	1.04	.27	.00	1.50	.56	.01
Constant	–1.35	.32	.00	–.85	.30	.00	–1.57	.35	.00	-2.62	.68	.00
N		5,014			6,512			4,285			1921	

Notes. Table entries for defection in presidential elections are maximum likelihood logit estimates with estimated standard errors. Table entries for defection in House elections are maximum likelihood hierarchical logit estimates with their estimated standard errors. The hierarchical model contains a random intercept across states and congressional districts (estimated variance component is .025, *ns*).

TABLE A6.11. *EFFECTS OF ANXIETY AND ENTHUSIASM ON VOTE INTENTION, 1980–2004*

Variable	*B(SE)*
Party ID	1.06 (.14)*
Issues	2.09 (.40)*
In-anxiety	.60 (.32)^
Out-anxiety	.28 (.25)
In-enthus	–.56 (.28)*
Out-enthus	–1.05 (.31)*
PID x In-Anx	–.65 (.19)*
PID x Out-Anx	.52 (.19)*
PID x In-Enthus	1.89 (.20)*
PID x Out-Enthus	–1.79 (.20)*
Issues x In-Anx	–.56 (.62)
Issues x Out-Anx	–.96 (.54)^
Issues x In-Enthus	–1.05 (.59)^
Issues x Out-Enthus	3.80 (.62)*
Candidate evaluations	7.23 (.21)*
Age	.02 (.01)
Gender	.02 (.04)
Black	–.32 (.07)*
Hispanic	–.02 (.02)
Education	.19 (.08)*
Income	–.05 (.08)
Interest	–.04 (.07)
Cut 1	–4.77 (.24)*
Cut 2	.51 (.02)*
N	8,512

Notes. ANES cumulative file, 1980–2004. Entries are ordered probit coefficients and standard errors.
$*p < .05$; $^p < .10$.

TABLE A6.12. *EFFECTS OF ANXIETY AND ENTHUSIASM ON CANDIDATE EVALUATIONS, 2008*

Variable	*B(SE)*
Lagged evaluation	.38 (.04)*
Age	–.04 (.02)
Male	–.02 (.01)^
Black	.00 (.02)
Education	–.06 (.02)*
Income	–.06 (.03)*
Republican	.29 (.04)*
Issue preferences	.19 (.08)*
In-anxiety	.04 (.08)
Out-anxiety	–.09 (.04)*
In-enthusiasm	–.11 (.04)*
Out-enthusiasm	.11 (.06)^
Rep x In-Anx	–.05 (.10)
Rep x Out-Anx	.05 (.06)
Rep x In-Enth	.23 (.06)*
Rep x Out-Enth	–.44 (.08)*
Issues x In-Anx	–.03 (.16)
Issues x Out-Anx	.16 (.10)^
Issues x In-Enth	–.09 (.11)
Issues x Out-Enth	.27 (.16)^
Constant	.19 (.04)*
R^2	.71
N	1,079

Notes. ANES 2008 Panel. Entries are OLS coefficients and standard errors.
*$p < .05$; ^$p < .10$.

CHAPTER 7

TABLE A7.1. *PARTISAN CHANGE, 1992–1994*

	Unsorted Respondents						Sorted Respondent					
	Health Insurance			Moral Traditionalism			Health Insurance			Moral Traditionalism		
Variable	*B*	*SE*	*p*	*B*	*SE*	*p*	*B*	*SE*	*p*	*B*	*SE*	*p*
Age	1.60	.99	.11	–.17	.70	.81	–.27	.49	.59	.38	.63	.54
Male	.17	.50	.74	–.03	.32	.93	.06	.25	.82	.09	.31	.79
Black	.68	.92	.46	.35	.53	.51	–.35	.42	.40	–.11	.55	.85
Education	–1.24	.83	.13	–.28	.67	.68	–.31	.52	.56	–.38	.58	.51
Income	2.32	1.02	.02	.24	.66	.71	–.06	.49	.90	.52	.59	.38
Strength	–.63	.70	.37	–1.19	.47	.01	–1.33	.31	.00	–1.53	.47	.00
Interest	.28	.74	.71	–.74	.51	.14	–.45	.39	.25	–.37	.50	.46
Sophistication	–.86	1.00	.39	–.98	.76	.20	–.28	.54	.61	–.23	.70	.74
Consistent	–1.81	1.14	.11	–.79	.74	.29	–.76	.50	.13	–1.20	.68	.08
Conflicting	3.38	1.26	.01	1.37	.98	.16	.51	.75	.50	.88	.88	.32
Constant	–2.02	.99	.04	.55	.55	.32	.24	.39	.53	–.57	.50	.26
Pseudo-R^2		.28			.15			.17			.18	
N		85			145			314			278	

Notes. ANES 1992–1994 Panel. Entries are probit coefficients and standard errors. Dependent variable is coded "1" for citizens who changed partisan identity, and "0" for those who remained stable from 1992 to 1994.

CHAPTER 8

TABLE A8.1. *EFFECTS OF PARTISANSHIP AND GDP GROWTH ON RETROSPECTIONS ACROSS LEVEL OF PARTISAN STRENGTH*

	Leaning			Weak			Strong		
Variable	*B*	*SE*	*p*	*B*	*SE*	*p*	*B*	*SE*	*p*
Age	−.02	.02	.35	−.03	.02	.04	−.02	.02	.27
Female	−.03	.01	.00	−.05	.01	.00	−.05	.01	.00
Black	−.05	.01	.00	−.04	.01	.00	−.05	.01	.00
Education	.04	.02	.01	.05	.01	.00	.06	.01	.00
Income	.02	.02	.19	.01	.01	.59	.02	.01	.17
Unemployed	−.04	.02	.03	−.06	.02	.00	−.04	.02	.03
In-party	.01	.02	.59	.03	.02	.08	.03	.02	.11
GDP growth	.02	.01	.19	.03	.01	.00	.03	.01	.01
Interest	−.11	.03	.00	−.04	.02	.15	−.05	.03	.09
Sophistication	−.04	.03	.24	−.03	.02	.24	−.05	.03	.06
Consistent	−.17	.04	.00	−.10	.03	.00	−.10	.03	.00
Conflicting	.19	.05	.00	.10	.04	.02	−.10	.05	.06
In-Party x Int.	.07	.03	.02	.06	.03	.03	.12	.03	.00
In-Party x Soph	−.02	.03	.61	.03	.02	.25	.04	.03	.12
In-Party x Conf.	−.34	.05	.00	−.23	.04	.00	−.21	.05	.00
In-Party x Cons.	.26	.04	.00	.18	.03	.00	.20	.03	.00
GDP x Int.	.02	.01	.01	.00	.01	.48	.00	.01	.75
GDP x Soph	.02	.01	.00	.01	.00	.05	.01	.01	.17
GDP x Conf.	−.01	.01	.35	.01	.01	.46	.05	.01	.00
GDP x Cons.	.01	.01	.14	.01	.01	.27	.00	.01	.98
Constant	.34	.05	.00	.30	.05	.00	.30	.05	.00
SD (constant)	.10	.02		.09	.02		.10	.02	
SD (residual)	.23	.00		.22	.00		.23	.00	
N		3,498			4,719			4,332	
Years		11			11			11	

Notes. Entries are restricted maximum likelihood coefficients and standard errors. Model includes random intercepts for year. Dependent variable is economic retrospections, where higher values indicate more positive assessments. GDP, gross domestic product.

TABLE A8.2. *VOTING BEHAVIOR DYNAMICS ACROSS PARTISAN STRENGTH*

				Weak			Strong		
Variable	*B*	*SE*	*p*	*B*	*SE*	*p*	*B*	*SE*	*p*
Age	.13	.24	.59	.04	.22	.87	–.27	.30	.38
Female	–.15	.10	.12	.07	.09	.45	–.17	.12	.18
Black	–1.07	.19	.00	–.89	.17	.00	–.59	.20	.00
Education	.17	.18	.36	.19	.17	.26	.21	.23	.37
Income	–.11	.20	.59	.57	.18	.00	.15	.26	.55
Unemployed	–.32	.29	.26	.09	.27	.76	–.13	.34	.70
Retrospections	.25	.54	.65	1.09	.44	.01	.85	.68	.21
Republican	.64	.28	.02	1.24	.23	.00	2.03	.42	.00
Economic issues	–.80	.73	.28	.48	.56	.39	.24	.94	.80
Social issues	.87	.59	.14	–.02	.43	.96	.30	.67	.66
Interest	–.66	.70	.35	–.86	.62	.17	–.41	.84	.63
Sophistication	–2.35	.61	.00	–1.19	.56	.03	–1.25	.72	.08
Consistent	–2.98	1.10	.01	–.62	.83	.45	–.69	.96	.47
Conflicting	4.31	1.08	.00	2.08	1.04	.05	–3.22	1.70	.06
Rep x Interest	–.45	.41	.26	.28	.36	.43	–.76	.55	.17
Rep x Soph.	1.01	.36	.01	–.20	.33	.55	1.56	.48	.00
Rep x Cons.	5.99	.59	.00	4.93	.54	.00	3.14	.68	.00
Rep x Conf.	–6.47	.60	.00	–4.61	.57	.00	–3.31	.94	.00
Retros x Int.	.78	.75	.30	.55	.65	.39	.79	.87	.36
Retros x Soph	1.13	.70	.11	–.35	.62	.57	–.46	.76	.55
Retros x Consis.	–.30	1.08	.78	.48	.94	.61	–.55	1.08	.61
Retros x Conf.	–2.55	1.13	.03	–.17	1.06	.87	1.03	1.49	.49
Econ x Int.	1.26	1.06	.24	.47	.91	.60	.66	1.24	.60
Econ x Soph.	2.06	.98	.04	1.62	.82	.05	.32	1.01	.75
Econ x Cons.	–1.11	1.68	.51	–3.68	1.34	.01	–1.61	1.58	.31
Econ x Conf.	.94	1.60	.56	.03	1.56	.98	7.85	2.52	.00
Social x Int.	.24	.82	.77	.71	.69	.30	–.44	.88	.62
Social x Soph.	.19	.74	.80	1.17	.63	.06	1.53	.80	.06
Social x Cons.	1.38	1.22	.26	–1.12	1.02	.27	–1.00	1.13	.38
Social x Conf.	–.35	1.17	.76	.23	1.13	.84	2.87	1.72	.10
Constant	–.20	.50	.70	–1.23	.44	.01	–1.31	.70	.06
Pseudo-R^2		.49			.49			.81	
N		1,381			1,783			2,125	

Notes. Entries are restricted maximum likelihood coefficients and standard errors. Model includes random intercepts for year. Dependent variable is economic retrospections, where higher values indicate more positive assessments.

Appendix B: Question Wording for the Traditional Engagement Variables

Throughout the book, we have treated partisan strength, interest in politics, and political sophistication as control variables. As our analyses using the ANES cumulative file cover almost 30 years of electoral history, we have operationalized these "competitor" variables using indicators that are consistently available in the ANES. Those indicators are shown in the following sections.

PARTISAN STRENGTH

Our partisan strength measure is based on the standard ANES item battery for partisanship. The first question in this battery is as follows:

> Generally speaking, do you usually think of yourself as a Republican, a Democrat, an Independent, or what?
>
> If the person indicates Democrat or Republican, then the follow-up question is as follows:
>
> Would you call yourself a strong Democrat/Republican or a not very strong Democrat/Republican?
>
> For respondents who initially say they are Independents, the follow-up is as follows:
>
> Do you think of yourself as closer to the Republican or Democratic Party?

Taken together, the three items produce the seven-point partisan identification scale: 0 = strong Democrat; 1 = weak Democrat; 2 = leaning Democrat; 3 = true Independent; 4 = leaning Republican; 5 = weak Republican; and 6 = strong Republican.

To obtain the partisan *strength* measure, we fold this scale around the category of true Independents. Consequently, the partisan strength scale has four categories: 0 = true Independent; 1 = leaning partisan; 2 = weak partisan; and 3 = strong partisan.

INTEREST IN POLITICS

Our measure of interest in politics is based on two items that tap interest in elections and public affairs. The first component is based on the following question:

> Some people don't pay much attention to political campaigns. How about you, would you say that you have been very much interested, somewhat interested, or not much interested in following the political campaigns (so far) this year?[1]

The second component was measured using the following question:

> Some people seem to follow what's going on in government and public affairs most of the time, whether there's an election going on or not. Others aren't that interested. Would you say you follow what's going on in government and public affairs most of the time, some of the time, only now and then, or hardly at all?

We recoded both items so that high values reflect a high level of interest. We then added the two components together and scaled the resulting measure to have a 0–1 range. For the period 1980–2004, the two items correlate at .51.

POLITICAL SOPHISTICATION

We measure political sophistication as a function of objective and subjective knowledge. The objective measure reflects knowledge of the composition of the House of Representatives:

Do you happen to know which party had the most Congressmen in Washington before the election this/last month?

This was coded 1 for a correct answer and 0 for an incorrect answer. The subjective level of knowledge is based on the assessment by the interviewer. At the end of the interview, each interviewer was asked whether the respondent's general level of information about politics and public affairs seemed (1) very high, (2) fairly high, (3) average, (4) fairly low, or (5) very low. We recoded this item so that high values reflect higher knowledge. We added the two items and scaled them to a 0–1 range. For the period 1980–2004, the two measures correlate at .39.

1. Minor deviations in the wording of this (and the other) item occurred from survey to survey.

Appendix C: Independents Versus Partisans: Contrasts in Civic Virtue

> Identifying too completely with a group threatens to crowd out [our] moral capacity, to undercut the independence of mind so necessary if the voice of conscience is to be heard. Better to be men and women, independents all, than partisans.
>
> –*Muirhead (2006)*

We compare the performance of Independents to that of univalent and ambivalent partisans on the following tasks: (1) the degree of opinion holding on the economy and policy issues; (2) the accuracy of perceptions about the economy and the policy stands of presidential candidates; (3) the degree to which material interest informs economic policy preferences; and (4) voting behavior.

OPINIONATION

We first consider a basic criterion of civic virtue: holding opinions on issues of the day. Successful policy inputs require both that citizens hold crystallized opinions on salient election issues and that they know where the candidates stand on them. This assumption is embedded in all models of issue voting (Downs, 1957; Rabinowitz & Macdonald, 1989; Schofield, 2008). Choosing candidates on the basis of issue agreement remains one of the primary vehicles for citizens to communicate the policy direction they desire. It is also important that citizens hold beliefs about other aspects of the political landscape, such as the performance of the economy. If these questions are met with a blank stare (or a reflexively biased response), then it would be nearly impossible for citizens to hold politicians accountable and steer them in the desired policy direction. A certain degree of opinionation is thus a prerequisite for two key mechanisms of a democratic polity: accountability and control over policy.

How, then, do Independents compare to ambivalent and univalent partisans in this regard? To find out, we counted the number of "don't know" responses on the following "issues": the state of the economy, ideological self-placement, and preferences on jobs, government spending, health care, defense spending, relationship with the USSR/Russia, aid to Blacks, and the role of women. We model the number of "don't' knows" as a function of partisanship (1 = Independent; 0 = partisan), interest in politics, sophistication, and the same set of demographics we have used throughout the book. For attached respondents, we also consider partisan strength and ambivalence.[2] We continue our strategy of converting the estimation results into predicted values; here we compare Independents to both groups of partisans. The predictions are shown in Figure C1 in the form of gray bars representing the expected number of "don't know" responses.

The bars show that Independents fare worse than either ambivalent or univalent partisans. The expected number of "don't know" responses for Independents is around one (out of nine); this value is cut in half for the two partisan groups (the differences are significant at the .01 level). What about "don't know's" for candidate issue placements? These results—collapsed across Democratic and Republican presidential candidates—are shown in the white bars in Figure C1, and they reveal that here too Independents are the least "opinionated." As before, the significant differences are between Independents on one hand (who were unable to respond to about 3 of the 14 candidate placement questions), and univalent and ambivalent partisans on the other (who failed to respond to about 2 of the questions).[3] While Independents fare somewhat worse than partisans on both counts, the effectiveness of accountability and policy signaling also requires that citizens hold *accurate* perceptions. It is possible that while Independents are less inclined than partisans to place candidates in policy space (or to offer assessments of the economy), their judgments may be just as (or more) accurate when they do.

---

2. The specific model that we estimate is a negative binomial regression.

3. The significance of these contrasts should not be understated. In our comparisons, political interest and sophistication are held constant and are set to relatively high (median) levels. Thus, we give Independents a bit of an advantage, as they tend to be less interested and knowledgeable than partisans, a difference that we ignore in the present analysis. Despite this advantage, levels of opinionation among Independents still come out worse than among ambivalent (or univalent) partisans. The conclusion, then, is that the latter look more virtuous than the former.

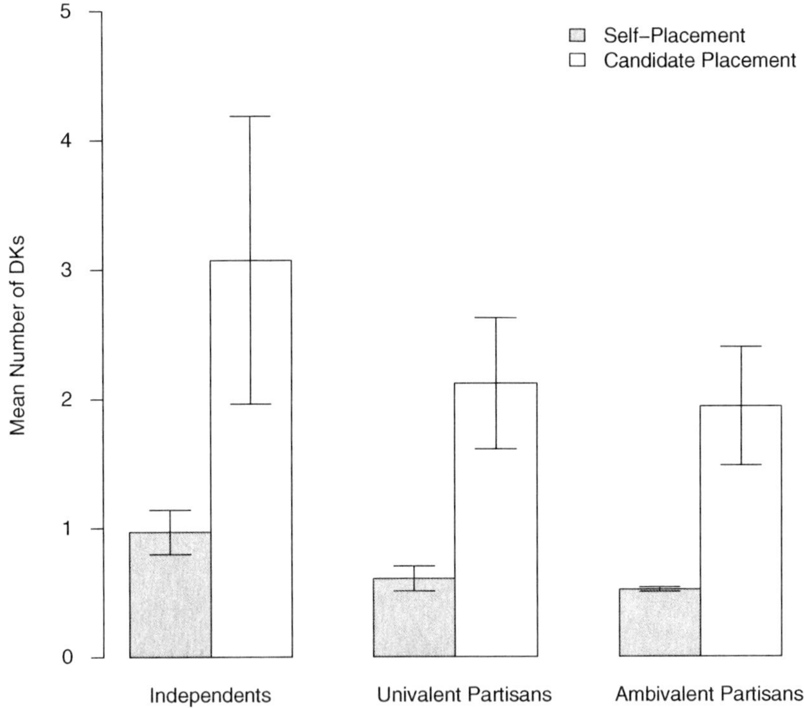

Figure C1. Opinionation Among Independents, Univalent, and Ambivalent Partisans.

Notes. The figure shows the expected number of "don't know" responses. The height of each bar represents the predicted count. The capped line represents the 95 percent confidence interval.

PERCEPTUAL ACCURACY

We demonstrated in Chapter 5 that the political perceptions of univalent partisans are shot through with motivated bias. For example, their judgments about economic performance are strongly dictated by whether they are partisan supporters or opponents of the president. As unattached citizens lack such "directional" motivation, this may be one arena in which they do a better job of getting it right. Lacking loyalty to either political party, there is no psychological incentive to view economic performance as better or worse than it truly is; nor is there an incentive to think of the policy stands of candidates as closer (or more distant) to one's own preferences than they really are. Little cognitive dissonance should thus arise in perceiving the objective performance of the government or the objective positions of candidates.

As far as bias goes, then, Independents may have an advantage. As we demonstrated in Chapter 5, however, there is another key driver of perceptual accuracy: the motivation to seek out and use diagnostic information about political reality. If Independents manage to acquire this information in sufficient amounts, they should fare well. If, however, they are apathetic, it is less clear how they will stack up against univalent partisans. Having laid out the relevant theoretical considerations, it is time to consider the empirical evidence. We do so in two stages. First, we analyze the accuracy of economic retrospections, a topic with important implications for the democratic mechanism of accountability. Next, we consider the accuracy of candidate placements, a topic relevant to the democratic mechanism of policy signaling. In both cases, our analyses are patterned after those reported in Chapter 5.

Economic Perceptions

Using the 1980–2004 ANES, we predict responses to the question of whether the economy improved, worsened, or stayed the same over the past year from a model that includes yearly change in unemployment and our usual set of demographic controls.[4],[5],[6] Our analysis focuses on the probability of stating that the economy worsened when in fact it did, or improved when this was true. We first simulate a bad economy, that is, one in which unemployment grew. Here *in-partisans* have an incentive to distort their perceptions upward (i.e., to perceive economic conditions as better than they really are); hence, we compare Independents to univalent and ambivalent *in*-partisans. We conducted the simulation based on the economy of 1982, a year in which unemployment worsened considerably. Next, we simulate a good economy, that is, one in which unemployment decreased. In this case it is *out-partisans* who have an incentive to form biased impressions (i.e., to perceive the economy as worse than it really is). We thus compare Independents to univalent and ambivalent *out*-partisans. For this comparison we simulated the economy of

4. We repeated the analysis using GDP growth (see Chapter 5). Since the results are analogous, we report only one set here.

5. We estimated an ordered logit model.

6. We also include political interest and sophistication, both as first-order terms and as product terms with change in unemployment. In the models for in- and out-partisans, we include partisan strength and ambivalence.

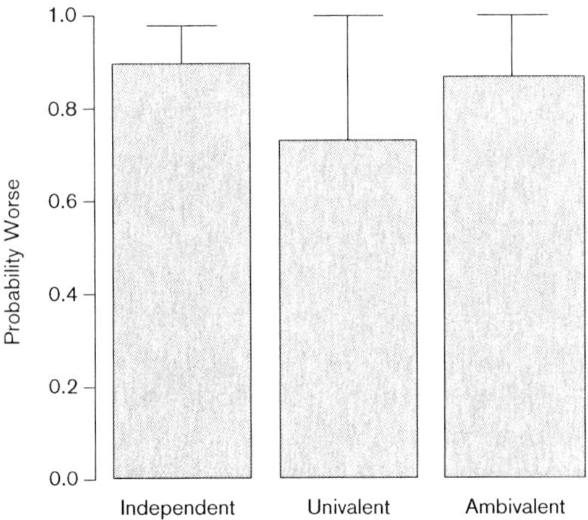

Panel B: Independents and Out-Partisans in a Good Economy

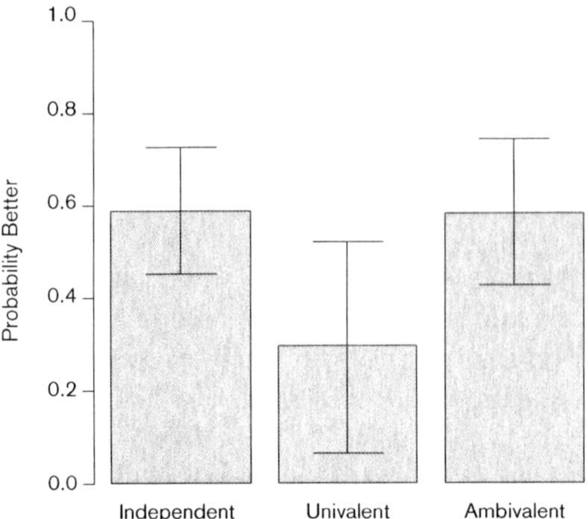

Figure C2. Economic Retrospections Among Independents, Univalent, and Ambivalent Partisans, 1980–2004 ANES.

Notes. The figures show the predicted probability that a given respondent correctly perceives the change in the economy over the past year. The height of each bar represents the predicted probability. The capped lines give the 95 percent confidence intervals.

1984, a year in which unemployment improved by a considerable amount.[7] The comparisons are shown in the panels of Figure C2.[8]

The figure reveals that Independents do a better job than univalent partisans in perceiving economic change. Consider first the contrast between Independents and in-partisans in a bad economy (Panel A). Ambivalent in-partisans and Independents have about the same probability of recognizing the downturn, whereas univalent in-partisans are about 10 percentage points less inclined to do so.[9] The comparisons in an improving economy are more dramatic (see Panel B). Again, it is Independents and ambivalent out-partisans who recognize the facts. For both groups, the most likely simulated response is that the economy has improved. Univalent out-partisans, however, are far less likely to acknowledge the facts. The most likely simulated response for this group is the lukewarm verdict of "stayed the same."

Perceptions of Candidate Issue Stands

The task of assessing the state of the economy is not particularly demanding. News about unemployment, economic growth, and the like is prominently reported in the media and trickles down to even the least involved citizens. It may thus not come as a surprise to learn that Independents on the whole did reasonably well in judging economic change. Information about the policy stands of presidential candidates is more difficult to come by, as the media pay more attention to the horserace aspect of elections than to issues (Cappella & Jamieson, 1997; Patterson, 1994). Independents may thus be comparatively less likely to possess the information needed to accurately perceive where the candidates stand—and to vote accordingly.

We begin by considering reversals in the ideological placement of presidential candidates. Throughout the post–World War II period, Republican candidates have operated to the right of Democrats, and our interest here is whether unattached citizens are comparatively less aware of this basic fact.

7. The advantage of selecting these years for our comparisons is that the presidency remained constant.

8. The simulations assume that the individual is a White, employed, average-aged female with median levels of income, education, interest, and sophistication. In the case where the simulated respondent is a partisan, a median level of partisan strength is assumed.

9. The difference between univalent and ambivalent in-partisans is statistically significant at the .05 level. Since different models were estimated for Independents and partisans, no significance level for the difference between Independents and univalent in-partisans could be computed.

For elections between 1980 and 2004, we coded whether a respondent placed the candidates correctly (i.e., Democrats to the left of Republicans). The results are graphed in the gray bars in Figure C3 and show that Independents compare unfavorably to both types of partisans.[10] The probability of an ideological reversal among the former is approximately .15; among partisans (of either variety) it drops to .10.

We next examine placements on specific issues. Here we consider the absolute distance between a respondent's placement of a candidate and the mean

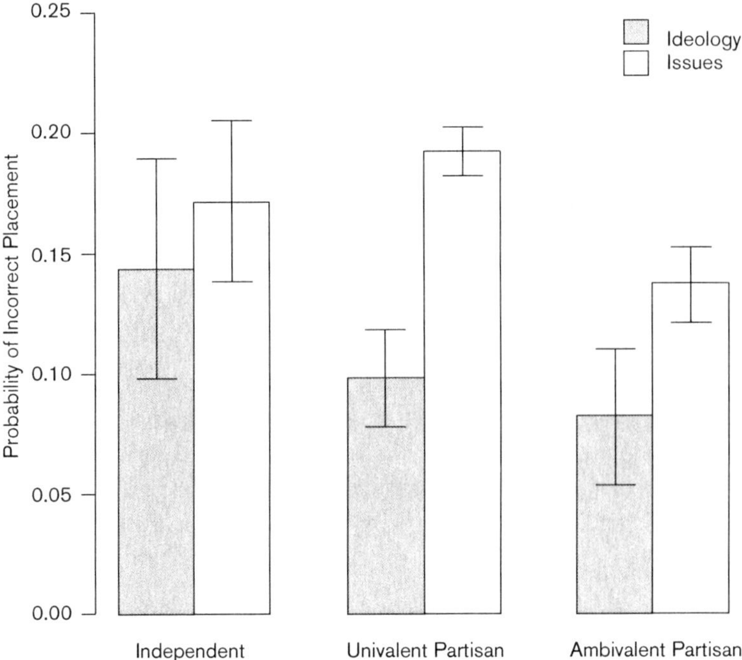

Figure C3. Accuracy in the Perceptions of Candidate Ideology and Issue Placements, 1980–2004 ANES.

Notes. The figure shows the predicted probability of correctly placing the candidates on policy issues and ideological orientation. The height of the bars corresponds to the predicted probability. The capped lines give the 95 percent confidence intervals.

10. We conducted a logit analysis. For the simulation, it is assumed that the individual is of average age, White, female, and possesses median levels of education and income. For partisans, partisan strength is set to the median. The distinction between univalent and ambivalent partisans is made in the usual manner.

placement for that candidate and issue in the sample as a whole.[11] These distances were averaged across all issues and both candidates to obtain a composite index of *perceptual error*. We dichotomized this measure, considering the error to be "large" if the average distance exceeded two units (on a seven-point scale).[12] We add candidate *clarity* to the usual right-side variables, which captures the distinctiveness of the candidates' positions in a given election year (e.g., the differences in 1984 were larger than those in 2000).[13] We expect perceptual errors to be smallest for ambivalent partisans. The expected relative performance of the other two groups is less clear. On one hand, Independents lack the motivation to systematically distort their perceptions. On the other, their lack of involvement may deprive them of the necessary information to get it right. So what do the results show? The white bars in Figure C3 reveal that ambivalent partisans exhibited the fewest errors of perception (about 2 percent), and univalent partisans exhibited the most errors (about 5 percent). Independents, meanwhile, scored in between (and statistically *better* than univalent partisans, though the difference was small).

ECONOMIC POSITION AND POLICY PREFERENCES

In Chapter 4, we used panel data to examine how voters updated their economic policy preferences over the course of the 2008 presidential election. We found that univalent partisans responded to campaign messages primarily on the basis of partisan cues, and that ambivalent partisans responded on the basis of their own economic circumstances. Here we examine how Independents fare in this regard. In updating their preferences, do unattached citizens consult their own economic predicaments? Absent a reflexive commitment to one side or the other in such debates, one might expect that they would. To find out, we construct an updating model from the 2008 ANES panel study that includes all of the usual controls, a lagged measure of economic policy preferences, and interactions between income and personal economic insecurity on

11. This is a common strategy in the measurement of party positions (e.g., Steenbergen & Marks, 2007).

12. The dichotomization does not greatly affect the results. A regression of the perceptual error onto the same set of predictors produces a similar pattern with significant positive effects of Independence and consistent considerations, and a significant negative effect of conflicting considerations. The cutoff of two units that we use here corresponds roughly to around 40 percent of the observed range of perceptual errors. It was chosen because a two-unit error is a serious distortion, which comes about when an individual places candidates on the wrong side of the issues.

13. We performed a logit analysis.

one hand and ambivalence and the engagement variables on the other. The predicted values from the two analyses (one using income as the key predictor and the other using economic insecurity) are shown in Figures C4 and C5. As both graphs clearly indicate, personal economic considerations matter only for ambivalent partisans.[14]

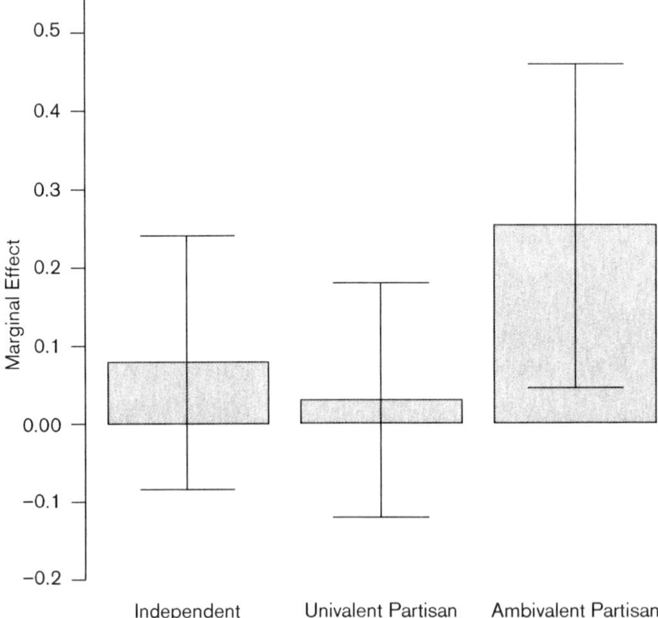

Figure C4. Marginal Effects of Income on Economic Policy Attitudes Among Independents, Univalent and Ambivalent Partisans, 2008 ANES.

Notes. The figure shows the estimated marginal effect of income measured in January on economic policy preferences measured in October, controlling for lagged preferences in June. The height of the bars represents the estimated marginal effect. The capped lines give the 95 percent confidence intervals.

---

14. Recall that the items comprising the economic insecurity scale were whether in the past year, one (and one's family) (a) was/were better or worse off than a year ago; (b) put off making planned purchases (including medical and dental treatments); (c) borrowed money from relatives, friends, or a financial institution to make ends meet; (d) dipped into savings; (e) looked for a second job or worked more hours at one's present job; (f) saved money; and (g) fell behind on a rent or house payment. Together, these items provide a broad and internally consistent portrait of an individual's current economic predicament ($\alpha = 76$). We recoded each item to a 0–1 to one scale and averaged them to form a composite measure of personal economic insecurity (where 0 = insecure; 1 = secure).

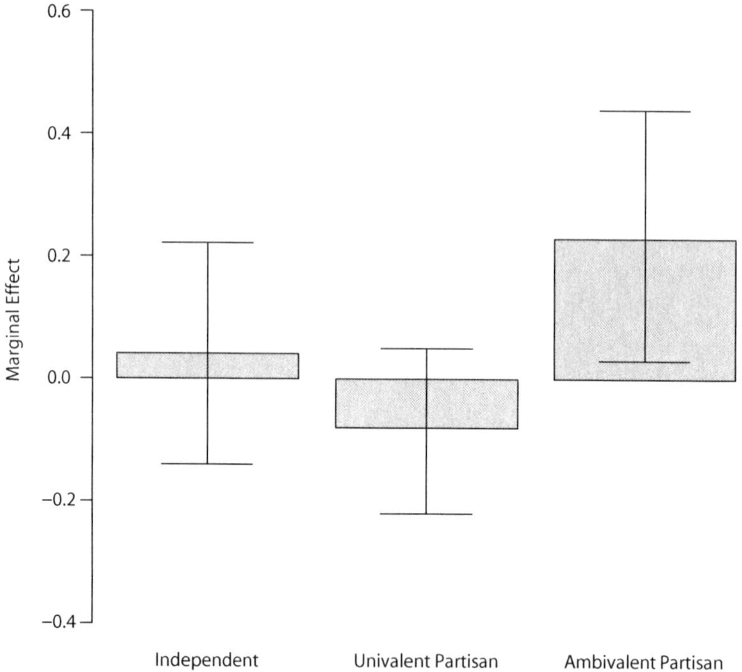

Figure C5. Marginal Effects of Personal Economic Insecurity on Economic Policy Attitudes Among Independents, Univalent and Ambivalent Partisans, 1992–1994 ANES.

Notes. The figure shows the estimated marginal effect of personal economic insecurity measured in 1992 on economic policy preferences in 1994, controlling for lagged preferences in 1992. The heights of the bars represent the estimated marginal effects. The capped lines give the 95 percent confidence intervals.

DETERMINANTS OF VOTE CHOICE

Citizens who lack an attachment to one of the political parties are less politically active than other citizens (e.g., they vote less; they are less attentive to campaigns). This is a well-established finding (see Green et al., 2002; Keith et al., 1992) and one that comes out in our research as well (we spare the reader the details). But what about those Independents who do vote? In the absence of a partisan identity, on what basis do they make their choices? Following the logic of our theoretical model, we might expect Independents—in an effort to reach their confidence thresholds—to turn to their policy preferences. This may well be the case. However, as they are less interested in politics than attached voters, they are also likely to have lower confidence thresholds. Therefore, they may simply turn to other cues, such as the nature of the times

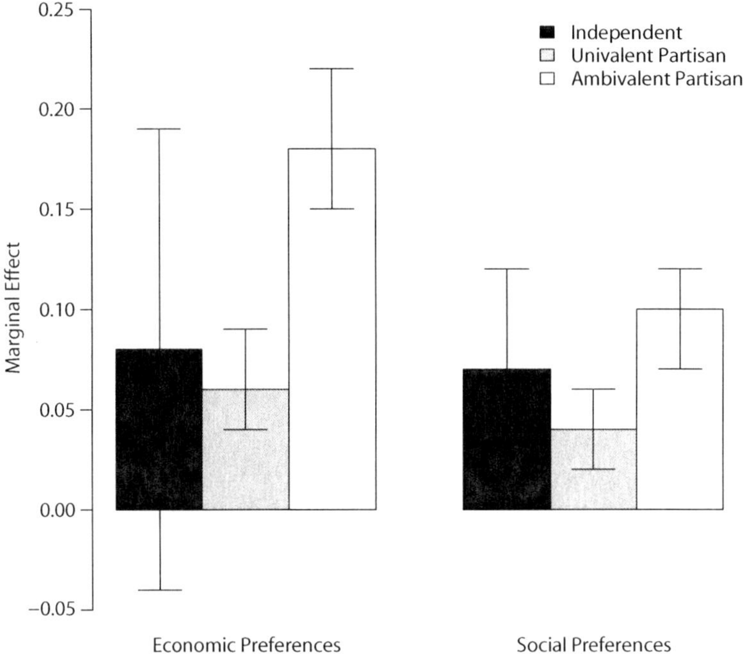

Figure C6. Marginal Effects of Policy Preferences on Candidate Evaluations Among Independents, Univalent and Ambivalent Partisans, ANES Cumulative File.
Notes. The figure shows the estimated marginal effect of economic and social policy preferences on presidential candidate evaluations. The heights of the bars correspond to the marginal effects. The capped lines give the 95 percent confidence intervals.

(e.g., economic performance) or the candidates' perceived personal qualities. In either case, we repeat the vote choice analysis from the last chapter, this time including Independents. As before, we constructed separate scales capturing economic and social policy preferences.

The results, shown in Figure C6, replay what we have already seen: Ambivalent partisans are issue voters, whereas univalent partisans are not. This is especially true for economic issues, where the former consult their preferences at a rate of three times that of the other two groups. The right side of Figure C6 presents a more interesting finding: While all three groups rely to some extent on social issues, Independents rely on them significantly more than do univalent partisans. Thus, although unattached citizens are less likely than other citizens to turn out, those who do cast a ballot rely to a modest extent on their policy preferences—at least as much, and perhaps *more so* than univalent partisans.

References

Abelson, R. P. (1959). Models of resolution of belief dilemmas. *Journal of Conflict Resolution, 3*, 343–352.

Abelson, R. P., Kinder, D. R., Peters, M. D., & Fiske, S. T. (1982). Affective and semantic components in political person perception. *Journal of Personality and Social Psychology, 42*, 619–630.

Abramowitz, A. (2010). *The disappearing center: Engaged citizens, polarization, and American democracy*. New Haven, CT: Yale University Press.

Abramowitz, A. I., & Saunders, K. L. (1998). Ideological realignment in the U.S. electortate. *Journal of Politics, 60*, 634–652.

Bartels, L., & Achen, C. H. (2006). It feels like we're thinking: The rationalizing voter and electoral democracy. Prepared for presentation at the Annual Meeting of the American Political Science Association, Philadelphia, August 30–September 3, 2006.

Adams, G. D. (1997). Abortion: Evidence of an issue evolution. *American Journal of Political Science, 41*, 718–737.

Alesina, A., & Rosenthal, H. (1989). Partisan cycles in congressional elections and the macroeconomy. *American Political Science Review, 83*, 373–398.

Allport, G. W. (1954). *The nature of prejudice*. Cambridge, MA: Perseus Books Althaus, S. L. (1998). Information effects in collective preferences. *American Political Science Review, 92*, 545–558.

Althaus, S. L., & Kim, Y. M. (2006). Priming effects in complex information environments: Reassessing the impact of news discourse on presidential approval. *The Journal of Politics, 68*, 960–976.

Alwin, D. F., & Krosnick, J. A. (1991). Aging, cohorts, and the stability of sociopolitical orientations over the life span. *American Journal of Sociology, 97*, 169–195.

Alvarez, R. M., & Brehm, J. (1995). American ambivalence toward abortion policy: Development of a heteroskedastic probit model of competing values. *American Journal of Political Science, 39*, 1055–1082.

Alvarez, R. M., & Brehm, J. (1997). Are Americans ambivalent toward racial policies? *American Journal of Political Science, 41*, 345–374.

Alvarez, R. M., & Brehm, J. (2002). *Hard choices, easy answers: Values, information, and American public opinion*. Princeton, NJ: Princeton University Press.

Amodio, D. M., Jost, J. T., Master, S. L., & Yee, C. M. (2007). Neurocognitive correlates of liberalism and conservatism. *Nature Neuroscience, 10*, 1246–1247.

Anderson, T. W., & Hsiao, C. (1982). Formulation and estimation of dynamic models using panel data. *Journal of Economics, 18*, 47–82.

Ariely, D. (2009). *Predictably irrational: The hidden forces that shape our decisions*. New York: Harper Collins.

Bartels, B. L., Box-Steffensmeier, J. M., Smidt, C. D., & Smith, R. M. (2011). The dynamic properties of individual-level party identification in the United States. *Electoral Studies, 30*, 210–222

Bartels, L. M. (1996). Uninformed votes: Information effects in presidential elections. *American Journal of Political Science, 40*, 194–230.

Bartels, L. M. (2000). Partisanship and voting behavior, 1952–1996. *American Journal of Political Science, 44*, 35–50.

Bartels, L. M. (2002). Beyond the running tally: Partisan bias in political perceptions. *Political Behavior, 24*, 117–150.

Bartels, L. M. (2006). What's the matter with what's the matter with Kansas? *Quarterly Journal of Political Science, 1*, 201–226.

Bartels, L. M. (2008). *Unequal democracy: The political economy of the New Gilded Age*. Princeton, NJ: Princeton University Press.

Basinger, S. J., & Lavine, H. (2005). Ambivalence, information, and electoral choice. *American Political Science Review, 99*, 169–184.

Bassili, J. N. (1995). On the psychological reality of party identification: Evidence from the accessibility of voting intentions and of partisan feelings. *Political Behavior, 17*, 339–358.

Beck, P. A., Baum, L., Clausen, A. R., & Smith, C. E., Jr. (1992). Patterns and sources of ticket splitting in subpresidential voting. *American Political Science Review, 86*, 916–928.

Ben-Akiva, M., & Boccara, B. (1995). Discrete choice models with latent choice sets. *International Journal of Research in Marketing, 12*, 9–24.

Berelson, B. R., Lazarsfeld P. F., & McPhee W. N. (1954). *Voting: A study of opinion formation in a presidential election*. Chicago, IL: University of Chicago Press.

Berinsky, A. J. (2006). *Silent voices: Public opinion and political participation in America*. Princeton, NJ: Princeton University Press.

Black, E., & Black, M. (2002). *The rise of Southern Republicans*. Cambridge, MA: Harvard University Press.

Boninger, D. S., Krosnick, J. A., & Berent, M. K. (1995). Origins of attitude importance: Self-interest, social identification, and value relevance. *Journal of Personality and Social Psychology, 68*, 61–80.

Borgida, E., Federico, C. M., & Sullivan, J. L. (2009). *The political psychology of democratic citizenship*. New York: Oxford University Press.

Botvinick, M. M., Cohen, J. D., & Carter, C. S. (2004). Conflict monitoring and anterior cingulate cortex: An update. *Trends in Cognitive Sciences, 8*, 539–546.

Box-Steffensmeier, J. M., & Smith, R. (1996). The dynamics of aggregate partisanship. *American Political Science Review, 90*, 567–580.

Box-Steffensmeier, J. M., & Smith, R. (1997, April 9–12). *Heterogeneity and individual party identification*. Paper presented at the 1997 Annual Meeting of the Midwest Political Science Association, Chicago, IL.

Brader, T. (2006). *Campaigning for hearts and minds: How emotional appeals in political ads work*. Chicago, IL: University of Chicago Press.

Brady, H. E., & Sniderman, P. M. (1985). Attitude attribution: A group basis for political reasoning. *American Political Science Review, 79*, 1061–1078.

Bruner, J. S. (1957). On perceptual readiness. *Psychological Review, 64*, 123–152.

Bruner, J. S., & Goodman, C. C. (1947). Values and needs as organizing factors in perception. *The Journal of Abnormal and Social Psychology, 42*, 33–44.

Burden, B. C., & Kimball, D. C. (2004). *Why Americans split their tickets: Campaigns, competition, and divided government*. Ann Arbor: University of Michigan Press.

Burnham, W. D. (1970). *Critical elections and the mainsprings of American politics*. New York: Norton.

Cacioppo, J. T., & Gardner, W. L. (1999). Emotion. *Annual Reviews: Psychology, 50*, 191–214.

Cacioppo, J. T., Gardner, W. L., & Berntson, G. G. (1997). Beyond bipolar conceptualizations and measures: The case of attitudes and evaluative space. *Personality and Social Psychology Review, 1*, 3–25.

Cameron, J. E. (2004). A three-factor model of social identity. *Self & Identity, 3*, 239–262.

Campbell, A., Converse, P. E., Miller, W. E., & Stokes, D. E. (1960). *The American voter*. New York: Wiley.

Campbell, A., Gurin, G., & Miller, W.E. (1954). *The voter decides*. Evanston, IL: Row Peterson.

Campbell, A., & Miller, W. E. (1957). The motivational basis of straight and split ticket voting. *American Political Science Review, 51*, 293–312.

Campbell, J.E. (1985). Explaining presidential losses in midterm congressional elections. *Journal of Politics*, 47, 1140-1157.

Cantril, A. H., & Cantril, S. D. (1999). *Reading mixed signals: Ambivalence in American public opinion about government*. Washington, DC: Woodrow Wilson Center Press.

Caplan, B. (2007). *The myth of the rational voter: Why democracies choose bad policies*. Princeton, NJ: Princeton University Press.

Cappella, J. N., & Jamieson, K. H. (1997). *Spiral of cynicism: The press and the public good*. New York: Oxford University Press.

Carmines, E. G., McIver, J. P., & Stimson, J. A. (1987). Unrealized partisanship: A theory of dealignment. *Journal of Politics, 49*, 376–400.

Carmines, E. G., & Stimson, J. A. (1980). The two faces of issue voting. *American Political Science Review, 74*, 78–91.

Carsey, T. M., & Layman, G. C. (2006). Changing sides or changing minds? Party identification and policy preferences in the American electorate. *American Journal of Political Science, 50*, 464–477.

Carver, S., & White, T. L. (1994). Behavioral inhibition, behavioral activation, and affective responses to impending reward and punishment. The BIS/BAS scales. *Journal of Personality and Social Psychology, 67*, 319–333.

Chaiken, S. (1987). The heuristic model of persuasion. In M. P. Zanna, J. M. Olson, & C. P. Herman (Eds.), *Social influence: The Ontario Symposium, vol. 5* (pp. 3–39). Hillsdale, NJ: Lawrence Erlbaum.

Chaiken, S., Liberman, A., & Eagly, A. H. (1989). Heuristic and systematic information processing within and beyond the persuasion context. In J. Uleman & J. Bargh (Eds.), *Unintended thought* (pp. 212–252). New York: Guilford Press.

Chaiken, S., & Trope, Y. (1999). *Dual-process theories in social psychology*. New York: The Guilford Press.

Chong, D., & Druckman, J. N. (2007). Framing theory. *Annual Review of Political Science, 10*, 103–126.

Clarke, H. D., & McCutcheon, A. L. (2009). The dynamics of party identification reconsidered. *Public Opinion Quarterly, 73*, 704–728.

Cohen, G. L. (2003). Party over policy: The dominating impact of group influence on political beliefs. *Journal of Personality and Social Psychology, 85*, 808–822.

Conover, P. J., & Feldman, S. (1986). The role of inference in the perception of political candidates. In R. R. Lau & D. O. Sears (Eds.), *Political cognition: The 19th Annual Carnegie Symposium on Cognition* (pp. 127-158). Hillsdale, NJ: Erlbaum.

Conover, P. J., & Feldman, S. (1989). Candidate perception in an ambiguous world: Campaigns, cues, and inference processes. *American Journal of Political Science, 33*, 912–940.

Converse, P. E. (1964). The nature of belief systems in mass publics. In D. Apter (Ed.), *Ideology and discontent* (pp. 206-261). New York: Free Press.

Converse, P. E. (1966). The concept of a normal vote. In A. Campbell, P. E. Converse, W. E. Miller, & D. E. Stokes (Eds.), *Elections and the political order* (pp. 9–39). New York: Wiley.

Cooper, J., Zanna, M. P., & Taves, P. A. (1978). Arousal as a necessary condition for attitude change following induced compliance. *Journal of Personality and Social Psychology, 36*, 1101–1106.

Craig, S. C., & Martinez, M. D. (2005). *Ambivalence and the structure of political opinion*. New York: Palgrave Macmillan.

Craig, S. C., Martinez, M. D., & Kane, J. G. (2005). Core values, value conflict, and citizens' ambivalence about gay rights. *Political Research Quarterly, 58*, 5–17.

Cunningham, W. A., Johnson, M. K., Gatenby, J. C., Gore, J. C., and Banaji, M. R. (2003). Neural components of social evaluation. *Journal of Personality and Social Psychology, 85*, 639–649.

Dalton, R. J., & Wattenberg, M. P. (2002). *Parties without partisans: Political change in advanced industrial democracies*. New York: Oxford University Press.

Dancey, L., & Goren, P. (2010). Party identification, issue attitudes, and the dynamics of political debate. *American Journal of Political Science*, 54(3), 686–699.

Delli Carpini, M. X. & Keeter, S. (1996). *What Americans know about politics and why it matters*. New Haven, CT: Yale University Press.

De Weerd, M., & Klandermas, B. (1999). Group identification and political protest: Farmers' protest in the Netherlands. *European Journal of Social Psychology*, 29, 1073–1095.

Dewey, J. (1927/1954). *The public and its problems*. New York: Holt Publishers.

Dewey, J. (1933/1997). *How we think*. Mineola, NY: Dover Publications.

Dionne, E. J. (1991). *Why Americans hate politics*. New York: Touchstone.

Ditto, P. H., & Lopez, D. F. (1992). Motivated skepticism: Use of differential decision criteria for preferred and nonpreferred conclusions. *Journal of Personality and Social Psychology*, *63*, 568–584.

Downs, A. (1957). *An economic theory of democracy*. New York: Harper and Row.

Druckman, J. N. (2001). Evaluating framing effects. *Journal of Economic Psychology*, *22*, 91–101.

Druckman, J. N., & Lupia, A. (2000). Preference formation. *Annual Review of Political Science*, *3*, 1–24.

Druckman, J. N., Green, D. P., Kuklinski, J. H., & Lupia, A. (2011). *Cambridge handbook of experimental political science*. Cambridge, UK: Cambridge University Press.

Duch, R. M., Palmer, H. D., & Anderson, C. J. (2000. Heterogeneity in perceptions of national economic conditions. *American Journal of Political Science*, *44*, 635–652.

Duckitt, J., Callaghan, J., Wagner, C. (2005). Group identity and intergroup attitudes in South Africa: A multidimensional approach. *Personality and Social Psychology Bulletin*, *31*, 633–646.

Duelfer, C. (2004). *Comprehensive report of the special advisor to the DCI on Iraq's WMD*. Retrieved May 2012, from http://www.lib.umich.edu.libproxy.cc.stonybrook.edu/govdocs/duelfer.html.

Dunning, D. (1999). A newer look: Motivated social cognition and the schematic representation of social concepts. *Psychological Inquiry*, *10*, 1–11.

Eagly, A. H., & Chaiken, S. (1993). *The psychology of attitudes*. Orlando, FL: Harcourt Brace Jovanovich College Publishers.

Ellemers, N., Kortekaas, P., & Ouwerkerk, J. (1999). Self-categorization, commitment to the group and social self-esteem as related but distinct aspects of social identity. *European Journal of Social Psychology*. *28*, 371–398.

Erikson, R. S. (2009). The American voter and the economy, 2008. *PS: Political Science and Politics*, *42*, 467–471.

Erikson, R. S., MacKuen, M. B., & Stimson, J. A. (1998). What moves macropartisanship? A response to Green, Palmquist and Schickler. *American Political Science Review*, *92*, 901–912.

Erikson, R. S., MacKuen, M. B., & Stimson, J. A. (2002). *Macropolity*. Cambridge, England: Cambridge University Press.

Fabrigar, L. R., MacDonald, T. K., & Wegener, D. T. (2005). The structure of attitudes. In D. Albarracin, B. T. Johnson, & M. P. Zanna (Eds.), *Handbook of attitudes and attitude change* (pp. 79–124). Mahwah, NJ: Erlbaum.

Fazio, R. H. (1990). Multiple processes by which attitudes guide behavior: The MODE model as an integrative framework. In M. P. Zanna (Ed.), *Advances in experimental social psychology, vol. 23* (pp. 75–109). San Diego, CA: Academic Press, Inc.

Fazio, R. H. (1995). Attitudes as object-evaluation associations: Determinants, consequences, and correlates of attitude accessibility. In R. E. Petty & J. A. Krosnick (Eds.), *Attitude strength: Antecedents and consequences* (pp. 247–282). Mahwah, NJ: Erlbaum.

Fazio, R. H., Sanbonmatsu, D. M., Powell, M. C., & Kardes, F. R. (1986). On the automatic activation of attitudes. *Journal of Personality and Social Psychology, 50*, 229–238.

Feldman, S. (1988). Structure and consistency in public opinion: The role of core beliefs and values. *American Journal of Political Science, 32*, 416–440.

Feldman, S. (1989). Measuring issue preferences: The problem of response instability. *Political Analysis, 1*, 25–60.

Feldman, S. (2003). Values, ideology, and the structure of political attitudes. In D. O. Sears, L. Huddy, & R. Jervis (Eds.), *Oxford handbook of political psychology* (pp. 477–510). New York: Oxford University Press.

Feldman, S., & Conover, P. J. (1983). Candidates, issues and voters: The role of inference in political perception. *Journal of Politics, 45*, 810–839.

Feldman, S., & Johnston, C. D. (2009, August 31–September 3). *Understanding political ideology: The necessity of a multi-dimensional conceptualization*. Paper presented at the Annual Meeting of the American Political Science Association, Toronto, Canada.

Festinger, L. (1957). *A theory of cognitive dissonance*. Evanston, IL: Row, Peterson.

Fiorina, M. (1981). *Retrospective voting in American national elections*. New Haven, CT: Yale University Press.

Fiorina, M. (1996). *Divided government*. Boston, MA: Allyn & Bacon.

Fischle, M. (2000). Mass responses to the Lewisnky scandal: Motivated reasoning or Bayesian updating. *Political Psychology, 21*, 135–159.

Fiske, S. T. (1992). Thinking is for doing: Portraits of social cognition from daguerreotype to laserphoto. *Journal of Personality and Social Psychology, 63*, 877–889.

Fiske, S. T. (2003). *Social beings: A core motives approach to social psychology*. New York: Wiley and Sons.

Fiske, S. T., Kinder, D. R., & Larter, W. M. (1983). The novice and the expert: Knowledge based strategies in political cognition. *Journal of Experimental Social Psychology, 19*, 381–400.

Fiske, S. T., & Taylor, S. E. (2008). *Social cognition: From brains to culture*. New York: McGraw-Hill.

Forgas, J. P. (1995). Mood and judgment: The affect infusion model (AIM). *Psychological Bulletin, 117*, 39–66.

Frank, T. (2004). *What's the matter with Kansas: How conservatives won the heart of America*. New York: Metropolitan Books.

Franklin, C. H., & Jackson, J. E. (1983). The dynamics of party identification. *American Political Science Review, 77*, 957–973.

Frenkel-Brunswik, E. (1949). Intolerance of ambiguity as an emotional and perceptual personality variable. *Journal of Personality, 18*, 108–143.

Gaertner, S. L., & Dovidio, J. F. (1986). The aversive form of racism. In J. F. Dovidio & S. L. Gaertner (Eds.), *Prejudice, discrimination, and racism* (pp. 61–89). San Diego, CA: Academic Press.

Gaines, B. J., Kuklinski, J. H., & Quirk, P. J. (2007). The logic of survey experiment reexamined. *Political Analysis, 15*, 1–20.

Gawronski, B., & Bodenhausen, G. V. (2006). Associative and propositional processes in evaluation: An integrative review of implicit and explicit attitude change. *Psychological Bulletin, 132*, 692–731.

Gelman, A., Park, D., Shor, B., & Cortina, J. (2008). *Red state, blue state, rich state, poor state: Why Americans vote the way they do*. Princeton, NJ: Princeton University Press.

Gerber, A., & Green, D. P. (1998). Rational learning and partisan attitudes. *American Journal of Political Science, 42*, 794–818

Gerber, A., & Green, D. P. (1999). Misperceptions about perceptual bias. *Annual Review of Political Science, 2*, 189–210.

Glass, D. P. (1985). Evaluating presidential candidates: Who focuses on their personal attributes? *Public Opinion Quarterly, 49*, 517–534.

Gomez, B. T., & Wilson, J. M. (2001). Political sophistication and economic voting in the American electorate: A theory of heterogeneous attribution. *American Journal of Political Science, 45*, 899–914.

Goren, P. (2004). Political sophistication and policy reasoning: A reconsideration. *American Journal of Political Science, 48*, 462–478.

Goren, P. (2005). Party identification and core political values. *American Journal of Political Science, 49*, 881–896.

Goren, P. (2012). *On voter competence*. New York: Oxford University Press.

Goren, P., Federico, C. M., & Kittilson, M. C. (2009). Source cues, partisan identities, and political value expression. *American Journal of Political Science, 53*, 805–820.

Granberg, D. (1993). Political perception. In S. Iyengar & W. J. McGuire (Eds.), *Explorations in political psychology* (pp. 70–112). Durham, NC: Duke University Press.

Gray, J. (1981). The psychophysiology of anxiety. In R. Lynn, R. (Ed.), *Dimensions of personality* (pp. 233–252). New York: Pergamon.

Gray, J. A. (1987). *The psychology of fear and stress*. Cambridge, England: Cambridge University Press.

Green, D. P. (1990). Rebuttal to Jacobson's "New evidence for old arguments." *American Journal of Political Science, 34*, 363–372.

Green, D. P., & Palmquist, B. (1990). Of artifacts and partisan instability. *American Journal of Political Science, 34*, 872–902

Green, D. P., Palmquist, B., & Schickler, E. (2002). *Partisan hearts and minds: Social identities of voters*. New Haven, CT: Yale University Press.

Green, D. P., & Yoon, D. H. (2002). Reconciling individual and aggregate evidence concerning partisan stability: Applying time-series models to panel survey data. *Political Analysis, 10*, 1–24.

Greene, S. (2002). The social-psychological measurement of partisanship. *Political Behavior, 24*, 171–197.

Greene, S. (2005). The structure of partisan attitudes: Reexamining partisan dimensionality and ambivalence. *Political Psychology, 26*, 809–822.

Greenwald, A. G., Banaji, M. R., Rudman, L. A., Farnham, S. D., Nosek, B. A., & Mellott, D. S. (2002). A unified theory of implicit attitudes, stereotypes, self-esteem, and self-concept. *Psychological Review, 109*, 3–25.

Habermas, J. (1998). *Between facts and norms, contributions to a discourse theory of law and democracy*. Cambridge, MA: The MIT Press.

Heider, F. (1958). *The psychology of interpersonal relations*. New York: Wiley,

Herek, G. M. (1986). The instrumentality of attitudes: Toward a neofunctional theory. *Journal of Social Issues, 42*, 99–114.

Herrnson, P. S. (2000). *Congressional elections: Campaigning at home and in Washington*. Washington, DC: CQ Press.

Hetherington, M. J. (1996). The media's role in forming voters' national economic evaluations in 1992. *American Journal of Political Science, 40*, 372–295.

Hetherington, M. J. (2001). Resurgent mass partisanship: The role of elite polarization. *American Political Science Review, 95*, 619–631.

Hetherington, M. J., & Weiler, J. D. (2009). *Authoritarianism and polarization in American politics*. Cambridge, England: Cambridge University Press.

Highton, B., & Kam, C. (2011). The long-term dynamics of partisanship and issue orientations. *Journal of Politics, 73*, 202–215.

Hillygus, D. S., & Shields, T. G. (2008). *The persuadable voter: Wedge issues in presidential campaigns*. Princeton, NJ: Princeton University Press.

Hochschild, A. (1981). *What's fair? Americans' attitudes toward distributive justice*. Cambridge, MA: Harvard University Press.

Hochschild, J. (2000). Where you stand depend on what you see: Connections among values, perceptions of fact, and prescriptions. In J. H. Kuklinski (Ed.), *Citizens and politics: Perspectives from political psychology* (pp. 313-340). New York: Cambridge University Press.

Holbrook, A. L., Krosnick, J. A., Visser, P. S., Gardner, W. L., & Cacioppo, J. T. (2001). Attitudes toward presidential candidates and political parties: Initial optimism, inertial first impressions, and a focus on flaws. *American Journal of Political Science, 45*, 930–950.

Houston, D. A., & Fazio, R. H. (1989). Biased processing as a function of attitude accessibility: Making objective judgments subjectively. *Social Cognition, 7*, 51–66.

Huckfeldt, R., Levine, J., Morgan, W., & Sprague, J. (1999). Accessibility and the political utility of partisan and ideological orientations. *American Journal of Political Science, 43*, 888–911.

Huckfeldt, R., & Sprague, J. (2000). Political consequences of inconsistency: The accessibility and stability of abortion attitudes. *Political Psychology, 21*, 57–79.

Huddy, L. (2001). From social to political identity: A critical examination of social identity theory. *Political Psychology, 2*, 127–156.

Huddy, L. (2003). Group identity and political cohesion. In D. O. Sears, L. Huddy, & R. Jervis (Eds.), *Oxford handbook of political psychology* (pp. 511–558). New York: Oxford University Press.

Iyengar, S., & Hahn, K. S. (2009). Red media, blue media: Evidence of ideological selectivity in media use. *Journal of Communication, 59*, 19–39.

Iyengar, S., & Kinder, D. R. (1987). *News that matters: Television and American opinion.* Chicago, IL: University of Chicago Press.

Jackman, S., & Sniderman, P. M. (2002). Institutional organization of choice spaces: A political conception of political psychology. In K. R. Monroe (Ed.), *Political psychology* (pp. 209–224). Mahwah, NJ: Erlbaum.

Jacobs, L. R., & Shapiro, R. Y. (2000). *Politicians don't pander: Political manipulation and the loss of democratic responsiveness*. Chicago, IL: University of Chicago Press.

Jacobs, L. R., & Shapiro, R. Y. (2010). Simulating representation: Elite mobilization and political power in health care reform. *The Forum, 8*.

Jacobson, G. C. (2001). *The politics of Congressional elections*. Boston, MA: Longman.

Jacobson, G. C. (2010). Perception, memory, and partisan polarization on the Iraq war. *Political Science Quarterly, 125*, 31–56.

Jacoby, W. J. (2006). Value choices and American public opinion. *American Journal of Political Science, 50*, 706–723.

Jennings, M. K., Markus, G. B., & Niemi, R. G. (1991). *Youth-parent socialization panel study, 1965–1982: Three waves combined*. Ann Arbor: University of Michigan, Center for Political Studies/Survey Research Center [producers], Ann Arbor: Inter-university Consortium for Political and Social Research [distributor].

Jennings, M. K., & Niemi, R. G. (1981). *Generation and politics: A panel study of young adults and their parents*. Princeton, NJ: Princeton University Press.

Jerit, J. (2009). How predictive appeals affect policy opinions. *American Journal of Political Science, 53*, 411–426.

Johnston, R. (2006). Party identification: Unmoved mover or sum of preferences? *Annual Review of Political Science, 9*, 329–351.

Jonas, K., Diehl, M., & Bromer, P. (1997). Effects of attitudinal ambivalence on information processing and attitude-intention consistency. *Journal of Experimental Social Psychology, 33*, 190–210.

Jost, J. T., Federico, C. M., & Napier, J. L. (2009). Political ideology: Its structure, functions, and elective affinities. *Annual Review of Psychology, 60*, 307–337.

Jost, J. T., Glaser, J., Kruglanski, A. W., & Sulloway, F. J. (2003). Political conservatism as motivated social cognition. *Psychological Bulletin, 129*, 339–375.

Kahneman, D. (2011). *Thinking, fast and slow*. New York: Farrar, Straus, and Giroux.

Kam, C. D. (2005). Who toes the party line? Cues, values, and individual differences. *Political Behavior, 27*, 163–182.

Katz, D. (1960). The functional approach to the study of attitudes. *The Public Opinion Quarterly, 24*, 163–204.

Katz, I., & Hass, R. G. (1988). Racial ambivalence and American value conflict: Correlational and priming studies of dual cognitive structures. *Journal of Personality and Social Psychology, 55*, 893–905.

Katz, I., Wackenhut, J., & Hass, R. G. (1986). Racial ambivalence, value duality, and behavior. In J. F. Dovidio & S. L. Gaertner (Eds.), *Prejudice, discrimination, and racism* (pp. 35–60). San Diego, CA: Academic Press.

Keele, L., & Wolak, J. (2008). Contextual sources of ambivalence. *Political Psychology, 29*, 653–673.

Keith, B. E., Magleby, D. B., Nelson, C. J., Orr, E., & Westleye, M. C. (1992). *The myth of the independent voter*. Berkeley: University of California Press.

Kelly, C. (1988). Intergroup differentiation in a political context. *British Journal of Social Psychology, 27*, 319–332.

Kerns, J. G., Cohen, J. D., MacDonald III, A. W., Cho, R. Y., Stenger, V. A., Carter, C. S. (2004). Anterior cingulate conflict monitoring and adjustments in control. *Science, 303*, 1023–1026.

Kessel, J. H. (1980). *Presidential campaign politics: Coalition strategies and citizen response*. Homewood, IL: Dorsey Press.

Key, V. O. (1955). A theory of critical elections. *Journal of Politics, 17*, 3–18.

Key, V. O. (1959). Secular realignment and the party system. *Journal of Politics, 21*, 198–210.

Kinder, D. R. (2006). Belief systems today. *Critical Review, 18*, 197–216.

Kinder, D. R., & Sanders, L. M. (1996). *Divide by color: Racial politics and democratic ideals*. Chicago, IL: Chicago University Press.

Knobloch-Westerwick, S., & Meng, J. (2009). Looking the other way: Selective exposure to attitude-consistent and counter-attitudinal political information. *Communication Research, 36*, 426–448.

Krosnick, J. A. (1991). Response strategies for coping with the cognitive demands of attitude measures in surveys. *Applied Cognitive Psychology, 5*, 213–236.

Kruglanski, A. W., Pierro, A., Mannetti, L., & De Grada, E. (2006). Groups as epistemic providers: Need for closure and the unfolding of group-centrism. *Psychological Review, 113*, 84–100.

Kruglanski, A. W., & Webster, D. M. (1996). Motivated closing of the mind: "Seizing"and"freezing." *Psychological Review, 103*, 263–283.

Kuklinski, J. H., & Hurley, N. L. (1994). On hearing and interpreting political messages: A cautionary tale of citizien cue-taking. *Journal of Politics, 56*, 729–751.
Kuklinski, J. H., & Quirk, P. J. (2000). Reconsidering the rational public: Cognition, heuristics, and mass opinion. In A. Lupia, M. D. McCubbins, & S. L. Popkin (Eds.), *Elements of reason cognition choice and the bounds of rationality* (pp. 153–182). New York: Cambridge University Press.
Kuklinski, J. H., Quirk, P. J., Jerit, J., & Rich, R. F. (2001). The political environment and citizen competence. *American Journal of Political Science, 45*, 410–424.
Kuklinski, J. H., Quirk, P. J., Jerit, J., Schwieder, D., & Rich, R. F. (2000). Misinformation and the currency of democratic citizenship. *Journal of Politics, 62*, 790–816.
Kuklinski, J. H., Quirk, P. J., & Peyton, B. (2008). Issues, information flows, and cognitive capacities: Democratic citizenship in a global era. In P. F. Nardulli (Ed.), *Democracy in the 21st century: International perspectives* (pp. 115–133). Urbane: University of Illinois Press.
Kuklinski, J. H., & West, D. M. (1981). Economic expectations and voting behavior in United States House and Senate elections. *American Political Science Review, 75*, 436–447.
Kunda, Z. (1990). The case for motivated reasoning. *Psychological Bulletin, 108*, 480–498.
Ladd, E. C., & Hadley, C. D. (1975). *Transformations of the American party system: Political coalitions from the New Deal to the 1970s*. New York: Norton.
Ladd, J. M., & Lenz, G. S. (2008). Reassessing the role of anxiety in vote choice. *Political Psychology, 29*, 275–296.
Lane, R. E. (1962). *Political ideology: Why the American common man believes what he does*. Oxford, England: Free Press of Glencoe.
Lane, R. E. (1973). Patterns of political belief. In J. Knutson (Ed.), *Handbook of political psychology* (pp. 83-116). San Francisco, CA: Jossey-Bass.
Lau, R. R. (2003). Models of decision-making. In D. O. Sears, L. Huddy, & R. Jervis (Eds.), *Oxford handbook of political psychology* (pp. 19–59). New York: Oxford University Press.
Lau, R. R., & Redlawsk, D. P. (1997). Voting correctly. *American Political Science Review, 91*, 585–598.
Lau, R. R., & Redlawsk, D. P. (2001). Advantages and disadvantages of cognitive heuristics in political decision making. *American Journal of Political Science, 45*, 951–971.
Lau, R. R., & Redlawsk, D. P. (2006). *How voters decide: Information processing during election campaigns*. New York: Cambridge University Press.
Lavine, H. (2001). The electoral consequences of ambivalence toward presidential candidates. *American Journal of Political Science, 45*, 915–929.
Lavine, H., Borgida, E., & Sullivan, J. L. (2000). On the relationship between attitude involvement and attitude accessibility: Toward a cognitive-motivational model of political information processing. *Political Psychology, 21*, 81–106.

Lavine, H., & Gschwend, T. (2007). Issues, party and character: The moderating role of ideological thinking on candidate evaluation. *British Journal of Political Science, 37*, 139–163.

Lavine, H., Huff, J. W., Wagner, S. H., & Sweeney, D. (1998). The moderating influence of attitude strength on the susceptibility to context effects in attitude surveys. *Journal of Personality and Social Psychology, 75*, 359–373.

Lavine, H., & Steenbergen, M. (2005). Group ambivalence and electoral decision-making. In S. C. Craig & M. D. Martinez (Eds.), *Ambivalence, politics, and public policy* (pp. 1–26). New York: Palgrace Macmillan.

Layman, G. (2001). *The great divide*. New York: Columbia University Press.

Layman, G. C., & Carsey, T. M. (2002). Party polarization and "conflict extension" in the American electorate. *American Journal of Political Science, 46*, 786–802.

Lazarsfeld, P. F., Berelson, B. R., & and Gaudet, H. (1948). *The people's choice: How the voter makes up his mind in a presidential campaign*. New York: Columbia University Press.

Lebo, M. J., & Cassino, D. (2007). The aggregated consequences of motivated reasoning and the dynamics of partisan presidential approval. *Political Psychology, 28*, 719–746.

Lenz, G. S. (2009). Learning and opinion change, not priming: Reconsidering the priming hypothesis. *American Journal of Political Science, 53*, 821–837.

Levendusky, M. (2009). *The partisan sort: How liberals became Democrats and conservatives became Republicans*. Chicago, IL: University of Chicago Press.

Levendusky, M. (2010). Clearer cues, more consistent voters: A benefit of elite polarization. *Political Behavior, 32*, 111–131.

Lewis-Beck, M. S., & Stegmaier, M. (2000). Economic determinants of electoral outcomes. *Annual Review of Political Science, 3*, 183–219.

Lieberman, M. D. (2007). Social cognitive neuroscience: A review of core processes. *Annual Review of Psychology, 58*, 259–289.

Lieberman, M. D., Schreiber, D., & Ochsner, K. N. (2003). Is political cognition like riding a bicycle? How cognitive neuroscience can inform research on political thinking. *Political Psychology, 24*, 681–704.

Lippmann, W. (1922). *Public opinion*. New Brunswick, NJ: Transaction Publishers.

Lipset, M. (1963). The value patterns of democracy: A case study in comparative analysis. *American Sociological Review, 28*, 515–531.

Lodge, M., & Taber, C. (2000). Three steps toward a theory of motivated political reasoning. In A. Lupia, M. D. McCubbins, & S. L. Popkin (Eds.), *Elements of reason: Cognition, choice and the bounds of rationality* (pp. 183–213). New York: Cambridge University Press.

Lodge, M., & Taber, C. S. (2005). The automaticity of affect for political leaders, groups, and issues: An experimental test of the hot cognition hypothesis. *Political Psychology, 26*, 455–482.

Lord, C. G., Ross, L., & Lepper, M. R. (1979). Biased assimilation and attitude polarization: The effects of prior theories on subsequently considered evidence. *Journal of Personality and Social Psychology, 37*, 2098–2109.

Lupia, A., & McCubbins, M. D. (1998). *The democratic dilemma: Can citizens learn what they need to know?* Cambridge, England: Cambridge University Press.

MacKuen, M. B., Erikson, R. S., & Stimson, J. A. (1989). Macropartisanship. *American Political Science Review, 83*, 1125–1142.

MacKuen, M., Wolak, J., Keele, L., & Marcus, G. E. (2010). Civic engagements: Resolute partisanship or reflective deliberation. *American Journal of Political Science, 54*, 440–458.

Manin, B. M., Przeworski, A., & Stokes, S. C. (1999). Elections and representation. In A. Przeworski & S. C. Stokes (Eds.), *Democracy, accountability, and representation* (pp. 29–54). Cambridge, England: Cambridge University Press.

Mansbridge, J. J. (1990). *Beyond self-interest*. Chicago, IL: Chicago University Press.

Marcus, G. (2002). *The sentimental citizen: Emotion in democratic politics*. University Park: Pennsylvania State University Press.

Marcus, G. E. (1988). The structure of emotional response: 1984 presidential candidates. *American Political Science Review, 82*, 737–761.

Marcus, G. E., & MacKuen, M. B. (1993). Anxiety, enthusiasm, and the vote: The emotional underpinnings of learning and involvement during presidential campaigns. *American Political Science Review, 87*, 672–685.

Marcus, G. E., MacKuen, M., & Neuman, W. R. (2009, July 14). *Measuring subjective emotional response redux: New evidence on alternative measurement methods*. Paper presented at the Annual Meeting of the ISPP 32nd Annual Scientific Meeting, Trinity College, Dublin, Ireland.

Marcus, G. E., Neuman, W. R., & MacKuen, M. (2000). *Affective intelligence and political judgment*. Chicago, IL: University of Chicago Press.

Markus, H., & Zajonc, R. B. (1985). The cognitive perspective in social psychology. In G. Lindzey & E. Aronson (Eds.), *Handbook of social psychology* (pp. 137–229, 3rd ed.). New York: Random House.

McCarty, N. M., Poole, K. T., & Rosenthal, H. (2006). *Polarized America: The dance of ideology and unequal riches*. Boston, MA: MIT Press.

McClosky, H., & Zaller, J. (1984). *The American ethos: Public attitudes toward capitalism and democracy*. Cambridge, MA: Harvard University Press.

Meffert, M. F., Guge, M., & Lodge, M. (2004). The consequences of multidimensional political attitudes. In W. E. Saris & P. M. Sniderman (Eds.), *Studies in public opinion: Attitudes, nonattitudes, measurement error, and change* (pp. xx–xx). Princeton, NJ: Princeton University Press.

Mendelberg, T. (2002). The deliberative citizen: Theory and evidence. In M. X. Delli Carpini, L. Huddy, & R. Y. Shapiro (Eds.), *Political decision making, deliberation and participation* (pp. 151–193). New York: Emerald Group.

Meltzer, A. H., & Richard, F. S. (1981). A rational theory of the size of government. *Journal of Political Economy, 89*, 914–927.

Milbrath, L. W., & Goel, M. L. (1977. *Political participation*. Chicago, IL: Rand McNally.

Mill, J. S. (1859/1998). *On liberty and other essays*. Oxford, England: Oxford University Press.

Miller, A. H., & Wlezien, C. (1993). The social group dynamics of partisan evaluations. *Electoral Studies, 12*, 5–22.

Miller, A. H., Wlezien, C., & Hildreth, A. (1991). A reference group theory of partisan coalitions. *Journal of Politics, 53*, 1134–1149.

Miller, J. M. (2000). *Threats and opportunities as motivators of political activism.* Unpublished Ph.D. dissertation, The Ohio State University, Columbus.

Miller, W. E. (1991). Party identification, realignment, and party voting: Back to the basics. *American Political Science Review, 85*, 557–568.

Mondak, J. J. (1994). Cognitive efficiency and the congressional vote: The psychology of coattail voting. *Political Research Quarterly, 47*, 151–175.

Mook, D. G. (1983). In defense of external validity. *American Psychologist, 38*, 379–387.

Moskowitz, G. B., Skurnik, I., & Galinsky, A. (1999). The history of dual process notions; The future of preconscious control. In S. Chaiken & Y. Trope (Eds.), *Dual process models in social psychology* (pp. 12–36). New York: Guilford.

Muirhead, R. (2006) A defense of party spirit. *Perspectives on Politics*, 4, 713–727.

Mulligan, K. (2011). Partisan ambivalence, split-ticket voting, and divided government. *Political Psychology, 32*, 505–530.

Murakami, M. H. (2008). Paradoxes of democratic accountability: Polarized parties, hard decisions, and no despot to veto. *Critical Review: A Journal of Politics and Society, 20*, 91–113.

Muthén, L. K., & Muthén, B. (2007). *MPLUS*. Los Angeles, CA: Muthen & Muthen.

Mutz, D. C. (2006). *Hearing the other side: Deliberative versus participatory democracy.* Cambridge, England: Cambridge University Press.

Nelson, T. E. (1999). Group affect and attribution in social policy opinion. *Journal of Politics, 61*, 331–362.

Nelson, T. E., & Kinder, D. R. (1996). Issue frames and group-centrism in American public opinion. *The Journal of Politics, 58*, 1055–1078.

Neuman, W. R. (1986). *The paradox of mass politics: Knowledge and opinion in the American electorate*. Cambridge, MA: Harvard University Press.

Nie, N., Verba, S., & Petrocik, S. (1976). *The changing American voter*. Cambridge, MA: Harvard University Press.

Nisbett, R. E., & Ross, L. (1980). *Human inference: Strategies and shortcomings of social judgment*. Englewood Cliffs, NJ: Prentice-Hall.

Norpoth, H., & Rusk, J. G. (1982). Partisan dealignment in the American electorate: Itemizing the deductions since 1964. *American Political Science Review, 76*, 522–537.

Nowak, A., Vallacher, R. R. (1998). *Dynamical social psychology*. New York: Guilford.

Oakes, P. J., & Turner, J. C. (1980). Social categorization and intergroup behavior: Does minimal intergroup discrimination make social identity more positive? *European Journal of Social Psychology, 10*, 295–301.

Ottati, V. C., & Wyer, R. S. (1990). The cognitive mediators of political choice: Toward a comprehensive model of political information processing. In J. A. Ferejohn & J. H. Kuklinski (Eds.), *Information and democratic processes* (pp. 186–218). Urbana: University of Illinois Press.

Page, B.I., & Jacobs, L.R. (2009). *Class War? What Americans Really Think About Economic Inequality*. Chicago: Chicago University Press.

Page, B. I., & Jones, C. C. (1979). Reciprocal effects of policy preferences, party loyalties and the vote. *American Political Science Review, 73*, 1071–1089.

Payne, J. W., Bettman, J. R., & Johnson, E. J. (1993). *The adaptive decision maker*. New York: Cambridge University Press.

Pearce, C. S. (1877). The fixation of belief. *Popular Science Monthly, 12*, 1–15.

Perlstein, R. (2001). *Before the storm: Barry Goldwater and the unmaking of the American consensus*. New York: Hill and Wang.

Perlstein, R. (2008). *Nixonland: The rise of a President and the fracturing of America*. New York: Simon & Schuster.

Petrocik, J. R. (1974). An analysis of intransitivities in the index of party identification. *Political Methodology, 1*, 31–48.

Petty, R. E., & Cacioppo, J. T. (1979). Issue involvement can increase or decrease persuasion by enhancing message-relevant cognitive responses. *Journal of Personality and Social Psychology, 37*, 1915–1926.

Petty, R. E., & Cacioppo, J. T. (1986). *Communication and persuasion: Central and peripheral routes to attitude change*. New York: Springer-Verlag.

Petty, R. E., Cacioppo, J. T., & Goldman, R. (1981). Personal involvement as a determinant of argument-based persuasion. *Journal of Personality and Social Psychology, 41*, 847–855.

Petty, R. E. (1994). Two routes to persuasion: State of the art. In G. d'Ydewalle, P. Eelen, & P. Bertelson (Eds.) *International perspectives on psychological science* (Vol. 2, pp. 229–247). Hillsdale, NJ: Erlbaum.

Petty, R. E., & Wegener, D. T. (1999). The elaboration-likelihood model: Current status and controversies. In S. Chaiken & Y. Trope (Eds.), *Dual-process theories of social psychology* (pp. 41–72). New York: The Guilford Press.

Pierce, J. C., & Hagner, P. R. (1982). Conceptualization and party identification: 1956–1976. *American Journal of Political Science, 26*, 377–387.

Pierro, A., Manetti, L., Kruglanski, A. W., & Sleeth-Keppler, D. (2004). Relevance override: On the reduced impact of cues under high motivation conditions of persuasion studies. *Journal of Personality and Social Psychology, 86*, 252–264.

Pollock, P. H. (1983). The participatory consequences of internal and external political efficacy: A research note. *Western Political Quarterly, 36*, 400–409.

Pomper, G. M. (1972). From confusion to clarity: Issues and American voters, 1956–1968. *American Political Science Review, 66*, 415–428.

Poole, K. T., & Rosenthal, H. (1997). *Congress: A political-economic history of roll call voting*. New York: Oxford University Press.

Popkin, S. L. (1994). *The reasoning voter: Communication and persuasion in presidential campaigns*. Chicago, IL: University of Chicago Press.

Priester, J. R., & Petty, R. E. (1996). The gradual threshold model of ambivalence: Relating the positive and negative bases of attitudes to subjective ambivalence. *Journal of Personality and Social Psychology, 71*, 431–449.

Putz, D. W. (2002). Partisan conversion in the1990's: Ideological realignment meets measurement theory. *Journal of Politics, 64*, 1199–1209.

Rabinowitz, G., & Macdonald, S. E. (1989). A directional theory of issue voting. *American Political Science Review, 83*, 93–121.

Rahn, W. M. (1993). The role of partisan stereotypes in information processing about political candidates. *American Journal of Political Science, 37*, 472–496.

Redlawsk, D. (2008, August 28–31). *Examining decision making using dynamic process tracing experiments*. Paper presented at the Annual Meeting of the APSA in Boston, MA.

Redlawsk, D. P. (2002). Hot cognition or cool consideration? Testing the effects of motivated reasoning on political decision making. *Journal of Politics, 64*, 1021–1044.

Rokeach, M. (1973). *The nature of human values*. New York: John Wiley.

Rosenstone, S. J., Behr, R. L., & Lazarus, E. H. (1996). *Third parties in America: Citizen response to major party failure*. Princeton, NJ: Princeton University Press.

Rosenstone, S. J., & Hansen, J. M. (2002). *Mobilization, participation, and democracy in America*. New York: Longman.

Rudolph, T. J. (2011). The dynamics of ambivalence. *American Journal of Political Science, 55*, 561–573.

Rudolph, T. J., & Popp, E. (2008). An information processing theory of ambivalence. *Political Psychology, 28*, 563–585.

Schofield, N. (2008). *The spatial model of politics*, New York: Routledge.

Schofield, N. (2009). *The political economy of democracy and tyranny*. Munich, Germany: Oldenbourg.

Schudson, M. (1998). The good citizen: A history of American civic life. New York: The Free Press.

Schumpeter, J. (1942). *Socialism, capitalism and democracy*. New York: Harper and Bros.

Schumpeter, J. (1994). *History of economic analysis*. New York: Oxford University Press.

Schwartz, S. H. (1992). Universals in the content and structure of values: theoretical advances and empirical tests in 20 countries. In M. P. Zanna (Ed.), *Advances in experimental social psychology* (Vol. 25, pp. 1–65). San Diego, CA: Academic Press.

Sears, D. O., & Funk, C. L. (1991). The role of self-interest in social and political attitudes. In M. P. Zanna (Ed.), *Advances in experimental social psychology* (Vol. 24, pp. 1–91). San Diego, CA: Academic Press.

Sen, A. (1990). Rational fools: A critique of the behavioral foundations of economic theory. In J. Mansbridge (ed.), *Beyond self-interest* (pp .25-43). Chicago, IL: University of Chicago Press.

Sen, A. (1978). On the labour theory of value: Some methodological issues. *Cambridge Journal of Economics, 2*, 175–190.

Sengupta, J., & Johar, G. V. (2001). Contingent effects of anxiety on message elaboration and persuasion. *Personality and Social Psychology Bulletin, 27*, 139–150.

Sherman, D. K., & Cohen, G. L. (2002). Self-affirmation and the reduction of defensive biases. *Current Directions in Psychological Science, 11*, 119–123.

Simon, H. A. (1955). A behavioral model of rational choice. *Quarterly Journal of Economics, 69*, 99–188.

Simon, H. A. (1957). *Models of man: Social and rational*. Oxford, England: Wiley.

Smith, B. M., Bruner, J. S., & White, R. W. (1956). *Opinions and personality*. Oxford, England: Wiley.

Smith, E. R. A. N. (1989). *The unchanging American voter*. Berkeley: University of California Press.

Smith, M. (2007). *The right talk: How conservatives transformed the Great Society into the economic society*. Princeton: Princeton University Press.

Sniderman, P. M. (2000). Taking sides: A fixed choice theory of political reasoning. In A. Lupia, M. D. McCubbins, & S. L. Popkin, *Elements of reason: Cognition, choice, and the bounds of rationality* (pp. 67–84). New York: Cambridge University Press.

Sniderman, P. M., Brody, R. A., & Tetlock, P. E. (1991). *Reasoning and choice: Explorations in political psychology*. Cambridge, England: Cambridge University Press.

Sorauf, F. J. (1972). *Party politics in America*. Boston, MA: Little, Brown.

Steenbergen, M. R., & Brewer, P. R. (2004). Policy attitudes in the political culture of ambivalence. In W. E. Saris & P. M. Sniderman (Eds.), *Studies in public opinion: Attitudes, nonattitudes, measurement error, and change* (pp. 93–132). Princeton, NJ: Princeton University Press.

Steenbergen, M.R., & Marks, G. (2007). Evaluating expert judgments. *European Journal of Political Research, 46*, 347–366.

Sweeney, P. D., & Gruber, K. L. (1984). Selective exposure: Voter information preferences and the Watergate affair. *Journal of Personality and Social Psychology, 46*, 1208–1221.

Taber, C. (2003). Information processing and public opinion. In D. O. Sears, L. Huddy, & R. Jervis (Eds.), *Oxford handbook of political psychology* (pp. 433–476). New York: Oxford University Press.

Taber, C. S., & Lodge, M. (2006). Motivated skepticism in the evaluation of political beliefs. *American Journal of Political Science, 50*, 755–769.

Taber, C. S., & Steenbergen, M. R. (1995). Computational experiments in electoral behavior. In M. Lodge (Ed.), *Political judgment: Structure and process* (pp. 141–178). Ann Arbor: University of Michigan Press.

Tajfel, H. (1978). *Introducing social psychology*. Harmondsworth, England: Penguin.

Tajfel, H., & Turner, J. C. (1979). An integrative theory of intergroup conflict. In W.G. Austin & S. Worchel (Eds.), *Social psychology of intergroup relations* (pp. 34–47). New York: Brooks/Cole.

Thomsen, C. J., Borgida, E., & Lavine, H. (1995). The causes and consequences of personal involvement. In R. E. Petty & J. A. Krosnick (Eds.), *Attitude strength and consequences* (pp. 191–214). Hillsdale, NJ: Erlbaum.

Thompson, M. M., Zanna, M. P., & Griffin, D. W. (1995). Let's not be indifferent about (attitudinal) ambivalence. In R. E. Petty & J. A. Krosnick (Eds.), *Attitude strength: Antecedents and consequences* (pp. 361–386). Hillsdale, NJ: Lawrence Erlbaum.

Thorisdottir, H., & Jost, J. T. (2011). Motivated closed-mindedness mediates the effect of threat on political conservatism. *Political Psychology, 32*, 785–811.

Todorov, A., Fiske, S. T., & Prentice, D. A. (2011). *Social neuroscience: Toward understanding the underpinnings of the social mind.* New York: Oxford University Press.

Tomarken, A. J., & Keener, A. M. (1998). Frontal brain asymmetry and depression: A self-regulatory perspective. *Cognition and Emotion, 12*, 387–420.

Tomz, M., Wittenberg, J., & King, G. (2003). *CLARIFY: Software for interpreting and presenting statistical results.* Stanford, CA: Stanford University.

Valentino, N. A., & Sears, D. O. (2005). Old times there are not forgotten: Race and partisan realignment in the contemporary south. *American Journal of Political Science, 49*, 672–688.

Vavreck, L., & Rivers, D. (2008). The 2006 cooperative congressional election study. *Journal of Elections, Public Opinion and Parties, 18*, 355–366.

Verba, S., Schlozman, K. L., & Brady, H. (1995). *Voice and equality: Civic voluntarism in American politics.* Cambridge, MA: Harvard University Press.

Visser, P. S., & Mirabile, R. R. (2004). Attitudes in the social context: The impact of social network composition on individual-level attitude strength. *Journal of Personality and Social Psychology, 87*, 779–795.

Watson, D., & Tellegen, A. (1985). Toward a consensual structure of mood. *Psychological Bulletin, 98*, 219–235.

Watson, D., Wiese, D., Vaidya, J., & Tellegen, A. (1999). The two general activation systems of affect: Structural findings, evolutionary considerations, and psychobiological evidence. *Journal of Personality and Social Psychology, 76*, 820–838.

Wattenberg, M. P. (1998). *The decline of American political parties, 1952–1996.* Cambridge, MA: Harvard University Press.

Wattenberg, M. P. (1981). The decline of political partisanship in the United States: Negativity or neutrality? *American Political Science Review, 75*, 941–950.

Weisberg, H. F., & Greene, S. H. (2003). The political psychology of party identification. In M. B. MacKuen & G. Rabinowitz (Eds.), *Electoral democracy* (pp. 83–124). Ann Arbor, MI: University of Michigan Press.

Weisberg, H. F., Haynes, A. A., & Krosnick, J. A. (1995). Social group polarization in 1992. In H. F. Weisberg (Ed.), *Democracy's feast: Election in America.* Chatham, NJ: Chatham House.

Wells, C., Reedy, J., Gastil, J., & Lee, C. (2009). Information distortion and voting choices: The origins and effects of factual beliefs in initiative elections. *Political Psychology, 30*, 953–969.

Wolak, J., MacKuen, M., Keele, L., Marcus, G. E., & Neuman, W. R. (2003, April 3–6). *How the emotions of public policy affect citizen engagement and public deliberation*. Paper prepared for presentation at the Annual Meeting of the Midwest Political Science Association, Chicago, IL.

Wolfinger, R. E., & Rosenstone, S. J. (1980). *Who votes?* New Haven, CT: Yale University Press.

Zaller, J. (1992). *The nature and origins of mass opinion*. Cambridge, England: Cambridge University Press.

Zaller, J., & Feldman, S. (1992). A simple theory of the survey response: Answering questions versus revealing preferences. *American Journal of Political Science, 36*, 579–616.

Zaller, J., & Hunt, M. (1994). The rise and fall of candidate Perot: Unmediated versus mediated politics—part I. *Political Communication, 11*, 357–390.

Zaller, J., & Hunt, M. (1995). The rise and fall of candidate Perot: The outsider versus the political system—part II. *Political Communication, 12*, 97–123.

INDEX

Note: Page numbers followed by n, *f* and *t* refer to notes, figures and tables.